Transforming Children's Mental Health Policy into Practice

Transforming Children's Mental Health Policy into Practice

Lessons from Virginia and Other States' Experiences Creating and Sustaining Comprehensive Systems of Care

Robert Cohen and Allison B. Ventura

LEXINGTON BOOKS
Lanham • Boulder • New York • London

Published by Lexington Books
An imprint of The Rowman & Littlefield Publishing Group, Inc.
4501 Forbes Boulevard, Suite 200, Lanham, Maryland 20706
www.rowman.com

Unit A, Whitacre Mews, 26-34 Stannary Street, London SE11 4AB

British Library Cataloguing in Publication Information Available

Library of Congress Cataloging-in-Publication Data

Names: Cohen, Robert, 1941– author. | Ventura, Allison B., author.
Title: Transforming children's mental health policy into practice : lessons from Virginia
     and other states' experiences creating and sustaining comprehensive systems of care /
     Robert Cohen and Allison B. Ventura.
Description: Lanham : Lexington Books [2016] | Includes bibliographical references
     and index.
Identifiers: LCCN 2016042657 (print) | LCCN 2016045521 (ebook) |
     ISBN 9781498541121 (cloth : alk. paper) | ISBN 9781498541145 (pbk. : alk. paper) |
     ISBN 9781498541138 (Electronic)
Subjects: MESH: Mental Health Services | Child Health | Health Policy—legislation &
     jurisprudence | Child Behavior | Adolescent Behavior | Child | Adolescent | Virginia
Classification: LCC RJ501.A2 (print) | LCC RJ501.A2 (ebook) | NLM WM 30 AV8 |
     DDC 362.2083—dc23
LC record available at https://lccn.loc.gov/2016042657

∞ ™ The paper used in this publication meets the minimum requirements of American
National Standard for Information Sciences—Permanence of Paper for Printed Library
Materials, ANSI/NISO Z39.48-1992.

Printed in the United States of America

For

Lennox, Arya, and Sonya, my three awesome grandchildren

and

*Howard Cullum, Kim McGaughey, Nancy Ross, and all of the
other bold pioneers who embraced the vision and provided
leadership on the long, arduous journey to establish the
Comprehensive Services Act for at-Risk Youth and Families*

and

*Judy Krysik, Karin Kline, Sandra Lescoe, Andrea Hightower, and
Lois Sayrs, valued colleagues at the Center for Child Well-Being.*

—RC

For

My mentors, Nancy and Bob

and

My two boys, Julio and John David.

—ABV

Contents

Acknowledgments

We are grateful for all of the generous assistance we received in writing this book. We are particularly appreciative of the guidance and feedback we received from Susie Clare, Scott Reiner and Alan Saunders of the Office of Comprehensive Services in Virginia. Chuck Savage, who has the patience of a saint, provided invaluable assistance in researching and interpreting pertinent data on the Comprehensive Service Act (CSA) over several years. Mark Hinson and Betsy Clark of Hampton CSA for sharing your enduring passions of serving one child and one family at a time. Bill Hazel, Secretary of Health and Human Resources for the Commonwealth, has provided much appreciated encouragement and support.

Thanks to the many individuals who allowed us to pick their brains in our effort to try to understand the evolution, operation and impact of CSA and Systems of Care in other states. More than 40 persons involved in the development and implementation of comprehensive services for vulnerable children and families generously allowed us to interview them and gave us permission to quote them in this book. The number of contributors is too long to acknowledge in this note, but each individual is cited in the text and bibliography. The extended quote from Apter et. al at the beginning of Chapter 1 comes from a monograph published by the Bridge Program in 1978. Robert Cohen, the senior author of this book, was the original director of the Bridge Program and provided permission to include the quote.

This book could literally not have been written without the tireless efforts of Dana Schultz, who transcribed the more than 50 interviews conducted with key stakeholders who informed our understanding of the history and dynamics of CSA.

Finally, we wish to acknowledge the support of our wonderful spouses, Nancy Cohen and Julio Ventura, who were patient, empathic and supportive throughout this long and sometimes challenging process.

Preface

Pursuit of reform grabs headlines. In this media-dominated era, the public's appetite for rectifying systemic deficiencies, improper practice and fraudulent behavior seems insatiable. We are constantly inundated with discussions about how to remedy widespread problems in education, health, criminal justice, and the financial sector. Even sports are not immune from demands for reform, as recent outcries about violence on and off the gridiron have demonstrated.

Unfortunately, attention to reform is skewed, with considerable interest generated at the front end, when problems are uncovered. Outrage is expressed and policies and laws are debated and enacted. Much less attention is paid once the rules are changed or legislative proposals are codified. This disparity in curiosity and focus is apparent in the media's lack of coverage of what happens after the reform is actually implemented. And the decline in interest following the initial excitement is not limited to television, newspapers, and the internet; the scholarly community has not always given sufficient consideration to what happens after the reform proposals have been endorsed. There are exceptions, such as the brouhaha that erupted following the botched roll out of enrollment for the Affordable Health Care Act. However, generally, the amount of attention a reform initiative receives declines over the course of time. We do not track whether the improvement effort is working and what impact it is having. Is the transformation fulfilling its intended purpose? Is the reform being conducted in a manner consistent with its stated principles and goals? What outcomes have been produced: intended and unintended?

This book focuses on efforts to transform the way in which care was being provided to children and youth with serious emotional and mental health challenges and their families. A significant portion of the book is devoted to examining a comprehensive statewide children's behavioral health reform initiated in the Commonwealth of Virginia in the early 1990s. The statute enacted in 1993 was considered by many to be the most ambitious state-level blueprint in the nation for transforming services to at-risk youth, and is still in effect, though it has undergone significant modification. The service system established by this legislation continues to function.

The early chapters of the book chronicles the events and conditions that led to the reform movement in Virginia and the intricate planning process that produced this visionary legislation, known as the Comprehensive Services Act for At-Risk Youth and Families (CSA). We also provide a social ecological conceptual framework that is referenced throughout the book to assist the reader in understanding the importance of taking into account technical, organizational, governance, fiscal, and broader contextual factors as well clinical/programmatic issues in designing and managing a complex system of care. This framework also can be used as a guide in assessing the impact of these internal and external factors on the development and performance of the system as well as examining how the leadership adapted policy and practice in response to the influence of these forces.

The succeeding chapters describe the initial implementation and evolution of CSA over the next two decades. In these chapters, we recount and describe how the components of this comprehensive system have performed and assess the impact and effectiveness of the overall system. Considerable attention is given to exploring how broad contextual factors, including the prevailing political ideology, the manner in which government entities define their roles and relate to each other, and the status of the economy and how funding is allocated, shape the way the system functions and services are provided. Following an overall assessment of the impact and effectiveness of CSA in meeting its original goals, we offer several chapters that describe exemplary reform efforts in other states and localities, and how these efforts compare with Virginia's CSA system. The final chapter attempts to synthesize lessons learned from CSA and other comprehensive transformation efforts and provides guidelines and suggestions for individuals interested in establishing and sustaining comprehensive systems of care for children with significant behavioral health challenges and their families.

The impetus for writing this book came largely from our personal experiences with the mental health service delivery system. As behavioral health professionals, we have struggled to understand and navigate the complex, often fragmented network of individuals and organizations responsible for providing care for at-risk youth and their families. Our reactions to the obstacles and deficiencies we have encountered have spanned the gamut of concern, confusion, frustration, and rage, with an occasional moment of gratification or inspiration. Even with the advances that have been made in recent decades, families seeking help for a child with serious emotional or behavioral challenges frequently cannot obtain appropriate care and are often led to feel that they are completely responsible for their child's problems. Our exasperating experiences with the mental health system have prompted us to try to understand why services for these children are so inadequate and what can be done to improve access and quality of care.

Both of us are psychologists, trained to work with children with behavioral health challenges. Our graduate education provided us with a good understanding of theories of etiology and treatment, as well as scientific methodology and evidence related to children's mental health and mental illness. Our clinical training prepared us to diagnose and provide therapy for these troubled young people. We even had some exposure to prevention and early intervention approaches.

What our formal training did not prepare us for was the complexity of the child mental health service system and the multiple forces that influence, often in a negative way, our ability to provide children and families with the care and support they need. Our "real-world" experience has taught us that it is not sufficient to have elegant theories or clinically validated intervention techniques. Having sound clinical knowledge and skills does not assure effective treatment. Unless other factors relevant within and beyond the service system are appropriately addressed, positive outcomes are unlikely to occur. The extent to which the workforce is properly prepared and the degree to which child-serving agencies such as social services, juvenile justice, education, and mental health work collaboratively have a significant effect on the quality of care. Even basic social attitudes influence the type of care that is provided. Support for providing appropriate mental health services is dependent on whether policy makers and the general public believe that children with serious mental health challenges have a genetic/biological predisposition toward mental illness or have been raised improperly by their parents/caregivers, or have lapsed into moral turpitude.

At a broader level, contextual forces also shape direction and quality of behavioral health care for children and families. Political, economic, social, cultural, and technological factors play a significant role in determining how care is provided and whether it produces positive outcomes.

Recognizing the significant role that non-clinical factors have on the availability and quality of care for children stimulated our efforts to study and improve the child mental health system. Allison Ventura has focused on empowering the families she works with by utilizing evidence-based interventions and tailoring her treatment to the unique personal and cultural characteristics of the child and family. She has also devoted time to training families and service providers on state-of-the art treatment approaches. Robert Cohen shifted his focus from intervening with individual children and families, the orientation of his professional training, to a broader systems perspective. He has become involved in studying and creating change at the community and state levels, developing innovative programs and promoting policies that mobilize child, family, and community strengths in order to address behavioral health challenges. He has been active in planning, implementing, and evaluating comprehensive community-based systems of care for at-risk youth and their families.

In the past 30 years, there has been a significant shift in the prevailing philosophy and approach to serving children with severe emotional and behavioral challenges. The new orientation stresses the importance of tailoring services to the specific needs of the child, giving youth and families a greater voice in the treatment process and keeping children in their home communities by developing coordinated networks of services and supports within the community. This approach declares that simply treating the child's emotional and behavioral symptoms is not sufficient; policy makers and service providers must recognize the critical role of educational, social, cultural, financial, and spiritual factors in the well-being of the child and family, and take affirmative steps to ensure that these needs are met. Unlike earlier approaches, the current paradigm emphasizes the importance of mobilizing strengths of the family and community, as well as the child, rather than restricting the plan of care to simply satisfying needs.

This model, known as the System of Care (SOC) approach, acknowledges and addresses the multiple contextual factors that may impact the quality of care including making agencies more responsive to the needs of children and families, promoting interagency collaboration, and restructuring funding so the money follows the needs of the child rather than the family being required to meet the restrictive eligibility criteria of each funding source, thus creating a fragmented and non-responsive service system. The SOC approach also emphasizes the importance of providing an array of supports, including training, performance and outcome monitoring and continuous quality assurance/improvement activities.

Much has been written about System of Care initiatives. Articles and books have articulated the philosophy and goals of this comprehensive approach. Thoughtful analyses have offered guidance on strategies that facilitate critical infrastructure components and supports required to establish and manage effective systems. Supporting research and evidence-based practices have been presented to bolster advocacy and program design efforts, and exemplary statewide and local efforts have been highlighted.

This book has a somewhat different focus. When we embarked on this project, our goal was to look beneath the surface and examine what happens to an ambitious children's behavioral health reform effort over an extended period of time. We hoped to find answers to some of the questions that have piqued our interest in this subject. How has CSA evolved during its

20 years of operation? Has it succeeded in fulfilling its mission? How have internal and external forces impacted the development and performance of this comprehensive System of Care? Has CSA paid sufficient attention to the philosophical, programmatic, fiscal, organizational, accountability, and technological components of the system and maintained an appropriate balance among these requisite functions? What accounts for CSA's ability to withstand constant criticism and continue to function more than two decades after its inception?

Several methods were employed to obtain answers to these questions. We interviewed more than 50 individuals who had significant involvement in the development and implementation of CSA. The stakeholders interviewed included state and local government officials, legislators, parents of children with behavioral health challenges, service providers, and advocates. In addition, we reviewed more than 100 reports, data bases, and other primary source documents pertinent to CSA's policy and performance. We also drew on our own first-hand experience with this comprehensive system of care. Finally, we spoke with individuals and reviewed documents from other local and state system of care initiatives that have been identified as exemplary programs in order to understand how these systems function and how they compare to Virginia's CSA system.

Not unexpectedly, our examination of CSA and other System of Care transformation efforts, have revealed that the situation and dynamics of each locality and state are unique, and that one-size-fits-all, cookie-cutter approaches are not appropriate or productive. However, the successful efforts we reviewed did seem to share many common elements and processes. From our study of the CSA reform and other successful System of Care programs, we were able to glean some practical lessons and identify a set of principles and guidelines. We hope the caveats and the strategic guidance we offer prove useful to those interested in understanding and confronting the challenges and opportunities that must be addressed in order to improve care for at-risk youth and their families.

Foreword

Drs. Robert Cohen and Allison B. Ventura have done a great service in compiling this history of the Commonwealth of, Virginia's effort to improve the availability of, access to, and the quality of services designed to improve the lives of our at-risk youth. The Comprehensive Services Act (CSA) of 1992 created a system of blended and braided funding streams from existing agencies and provided for local decision-making under state supervision. Virginia now has 24 years of experience to share. As leaders look for innovative ways of addressing the issues that families and youth face in navigating the complicated systems that exist today, this experience, both the positives and negatives, can be of value.

Virginia, like most states, has developed state agencies along the lines of federal funding streams. We have Departments of Education, Juvenile Justice, Social Services, Behavioral Health, Health, and Medical Assistance Services (Medicaid). Some refer to these as silos. We call them our "cylinders of excellence." Similarly, programs exist at the federal, state, and local levels and in a sense are also silos. Unfortunately children and families do not fit neatly into the cylinders that exist. There is a lack of common terminology, common processes and procedures, and even common goals. There are restrictions on the use of funds that create barriers to truly integrated and seamless continuum of services for those who might benefit. Complicating the situation is the difficulty sharing information on both a clinical and financial level.

In today's environment, it is necessary to demonstrate the value of our programs. This includes an assessment of the outcomes and the costs and demands some efficiency. I believe that Virginia's Comprehensive Services Act was a visionary step in the right direction. As with most pioneering efforts, there have been successes and "learning opportunities." Drs. Cohen and Ventura have been diligent in sharing some of those opportunities.

Virginia is continuing to evolve our system. This past year, what we now call our "Office of Children's Services," provided support to 15,609 children across the state. Local teams did the assessment and developed the plans of care. Cost sharing is about 65% state and 35% local. We are working with the various state agencies to address issues of alignment and communication as well as oversight.

This book provides a look at the CSA within the historical and political contexts and with an eye toward service delivery innovations that have emerged over time, especially the system of care model. Additionally, the book sets Virginia's efforts within the framework of larger national trends in the systems that deliver services to children and families. I hope that our story will be of help to you.

William A. Hazel Jr., MD
Secretary of Health and Human Resources
Commonwealth of Virginia.

Part I

SETTING THE STAGE

Chapter 1

The Status of Care for At-Risk Youth Prior to the 1990s

THE UNCLAIMED CHILDREN

Robby squirms uncomfortably in his seat in the third grade classroom of a small city public school. The substitute teacher, who has just arrived, notices the boy but does not respond. The boy becomes more active, and finally leaves his seat and walks around the back of the classroom. He is becoming more agitated and speaks out in a loud, strained manner. The teacher, sensing the disruptive impact he may have on the other children, directs him to sit down. When this does not work, she becomes more anxious and moves toward the boy hoping that he will finally return to his seat. The boy becomes more agitated; the teacher feels less confident. They stand face to face, finding themselves in a small showdown. The teacher commands the boy to obey. The boy yells "no." Suddenly, because she does not know what else to do, the teacher grabs at the boy. She catches him by the hair and pulls him toward her. Robby, trying to escape, swings at her, striking her arm and stomach as he struggles. The teacher, more humiliated than hurt, lets go of him, walks out of the room, and goes directly to the principal's office. Since hitting a teacher automatically results in a five-day suspension, Robby is sent home, missing a week of school, and needing to keep himself occupied for that time without supervision or assistance.

Althea is a tall, slender 8-year-old girl, with a pretty smile which she seems reluctant to use. She is one of many children in a house her family shares with two other families. There are no men in this house. Althea is responsible for taking care of several of the younger children. Rarely does anyone take care of her, or even pay attention to what she is doing. In school she sits quietly in the back of the room. Because she does not cause any trouble the teacher does not have to give her much attention. Yet, the teacher is concerned about Althea. This little girl always seems to be lost. She is not responding to the teacher or her classmates, does not seem to be learning, does not even appear to know what is happening around her. Last year's teacher decided to have Althea repeat the grade. The teacher she has this year is also puzzled but knows that keeping her behind is not much of a solution. Yet, the teacher has 25 other children to worry about, and she does not know how much she can do with Althea.

Mike is 10 years old. He has never learned to read or write. He has never learned to express his feelings. His older brothers have been "in trouble" for as long as anyone can remember. They have been excluded from school frequently. One of his brothers has had difficulty with the police. Mike seems to be moving in the same direction as his brothers. There is nothing in his life which seems capable of deterring him from this destiny of alienation and punishment. His family lives in poverty. Rather than offering refuge, his home intensifies his confusion and frustration by presenting him with dirt, disorganization, and the absence of any stable adult figure. At school Mike feels out of place. He cannot follow what the teacher is saying. Sitting in a seat for long periods of time is too difficult; he feels trapped when he is in school. With increasing frequency he does not even bother coming to school in the morning.

Most of these children were doing poorly in school academically, if they were in school or doing any work at all. All of them had the additional burden of living in very chaotic and disordered homes (Apter et al., 1978, p. 2).

Ruth has had severe mental health problems since the age of two. She is agitated and miserably unhappy, imagines everyone is against her and strikes out at others at random. In fifth grade she was suspended from school for hitting a teacher and breaking her foot. Since then Ruth has been in and out of residential placements and psychiatric hospitals. She runs away from most placements and once fled in the winter without coat or shoes. Other places push her out. Last fall she was immediately discharged from a psychiatric hospital when she assaulted a physician. More recently, she was evicted from another inpatient setting when she was described as "dramatically aggressive." Now Ruth is at home and her behavior is deteriorating rapidly. Her parents feel helpless. They alternate between overprotecting Ruth and rejecting her. The programs to which Ruth has been referred to recently do not believe they can protect both her and the other children in her care. They claim to lack the resources required to provide Ruth the intensive services she needs. Ruth could benefit from long-term care provided by staff trained to work with children like herself. No such program has appeared, and Ruth may end up on the adult ward of a state hospital before one comes along (Ruth's state has no adolescent units) (Knitzer, 1982, p. 5).

These children and families are representative of the "unclaimed children," Jane Knitzer (1982) described in her shocking expose of the plight of children with serious emotional and behavioral challenges prior to the advent of the comprehensive Systems of Care approach. Knitzer and her research team conducted a comprehensive study of how these children were being served. Their investigation included surveys of state departments of mental health in all 50 states as well as site visits to numerous mental health programs, review of the professional literature, and interviews with experts in the field and other key stakeholders. Finally, the team met with state officials in four states and evaluated federal programs that provide funding or afforded protection for children with significant mental health problems. The findings of Knitzer's team were disturbing.

Knitzer found that two-thirds of all children and adolescents with serious emotional and behavioral issues did not receive any services. Youth with multiple problems and those who have been or are at risk of being hospitalized were especially not likely to receive appropriate mental health care. Children who are in the custody of child welfare or juvenile justice agencies and have been placed in out-of-home care also fared poorly.

Socioeconomic factors also played a role in who received suitable care. While nearly all parents received minimal assistance in locating services for their children and were frequently ignored or coerced by public agencies, families with fewer resources received even lesser help. Children from poor, disordered families, where parents often had their own mental health or substance-abuse problems, had even more difficulty accessing appropriate mental health care. Respite care and other support services to relieve stress for parents of troubled children were not available and advocacy to address these problems was minimal (Knitzer, 1982).

Knitzer's team discovered that state departments of mental health were providing few services for this population, and states that were developing services generally limited their efforts to traditional residential care rather than community-based alternatives that were more cost-effective. Only one state was making a concerted effort to close state-operated institutions for youth and establish less restrictive alternatives in the community, and several states regularly placed children and adolescents on adult inpatient units. Few states were allocating mental health resources to establish services for infants and young children, or encouraging development of nonresidential community-based programs that would permit children with mental health challenges to remain with their families. Only seven state departments of mental health had taken the preliminary measures required to develop a comprehensive, coordinated set of mental health services for children and their families. These states were systematically focusing on increasing the range of services available, replacing the traditional inflexible funding practices with more malleable allocation strategies and enhancing coordination among agencies and providers within a given geographic area (Knitzer, 1982).

The early efforts of these states heralded the emergence of a new model, a strikingly different approach for serving youth with serious behavioral health challenges. This new paradigm, which focused on engaging and empowering families to assist in providing individually tailored care in less restrictive settings, became known as the System of Care (SOC) approach. During the next decade, this new approach would be more fully articulated, attain wider acceptance among child-serving professionals and advocates as well as public officials, and begin to gain momentum (Burns & Hoagwood, 2002; Stroul & Friedman, 1986).

In addition to finding weak leadership and lack of involvement from state departments of mental health, Knitzer also identified a number of other systemic deficiencies. Less than half of the states reported that they had a specific unit dedicated to children's mental health in their departments of mental health. Only one-third tracked expenditures related to children's mental health services, and in those states where those data were accessible, the total spent was far less than what was required to meet the need.

Given the large number of children with significant mental health challenges who are in the care of child welfare, education and juvenile justice agencies, there was a serious lack of specialized assistance available for at-risk youth and families in these agencies. Child welfare agencies did little to prevent the removal of or reunion of these children with their families, and typically placed children with serious problems in inpatient hospital or residential treatment settings. Little effort was made to address the mental health need of children who had been abused or neglected. In education, where Public Law 94-142 mandated states to provide handicapped children with a free and appropriate education, children with severe emotional disturbance frequently were not afforded the rights of this federal act and were often suspended or excluded from school and given only instruction in their home without other services prescribed by the Education for All Handicapped Children Act.

In addition to the intra-agency deficiencies, little attention was given to enhancing coordination among education, child welfare, mental health, and juvenile justice departments. Many of these children had multiple needs and were being served by more than one child-serving agency. These agencies functioned for the most part in an autonomous manner, with minimal effort devoted to working together to address the needs of at-risk children in an integrated manner. This lack of collaboration produced a fragmented, inefficient service delivery system (Knitzer, 1982).

Knitzer (1982) also examined the role of the federal government in promoting and supporting effective care for troubled youth and their families. She concluded that federal support for community-oriented care was relatively weak, and that federal funding had shrunk by approximately 50 percent in recent years. In the past decade three targeted initiatives for developing mental health services for youth had been established and terminated. A fourth proposal for improving care for children and youth had been rejected by Congress.

The dismal status of child mental health services portrayed by Knitzer, appeared to be even bleaker, considering the lack of advocacy for this vulnerable population. Knitzer concluded that "there is only a limited voice on behalf of troubles children and adolescents who need mental health services." The lack of general youth advocacy and mental health organizations concentrating on this issue, left professionals, who have traditionally been strong advocates, "feeling isolated and ineffective" (Knitzer, 1982, xii).

Based on the findings of their investigation, Knitzer and her colleagues made a series of specific recommendations in six areas. Their proposed actions, designed to help public agencies "reclaim" responsibility of seriously disturbed children, included action items in the following domains:

- Strengthening services and systems of care within state mental health departments;
- Increasing the mental health policy focus on children;
- Protecting the rights of children and adolescents in need of mental health services;
- Increasing the response of non-mental health agencies to the mental health needs of children and adolescents;
- Maximizing the impact of existing federal programs;
- Increasing effective advocacy (Knitzer, 1982).

Knitzer's groundbreaking study along with the efforts of child mental health reform pioneers (including Mary Armstrong, Cliff Attkisson, Lenore Behar, Len Bickman, John Burchard, Barbara Burns, Elizabeth Costello, Karl Dennis, Bob Friedman, Barbara Friesen, Sybil Goldman, Mario Hernandez, Kimberly Hoagwood, Phil Leaf, Ira Lourie, Andres Pumariega, Sheila Pires, Abram Rosenblatt, Beth Stroul, and John Vandenberg) captured the attention of local, state, and federal officials as well as professionals and advocates. Interest in transforming children's mental health service accelerated, with much of the effort devoted to promoting and establishing comprehensive Systems of Care that cut across agency boundaries and engaged families and professionals in figuring out how to replace the traditional, rigid, institutional-oriented service model with a more flexible and collaborative child-focused, family-centered, community-based approach.

How much of this momentum was spurred by the stark picture Knitzer and others depicted, and what can be attributed to a general societal readiness for reform is difficult to discern. However, it can be stated unequivocally that beginning with the publication of Knitzer's *Unclaimed Children* in the early 1980s, the direction of focus shifted appreciably and the pace of action to improve care for at-risk youth and their families accelerated significantly.

The remainder of this chapter provides an overview of some of the key issues associated with child mental health reform. We begin with a brief description of the types of mental health challenges youth experience and their prevalence. Next, we present a historical perspective on how children's mental health has been defined and perceived along with an account on how treatment methods have evolved. Finally, we review the challenges that proponents of children's mental health were struggling with in the 1980s and some of the promising approaches that were being explored.

1-IN-5 CHILDREN

Mental health is not only a critical component of a child's well-being, but is also meaningful for the family and the greater community in which the child lives. It encompasses emotional and behavioral areas of health and often impacts physical well-being, relationships, and learning (Simpson et al., 2008). Approximately 13–20 percent of children in the United States struggle with a diagnosable mental disorder in a given year and an estimated $247 billion is being spent each year on child mental disorders (National Research Council and Institute of Medicine, 2009). Approximately one-fifth of these children are considered to have a severe behavioral health disorder (Costello et al., 1996). Although recognized as a prevalent problem for U.S. youth, only 20 percent of children with mental disorders are identified and receive mental health services (US Surgeon General, 2000).

Behavioral health disorders are manifested in many ways. The Diagnostic and Statistical Manual for Mental Disorders (DSM) published by the American Psychiatric Association (APA), is the most frequently used diagnostic classification system used in the United States. The fifth edition of DSM, released in 2013, lists more than 275 specific disorders, many of which are applicable to children and adolescents (APA, 2013). These diagnoses can be viewed in many ways, including the personal domain they affect, that is, neurodevelopmental, affect, behavioral; the severity of their impact on an individual's functioning; and the treatment modalities suitable for a particular disorder. There has been an ongoing debate on what causes these disorders, with most contemporary experts agreeing that both genetic and environmental factors contribute significantly (Kendler, Prescott, Myers, & Neale, 2003). While recent advances in genetic research have confirmed that some individuals are genetically predisposed to specific disorders, there is not yet a definitive explanation of the etiology of behavioral health disorders.

There has been speculation that the prevalence of some disorders has increased during the past several decades, with some experts citing increased societal stress and others pointing to more specific environmental factors such as toxins being ingested by vulnerable individuals. In regard to depression, epidemiological studies have concluded that the prevalence of depression has not changed in the last 40 years (Murphy, Laird, Monson, Sobol, & Leighton, 2000). Recent studies of the Autism spectrum indicate that that these disorders are on the rise, but are not able to fully explain the source of this increase (Hyman, 2000).

Historically, childhood depression, anxiety, substance abuse, and disruptive behaviors were typically thought to be primary, stand-alone diagnoses for children. There is now greater recognition that youth often experience more than one behavioral health challenge, for example, co-morbid depression and substance abuse, which increases the risk for that individual. There is also increased awareness of the role of trauma in the behavioral health of children and adolescents. Until recently, the prevalence and implications of child and adolescent trauma were largely overlooked. Trauma has now become a part of the mental health dialogue and an important piece of the puzzle. Clinicians, researchers, and agencies are employing a more trauma-informed lens when examining children and youth's symptomatologies. Trauma may now better explain some of the previously exhibited behavioral problems. In community samples, more than two-thirds of American children report experiencing a traumatic event by the age of 16, with traumatic events including sexual abuse, physical abuse, domestic violence, community and school violence, medical trauma, motor vehicle accidents, acts of terrorism, war experiences, natural and human-made disasters, suicides, and other traumatic losses (APA, 2008).

Several studies have focused specifically on at-risk trauma populations rather than general populations, such as juvenile justice or foster care. Abram and colleagues' (2004, 2007; cited in Fairbanks, 2008) Northwestern Juvenile Project of youth 10–18 years of age held in a detention center found that 84 percent reported multiple exposures to trauma, with a majority exposed to six or more. Stein and colleagues (2001; cited in Fairbanks) documented a high prevalence of exposure to violence among children in foster care. For instance, of 300 school-aged children (6–13 years) living in out-of-home placement and with foster parents, 85 percent were witnesses and 51 percent had been victims of violence. Unfortunately, few children in need of trauma-informed mental health services received them (Fairbanks, 2008). Findings from the National Survey of Child and Adolescent Well-Being (Burns et al., 2004) estimated that nearly half of the children in the child welfare system are in need of mental health services, yet only a quarter of these received any such services.

Violence associated with mental health disorders among youth appears to be on the rise. American children and their families have been dealing with mental and behavioral challenges for several centuries. For the most part these struggles were quiet and private and not a hot topic of public interest. All of that changed in the spring of 1999 at Columbine High School after two adolescent boys went on a shooting rampage killing 12 students and one teacher and then committing suicide. The Columbine massacre in Littleton, Colorado attracted much media coverage and grabbed the nation's attention. Debates began over gun control, school security, the nature of high school cliques and bullying, and the influence of violent movies and video games in the American society. It also started dialogue about the use pharmaceutical anti-depressants by teenagers and the status of mental health prevention and treatment for American youth. Unfortunately, school shootings have become a common event.

Although much attention has been directed at mass shootings and other acts of violence committed by young people, there is also a significant problem of young people harming themselves. Nonsuicidal self-injury (NSSI) among children and adolescents is on the rise. Community research studies have estimated that 7–24 percent of adolescents in the United States have engaged in some type of NSSI (e.g., Yates et al., 2008; Jacobson & Gould, 2007). More recent research has even begun to demonstrate that children as young as 7 years old report these NSSI behaviors as well (Barrocas et al., 2012). Why the increase in self-harm among American youth? Some correlations have been found between self-harming behaviors and childhood maltreatment and sexual abuse, depression, substance abuse disorders, and bullying (Peterson et al., 2008). There even seems to be a contagion effect of deliberate self-harm among adolescents, which has subsequently increased the attention and publicity about these behaviors.

Although the children and adolescents described above are not attempting to kill themselves, there is a large percentage of American youth who are in fact taking their lives. The National Institute of Mental Health (NIMH) found that suicide was the third leading cause of death for youth ages 15–24 (NIMH, 2014). According to National Alliance on Mental Illness's (NAMI) National Comorbidity Survey-Adolescent Supplement, approximately 11 percent of youth have a depressive disorder by the age of 18 (Uttaro & Mechanic, 1994). While some depressed youth kill themselves, others resort to medicating their depression with substances and alcohol. This only compounds the problem as there is a positive association between depression levels and problems with alcohol in adolescents, indicating that youth who both suffer from depression and alcohol abuse may be at higher risk for a suicide attempt (Danielson et al., 2003).

A BRIEF HISTORY

Most historical accounts of child mental health trace the first modern efforts to address children to the eighteenth century. Prior to that period, persons with mental illness who were delusional and having hallucinations were considered to be witches or possessed by the devil and were imprisoned or burned at the stake (Norman, 1911). More humane approaches gradually emerged, and in the mid-1700s orphanages were established by religious and charitable groups to care for children without a home. These organizations employed a mix of religious training and primitive psychological theory to address the abnormal behavior of children placed in their care. This approach, which later became known as "moral" treatment, was clearly more humane and compassionate than previous methods, though not very sophisticated by today's standards (Earle, 1838). It is interesting to note that during the first half of the nineteenth century, a significant number of American psychiatrists supported the notion that overstimulation of the brain due to too much study could lead to insanity (Makari, 1993).

During the nineteenth century treatment approaches continued to evolve. Stigma diminished slightly, though negative attitudes toward children with mental health challenges were still prevalent, as they are today. Previously all children with problems had been lumped together. In the early 1800s children who were placed in psychiatric hospitals were mixed in with adults. With growing awareness that the needs of children and adults were different, distinct programs were developed for children. The child-serving system also began to recognize that children had different needs which required different treatment approaches. Institutions began to differentiate among children with mental illness, developmental disabilities, and delinquency issues, and programs were tailored to meet the unique needs of these young persons. The prevailing orientation during this period was to remove children with serious mental health problems from their homes and treat them through a milieu approach with other children who had similar problems (Lyons, 2004).

The focus began to shift in the early twentieth century and the field of child mental health in this country began to acquire a distinctive identity. Ironically, the initial impetus for this approach came from the juvenile justice system, not from psychiatry or other traditional proponents of improving care for vulnerable children. Dissatisfied with the punitive methods that were being applied to young people who had been abandoned by their families and became entangled with the legal system, juvenile justice leaders opted for a different approach. Court clinics, offering mental health services, were established to assist judges interested in providing a corrective rather than punitive approach (Lourie & Hernandez, 2003).

Shortly after the establishment of clinics for delinquent youth, a similar movement began to address the needs of children with mental health disorders. In the early 1920s, child guidance clinics, comprised of clinical teams of psychiatrists, psychologists, and psychiatric social workers were established to provide comprehensive services for "maladjusted children." These clinics initially espoused a preventive as well as treatment mission. The clinics engaged in community outreach efforts to educate the public about mental illness, detect early warning signs, and actually attempt to prevent mental disorders. After a decade, the prevention/early intervention focus faded and the guidance clinics primarily operated under a medically oriented model designed to treat children with relatively mild emotional and behavioral issues in a community-based clinic setting (Horn, 1989).

In spite of the development of more humane and compassionate approaches to serving children with emotional and behavioral problems, a formal policy to ensure that appropriate, comprehensive child mental health services were provided was not established. In fact, some experts argue that the United States has never had a formalized policy or governmental commitment to ensure that at-risk children and their families receive these services (Lourie & Hernandez, 2003).

During the next half-century, a number of significant advances occurred in the treatment of mental illness. Many of these developments were primarily focused on adults, with children sometimes receiving derivative benefits. Thus, the deinstitutionalization and community mental health movements which began in the late 1950s and early 1960s were initially motivated by concern for the quality of care and civil rights of more than a half-million adults with severe mental illness who were languishing in aging, state-operated psychiatric hospitals. With improved psychotropic medication, policymakers believed that these individuals could be better served in the community. While the number of individuals residing in public psychiatric facilities decreased dramatically, dropping from 550,000 in 1955 to 193,000 in 1973, critics claim that the movement failed to achieve its goal of providing more humane and effective care to persons with severe mental illness (Ozarin & Sharfstein, 1978). The momentum to move individuals out of institutions was not matched by a comparable effort to establish a comprehensive, coordinated system of community-based services and supports, despite federal legislation such as the Community Mental Health Center (CMHC) Act of 1963 (Koyangi, 2007).

Most of the mental health reform attention during this period was focused on adults. The first major federal policy initiative for youth was the Joint Commission on the Mental Health of Children, established by Congress in 1965. In its 1970 report, Crisis in Child Mental Health, the Joint Commission proposed that resources be devoted to a shift in strategy toward optimizing human development. They recommended that significant resources be invested to develop comprehensive services to ensure the maintenance of health and mental health of children and youth, establish a broad range of remedial services for children with emotional and behavioral handicaps and their families, and create a child advocacy system at every level of government to ensure that these goals were effectively implemented (Joint Commission on Mental Health of Children, 1970).

Despite the gravity of the problems described by the Joint Commission and the broad set of recommendations presented in its report, not much progress occurred in providing care for children with severe mental health disorders in the 1970s. The federal CMHC program funded some service demonstration projects for children. However, the CMHC programs had limited impact, as states did not continue supporting these efforts when the federal funding expired.

Medicaid, which was established in 1965 as a public funding mechanism for persons on welfare, did not have an immediate impact on the provision of mental health services for children. However, several decades later, this federal payment program became a major source of support for children's behavioral health care. Today, Medicaid is the largest funder of the public children's mental health services and plays a significant role in shaping policy and practice.

Among the most significant policy actions during this period were the passage of Public Law 94-142 in 1974 and the Individuals with Disabilities Education Act in 1975. These federal laws mandated treatment in least restrictive settings for children with disabilities, including emotional and behavioral disorders and established the right to receive special education services for these children. Prior to enactment of Public Law 94-142, families with children with a serious emotional disturbance (SED) had few viable options. When the behavior of these children disrupted the educational routine in the classroom, schools were then able to exclude these youngsters from school without offering them remedial services.

President Carter established the President's Commission on Mental Health, which included a task panel on infants, children, and adolescents. The President's Commission identified children with SED, as well as adults with chronic mental illness, as underserved populations and recommended that comprehensive community-based service systems be developed to meet their needs. A National Plan for the Chronically Mentally Ill was established to implement the Commission's recommendations. Consistent with earlier efforts, most attention and resources were directed at developing state and local social/rehabilitation programs for adults with serious and persistent mental illness. Once again, children with SED received only a fraction of the resources and no serious effort was made to mount a systematic campaign to develop comprehensive care for youth (Lourie & Hernandez, 2003; President's Commission on Mental Health, 1978).

THE PACE QUICKENS

Efforts to improve care for children with SED began to gain momentum in the 1980s. Although the Joint Commission on Mental Health of Children and the President's Commission on Mental Health did not produce many tangible results, their findings and recommendations established a framework and series of strategies that served as a foundation for future reform efforts. Several developments contributed to the accelerated pace of progress. In addition to Knitzer's graphic depiction of the plight of children with serious emotional and behavioral challenges in *Unclaimed Children*, several grass-roots advocacy organizations helped to raise public awareness and apply pressure to public officials. The National Alliance on Mental Illness (NAMI), which had become a major force in promoting improved care for adults with severe and persistent mental illness, began to focus on children's issues as well. A new group, the Federation of Families for Children's Mental Health, comprised primarily of families with children with SED, emerged as a strong advocacy group in the late 1980s. Both of these groups concentrated on establishing strong partnerships with behavioral health professionals in their campaign to improve care for children.

The role of family-led advocacy groups was significant in several ways. Many of these families had first-hand experience with the fragmentation and inadequacy of the current service arrangement and were able to passionately articulate the frustration and inappropriate care they had encountered in seeking help for their children. These groups were also keenly aware of the historical pattern of blaming parents for the mental health problems of their children. With new research on genetic and biological influences and shifts in prevailing thinking among mental health professionals, these negative perceptions were being challenged. Parents in these grass-roots organizations, along with many professionals, began to advocate for a more enlightened view of the etiology of mental health disorders by educating policy makers and the general public about the negative impact of stigma as they advocated for improved services.

During this period, the role of child psychiatry became more prominent and there were and continue to be significant advances in psychopharmacological approaches for youth with SED. Many of the medications employed were originally designed for adults and often produced serious negative side effects in children. In recent years, more methodologically rigorous studies have been conducted on the impact of these medications on children and adolescents (McVoy & Finding, 2009).

Recognizing that children with SED interacted with multiple individuals and organizations within the community and that no single treatment modality or intervention could adequately address their multiple needs, child mental health experts focused on designing a more comprehensive approach to serving these children and their families. Their work was guided by recent developments in the field as well as an acknowledgment of the deficiencies in the manner with which services were being provided at that time. The primary problems of the approach during that period were that (a) children with SED were too often served in residential or other restrictive settings; (b) there was a dearth of community-based services and supports; (c) services focused exclusively on deficits and problems that did not take into account the strengths and assets of youth and families; (d) services were typically provided in cookie-cutter fashion, not tailored to the unique situation of the child and family; (e) families were typically not involved in the service planning and delivery process; and (f) mental health services, as well as efforts of other child-serving agencies, were poorly coordinated and collaboration among various levels of government was weak (Stroul & Friedman, 1986).

Chapter 2

The System of Care Paradigm Emerges

In the mid-1980s, several significant events propelled the development of a new service model. The federal Substance Abuse and Mental Health Services Administration (SAMHSA) launched the Child and Adolescent Service System Program (CASSP), which provided funding to states to strengthen their capacity to improve services for children with serious mental health challenges. Although the amount of funding allocated was limited, CASSP established a policy direction and provided a service system concept that guided future development. The model was further enhanced by the publication of *A System of Care for Children and Youth with Serious Emotional Disturbance* (Stroul & Friedman, 1986), which became the authoritative source for understanding the values, principles and goals of this comprehensive approach for serving at-risk youth. Stroul and Friedman offered a framework for addressing the deficiencies of the current service arrangement and developing a more responsive approach. Table 2.1 describes the original core values and guiding principles of the Systems of Care.

While this framework has been adjusted and enhanced over the next three decades, the basic tenets of Stroul and Friedman's initial monograph are still considered to be authoritative and are used by policymakers, administrators, service providers, and researchers to inform their efforts on behalf of at-risk children and families.

THE SYSTEMS OF CARE GAIN MOVEMENT FINDS TRACTION

Acceptance and adoption of the System of Care (SOC) approach accelerated significantly in the late 1980s and continued during the 1990s. The Robert Woods Johnson Foundation (RWJF) developed a program to support

Table 2.1   Core Values and Principles for the Systems of Care

Core Values	1. The system of care should be child-centered, with the needs of the child and family dictating the types and mix of services provided.
	2. The system of care should be community-based with the locus of services as well as management and decision-making responsibility resting at the community level.
Guiding Principles	1. Emotionally disturbed children should have access to a comprehensive array of services that address the child's physical, emotional, social and educational needs.
	2. Emotionally disturbed children should receive individualized services in accordance with the unique needs and potentials of each child, and guided by an individualized service plan.
	3. Emotionally disturbed children should receive services within the least restrictive, most normative environment that is clinically appropriate.
	4. The families and surrogate families of emotionally disturbed children should be full participants in all aspects of the planning and delivery of services.
	5. Emotionally disturbed children should receive services that are integrated, with linkages between child-caring agencies and programs and mechanisms for planning, developing and coordinating services.
	6. Emotionally disturbed children should be provided with case management or similar mechanisms to ensure that multiple services are delivered in a coordinated and therapeutic manner, and that they can move through the system of services in accordance with their changing needs.
	7. Early identification and intervention for children with emotional problems should be promoted by the system of care in order to enhance the likelihood of positive outcomes.
	8. Emotionally disturbed children should be ensured smooth transitions to the adult service system as they reach maturity.
	9. The rights of emotionally disturbed children should be protected, and effective advocacy efforts for emotionally disturbed children and youth should be promoted.
	10. Emotionally disturbed children should receive services without regard to race, religion, national origin, sex, physical disability or other characteristics, and services should be sensitive and responsive to cultural differences and special needs.

Source: Stroul & Friedman (1986).

localities interested in developing approaches based on the principles articulated by CASSP and Stroul and Friedman. Subsequent to the RWJF program, the Center for Mental Health Services of SAMHSA initiated a demonstration program designed to foster development of systems of care. More than 100 sites received funding to create comprehensive approaches to serving children with severe mental health challenges during the following decade.

Along with Virginia, several other states launched statewide initiatives to provide comprehensive, coordinated systems of care for children with behavioral health challenges. Perhaps the most notable early adoption of an innovative statewide system occurred in North Carolina. In 1979, when four adolescents with significant mental health challenges were adjudicated delinquent, the state was unable to provide appropriate services for these youth. Frustrated by this lack of capacity, District Court Judge George Bason of Wake County, worked with a team of attorneys and leadership from the state's mental health system, including Lenore Behar, director of children's mental health services, to construct a lawsuit that would address the deficiencies of the current system and ensure that appropriate services would be available. Their efforts led to a federal civil rights law suit, commonly referred to as *Willie M. v. Hunt* (the governor of North Carolina at the time) that challenged the failure of the state to provide adequate community-based treatment facilities for children considered violent or aggressive. The plaintiffs claimed that these children were being warehoused in large institutional settings, such as state mental health and juvenile training schools, where they were not receiving appropriate care (Soler & Warboys, 1990).

This class-action suit was settled in 1980, requiring the State to develop and fund community-based treatment programs for children with serious mental health problems. Over the course of the next 18 years, North Carolina established systems of care throughout the state to serve this population. These systems, which eventually provided care to more than 1600 children a year and cost more than $100 million annually, served as a model for other states and localities interested in transforming children's mental health services to a comprehensive, community-based system of care (Dodge, Kupersmidt, & Fontaine, 2000).

A key component of these Systems of Care demonstration projects was the utilization of a team-based, wraparound planning process to identify appropriate community-based services and natural supports for child and family, based on their strengths as well as their needs. The process, directed by the child and family, employed a team comprised of representatives from all pertinent child-serving agencies as well as the family and other informal sources of support. The team was responsible for developing, implementing, and evaluating an individualized comprehensive and coordinated plan of care. The Wraparound Model, which was based on SOC principles, called for flexibility to ensure provision of appropriate services and adequate funding, and urged participants to take into account the unique personal, cultural, and social conditions of the child and family (Burchard, Bruns, & Burchard, 2002; VanDenBerg & Grealish, 1998).

The Systems of Care approach has continued to gain acceptance and support nationally and has become widely acknowledged as the preferred method for serving children with serious behavioral health challenges and their families. Through its Children's Mental Health Initiative (CMHI), SAMHSA has provided nearly $1.6 billion in grants and cooperative agreements to implement nearly 200 local and statewide Systems of Care efforts in all 50 states, as well as in American Indian/Alaska Native Communities and several territories.

Both the U.S. Surgeon General's 1999 Report on Mental Health and President George W. Bush's New Freedom Commission on Mental Health supported the principles and goals of a collaborative, comprehensive approach to caring for at-risk youth and their families and made recommendations to address obstacles hampering expansion of system of care strategies (New Freedom Commission on Mental Health, 2003; U.S. Surgeon General, 1999).

Evaluations of the SOC approach have generally yielded positive results in terms of improving outcomes for children and families as well as furthering system reform (Stroul & Friedman, 2011; Stroul et al., 2014). The growing emphasis on requiring empirical data demonstrating that behavioral health treatment approaches actually achieve their intended purpose has produced evidence supporting the efficacy of many of the psychosocial interventions utilized in SOC programs (Burns & Hoagwood, 2002). Research on therapeutic interventions, including Cognitive Behavior, Exposure, and Multisystemic Therapies has shown that these modalities can help children with certain disorders. Likewise there is a growing base of empirical evidence supporting the effectiveness of certain parent training and family education/support practices (Gruttadaro, Burns, Duckworth, & Crudo, 2007).

Community-based strategies that are integral to the Systems of Care approach have also been validated through methodologically sound research studies. For instance, treatment foster care, which provides foster parents special training and additional supports to enable them to care for at-risk youth in a family-based setting, has proven to be a viable alternative for keeping young people in their community rather than being placed in a residential or institutional facility (e.g., Chamberlain, 2002; Farmer, Wagner, Burns, Richards, 2003). Youth placed in treatment foster care showed significant gains in social skills and had higher rates of achieving permanent placement than children who did not participate in this program (Reddy & Pfeiffer, 1997).

In recent years, the Wraparound service process has been enhanced for children with SED by assigning an individual coordinator to work with each child and family. In this model, the Individual Care Coordination (ICC) Model, the coordinator, who is assigned a relatively small caseload and receives close supervision from a behavioral health professional, is responsible for conducting a comprehensive assessment, developing a risk management and safety plan, and assembling a planning team of formal providers and natural support resources chosen by the family. The care coordinator then facilitates the development of an individualized care plan and ensures that services and supports articulated in the plan are in place and are well coordinated. Localities and states that have employed ICC in conjunction with high-quality Wraparound services have produced significant positive outcomes, including improvement in the youth functioning, decreases in involvement in juvenile justice and protective services, and declines in congregate care and out-of-community placements as well as significant reductions in per child and aggregate service costs (Simons, Pires, Hendricks, & Lipper, 2014).

One of the most significant developments in caring for individuals with behavioral health challenges, including children, is the increased recognition of the role that trauma plays in the manifestation of emotional and behavioral difficulties. The impact of posttraumatic stress disorders (PTSD) in military personnel and others exposed to violence has captured public attention and begun to influence policy. This awareness has also influenced the way we perceive and care for children. The SAMHSA, Center for Mental Health Services, created the National Center for Child Traumatic Stress (NCCTS). The purpose of the NCCTS is to develop and maintain a collaborative network structure, support resource and policy development and dissemination, and coordinate the network's national child trauma education and training efforts (SAMHSA, 2016). The NCCTS is part of the National Child Traumatic Stress Initiative (NCTSI). The purpose of NCTSI is to improve the quality of trauma treatment and services in communities for children, adolescents, and their families who experience or witness traumatic events, and to increase access to effective trauma-focused treatment and services for children and adolescents throughout the nation. The initiative is designed to address child trauma issues by creating a national network of grantees—the National Child Traumatic Stress Network (NCTSN)—that works collaboratively to develop and promote effective trauma treatment and services for children, adolescents, and their families exposed to a wide array of traumatic events (SAMHSA, 2016).

The number of at-risk youth who have experienced maltreatment or neglect, sexual abuse or community violence is staggering. Estimates of the number of youth involved in the juvenile justice system who have experienced childhood trauma range from 75 to 90 percent (Adams, 2010). In the general population, 80 percent of adolescents meet clinical criteria for having been exposed to a serious traumatic event and the average prevalence rate of PTSD among adolescents is 14 percent. The prevalence rate rises appreciably for adolescents who have experienced trauma associated with shame and deviance, with 57 percent of adolescence who have been sexually abused meeting criteria for PTSD. Adolescents with PTSD are three times more likely to make a suicide attempt than adolescents who do not have a history of trauma or PTSD, and 80 percent have a co-morbid substance-abuse problem (Gabbay, Oatis, Silva, & Hirsch, 2004; Nooner et al., 2012).

This enhanced awareness of the detrimental effects of trauma on children has altered the approach to serving at-risk youth in educational, mental health, juvenile justice, and social welfare settings as well as in the broader community. In addition to highlighting the importance of preventing exposure to trauma, there have been substantial shifts in the manner in which we care for these vulnerable individuals (Ko et al., 2008). For example, during the past half-century many of the prevailing treatment approaches for youth with serious behavioral challenges have been based on learning and reinforcement theories that prescribe reinforcing appropriate behavior and withholding rewards for inappropriate behavior. This behavioral contingency approach assumes that children will replace maladaptive behaviors with more appropriate alternatives if suitable environmental conditions and supports are provided.

One corollary of this orientation has been the use of supposedly nonpunitive controls for youth in treatment facilities who are exhibiting aggressive behavior. When a young person "goes off" and attempts to harm another individual or destroy property, treatment staff have been trained to mobilize a sufficient number of personnel to intervene in order to contain and remove the child from the immediate environment and allow him or her to calm down before processing the event in order to explore more appropriate ways to manage their frustration and anger. While there is an intuitive logic supporting this approach and it is certainly preferable to previous traditions of meting out punishment in response to disruptive behavior, this "contain and remove" strategy has some fundamental flaws when viewed from the emerging trauma-based perspective. A child who has previously been impacted by physical violence or sexual abuse, will likely perceive the experience of being "taken down" by a group of adults as an aggressive act, which may stimulate fear, helplessness, and other feelings associated with their original traumatic experience and cause considerable distress.

Beyond heightening awareness of the potential negative effects of staff physically intervening with a child to deal with disruptive behavior, the trauma model also provides caregivers with a different perspective on the source of the child's behavioral and emotional difficulties and offers an alternative pathway for working with youth and their families. While primitive views of the etiology of mental disorders as the work of the devil or witches no longer hold sway, many individuals, including staff of child-serving agencies, believed that the deviant behavior of children with SED was caused by inappropriate parenting or that these young people were able to control their responses and, in some instances, intentionally acted inappropriately. Workers with these views gravitated to behavioral contingency or "tough love" approaches that presumed children would terminate their disruptive/inappropriate behavior if it no longer generated desired outcomes or if alternative behaviors achieved better results for the child. Though there may be instances in which children willfully behave inappropriately, the research on the impact of trauma on an individual's brain and subsequent adaptation provides convincing evidence that refutes this view of children with PTSD. Neurobiological studies have demonstrated that traumatic stress affects many areas of the brain and has significant negative impact on normal development (Bremner, 2006). This interruption of normal brain development make children as well as adults susceptible to a number of mental disorders, including PTSD, depression, substance abuse, and dissociative personality disorder (Battle et al., 2004; Bremner, 2006; Franklin & Zimmer, 2001; Kessler et al., 1995).

With the introduction of an evidence-based perspective on the impact of traumatic stress and the emergence of trauma-informed treatment approaches, child-serving providers have had to rethink their previous positions on what causes behavioral health disorders and how to effectively treat young people experiencing these challenges. Approaches such as Collaborative Problem Solving and the Sanctuary model assert that delays in brain development of children who have been exposed to trauma has impeded their ability to acquire appropriate coping skills. The goal of these trauma-informed treatment approaches is to provide a healing environment for children who have experienced psychological and social trauma and help them acquire coping strategies that will enable them to deal more effectively with stress-producing situations (Bloom, 2000; Bloom & Sreedhar, 2008; Greene & Ablon, 2006; Rivard et al., 2003). These trauma-informed approaches recognize the importance of establishing a caring, understanding and nurturing culture within the therapeutic milieu and making a concerted effort to train staff and create a supportive organizational climate that will facilitate growth and healing for children served by their program (Bloom, 2005).

Trauma-informed care has had a significant impact on the attitudes and practice of child-serving personnel and agencies. In addition to providing effective treatment tools, trauma orientation has provided a conceptual framework that is compatible with the strengths-based, collaborative Systems of Care model. Having a shared non-judgmental, evidence-based perspective, makes it easier for staff, family members, and other stakeholders engaged in Systems of Care for at-risk youth to shed their previous biases and work together to provide comprehensive and compassionate care.

LOOKS GOOD, BUT WILL IT FLY?

The System of Care (SOC) model provided an elegant design for addressing long-standing problems in providing care for children with serious behavioral challenges and their families. The model offered a framework that would allow policy makers and practitioners to develop alternatives to placing children in restrictive, out-of-community placements, stigmatizing children and families, and eliminating the bureaucratic culture and fragmented relationships among child-serving agencies. The SOC paradigm advanced a vision and accompanying value statements and guiding principles for establishing a community-based network of services and supports that could respond to the unique strengths as well as needs of each child and family offered. Localities and states were given guidance for fostering collaboration among multiple stakeholders through interagency teams that engaged and empowered families to plan and implement coordinated community-based care responsive to the personal, social, and cultural circumstances of the child and family.

The SOC model was laudable in its intent. It was also ambitious and extremely complex. Successful implementation of the SOC model required commitment, ingenuity, and a significant shift in the orientation, policy, practice, and culture for participating organizations at all levels. Individuals and agencies needed to incorporate a new array of programmatic and organizational skills and tools, including the establishment of community-based services and supports to replace residential treatment programs where children with significant behavioral challenges had traditionally been placed. Execution of the SOC model also required a major realignment of relationships among stakeholders. Child-serving personnel, who were accustomed to working independently, would have to learn how to work collaboratively with other providers as well as family members. Historically, the relationship between professionals and consumers had been hierarchical, with providers generally dictating the terms of the service arrangement. A critical component of the SOC model is the engagement and empowerment of children and family members. In order to achieve these goals, professionals would need to redefine their relationship with consumers, shifting from a position of expert dispenser of wisdom on what is in the child's best interest to collaborative partner in planning and implementation of services.

Incorporating the technical and relational aspects of SOC posed a considerable challenge for policy makers, administrators, and practitioners. Participants had to overcome substantial obstacles and learn new skills. This challenge was made even more complicated by the need to address numerous contextual forces that had significant influence on how an SOC would function. Planners had to take into account political, economic, social, cultural, and technological factors, as well as programmatic concerns. Actualizing the SOC model required finding successful solutions during issues such as:

- Defining the roles, responsibilities, and relationships of participating local and state governmental entities in order to be consistent with the geopolitical dynamics of the area while conforming to the principles of the SOC. This task would be easier in states where the control of children's services was clearly in the control of either the local or state government. Resolution would be more difficult in states where both local and state governments viewed themselves as having legitimate authority in determining how services should be provided.

- Realigning a system of funding that was driven by existing program categories to one that was guided by the needs and strengths of individual children and families. Prior to SOC, funds were tied to specific program entities and consumers had to meet the eligibility criteria of an available service modality. The new approach called for services to be individually tailored and provided in a flexible and holistic manner. To be consistent with this SOC philosophy, policy makers had to figure out how to shift from a system in which consumers must fit into the stipulations of a program to an approach that enabled the funds to follow the needs of the children and families. Changing established funding patterns, especially when this required flexibility and blending of discrete funding sources would not be easy.
- Developing a common language and collaborative practice among the mental health, social services, education, and juvenile justice sectors, which were responsible for caring for most of the youth who would be served through an SOC approach. Each of these sectors had a distinct mission and unique operating procedures that were often incongruent with those of their sister agencies. Considerable effort would be required to replace the cultural and procedural barriers with organizational processes and structures that would foster a strength-based, collaborative approach to working with youth and families.
- Reconciling apparently competing political ideologies to ensure support from local- and state-elected officials and their appointees. For example, the SOC model emphasized the importance of encouraging innovation and flexibility, values consistent with the mission of private service providers. At the same time, there was concern for ensuring that children and families served through an SOC received appropriate care. The tension between promoting a free market approach and safeguarding consumers by employing accountability measures was palpable. Finding a reasonable balance between these competing priorities would require political sophistication.
- Providing the multiple supports required to effectively implement a comprehensive, collaborative consumer-centered SOC. Successful transformation from the existing fragmented, institutional-based service arrangement to a seamless, holistic System of Care requires leadership to provide sufficient training for stakeholders, create monitoring and evaluation data systems to track progress and guide improvement efforts, and establish

policies to incentivize and facilitate this holistic, cooperative approach. For instance, policy makers have to figure out how to balance protecting consumer privacy rights with establishing mechanisms to share client information needed by the various child-serving agencies to work collaboratively on behalf of the child and family.

As the SOC movement gained momentum, many localities and states began to develop comprehensive, collaborative programs for at-risk youth and their families. In the first decade a number of noteworthy systems of care were established, mostly at the local level. A few smaller states like Vermont created statewide programs, but most successful efforts were at the local community level. During the early years, many communities professed to have established comprehensive systems of care, but in many instances, child-serving systems were still incomplete and inadequate. John Lyons (2004), in his thoughtful analysis of the children's mental health system, entitled *Redressing the Emperor*, observes that "despite the focus on developing Systems-of-Care philosophy in the children's public mental health system, in most places the system primarily consists of its component parts and thus is a system in name only" (p. 14).

As noted earlier in this chapter, SOC is still considered the program of choice for children with serious and complex behavioral challenges and their families. Much progress has been made in the past decade to validate, improve, and expand this approach (Simons, Pires, Hendricks, & Lipper, 2014; Stroul & Friedman, 2011; Stroul et al., 2014). However, there are many areas of the country that do not have fully developed Systems of Care, and those that have been established are often vulnerable to political and economic threats to their continued functioning. Some of the difficulties stem from the complexity of behavioral health and this programmatic model, which make it difficult to achieve widespread understanding of the benefits of this comprehensive approach. The lack of a national policy requiring that comprehensive children's mental health services be established is emblematic of the frustration experienced by proponents attempting to obtain acceptance and support of the SOC concept from policy makers and other senior government officials.

This book focuses on the broad question of what it takes to establish and sustain a comprehensive SOC for at-risk youth and their families. The following chapters present case studies, review research and program literature, and offer perspectives of experts and other individuals who have played a significant role in planning, implementing, and evaluating local and state SOC models.

One of the overarching issues addressed in this book is what happens after the initial reform is achieved? Enacting legislation or achieving a shift in policy is impressive and important. But passing a law or promulgating a policy is not sufficient and does not ensure successful implementation of the intent of the transformation. And being able to establish a viable program does not necessarily translate to long-term effectiveness. Many innovative efforts have failed to live up to their initial promise, and in many instances, have been terminated. What factors have contributed to developing and maintaining responsive systems of care for at-risk youth and families? Which strategies enhance the probability of sustaining an effective SOC? Are there errors of omission or commission that may impede continued progress?

In our examination of Systems of Care that serve at-risk youth and their families, we identified several specific questions that seemed relevant to understanding the skills and conditions leaders and other stakeholders need to effectively fulfill the SOC mission and goals and sustain effective performance of their system over an extended period of time. Among the questions we explored are the following:

- Are there identifiable characteristics of successful SOCs? What are the unique attributes of leaders and localities/states that enable them to mount successful transformation campaigns?
- What has the leadership of the SOC done to sustain the initial momentum that propelled enactment of the initial transformation effort? What skills and strategies are needed to ensure long-term viability of the system different from those required to launch the reform? How have these exemplary programs been able to continue to provide necessary supports such as training, collection and analysis of relevant data, and quality improvement over an extended period of time?
- How have policy makers and administrators navigated and adapted to changing political, economic, and other contextual forces that potentially impacted their SOC?
- What guidance can be gleaned from how successful SOCs have defined roles and responsibilities of key stakeholders, including children and families, child-serving agencies, service providers, and local and state government entities? And have they been able to achieve a suitable balance between fostering a team-driven process and holding each stakeholder accountable for specific duties and tasks?
- How have proponents of SOC dealt with the traditional political dynamics found in many large bureaucratic systems? Which strategies seem to facilitate reducing silo-oriented, bureaucratic tendencies and promote a culture of team-driven, family-centered practice?
- Related to the issue of organizational culture, what steps can be taken to strengthen the voices of children and families in the planning and implementation of services?

- What are the critical elements required to establish and maintain collaborative relationships among staff of various child-serving agencies as well as between professionals and families?
- How have communities managed to establish an appropriate balance between providing least-restrictive, growth-enhancing opportunities for at-risk youth while ensuring that children and the community are safe?
- Have states and localities identified viable approaches for enabling funding to support the programmatic goals of their SOCs? What strategies have been employed to integrate financial resources into this flexible, collaborative model through blending or braiding multiple child-serving funding sources?
- Are there useful guidelines or strategies that have been employed to ensure an appropriate balance between encouraging innovation and local initiative and maintaining accountability to the core principles and goals of the system? How can SOCs integrate data-based monitoring and evaluation processes into a collaborative, family-driven, locally directed operational framework?
- Is it possible to anticipate negative unintended consequences of the reform effort or is this line of reasoning flawed, or even oxymoronic? How do SOCs cope with adverse outcomes when they occur?

The primary focus of this book is on Virginia's Comprehensive Services Act for At-Risk Youth and Families (CSA). Enacted in the early 1990s during one of the Commonwealth's worst economic recessions, CSA was, at that time, the most ambitious statewide transformation of services for children with SED in the nation. The next nine chapters describe the origin of the Act and how the SOC evolved over the next 20 years. Attention is given to how local and state leaders actualized the lofty vision proposed in the legislation through operating systems that took into account and integrated the multiple programmatic, fiscal, administrative, and technological facets of this interagency system. The narrative describes the challenges planners and administrators faced and how they coped with the broader contextual forces impacting the system as well as the programmatic issues. Successes as well as shortcomings are highlighted, using case examples and program reviews. Empirical data and the perspectives of key stakeholders are utilized to evaluate the performance of the system as well as construct a perspective on why CSA evolved as what factors and forces contributed to desired and unfavorable outcomes.

In the next three chapters, exemplary SOCs from other states and localities are described and analyzed. These efforts are compared to Virginia's CSA in order to provide a framework for understanding how public entities adapt SOC principles to the unique political, social, economic, and demographic conditions of their communities. The final chapter provides a synthesis of the efforts to establish and sustain SOCs for at-risk children and families during the past 25 years. In this concluding chapter, we attempt to cull lessons learned from Virginia and other SOC efforts and offer guidelines and recommendations for policy makers, administrators, practitioners, and advocates interested in promoting and developing systems of care for vulnerable children and their families.

Chapter 3

Why Virginia?

Mr. Jefferson's Virginia has a long history of conservatism. Often touted as the cradle of democracy, Virginia played a key role in the war to gain independence from the British monarchy and the establishment of the United States of America. Since that time the Old Dominion has been a fierce supporter of limiting the power of central authority and strict constructionist interpretation of the constitution. The Commonwealth's conservative social position has been evident in its position on slavery during the nineteenth century and the General Assembly's declaration of Massive Resistance to desegregation in the mid-twentieth century. Until recently, it has lagged behind many other states in recognizing the rights of gay and lesbian citizens.

During the nineteenth century and much of the twentieth century, Virginia was governed by Democrats whose views aligned with the Blue Dog Democrats who controlled the South. In the latter part of the twentieth century these Democrats were replaced by Republicans whose political orientation was equally conservative.

Fiscally, the Commonwealth has traditionally embraced a "pay as you go" approach to budgetary matters. The executive and legislative branches have been staunch supporters of keeping taxes low and limiting debt. Historically, Virginia has been a leader among states in its reluctance to accept federal funding. Many have argued that these conservative fiscal policies have led to insufficient funding for basic need of its citizenry. Most agree however, that the Commonwealth's prudent management of fiscal resources, as evidenced by its AAA bond ratings (i.e., the highest possible rating assigned to an issuer's bonds by credit rating agencies), has enabled Virginia to maintain a relative stable economy in relation to more free spending states.

With this conservative tradition, it seems unlikely at first glance that Virginia would enact the most visionary and ambitious statewide reform of how children with serious mental health challenges are served. However, the fact that the governor of Virginia proposed and the General Assembly passed the Comprehensive Services Act for At-Risk Youth and Families (CSA) seems less surprising when one considers some other characteristics and traditions of the Commonwealth.

Peter Wallenstein (2007) in his eloquent review of four centuries of Virginia history challenges the commonly held belief that the Old Dominion has been characterized by harmony, consensus, and continuity. He argues that closer scrutiny reveals tension, conflict, and change not just in recent years but as early as the Colonial period. The bold and visionary leadership that guided our country through its formative years was provided largely by George Washington, James Madison, Thomas Jefferson, and other Virginians. During the first part of the twentieth century the Commonwealth made considerable strides in improving education at primary, secondary, and higher levels. Although the Byrd organization played a critical role in trying to perpetuate segregation, in his early years as governor, Harry F. Byrd introduced significant reforms in how state government functioned, including creative and efficient approaches for constructing and financing highways. During the second half of the twentieth century, when Virginia became a two-party state, the Commonwealth was a leader in progressive state governance, introducing innovative government practices such as performance-based budgeting and forging public-private partnerships that promoted economic growth by enhancing production and delivery of goods and services and expanding international trade (Atkinson, 2006).

As we examine the factors that influence the passage of the CSA legislation, we should keep in mind that this odd hybrid of tradition and innovation may provide a partial explanation for why Virginia was able to enact such a bold and far-reaching blueprint for reforming the delivery of services for at-risk youth and their families. In the remainder of this chapter we will examine other factors that contributed to the Commonwealth's passage of this groundbreaking legislation.

BEFORE THE BEGINNING

Where does a reform begin? How does one pinpoint the precise events or set of forces and events that trigger the groundswell leading to significant policy change or enabling legislation? As one might expect with such complex social/political phenomena it is extremely difficult to hone in on a single precipitating factor or event. Instead, we tend to review the historical context and identify those actions and conditions that seem pertinent to the reform. Ultimately our selection of a point of origin is somewhat arbitrary.

A review of history about the provision of mental health services in the United States offers several potential starting points. The deinstitutionalization movement, which began in the late 1950s, moved the traditional locus of care for persons with serious mental illness away from state hospitals. The community mental health initiative, which started during the Kennedy administration in the 1960s, established in many communities local centers responsible for providing mental health services. Ironically, the initial focus of these centers was to provide preventive services and therefore did not focus on the population of people being discharged from state institutions. It was not until the late 1970s that communities began developing community-based services and supports aimed at helping persons with serious mental health challenges. The designers of these programs for individuals with chronic mental illness recognized the importance of incorporating the multiple physical, social, economic, and medical needs experienced by this population; theoretically, all needs had previously been addressed under the single roof of the state hospital. In response, they created community-based service models that addressed these multiple needs in an integrated manner, using multi-disciplinary teams that often brought services to where the patients resided (Stein & Santos, 1998).

Although children and adolescents with serious mental health challenges constituted a small segment of the state hospital census, many troubled youth were placed in residential treatment programs, often outside the communities where they lived. The shift in philosophy occurred later for children than adults, a trend consistent with the lower priority given to children's mental health issues. It was not until Jane Knitzer published *Unclaimed Children* (1982) and revealed the extent to which children with mental health get shortchanged, that policy makers began to give serious attention to this issue. The release of Beth Stroul and Bob Friedman's sentinel work on developing systems of care for children and youth with severe emotional disturbances (Stroul & Friedman, 1986) spawned reform activity at the local, state, and federal levels.

In Virginia, there are numerous events that might be viewed as triggers for the children's mental health reform movement. The Chapter 10 legislation, enacted by the General Assembly in response to deinstitutionalization, established Community Service Boards (CSB) in each locality. These CSB entities were responsible for the provision of publically supported mental health services in each community. In the years that followed, numerous commissions and special reports identified the shortcomings of mental health services for young people and offered recommendations for improving care.

For the purpose of this chronology we have chosen Governor Gerald Baliles' (1985–1989) term in office as the starting point. This decision has been made for two reasons. First, during this period the governor and legislature appropriated nearly $60 million in the mid-term biennial budget for community-based mental health services. During this period, the Secretary of Health and Human Resources, Eva Teig, and the Commissioner of the Department of Mental Health, Mental Retardation and Substances, Howard Cullum, were instrumental in procuring that appropriation. Teig was, and continues to be, a masterful navigator of the Commonwealth's political system as well as a strong proponent for children's mental health. She worked diligently with agency heads to establish a policy, financial and administrative infrastructure that would serve as a foundation for the future development of the State's comprehensive system of care for at-risk youth and their families. Cullum, a seasoned public manager and a visionary program developer, was appointed Secretary of Health and Human Resources, in the following gubernatorial term, and became the moving force behind the development and enactment of the CSA.

Baliles was also committed to improving community-based services for individuals with mental health disorders. At the time he took office, he had a clear sense of how he would address his priorities. According to his Secretary of Health and Human Resources, the Governor said, "I am doing transportation my first year; world trade and economic development, and education by my second year; and by my third year, a major mental health initiative" (E. Teig Hardy, personal communication, May 13, 2014). In addition to successfully persuading the General Assembly to appropriate an additional $63 million for community-based mental health services, Baliles and his leadership team addressed other shortcomings in the system, including problems in the child welfare system and lack of accreditation for state-operated mental health facilities.

During the Baliles administration a number of other significant events occurred that set the stage for the future legislation and put in motion actions that would culminate in the passage of the CSA several years later. One of those events was a conference held in April 1987 that focused on the relationship of parents of children with serious mental health problems and the professionals who serve them. The co-sponsors of the conference, the Virginia Treatment Center for Children (VTCC), the state's flagship public psychiatric hospital for youth and the National Alliance on Mental Illness (NAMI), the nation' most influential advocacy organization on behalf of persons with serious mental illness, recognized that relationships between these critical players were often strained and nonproductive. These organizations wanted to address the problems that created a rift between parents and professionals and lay the groundwork for establishing productive partnerships between these important stakeholder groups so they could work more effectively on behalf of at-risk children at both individual and broader system levels. The conference addressed the outmoded theories subscribed to by some professionals that children's mental health problems were caused in large part by the bad behavior of parents. According to these theories, which have since been shown to be spurious and are no longer viewed as credible, such as cold, rejecting mothers are responsible for their child's autism ("refrigerator mothers") (Bettelheim, 1967; Kanner, 1949) and parents who criticize or punish their children regardless of which choice they make, create a double-bind situation which may lead to the development of schizophrenia in later years (Bateson, Jackson, Haley & Weakland, 1956). The conference also presented examples of how collaborative efforts by parents and providers led to improved outcomes and provided models for how parent support groups could assist individual families as well as lead to significant change in children's mental health programs.

A group of parents attending this conference met subsequently to form a support group for parents of children with serious emotional disorders. Initially the group served as a setting where family members could discuss the challenges and frustrations they experienced with individuals who understood what they were experiencing. Recognizing that many of the difficulties they experienced stemmed from deficiencies in the mental health service system, the group quickly turned its attention to building capacity to enable them to advocate on behalf of children with mental health challenges and their families. The members of this small support group established the Parents and Children Coping Together (PACCT) organization in Virginia, which had a central leadership core as well as local chapters in all regions of the state. PACCT became involved in educating family members about children's mental health issues, including how to navigate the complicated and often fragmented service system. They also developed an effective network of parents who advocated with state and local officials to improve services for at-risk youth.

During the next few years PACCT became a powerful force for change in the Commonwealth. In the period leading up to the development of the CSA legislation, as well as during its formative years, PACCT provided a strong vehicle for parents to articulate their concerns and recommendations. Given the natural inclination of public officials to distrust the views of child-serving agencies and service providers because of the vested interests of these groups, the presence of a strong parent voice significantly enhanced the credibility of the message.

The pre-CSA momentum was also accelerated from another source outside of the group of mental health service providers who traditionally had been the leading advocates for improvement in care. Jeannie Baliles, the first lady of Virginia during the latter part of the 1980s expressed a strong interest in children's mental health. Mrs. Baliles became involved with the VTCC and subsequently created a state interagency task force charged with developing a plan to improve coordination of services for children. Mrs. Baliles played a pivotal role in facilitating cooperation among the state's child-serving agencies, including the departments of education, social services, juvenile justice, and mental health.

In the fall of 1987 the group responsible for interagency coordination sponsored a conference to address the current problems and future directions for serving children with serious mental health disorders. At this meeting, which was called the First Lady's Forum on Children's Mental Health, Jane Knitzer, whose seminal work, *Unclaimed Children*, was cited earlier in this chapter, spoke to participants about the scope of the problem and provided examples of innovative approaches for improving care. This was followed by presentations by workgroups of the interagency task force focused on innovative strategies for reducing fragmentation and improving services for these children. In addition to providers and consumers, the commissioners of the state's child-serving agencies as well as the cabinet secretaries responsible for these organizations were invited to attend. Because of Mrs. Baliles relationship with the governor, all of these high-level officials accepted the invitation.

At the end of the forum, which was held in a small auditorium at VTCC, the commissioners and cabinet secretaries were invited to come to the stage of the auditorium and offer brief remarks. Before they spoke, Mrs. Baliles, who was particularly concerned with the territorial inclination of the child-serving agencies and the disjointed manner in which services were delivered, stood in front of the auditorium and addressed the audience. She shared her concerns about how fragmented and ineffective services were and the importance of developing collaborative strategies. Then she turned to the officials assembled on the stage and told them she wanted them to work together to develop a plan for enhancing cooperation and collaboration among state child-serving agencies. She directed them to submit this plan to her within six months.

Clearly, the first lady did not have the legal or even administrative authority to direct these high-level officials to produce this plan. Yet she was able to use her bully pulpit position to encourage them to work together. The plan she requested was developed and served as a framework and guide for the children's interagency activity over the next few years. This work, most of which was not formally reflected in regulations or code, provided the foundation upon which CSA was eventually constructed (Cohen & Cohen, 2000).

One of the products of the deliberations among cabinet secretaries, agency heads and their staff was the formation of the State Interagency Consortium on Child Mental Health. The Consortium was governed by a board of state agency personnel, local providers, and family members. Among the accomplishments of this group was the establishment of two funding initiatives designed to provide integrated services to children in need of intensive mental health services. Funds for these initiatives were contributed by each state child-serving agency. The funds were removed from the control of the individual agencies and deposited in a common fund administered by the Consortium in order to allow flexibility and innovative use of these resources. In its first year of operation the Consortium was allocated $1.6 million.

The funds were used for two initiatives. *The State Interagency Pool Account*, encouraged local communities to apply for small grants to pay for individualized services for children whose needs could not be met within existing regulatory restrictions. Directors of mental health, social services education and other relevant child-serving agencies were required to provide written verification of their involvement. *The Local Interagency Service Projects* was designed to address critical gaps in the continuum of care of local communities. Proposals were solicited from communities interested in developing new services that would enhance coordinated service delivery. This initiative provided awards of up to $200,000 each for six localities. Similar to the requirement of the State Pool program, local officials were required to verify their participation in this local service coordination improvement initiative.

Over the course of the next three years nearly 250 requests were received from localities asking for funds to support individualized service plans for children. In 1988, its initial year of operation, 51 percent of requests were approved. By 1990, 79 percent were approved. The type of service requested also changed over time, with placement in residential care dropping from 50 percent to 21 percent over that same period of time and requests for service in home-based settings increasing (MacBeth, 1993).

These building blocks, the formation of the PACCT network that created a strong parent voice in policy deliberations, the First Lady's Forum, and subsequent establishment of the State Interagency Consortium on Child Mental Health, as well as the individualized child service plans and community development initiatives funded by the Consortium, provided important building blocks upon which the CSA would be constructed. Ironically, almost no one at that time would have predicted that such a grand edifice, the bold and ambitious system of care embodied in the CSA legislation, would rise so quickly from these significant but modest first steps.

AN UNLIKELY TIME FOR REFORM

In November 1989, L. Douglas Wilder was elected Governor of Virginia, becoming the first African-American in the nation to be elected to this high post since the reconstruction period of the nineteenth century. Wilder was part of a legendary group of black lawyers in Richmond who were instrumental in bringing an end to segregation in Virginia during the 1960s and

1970s. A savvy politician, Wilder was elected to the state Senate in 1969, and was also the first African-American elected to the senate body since Reconstruction. As a liberal in a conservative environment Wilder exerted relatively strong influence in the legislature through the key committee leadership positions he acquired over the years through seniority. In 1985, running with Gerald Baliles, he was narrowly elected to the post of Lieutenant Governor.

Unfortunately Governor Wilder's historic victory was quickly overshadowed by the state's largest fiscal crisis in modern history. The $2.8 billion budget shortfall Wilder faced when he took office in January 1990 surpassed all but the recent deficit resulting from the 2008 financial collapse. Wilder and his staff were forced to spend most of their time and energy figuring out how to balance the budget. Given Virginia's generally conservative position, the challenge of matching expenditures with revenue required making difficult spending cuts as raising taxes was not a politically acceptable option. Many well-established programs, including those within the Health and Human Resources Secretariat were seriously curtailed or, in some instances, eliminated.

Despite the shortfall and the drain of attention and energy required to deal with it, officials in the Wilder administration were able to muster enthusiasm and resources to address several critical problems, including the serious deficiencies of the child mental health system. Although some of the key players including the Secretary of Health and Human Resources and heads of the state child-serving agencies were logical leaders in the children's mental health reform effort, significant help also came from other unexpected sources of influence.

THE KEEPERS OF THE PURSE STEP UP

Toward the end of the Baliles administration, the State Department of Planning and Budget (DPB) became aware of the rising cost of placing at-risk children and adolescents in residential treatment programs. In response to their concern, the DPB conducted a thorough study of the extent to which residential treatment was being utilized, the types of children who were being placed in these settings and the cost of funding residential treatment programs. Under the leadership of Rob Lockridge, who managed the Health and Human Resources division, DPB staff reviewed every child who had spent more than 30 days in a group residential care setting paid for by at least one Virginia public agency in the fiscal year of 1989. Their findings surprised almost everyone, including individuals familiar with the children's service system in the Commonwealth.

When multiple placements for the same child were taken into account, there was a total of 4,993 youth with emotional or behavioral difficulties who were placed for more than 30 days in a group residential or state institution setting (i.e., state psychiatric hospital or correctional facility). Most of these young people were placed in facilities within Virginia, but more than 300 were placed outside the state. Almost half of the youth had two or more placements during the year, 80 percent were involved in two or more child-serving agencies, and nearly 20 percent were engaged with four agencies. Nearly 9 percent of the youth exhibited serious emotional or behavioral problems, almost as many children had major school-related problems, and two-thirds had been adjudicated by the courts (Virginia Department of Planning and Budget, 1990).

Equally surprising was the cost of placing these young people in residential care settings. The total cost for serving approximately 5,000 children was $93.6 million in the year the study was conducted. In the following fiscal year, 1990, the cost rose to $101 million (Virginia Department of Planning and Budget, 1990).

Although the initial purpose of the DPB study was to understand and highlight the considerable fiscal burden for Virginia, the study also served another purpose. In the course of conducting their research, the DPB staff learned how dysfunctional the current service system was. In their final report, DPB provided strategies for improving programmatic approaches as well as fiscal outcomes. Interestingly, their recommendations were quite similar to those that had been offered by experts in the child-serving community over the past few years.

Gail Ledford, Director of the Department for Administration of Human Services of Fairfax County in Northern Virginia recalls that the DPB study was a "catalyst, a big 'ah-ha' moment for what was to become CSA." Ledford, who was a lobbyist for the county at that time, notes that "Everybody in the whole system had a sense that we were serving thousands and thousands of children. The kid count was so dramatically less than we thought . . . but we were still spending those same big dollars" (G. Ledford, personal communication, August 3, 2010).

The importance of DPB and its residential care study in the formulation and establishment of CSA cannot be overstated. Howard Cullum, who served as Secretary for Health and Human Resources during the Wilder administration recalls "The budget office wanted to see some changes happen. They had the power because they were over all the state entities. Basically the budget office wanted to drive this" (H. Cullum, personal communication, July 27, 2010). The DPB's interest in this initiative was clearly related to the prospect of reducing expenditures for children's services and ending the outflow of state funds to residential facilities outside of Virginia. In addition, they understood that localities did not have a stake in controlling the cost of residential services as the current system relied solely on federal and state funds. The proposed funding formula for CSA required local governments to pay for a portion of services, giving them a tangible inducement to ensure that funds were expended judiciously.

Given DPBs interest in the financial ramifications as well as their support for the programmatic goals of CSA, they became champions of this ambitious reform initiative. Rob Lockridge, who directed the Health and Human Resources section of DPB at that time, explains the role of the budget office in convincing the state's leaders that change was needed. "If the secretary goes to the governor's office and his staff and says we need to change this program, it is important, but if numerous people go to the budget director, that has a lot more weight . . . because the budget office doesn't talk to the governor about things like that unless they felt there was a financial reason to do so" (R. Lockridge, personal communication, June, 2013).

Kim McGaughey, one of the lead researchers for the DPB study describes what may have been the initial step in conceptualizing the CSA. "My boss (Rob Lockridge) and I approached Howard (Cullum) and he was passionate about this and gave us suggestions on how to move forward. He said go for it. And so we worked it out that I would work for him out of his office" (K. McGaughey, personal communication, November 17, 2011). While Cullum served as the lead state official and spokesperson during the development of CSA legislation, Ms. McGaughey became the point person responsible for managing the complex, intricate planning process during the next several years.

IT TAKES A VILLAGE TO PLAN A REFORM

The planning process for CSA deserves a place in the Guinness Book of Records for the scope of its mission and activity as well as the diversity of the people participating in the planning process. The residential care study evoked considerable interest within the executive and legislative branches of state government. In response to the General Assembly's mandate to create a detailed implementation plan addressing the DPB study's recommendations, the governor established the Council on Community Services for Youth and Families to recommend fundamental, structural, and operational changes in the current system. The Council reported directly to the three cabinet secretaries responsible for children's services and was comprised of nearly 200 individuals including 145 public- and private-service providers, parents, child advocates, judges, university faculty, local and state government officials and personnel who were assigned to work groups created to address all aspects of the children's service system.

During the next 18 months members of the Council developed detailed blueprints for a system that would ensure that young people with serious emotional and behavioral challenges would be served appropriately in a cost-effective manner. The workgroups tackled a variety of issues including developing a model of community services, designing funding mechanisms, and establishing an interagency planning process. Recognizing that a strong infrastructure would be needed to sustain and enhance the service system, work groups also designed training, technical assistance, data tracking, utilization review, and program evaluation. There was also a group responsible for managing five local demonstration projects intended to test best practices in the field. The demonstration project initiative was supported by a $2.4 million two-year appropriation from the state legislature.

The work of the Council served, in many ways, as a microcosm and role model for the system of care that was eventually enacted. There was enormous synergy among the leadership and work group members of the Council. In planning the new system, participants were willing to discard traditional approaches and boundaries and consider innovative approaches for ensuring that at-risk youth received timely, holistic services provided in or as close to home as possible. Larry Jackson, who served as Commissioner of Social Services during that period observes "It was the right set of people coming together at the right time in an environment that was open to these ideas and with some people who were pushing it who had a lot of credibility on both sides of the political aisle and with the professional community and parent groups and others. I think everything just came together at the right time" (L. Jackson, personal communication, February 7, 2012).

The workgroups, which brought together people with very different perspectives, experience, and geographic and organizational affiliation met frequently during the 18-month planning period. Participants wrestled with complex funding, programmatic, and technical and governance issues, considered a range of alternative approaches, and eventually found ways to put aside their differences and reach consensus. A frequent refrain in these meetings was *let's look at what will work best for the children and families we are serving.*

At the leadership level, public executives, who often worked in silos, modeled proactive, collaborative problem solving as they put together the multiple components of this complex reform legislative proposal. Working under the leadership of Howard Cullum, the commissioners and directors of the departments of Social Services, Mental Health, Education, Juvenile Justice, and the Supreme Court worked diligently to develop an alternative approach to the territorial, segmented manner in which at-risk youth had traditionally served. Charles Kehoe, the Director of the Department of Youth and Family Services during the Wilder administration notes that for children who had

multiple disabilities or required services from more than one child-serving
agency:

> Everybody pointed the finger at the other guy and expected them to pick up the
> tab. So we felt that collaboration would be a good model to use and we pursued
> it. We were asked to see what would happen if we pooled all of our money and
> then communities would be able to draw down on that money. Some money
> would be added to the pool ... it would be allocated to communities based on
> need. We thought that would be better than each agency having to decide where
> a child fit. (C. Kehoe, personal communication, February 10, 2012)

To be clear, the deliberations were not always harmonious. The most con-
tentious issue, as might be expected, was funding. As stated above, the CSA
legislation called for agencies to place funding previously allocated to serve
at-risk youth into a central account in order to provide greater flexibility.
Once money was transferred to this pool the state and local child-serving
agencies that transferred their funds would no longer have control of these
financial resources. Kim McGaughey, who coordinated all of the planning for
CSA, remembers "there was a lot of distrust as to when we put all the funding
streams together and when we allocated them to localities, who was going to
lose. There were going to be losers and winners" (K. McGaughey, personal
communication, November 17, 2011).

At one of the final meetings of the planning council, Howard Cullum did
not mince words when he addressed the proposal to consolidate funding
streams. He told the audience, which included many of the key stakeholders
who would be impacted by this change, that he expected them to sit together
at a common table and place the funds allocated to at-risk youth on the table.
Then they would push their resources to the center of the table and remove
their hands. Ordinarily, the strongly grounded tradition of government agencies operating in silos and the power and inclination of local government to
resist state-imposed changes on how local agencies handled their resources
would have been sufficient to prevent the pooling of funds to move forward.
However, the dynamic leadership of Cullum and his staff and the clearly
articulated goals of CSA to promote an integrated approach for serving children and families sustained momentum which allowed the funding proposal
and other provisions of the act to move forward, at least until it reached the
General Assembly.

Governance was the other major controversial issue that the planners struggled with. In Virginia, both state and local governments are strong governing
bodies and exert considerable influence on shaping policy and managing
resources and programs. In contrast to states in which either the state or local
government is dominant and the other governing body is relatively weak, this

balance of power often creates tension when decisions are being made about the operational details of implementing policies and programs.

The designers of CSA tried to take into account how to best serve youth as well as how to ensure the political and practical viability of this innovative system of care. Most planners believed that strong local ownership and control were essential. The traditional system had been managed in a top-down manner, relying heavily on bureaucratic procedures. This approach not only fostered fragmented, non-responsive services but also discouraged localities from becoming enthusiastic participants in the children's mental health system. In response to the shortcomings of the current system, the Council endorsed a governance structure in which the locus of authority and accountability would reside with each locality. Responsibility and authority for CSA resided with the highest elected official of each locality, that is, mayor, county supervisor.

Two local management structures were included in the final plan. Each locality would establish a Community Policy and Management Team (CPMT) which would be responsible for developing, monitoring and modifying the guidelines and procedures for implementing CSA in their community. The CPMT would be appointed by the local governing body and would be comprised of the heads of the child-serving agencies of that locality as well as several at-large members including at least one parent of an at-risk child. The CPMTs would be responsible for managing the collaborative efforts in their community to more effectively serve the needs of troubled and at-risk youth and their families and optimize the use of state and local resources (Virginia Acts of Assembly, Chapter 837, § 2.1-752, April 15, 1992).

Each locality would also create a Family Assessment and Planning Team (FAPT), responsible for developing individualized service plans for each child and family referred to and found eligible for CSA services. Similar to the CPMT, staff of all child-serving agencies as well as at-large parent representatives would be standing members of each FAPT. Parents and children referred to FAPT were expected to actively collaborate with FAPT members and staff of the local CSA office to design an individualized plan for capitalizing on the strengths and addressing the needs of the eligible youth and family. This emphasis on family empowerment was one of the core tenets of CSA and was intended to serve as a counterbalance to the inclination of many child-serving agencies to plan based on organizational convenience rather than consumer need (Virginia Acts of Assembly, Chapter 837, § 2.1-754, April 15, 1992). The CSA referral system for families is visually depicted in Figure 3.1.

The local FAPT creates a menu of interventions from which to choose one that can best fit the individualized treatment planning needs of the child. Services range from: (a) preventive care (e.g., parenting education, coaching, and skills training; parent aides), (b) crisis management (e.g., respite care and

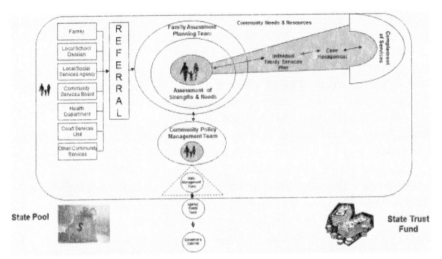

Figure 3.1   Overview of How the CSA System of Care was Integrated into Various Teams and Community Agencies for Referral, Funding, and Service Sources. *Source*: Created by R. Cohen (author).

mobile crisis services for children requiring immediate attention and interventions), (c) intensive in-home services (i.e., a short-term, solution-focused, counseling service provided in the home for children and youth who are at risk of being removed or who are transitioning back from an out-of-home placement due to a severe emotional or behavioral problem), (d) home-based counseling (i.e., clinical services provided in the home to children and families' identified needs), (e) outpatient psychotherapy (i.e., traditional evidenced-based individual and/or family therapy, such as cognitive behavioral therapy), and (f) intensive care coordination (i.e., an intensive case management service that links families with both informal and professional resources to provide services to either prevent a child from going into an out-of-home placement or to transition a child out of placement and stabilize them in the home). Creative and unique interventions are also sometimes available to youth, such as equine therapy which provides children with physical, mental and psychological challenges and provides opportunities to use equine activities—adapted and individualized for them—as recreation, socialization, and skill-building. Specialized treatments are also typically available for the FAPT to integrate into the child's individualized plan. For instance applied behavioral analysis therapy (ABA) for children on the autism spectrum, or substance-abuse assessment and treatment which may include detox, individual and/or group counseling, and random drug testing. Young adults requiring assistance with the transition into independent living can receive a variety of interventions to job readiness training, life skills coaching, and mental health skills building. Overall, the FAPT's goal was to create an individualized treatment plan to best help the family and child.

Although the architects of CSA were firmly committed to empowering localities they also recognized the need to ensure accountability as well as equity. Toward this end the state was given several roles and responsibilities related to effective implementation of the CSA. Some of these functions were specifically designed to provide support and assistance to localities. Training for those involved in the implementation of CSA at the local level was managed centrally for purposes of efficiency as well as to reduce burden on localities, especially smaller communities with limited resources. A central data base was established for organizing information and facilitating financial transactions. A State Executive Committee and Management Team designed similarly as their local counterparts, and including local government and private provider representatives, were established to work collaboratively with localities to provide assistance and address obstacles and concerns relating to CSA (Virginia Acts of Assembly, Chapter 837, § 2.1, April 15, 1992).

One of the core governance issues the Council grappled with was whether the state should mandate participation in CSA by all localities and local child-serving agencies as opposed to giving localities leeway in determining the extent to which they chose to be involved. This is a classic governance issue, with compelling arguments on both sides. Proponents of local choice argue that localities know best how to provide services for their citizens and should be allowed to manage their own activities and services, especially when the state or local government control produced additional financial burden for the locality.

Those in favor of limited central control call attention to the responsibility the central government has for ensuring that all citizens have equal access to critical services and resources. They believe that it is sometimes necessary to mandate participation by all government entities. When this issue was addressed by the planners of CSA, a majority concluded that anything short of full participation by all localities and local agencies would doom the program to failure. They asserted that allowing local entities to opt out of participating would significantly impede the ability of children and families to receive seamless, comprehensive services. They believed that if localities were given a choice in this matter, services for at-risk youth would eventually regress to the former silo-like, fragmented, unresponsive system they were trying to replace.

The Council decided to include strong language in its legislative proposal, requiring participation of all localities in CSA, as well as mandating full involvement of all child-serving agencies within the localities. When the final proposal for CSA was presented to the state legislature, this provision, mandating participation would become the source of considerable debate.

The irony of the state's strong stance on mandating local participation was not lost. Some members of the planning process noted that Virginia, which was often in the forefront of criticizing the Federal government for interfering with the rights of states for self-governance had now aggressively pursued the same position in relation to its own localities.

DRESS REHEARSAL

After 18 months of intensive planning by nearly 200 people, a lengthy final report was produced. A process that at least one senior official called "one of the most complex planning processes she had participated in" (J. Kusiak, personal communication, July 16, 2013), defied conventional wisdom and produced a thorough, detailed blueprint for substantively overhauling the service system for at-risk youth and their families. And that plan had the enthusiastic support of knowledgeable stakeholders from all sectors of the system, including local and state governments, private and public service providers, advocates and families. The proposed legislation described a set of core goals and objectives to guide the development and implementation the CSA system of care. These desired outcomes, based on nationally acknowledged principles of state-of-the-art practice for serving at-risk youth, provided a philosophical and conceptual framework for shaping how care should be delivered. The core objectives included:

- Ensure that services and funding are consistent with the Commonwealth's policy of preserving families and providing appropriate services in the least restricted environment, while protecting the welfare of children and maintaining the safety of the public;
- Identify and intervene early with young children and their families who are at risk of developing emotional or behavioral problems or both due to environmental, physical, or psychological stress;
- Increase interagency collaboration and family involvement in service delivery and management;
- Encourage a public and private partnership in the delivery of services;
- Provide communities flexibility in the use of funds and to direct decisions, authority, and accountability to communities who know best the needs of their youth and families (Virginia Acts of Assembly, Chapter 837, § 2.1-745, April 1, 1992).

Consistent with the overall approach of CSA, these objectives address not only the programmatic technology needed to effectively serve children, but also take into account the contextual forces that significantly impact the way in which services are delivered. By acknowledging and incorporating contextual forces such as funding, general state policy on the well-being of children and families as well as public safety, and governance issues, the planners believed they could ensure that CSA became a viable and sustainable service system.

As we follow the development and evolution of CSA we will return to these original objectives to help us assess the effectiveness of this act. As might be expected, some of these objectives have been more challenging than others, and progress has not always proceeded in a linear fashion (Virginia Acts of Assembly, Chapter 837, § 2.1-745, April 1, 1992).

In the fall of 1991 Governor Wilder, with the assistance of his senior staff, formally presented the proposed CSA legislation to the leaders of the General Assembly. As with all major legislation, considerable preliminary discussions had taken place between the chief proponents of the CSA and staff of the major legislative committee. Because of the critical financial issues attached to this bill, staff of the House Appropriations and Senate Finance Committees was involved in these discussions early in the process. Fortunately, the lead staff members for the Health and Human Resources subcommittees were strong advocates for children and families as well as skilled practitioners of the art of crafting successful legislation. Steve Harms, of the Senate Finance Committee, had been a social worker before joining the legislature, and Jane Kusiak, of the House Appropriations Committee had a strong background in children's policy and was a passionate supporter of well-designed initiatives that addressed the needs of vulnerable children.

The budget crisis the Commonwealth was experiencing at that time consumed a considerable amount of time and energy of key legislative and executive officials and there was not much enthusiasm for new initiatives, given the large number of programs that were being cut in response to reduced revenue. Despite these obstacles, senior staff of the executive and legislative branches were able to reach agreement about the potential value of the core mission, principles and objectives and began to speak with key members of the House of Delegates and Senate to obtain support. The consensus among staff from both branches of government was clearly facilitated by the financial benefits they perceived in this proposal. These seasoned policy staff saw the potential value of fiscal resources being used more effectively to serve at-risk youth as well as enhancing efficiency by reducing fragmentation and creating more flexibility and accountability at the local level.

In preparing the legislative proposal the CSA planners struggled with two important issues that would potentially impact the fate of the legislation. The first matter involved how the pooled resources would be redistributed to localities. Knowing that the financial crisis the state faced had heightened sensitivity about the fiscal impact of any legislation and the unlikely availability of new resources. Therefore considerable attention was given to ensure that the distribution methodology was equitable and did not significantly harm any local government entity. The formula they finally agreed upon was based on population and poverty. Localities would receive a share of the total funds equal to the percentage of the state's population residing in their city or county, adjusted for the proportion of residents who fell below the established poverty income level.

The second sensitive issue concerned governance. As noted earlier, the Council had attempted to move the locus of control to the local level while also ensuring equity and accountability. The legislative proposal presented to the General Assembly took a strong stand on requiring participation. All localities in the Commonwealth were mandated to participate in the system and involvement in CSA was obligatory for all child-serving agencies in each of the localities.

Over the course of the 1992 General Assembly session the CSA legislative proposal was thoroughly vetted. In addition to receiving briefings and questioning, senior officials in the Wilder administration legislators heard from child advocates, lobbyists representing a range of special interest groups, and constituents from their home district. They were particularly interested in the views of the two organizations representing local government, the Virginia Municipal League (VML), a nonpartisan not-for-profit organization that represented cities and towns, and the Virginia Association of Counties (VACO), primarily focused on county government.

Leadership from VML and VACO had been active participants in the CSA planning process. Betty Long, representing VML and Dean Lynch of VACO had become strong supporters of the CSA approach and had contributed to the work of the Council. When the proposal was brought to the General Assembly it received intense scrutiny from the constituents of VML and VACO. Based on their analysis of the bill they concluded that implementation of the proposed distribution formula, some localities, particularly the large, wealthy suburban cities and counties, would suffer significant losses in relation to their current allocations. They were also uncomfortable with the strong mandate for participation imposed by the bill.

Toward the end of the legislative session the bill was partially enacted but without inclusion of a funding formula or other vital components needed to implement the system. Without a funding mechanism, services could not be paid for, rendering the legislation impractical. Although both parties were generally favorably disposed to the CSA concept, the negative fallout from the fiscal distribution formula and the objection of local government and agency officials to being required by the state to participate proved to be insurmountable obstacles. The 1992 General Assembly closed without producing viable CSA legislation.

TWO'S A CHARM

Supporters of CSA were disappointed but not disheartened. They went back to the drawing board to address the concerns that had led to the bill's defeat. The level of commitment of the Wilder administration was most seriously tested by the funding distribution issue. The only way to rectify the loss of funds by some localities would be to add additional dollars to the CSA budget. The Commonwealth was still experiencing serious fiscal problems and the price tag to hold localities harmless from losses they would incur under the new formula was large. After much deliberation the Governor decided to provide an additional $7 million dollars to the CSA budget request submitted to the 1993 session of the General Assembly.

A lively debate ensued about the merits and disadvantages of requiring local participation. Staunch proponents of the CSA model argued that loosening the full participation requirement would weaken the essential interagency bond required to deliver seamless, holistic services and dilute the impact of the program. Supporters of CSA who were more focused on the logistics of transforming the plan into a functional statewide system of care were willing to be more flexible. They contended that it was essential to ease the mandate clause if they expected the legislation to be enacted.

When the General Assembly convened, it was apparent that local governments were united in their opposition to the participation mandate and their support would be essential for the passage of CSA legislation. After considerable negotiation an agreement was reached. All localities would be required to participate in CSA. However, the language of the mandate was tweaked from requiring all child-serving agencies in the locality to be involved to encouraging them to participate. This seemingly minor change in language would later prove to have a significant impact on how the CSA developed and evolved.

On March 15, 1993, the House passed House Bill 1748 and two days later Senate Bill 783 and the CSA became part of the code of the Commonwealth.

AGAINST THE ODDS

How did this visionary children's mental health reform initiative surmount the multiple obstacles it faced to become enacted as the system of care for the entire State of Virginia? As with most successful complex policy endeavors, success was dependent upon multiple forcers converging at an opportune time.

A key factor in bringing the vision to fruition was the hard work and commitment of a core group of individuals passionately committed to the philosophy and principles underlying the Comprehensive Services Act.

Many of these individuals, such as Howard Cullum, Kim McGaughey, Rob Lockridge, Jane Kusiak, and Steve Harms occupied positions of influence at the highest level of state government. The fact that several of these leaders were intimately involved with fiscal policy and decisions was a major asset as was the political savvy these individuals brought to the process. The involvement of a broad spectrum of stakeholders in the thorough planning process also contributed to the successful outcome. Representatives from virtually all groups with an interest in the issue had an opportunity to provide input during the nearly three years from its inception to the passage of the CSA legislation. Although all of the participants did not agree on all aspects of the plan their involvement enabled them to develop a strong commitment to the mission and purpose of the act. When disagreement arose the stakeholders were able to play an active role in negotiating resolution.

Attention to detail was a critical factor in being able to actualize this complex vision. During the 18-month planning period prior to submission of the legislative proposal, literally hundreds of meetings were held to work on specific issues and concerns. The investment of time and energy by senior leaders was unprecedented. Every Wednesday morning Howard Cullum met with the commissioners and directors of the state's major child-serving agencies for an hour and a half to resolve questions and problems that had arisen during the past week. This concentrated effort not only allowed timely resolution of potential obstacles but also created a foundation and model for future collaboration among these agencies.

As noted earlier, Virginia has a paradoxical relationship with social issues. With its strong conservative political tradition and reactionary stance to issues such as racial integration, one would not expect the Commonwealth to be an incubator for innovation. Yet in many ways the state's management philosophy and practice paved the way for the passage of such progressive legislation. Virginia's long-standing tradition of appointing high-level administrative staff on the basis of professional rather than political credentials, in both the executive and legislative branches was clearly an asset in this case. The senior staff who briefed elected officials was viewed as credible by the political leaders as well as the multiple constituents who influence government policy. The reports they prepared were based on empirical data and thoughtful analysis which provided a sense of legitimacy to their recommendations.

Virginia also had experience utilizing partnerships to effectively actualize policies and programs. The CSA built on this precedent. With its strong focus on empowering localities and encouraging municipalities to forge partnerships with private providers to deliver services, the act was perceived as an extension of the trend toward building public-private partnerships. The redefined relationship between localities and the state in the CSA legislation was also viewed as an example of 'good government.'

The manner in which the legislature functioned in the early 1990s was quite different from today's strident partisanship and gridlock. During the period in which CSA was enacted Democrats held a clear majority. Republicans, however often joined with Democrats to sponsor and support important legislation. Robert Bloxom, a Republican who represented the Eastern Shore for many years in the House of Delegates, recalls how bills were processed:

> Once you were elected, party was not a factor. You became focused on what the problems were and what solutions were and the Democrats and Republicans and Independents sat around the table and talked about these problems. And then you went to the floor with it or to the Finance Committee on the Senate side and really got some things accomplished. (B. Bloxom, personal communication, November 2012)

Bloxom and other Republicans supported the proposal to develop a statewide system for vulnerable children and worked closely with the majority Democrats to craft a viable bill. This sense of bipartisanship, which was vital to the passage of the CSA legislation, has been a continuing theme in the evolution of this system. As will become apparent later, champions for CSA have come from both sides of the aisle.

At that time, the relationship between the executive branch and the legislature was more professional and less rancorous than today. Some of that tone was due to the general political zeitgeist. Credit for this productive relationship should also be given to the time spent by administrative officials to educate legislators on the issues and proposed solutions. Eva Teig Hardy recalls that as a result of conducting systematic studies and spending so much time explaining, discussing critical issues and writing legislation, members of the General Assembly, particularly members of the Senate and House Finance Committees had considerable knowledge about everything that was happening. "When Howard (Cullum) stood in front of a committee, he brought tremendous credibility. So when he said there was a problem of major proportion, those members, both Republicans and Democrats really listened and worked together with us to put together solutions" (E. Teig Hardy, personal communication, May 13, 2014).

A number of less tangible contextual factors likely contributed to the passing of this groundbreaking legislation. In 1989, in response to concerns about the well-being of children in the Commonwealth, the General Assembly established the Commission on Youth to deal with policy and provide assistance on matters related to young people. Comprised of members of both divisions of the legislature, the state agency personnel and other knowledgeable individuals, the Commission conducts studies and produces reports examining state-of-the-art research and practice. Although the Commission was not formally associated with the development of the CSA legislation, the work of this body had heightened the legislature's awareness of the problems experienced by youth and their families, made them aware of issues related to at-risk youth and helped them become attuned to the need for comprehensive reform.

The CSA's endeavor was also aided by the string of previous executive and legislative activities aimed at improving services for vulnerable youth. It would be difficult to establish a causal relationship, but it seems apparent that the multiple reports, commissions and task forces cited earlier laid a foundation and provided momentum that aided the CSA planners to create and gather support for this ambitious legislation.

Finally, timing and even serendipity played a role in facilitating passage of the CSA legislation. How do we account for the large and diverse group of passionate advocates being in prominent positions at the same time? What role did the recently established statewide parent advocacy group (PACCT) have on this effort? To what extent did the national movement for reforming children's mental health influence the initiative in Virginia?

In exploring what contextual factors may have aided the surprising enactment of this comprehensive reform, one question continued to rise to the surface. Did the enormous fiscal crisis Virginia was experiencing during the Wilder administration have a paradoxical effect on the successful passing of CSA legislation? It is tempting to conjecture that given the amount of attention and activity devoted to laying off staff and cutting programs, the Administration viewed the CSA as a potentially positive legacy and therefore invested extraordinary energy to ensuring its passage.

Clearly the Administration worked diligently prior to and during the two legislative sessions to create a viable plan and garner support for the CSA legislation. William Mims, a Republican, who later served as Attorney General and a member of the Supreme Court in Virginia, was a freshman delegate during the 1992–1993 General Assembly session. He recalls that when the CSA legislation encountered resistance, Lieutenant Donald Beyer, a Democrat, visited him in his office to persuade him to support the bill (W. Mims, personal communication, December 13, 2011).

None of the senior officials involved in the establishment of CSA confirmed that the exceptional effort to ensure passage was an attempt to create a legacy. Thus there is no direct evidence to support the legacy hypothesis. Regardless of the actual intention, it is reasonable to conclude that the confluence of forces that came together to enable passage of this unique legislation was extraordinary.

Chapter 4

Inside the Act

What the CSA Legislation Promised and Required

Navigating CSA through the planning and legislative processes had been a formidable endeavor. Implementing the legislation in the 138 localities in Virginia posed an even more daunting challenge. This transformative legislative package was indeed comprehensive, requiring local and state administrators to make significant changes in not only how at-risk youth were cared for but also how services were organized, governed, and funded. Although the focus of CSA was to provide services to at-risk youth and families in a more responsive and appropriate manner, those involved in implementation recognized the importance of effectively managing the context in which care would be delivered.

Fragmentation, discontinuity, and bureaucrat convenience had hampered the provision of services prior to the enactment of CSA. While the new legislation contained structural provisions to address these impediments, those familiar with the human services delivery system were aware that changing traditional ways of providing services would not be easy. Modifying the Code of Virginia did not ensure that the behavior of service providers and government agencies would fall into line with the intent and stipulations of the act.

Furthermore, the individuals who crafted this legislation knew that regardless of how careful and thorough they had been, it was impossible to address all of the issues that might arise. It was difficult to anticipate all potential service, funding, and governance dilemmas that might arise. In addition, reform of this magnitude is bound to produce unintended consequences.

These complexities were further intensified by the change in political leadership at the state level just as the CSA legislation was scheduled to be implemented. The period of initial implementation of CSA occurred at the tail-end of Governor Wilder's term, under whom CSA was developed. Wilder was a Democrat. The new governor, George Allen was a Republican.

When Allen took office, virtually all of the senior officials involved with the establishment of CSA were replaced with new administrators not familiar with this bold endeavor and did not possess institutional memory pertaining to children's mental health services. As will become apparent later, Virginia's one-term limit for governors and the frequent turnover of senior leadership which inevitably disrupted continuity would create challenges for developing and sustaining CSA during the next twenty years.

In the next two chapters we will cover the early implementation of CSA. This chapter offers a description of the specific provisions of the CSA legislation, including who was eligible to participate and what were the core processes and structures designated to plan and provide services. As mentioned earlier, support functions such as funding, management, and governance were identified during the initial planning as critical requisites for effective implementation. How services were going to be paid for and administered, as well as how staff were to be trained and supported will also be described.

In Chapter 5 we turn our attention to the initial rollout of CSA and the issues and challenges encountered during this period. What steps did state officials take to ensure that operations at the local and state levels were consistent with the principles, values, standards, and goals of the enabling legislation? How did local governments and providers accept the CSA model and procedures? Was there uniform acceptance or was there wide variations among localities? Were the supports articulated in the CSA legislation, including appropriate training and a functional data base put into place? Did issues arise that the planners of CSA had not addressed or did implementation of this system produce results that were not anticipated or intended? Once the CSA was built did the children and families come?

Although the primary purpose of these two chapters is to provide a narrative describing how the CSA legislation was transformed into practice during the early years, some space will be allotted to preliminary observations on how effectively this system of care met its intended goals. A more though evaluation will be presented in later chapters.

A BRIEF PRIMER ON CORE COMPONENTS OF THE CSA

The enabling legislation that established the Comprehensive Services Act for At-Risk Youth and Families filled 13 single-spaced pages with details and provisions. In addition to stating CSA's intent and purpose, the CSA Code describes the core functions of the system, the individuals and agencies required to participate along with their duties and responsibilities, and the organizational structures created to establish policy as well as oversee, manage, and support the service delivery system. Sections of the Code identify who is eligible for CSA services, how they are referred and assessed, and how services are paid for. Given CSA's emphasis on empowering localities, coordinating efforts among child-serving agencies and providing flexibility to ensure that services were individually tailored, considerable attention is given to the structures and functions put in place to achieve these goals.

Definitions are provided for individuals and entities involved in the administration of CSA as well as their duties and responsibilities. Attention is given to the importance of assuring quality and accountability, and the Code delineates who are responsible for these functions. Sections of the Code are also devoted to ensuring the rights and safety of participants, including language addressing due process, confidentiality, and licensing/certification of service providers.

Interestingly, within this extensive legislative package there is little mention of specific treatment modalities or service approaches. At first glance it appears odd that a law devoted to improving services for at-risk youth would not be more explicit about the service modalities to be employed. However, the crafters of this legislation had several reasons for not prescribing specific service components.

First, a core guiding principle of the CSA legislation was to encourage localities to be flexible and responsive in developing individual service plans for at-risk youth and their families. They wanted officials and service providers at the local level to adhere to the basic principles of being child-centered, family-focused and community-based when considering how to best serve youth enrolled in CSA. However, they also wanted planners and providers to avoid cookie-cutter approaches. By not prescribing specific service modalities in the statute they hoped service providers would incorporate the natural strengths and resources of the local community as well as more traditional service techniques and programs.

For example, school-age children whose parents work are most likely to engage in high-risk behaviors during the period between when school lets out and their caregiver returns home. Traditionally, these children might be enrolled in a structured after-school program. However, some communities do not have formal programs for this purpose and the cost of establishing and operating this type of service can be costly. The CSA legislation encouraged localities to explore innovative approaches to responding to reducing risk and building strengths. In the case of the child who lacks supervision in the afternoon, a community might hire a high school student to mentor and supervise the child during this vulnerable time of day. This innovative child-specific approach would offer meaningful experience and modest income for the high school student as well as provide a less expensive alternative for reducing risk.

A second reason for not stipulating specific service modalities and programs in the CSA legislation was the recognition that the field of children's behavioral health was rapidly evolving. Clinical and service research and shifts in the conceptual/philosophical perspectives of experts continually produced new therapies and service modalities. Although many traditional care approaches continued to be endorsed and utilized, some previously accepted services had been replaced with modalities that had shown to be more effective. The framers of the CSA legislation did not want to lock the system into service modalities that might become outdated or create a situation requiring the legislature to constantly amend the Act to keep pace with changes in the field. Therefore they opted to omit reference to specific therapies and service modalities in order to allow the system to adapt more readily to advances in technology.

Who Is Eligible for CSA?

The CSA was intended to serve young people with complex needs who could not readily be served by a single child-serving agency. The system was also established to reduce the prevailing tendency to place youth with intensive service needs in residential treatment centers outside of the child's community and sometimes outside of the Commonwealth of Virginia. The legislation stipulated that in order to be eligible for funding through the CSA a child or youth must meet one or more of the criteria specified in subdivisions 1 through 4 below:

1. Have emotional or behavioral problems which:
   a. Have persisted over a significant period of time or, though only in evidence for a short period of time, are of such a critical nature that intervention is warranted;
   b. Are significantly disabling and are present in several community settings (such as home, school, or with peers); and
   c. Require services or resources that are unavailable or inaccessible, or that are beyond the normal agency services or routine collaborative processes across agencies, or require coordinated interventions by at least two agencies.
2. . . . is at imminent risk of entering purchased residential services.
3. . . . requires placement for purposes of special education in approved private special education programs.
4. . . . has been placed in foster care through a parental agreement between a local social services agency or public agency, or is entrusted to a local social services agency by his parent or guardian, or has been committed to the agency by a court of competent jurisdiction (Virginia Acts of Assembly, Chapter 837, § 2.1-758, April 15, 1992).

To be eligible for CSA funding, an individual had to be either less than 18 years of age or if eligible for mandated services of the participating state agencies, including special education and foster care services, the person could receive funding through 21 years of age.

How Do Youth Obtain Services through CSA?

The authors of the CSA legislation wanted to ensure that services provided under this new system were easy to access and considered the family's perspective in the planning process. Services were to be delivered in a comprehensive and coordinated fashion and provided in the least restrictive, most appropriate environment. In addition, CSA services were to be tailored to the unique situation of each family and should take into consideration the strengths as well as the needs of the child and family.

In order to achieve these goals the CSA, statute established a Family Assessment and Planning Team (FAPT) responsible for coordinating and managing the provision of services for each eligible child and family. Each locality was mandated to have at least one FAPT, and larger cities and counties could establish multiple FAPTs. Consistent with the goal of being user-friendly, referrals were accepted from many sources including all child-service agencies as well as self-referrals from families seeking help. FAPT's were required to have representatives from each local child-serving agency, including education, social services, mental health, and juvenile justice. FAPTs also were required to have a parent with a child with a history of emotional and/or behavioral problems serve as a standing member of the team.

Each locality was given leeway to establish specific procedures for conducting the functions of the FAPT. However, all FAPTs were expected to perform a core list of mandated functions in accordance with the prescribed CSA principles. One of the central functions of the FAPT was to develop individualized service plans for youth referred for CSA services. Once the referral was made, the child and family were invited to a team meeting where the needs and strengths of the child and family would be assessed. Through discussion among FAPT members and the family, a list of goals and objectives would be established and a service plan would be developed. As stated above, service options were not limited to traditional modalities or programs. FAPT participants were encouraged to consider innovative approaches, including utilizing resources of the immediate and extended family as well as other informal supports. Unlike many conventional assessment processes the child and family members were viewed as key members of the planning effort and their input was to be actively sought.

Once the service plan was established, the FAPT was expected to identify the specific providers and other sources that could best provide the services and supports included in the plan. The task of working with the child and family to implement the plan was often delegated to a specific FAPT staff member or contractor, often a case manager. That individual was responsible for assuring that the services identified in the plan were provided in a timely, appropriate, coordinated, and effective manner. This staff member was also supposed to check in with and provide support to the family regularly while the child was receiving CSA services.

WHAT DID CSA PUT IN PLACE TO ENSURE THAT SERVICES WOULD BE PROVIDED AS PROMISED?

Many jurisdictions in the United States had already articulated the system of care principles, stating that services would be delivered in a seamless, child-centered, family-focused, community-based manner. The real challenge was to actually provide care consistent with these criteria. At the time CSA was enacted few programs were actually implementing systems of care that adhered to these guiding principles. The small number of successful programs operating in the early 1990s, generally, were confined to serving discrete geographic areas such as a city or county.

The diverse panel of individuals who planned CSA recognized that lofty intentions and principles were not sufficient. Actualizing a comprehensive, coordinated, and responsive system required a strong infrastructure that addressed the core functions needed to support an effective service delivery system. These essential functions included a flexible and responsive mechanism to pay for individualized service plans and a governance structure that encouraged and incentivized cooperation and coordination within localities as well as among local, state, and federal government entities.

A sound infrastructure also had to provide mechanisms for planning, managing, monitoring and evaluating the service system in order to ensure efficiency, fidelity, productivity, and accountability. Successful implementation of these management functions required a comprehensive data base to track service utilization, outcomes, and financial transactions as well as other key performance indicators. Finally, continuous education and training needed to be provided for all stakeholders participating in CSA to assure that they understood and could effectively participate in this unique system. This training needed to be comprehensive and be directed at consumers, and government officials as well as service providers.

Paying for Services

To their credit the authors of the CSA legislation addressed these infrastructure issues in considerable detail, which partially accounts for the hefty size of this Act. Two funding mechanisms were constructed. The state pool, which is the larger of the two, consolidated funds from eight categorical agency funding sources. This pool was established in order to provide local communities with financial resources to pay for services included in the individual service plans developed by FAPTs. In addition to supporting services for specific children and families, the state pool had several specific purposes. These include: (1) placing authority for program and funding decisions at the local level, (2) providing greater flexibility for purchasing services based on the strengths and needs of youth, and (3) reducing disparity and inadvertent fiscal disincentives for providing services due to differing local required match rates for various funding streams (Virginia Acts of Assembly, Chapter 837, § 2-1-757, April 15, 1992).

In order to create this single flexible source of funding several critical decisions had to be made. Although these actions were necessary to move CSA from its conceptual to its operational phase, in several instances the long-term consequences of these decisions were profound and sometimes unintended. For example, CSA was predicated on the premise that providing services consistent with system of care principles required blending traditional funding sources to allow flexibility and innovation. Two of these traditional funding sources were entitlement programs funded by the federal government: special education and foster care. To obtain approval to blend these funds into the state pool the Commonwealth had to guarantee to the respective federal agencies that these children would receive services for which they were entitled. The senior staff of the state was reluctant to establish a distinction among children to be served by CSA but recognized that implementation of the system was not feasible without inclusion of the funds provided by federal entitlement programs. Therefore, they accepted the conditions imposed by the federal government and were granted a waiver to include special education and child welfare funds in the state pool.

Initially, it was hoped that the special conditions for ensuring that youth eligible for federal entitlements would receive services could be managed in a seamless and unobtrusive manner and would not adversely affect the service delivery system. It soon became apparent, however, that young people eligible for federal entitlements, who were referred to as "mandated" youth, were receiving preferential treatment. This was less of a problem when the demand for services was less than the availability of financial resources. As the CSA grew and the number of youth seeking services increased, this distinction became more significant. In many communities there was only enough money available to serve the "mandated" children, and those who were "non-mandated" were unable to access care.

This two-tiered distinction was further exacerbated by the fact that many of the non-mandated youth were clients of the juvenile justice system who had previously been supported by several funding streams controlled by the state Department of Youth and Family Services. When these funding categories were dissolved and the funds were put into the State Pool, local judges and juvenile justice program administrators were left without resources to use to provide community services for young people placed in their care.

The preferential care scenario created by the terms required to obtain a federal waiver became the first, and possibly most, serious unintended consequence of the CSA. For a system designed to enhance rational and equitable provision of services the distinction between mandated and non-mandated youth posed a formidable dilemma.

The second funding mechanism established by CSA was the state trust fund. The planners of CSA recognized that simply providing funds for individual youth already engaged in high-risk behavior was not sufficient. Some communities did not have sufficient capacity to offer services and programs for this population. In addition, there were many younger children who had not yet experienced serious difficulty but who showed early warning signs. The state trust fund was created to provide funds for early intervention services, as well as to assist localities cover infrastructure costs associated with developing community-based services for troubled youth who could be appropriately and effectively served at home or community (Virginia Acts of Assembly, Chapter 837, § 2.1-759, April 15, 1992).

How Was the CSA System Governed and Managed?

One of the most unique features of CSA was its stated intention to empower each locality to design and implement the provision of services in line with the conditions and circumstances of its own community. This bottom-up approach represented a stark contrast to the traditional service delivery approach in which the state dictated the manner in which services were to be provided, including making decisions regarding how youth requiring expensive care would be served. In designing the CSA system, planners paid particular attention to the governance and management structures. They wanted to assure that appropriate authority and tools were provided to localities while also offering guidance and support to local leaders. The planners also wanted to provide some oversight to ensure that youth in all localities had access to appropriate care and that local service systems adhered to the core principles of CSA.

The initial CSA governance/management structure was comprised of four entities: two local- and two state-level bodies. The legislation mandated that each structure include standing members representing the key stakeholder groups: senior administrators of state child-serving agencies, including health, mental health, education, social services, juvenile justice, and the

Figure 4.1   Initial CSA Governance/Management Structure Was an Inverted Pyramid of Power Comprised of Four Entities: Two Local-Level and Two State-Level Bodies. *Source*: Created by A. B. Ventura (author).

courts; a private service provider representative; and parents of a child with emotional/behavioral problems. These entities were structured in a manner resembling an inverted pyramid, with local decision-making bodies at the top of the organizational chart and state at the base, providing assistance and support as needed. See Figure 4.1 for how the CSA was structured.

In each locality the governing body of the participating city or county was charged with establishing a Community Policy and Management Team (CPMT) that would be responsible for the planning, implementation, and monitoring of the CSA system for that locality. The members of the CPMT were appointed by the local governing body and included, at a minimum, local agency heads or their designees of mental health, school, social services, health and juvenile court services, as well as a representative of a private children's service provider agency or association, and a parent representative who was not employed by a public or private program. Although local governing could appoint a local government official, law-enforcement official, or representative of another public agency as a member of the CPMT, these appointments were not mandated.

Each CPMT was required to establish and appoint one or more FAPTs depending on the needs of that community. FAPTs were responsible for assessing the needs and strengths of eligible youth and families, developing individualized service plans, ensuring that the plans are appropriately implemented, and monitoring the provision of services.

Each FAPT was responsible for conducting assessments of all eligible youth referred to CSA. They were charged with evaluating the needs and strengths of the child and family. Based on their assessment, the FAPT was to identify and determine the appropriate complement of services required to meet their unique needs of that child and family.

Specific powers and duties of the FAPT included reviewing referrals, ensuring family participation of families in all aspects of assessment, planning and implementation of services, and developing individual service plans that provide appropriate and cost-effective services. FAPTs also were tasked with referring the youth and family to community agencies in accordance with their individual service plans and designating an individual responsible for monitoring and reporting on the youth and family's progress. Finally, FAPTs were charged with recommending to the CPMT expenditures to be made from the state pool of funds (Virginia Acts of Assembly, Chapter 837, § 2.1-754, April 15, 1992).

The CPMT was given responsibility for managing cooperative efforts in each community in order to better serve troubled and at-risk youth and their families as well as maximizing the use of state and community resources. Each team was responsible for:

1. Developing interagency policies and procedures for governing the provision of services to children and families in their community;
2. Developing interagency fiscal policies to determine how eligible populations can access state pool of funds;
3. Coordinating long-range, community-wide planning to ensure development of resources and services needed by children and families in their community;
4. Establishing policies governing referrals and reviews of families to the FAPT;
5. Establishing quality assurance and accountability procedures for utilization of programs and management of funds;
6. Establishing procedures for obtaining bids for developing new services;
7. Managing funds in the interagency budget allocated to the community from state and other sources;
8. Authorizing and monitoring expenditure of funds by each FAPT;
9. Submitting grant proposals that will benefit the community to the state trust fund and entering into contracts for provision or operation of services if approved;
10. Serve as the locality's liaison to the State Management Team (SMT), providing reports on programmatic and fiscal operations, as well as recommendations for improving the service system (Virginia Acts of Assembly, Chapter 837, § 2.1-752, April 15, 1992).

The CSA legislation prescribed two state-level entities to provide guidance and support for the local management/governance structures. The SMT served as a link between the CPMTs at the local level and the body designated to establish policy and provide oversight for the Act, the State Executive Council (SEC).

The SMT was comprised of representatives from the State's five major child-serving agencies: social services, education, mental health, mental retardation and substance abuse, health, and juvenile justice. The team also included a parent representative who was not an employee of an organization that provided services to children, a representative of a private organization or association of child- and family-service providers, a juvenile and domestic relations court judge, and one individual from each of the five geographic areas of the Commonwealth who is representative of the different stakeholder participating in local CPMTs. Members of the SMT were to be appointed by and responsible to the SEC. The team was tasked with electing a chairman from its membership each year.

Initially the SMT was charged with developing and recommending to the SEC program specific fiscal policies that promoted and supported cooperation and collaboration to at-risk and troubled youth and their families. They also were responsible for providing training and technical assistance to state and local agencies and to serve as liaison to participating state agencies by serving as fiscal agent, designing and implementing an interagency tracking and evaluation system, and providing training and technical assistance (Virginia Acts of Assembly, Chapter 837, § 2.1-747, April 15, 1992).

The authors of the CSA legislation recognized that bringing together the diverse state and local entities needed for a genuinely collaborative system of care would require effective leadership. Strong communication and mediation skills, as well as a clear understanding of and commitment to the purpose and goals of the Act, were essential but not sufficient. The leadership also had to possess the authority and resources to make difficult decisions and implement this complex enterprise that was dependent upon cooperation among organizations that did not always have a history of working well together.

The SEC was established to oversee the administration of CSA. Its membership paralleled the SMT. Members of the SEC included the heads of the major state child agencies, an elected or appointed local official, a parent, and a representative. The non-state agency representatives were to be appointed by the Governor. Similar to the SMT, the members elected a chair each year.

The state child-serving agencies that were required to participate in CSA functioned under the authority of three different secretariats: health and human resources, education, and public safety. Initially, the CSA legislation did not provide clarification on the role of the three Secretaries in relation to supervision of CSA and management of the SEC. Eventually senior state officials recognized the administrative challenge posed by this lack of clear authority. They believed a single cabinet head should be responsible in order to ensure clear and efficient direction for this complex endeavor. In 2000, the legislature amended the Act to authorize the Secretary of Health and Human Resources to serve as the lead Secretary for CSA, working with the Secretaries of Education and Public Safety to facilitate interagency collaboration. The amended CSA legislation stipulated that in this capacity the Secretary of Health and Human Resources would report to and act on behalf of the Governor (Virginia Acts of Assembly, § 2.1-5114, April 9, 2000). Despite this legislative effort to clarify leadership authority, the initial concern that some of the participating agencies are not directly under the jurisdiction of the Health and Human Resource Secretariat continues to make it difficult to achieve seamless cooperation and coordination among these agencies.

The SEC was given responsibility for overseeing CSA and making decisions required to fulfill its purposes. Its powers and duties included appointing members of the SMT, establishing interagency programmatic and fiscal policies to be developed by the SMT, providing a process for public participation related to the development of guidelines to support the program and fiscal purposes of the Act, and overseeing administration of state interagency policies governing the use, distribution, and monitoring of funds in the state pool and trust funds. The SEC was also charged with providing administration of essential functions that support the work of the SMT and reviewing and taking appropriate action on issues brought before it by the SMT.

In addition, the SEC was mandated to advise the Governor and appropriate Cabinet Secretaries on proposed policy and operational changes related to enhancing interagency functioning, oversee early intervention initiatives as well as efforts to provide uniform assessment, plan of care, service monitoring, and ongoing review of the status of youth and families served by local government. The initial CSA legislation directed the SEC to provide oversight for developing uniform guidelines for documentation, utilization management, data collection standards and outcome measures including how many youth were served by CSA, length of stay in residential facilities, and the match between actual placement in treatment settings and the proportion suggested to be placed by the uniform assessment instrument. SEC also was given a major role in overseeing the development of dispute resolution procedures for CPMTs charged with failing to comply with provisions of the Act and to deny funding to CPMTs when it has been determined that they have failed to comply with these provisions. The SEC was required to produce and provide to the General Assembly and CPMTs biennially a comprehensive progress report and plan for the following two-year period (Virginia Acts of Assembly, § 2.1-746, April 15, 1992).

It was apparent that much thought had been given to how to effectively actualize the grand principles and goals of the CSA. The enabling legislation spelled out all of the key functions that had to be performed to ensure that services provided through CSA were individually tailored, comprehensive, family-focused and community-based. The Act consistently emphasized the importance of empowering localities to develop and implement a system consistent with the unique conditions of their local communities. At the same time, the legislation acknowledged the importance of striking a balance between providing localities flexibility and ensuring that all at-risk youth and their families received services that were sufficient to meet their needs and consistent with system-of-care principles. By assigning authority and responsibility to governing bodies at the local and state levels, the architects of CSA hoped to achieve an appropriate balance between encouraging and incentivizing locally driven service systems and support and accountability mechanisms that could be best provided centrally by the Commonwealth (Virginia Acts of Assembly, Chapter 837, § 2.1-747, April 15, 1992).

When the CSA went live in July 1993 the most pressing question was how this eloquent and thorough legislation would play in real-life conditions.

Part II

1993–2001

Chapter 5

The Curtain Rises

The Early Years

The task of implementing CSA would have been challenging under ideal circumstances. The Commonwealth's intention to allow local officials to tailor service systems to the unique conditions of each locality added an additional level of complexity. State officials wanted to ensure that all children eligible for CSA services were treated equitably, consistent with the principles, standards, and goals of the CSA legislation. At the same time, the individuals responsible for implementing CSA were mindful of the values and tradition of local prerogative in Virginia and wanted to empower localities to adapt the CSA service system to local conditions.

This tension between ensuring uniformity and respecting individual differences among localities posed an interesting dilemma, succinctly described by the CSA Coordinator for three small jurisdictions in Southern Virginia, Bud Sedwick, who has been involved in CSA since its inception:

> In the beginning we were told every locality should develop the program that was best for them and we also found out the weakness of CSA was that every community developed the program that was best for them. . . . It was tough without some level playing field. . . . We just did what we felt was best. (B. Sedwick, personal communication, April 21, 2013)

In addition to the local-state tensions, several other factors and forces influenced the initial implementation of CSA and subsequently the effectiveness of this ambitious new system. In addition to the obvious challenge of preparing a large and diverse set of stakeholders to understand and participate in a complex, collaborative service system that in many ways contrasted philosophically and operationally with traditional practice, they had to contend with several major sociopolitical forces. The two most powerful influences were, not surprisingly, money and power. In the next section we will focus on how both of these highly charged forces were allocated under CSA and the significant impact these changes had on the initial implementation of CSA. Consistent with other aspects of CSA's evolution, there was wide variation among localities across the state in how the distribution of money and power played out.

WINNERS AND LOSERS

The notion of consolidating all of the funds from multiple child-serving accounts into one large budget pool was appealing in several ways. Programmatically, it provided flexibility for localities to tailor service plans to the unique needs and strengths of young people without being constrained by eligibility and service limitations imposed by specific funding sources. Proponents also believed that pooling funds would ensure that children would receive better care in their communities by serving them collaboratively through a single team rather than requiring families to go from one agency to another (A. Atkinson, personal communication, May 2013).

From a fiscal perspective, state legislators saw the advantage of providing a structured formulaic role for local governments to participate in funding services for at-risk youth. Bill Murray, who has served in multiple roles in the executive and legislative branches of state government in Virginia, including legislative director for Governors Warner and Kaine, believes the General Assembly saw benefit in this arrangement, which gave local government legislative bodies "skin in the game" by requiring a local match for state funds they received. Previously, local government legislatures often chose the most expensive rather than the most effective programs because spending decisions did not have an impact on local financial resources. The state also liked the simplicity of dealing with a single budget line rather than multiple smaller accounts. The availability of a larger pool of resources gave local teams greater ability to serve children and families and allowed them to spend money on prevention to avoid significant costs later on (W. Murray, personal communication, July 16, 2013).

According to Senator Ed Houck, a strong advocate for children in the state senate, "There was a pretty compelling case that not only could you do a better job of helping children but you could also do it more economically because if the funding streams were all intended to serve the child or family, then having it fragmented meant there was often duplication" (E. Houck, personal communication, March 22, 2013).

Although the CSA legislation provided clear benefits and opportunities, some stakeholders viewed these changes negatively, in part because of the adverse impact they perceived for their own organizations and agencies. Pat Harris, a private provider who was involved in planning for CSA, believes that not everyone involved embraced the value of blending funds. "Before CSA there was a lot of territoriality . . . all the pots of money were combined and then everybody was supposed to play nice with each other. But immediately what happened is that the agencies tried to hang on to their money" (P. Harris, personal communication, October 2011).

Local social service departments, for example, were required to contribute large amounts of their budget to the CSA state pool. While there was an expectation that youth eligible for this child protective services funding would receive care through CSA, the local social services agencies still retained responsibility for these young people. Some social service workers and administrators viewed this as unreasonable and entered the initial implementation phase of CSA with negative attitudes. Some directors of social service had been in their jobs for a long time and believed their freedom was being threatened (A. Saunders, personal communication, September 23, 2011). Larry Jackson, who served as Commissioner of Social Services for the state during the establishment of CSA, believes that most urban directors responded well. However, some directors in rural areas were reluctant to participate because they felt they were being "put upon financially." Jackson attributes the reluctance of these directors to their lack of understanding of what was happening and what role they needed to play (L. Jackson, personal communication, February 7, 2012).

Jane Kusiak, who served as Deputy Director for the House Appropriations Committee in the early 1990s, noted another unintended negative consequence associated with the consolidation of funding:

> Unfortunately, when an agency has a specific program, it's like your child. They adopt it, they protect it, they do whatever they can to advocate for it. When these programs went into a central pool there was this sense that we no longer have to take care of this problem child. Now it's someone else's problem. (J. Kusiak, personal communication, July 16, 2013)

Similar reactions occurred in some local special education programs, but the dynamic in this situation played out differently. Historically, education departments have functioned more autonomously than other child-serving agencies. This is due, in part to education's broader constituency base. Because primary and secondary education is mandated for all children, most families have children attending schools. A smaller proportion of the population is enrolled in social service, mental health, and juvenile justice programs. Additionally, many of the youth involved in these agencies are from less socially and economically advantaged families, giving these consumers less political clout. Therefore local school systems, with their large, broad-based constituencies are in a better position to influence policy and determine how local education programs will function.

As a result, some local school systems were able to choose to not fully participate in the coordinated programmatic and fiscal efforts prescribed by the CSA legislation. This ability to opt out was made possible through modifications made to the original legislation, giving localities additional flexibility to determine how local education agencies would be involved in the CSA process. These changes were made during negotiations in the General Assembly and were granted in order to secure the votes of reluctant legislators needed to pass the CSA legislation. As CSA evolved, it became apparent that this compromise, as well as other strategic decisions made during its formulation and planning, had a significant impact on how CSA was able to actualize its original purpose and goals.

The decision to distinguish between mandated and non-mandated children arguably had a more profound unintended effect on CSA and its effectiveness than any other policy deliberation. By establishing a preferred eligibility path for youth receiving federally mandated child protective or special education services, CSA created a two-tiered system which had serious consequences for youth not enrolled in these mandated programs as well as the agencies responsible for serving these children and adolescents. Leah Hamaker, Senior Policy Analyst for the Virginia Commission on Youth, describes how the distinction between mandated and non-mandated youth played out:

> In the beginning there were winners and there were losers and the winners were those children mandated to receive services by the federal government, which were foster care, at risk of foster care and special education kids. And the losers were the ones who had to throw money in the pot, which was juvenile justice and mental health funding appropriations that were taken away and used to support CSA. What juvenile justice and mental health (agencies) got out of CSA for the non-mandated children was very limited. (L. Hamaker, personal communication, May 2013)

Lelia Hopper, who helped to draft the CSA legislation, worked with the juvenile court judges during the early years of CSA. She believes that most juvenile court judges dealing with children who come before the court on delinquency charges do not view their responsibility as simply deciding on the narrow legal issues of whether the child committed the crime. The judges and the Department of Youth Services, which were responsible for serving many youth who come before the court, wanted to understand why the child was involved in deviant activity and what can be done to address the underlying issues in order to prevent a recurrence. According to Hopper, "When the money the Department of Youth Services brought to the table was folded into all of the rest of this money . . . the feeling was that they kind of got left out of having services available for CSA to fund children who were before the court because of delinquency or truancy" (L. Hopper, personal communication, June 5, 2013).

Youth served by public mental health agencies were also considered non-mandated, but the funding dynamics for mental agencies was quite different from what occurred in youth services. The courts and juvenile justice agencies contributed a significant amount of money to the CSA pool and then discovered that youth they were responsible for were considered lower priority recipients for these funds because of their non-mandated status. The Department of Mental Health, Mental Retardation, and Substance Abuse (DMHMRSAS), however, contributed very little to the CSA state pool. DMHMRSAS (which has recently been renamed the Department of Behavioral Health and Developmental Services) was the state agency responsible for managing, funding, and regulating public mental health services. This agency had direct operational responsibility for a number of state hospitals and residential centers for individuals with developmental disabilities. They also were charged with providing funding and oversight for 40 local Community Services Boards (CSB) which provided services for localities throughout the Commonwealth. The CSBs did not have a direct management reporting relationship to DMHMRSAS but were dependent on the state agency for much of their funding as well as support and regulatory services.

When CSA was launched, CSBs did not have a designated budget line for children's mental health services. They received funding through DMHMRSAS from a relatively small block of money from the federal or state government that was not specifically tied to children and adolescents. Therefore, when agencies were required to put money into the CSA funding pool, the state mental agency and the CSBs contributed very little (H. Cullum, personal communication, July 27, 2010).

The contrast between the small amount of funding contributed by the state's mental health authority and the significant extent of behavioral health needs manifested by youth enrolling in CSA did not go unnoticed. The irony of this discrepancy between investment and need became more apparent as CSA evolved. Administrators, providers, families, and advocates became acutely aware of the significant behavioral health challenges experienced by youth referred to CSA and the limited availability of mental health expertise. Many youth served by CSA suffered from mental health disorders that remained undiagnosed and insufficiently treated due to the absence of adequate knowledge among CSA providers and the lack of timely access to child psychiatrists and other behavioral health professionals (Joint Legislative Audit and Review Commission, 2007).

As localities began to implement CSA, it became obvious that the changes in how money and power were allocated were having a significant impact on how the system was functioning. The reluctance of some local agencies to give up traditional patterns of functioning autonomously impeded efforts to foster collaborative planning and delivery of services. The mandated/non-mandated dichotomy became especially problematic when localities realized that the resources available were insufficient to meet the growing demand for services. FAPTs and CPMTs had to make difficult decisions on how to allocate scarce resources given the requirement to serve mandated youth. These limitations often led to the dilemma of communities being forced to provide service to a mandated child even when his or her situation was not as dire as a non-mandated youth seeking service. Some communities did not have sufficient funds to serve anyone but the mandated population, leaving non-mandated individuals without access to care (Joint Legislative Audit and Review Commission, 1998).

DID THE STATE FULFILL ITS PROMISE TO PROVIDE INFRASTRUCTURE AND SUPPORT?

The key stakeholders involved in the establishment of CSA argued vigorously that the success of this system of care was dependent on the availability of sufficient resources, infrastructure, and technical assistance. In response to these expressed concerns the crafters of the legislation incorporated specific stipulations about providing training, establishing databases and processes that would enable localities and state officials to track and evaluate progress, and offering technical assistance to all participants to assist in the implementation of this grand and complex vision.

The importance of providing timely and appropriate support was further accentuated by the contextual dynamics described earlier. The CSA legislation called for drastic changes in practice methods for administrators and providers. Many key stakeholders, particularly at the local level, were still skeptical about this new model and required assistance in understanding and implementing the Act. Working through tensions between local and state governments, and overcoming the barriers impeding child-serving agencies to move from a silo mentality to a collaborative approach of working with at-risk youth and families would also require considerable discussion, education, and support.

These would be formidable challenges under ideal circumstances. They were made more difficult by two contextual factors. First, the legislation called for full implementation to occur simultaneously across the entire state. There was no provision for incremental implementation, either in the scope of functions or number of localities. Everything was scheduled to begin on July 1, 1993. The second complication was precipitated by the election calendar. The gubernatorial election was held in November 1993. Since the governor in Virginia is limited to one four-year term, the task of implementing this complex system fell on the shoulders of the new governor and his administration. The situation was further complicated when the citizens of the Commonwealth elected George Allen in the fall of 1993. Allen, a Republican, would most likely replace most of the senior officials who established CSA during the previous Democratic administration with his own cabinet secretaries and agency heads.

The changing of the guard was swift and in some instance, brutal. Demis Stewart, who played a pivotal role in the development of CSA while she worked at the Virginia Department of Social Services, describes the transition at her agency. "One Friday at 4:00pm all of the sudden a state police officer shows up in your office and says you're done; you have an hour to clean out your desk. There were 200 of us" (D. Stewart, personal communication, February 2012).

The loss of so many senior state officials, most of whom served at the pleasure of the governor, erased much of the institutional memory and knowledge pertaining to CSA. Those who replaced the former leaders had a steep learning curve, especially in light of CSA having been operational for barely six months. Although the new state administrators were able to ensure that the basic administrative and fiscal structures continued to operate, they had neither the knowledge nor time to put in place some of the critical infrastructure and support functions contained in the statute.

Perhaps the most critical support function at that time was training. Effective implementation of CSA required participants to understand the value as well as the skills involved in working collaboratively with and on behalf of young people and their families. Charlotte McNulty, who directed a CSB and served on a local CPMT remembers that localities were not given direction or support when CSA began:

> We got a few rules that we were supposed to follow and then we just had to flounder and figure it out. I think that's why you will find the implementation in 130 localities is different from on locality to the next. I don't think the upfront effort was put there to help localities really understand what was being expected of them. (C. McNulty, personal communication, August 25, 2011)

McNulty argues that you cannot legislate collaboration. People do not have to talk to each other if they do not want to, especially when there are no consequences, which was the case with CSA. Therefore training and technical assistance are critical to building an effective collaborative system of care.

To be fair, the administrators of CSA offered some training and technical assistance to localities in the early years. The magnitude and scope of these efforts was, however, severely impeded by limited resources to support these activities as well as lack of role clarity among the various entities responsible for administering CSA (Joint Legislative Audit and Review Commission, 1998).

Similar criticisms were directed at other important support functions identified in the planning process and subsequent legislation as requisites for successful implementation of CSA. During the first years of operation there was inadequate state monitoring and oversight of CSA activities at the local level. In addition, a uniform data reporting system was not established. The absence of adequate monitoring and reporting systems seriously hampered efforts to understand and address important issues such as who was enrolled in CSA, how they were being served, whether "best "practices were being utilized, how funds were being spent, and the extent to which the system was producing effective outcomes. This lack of data and oversight procedures made it extremely difficult to ensure that localities were complying with the CSA legislation and acting in a responsible manner (Joint Legislative Audit and Review Commission, 1998).

In some instances, even serious problems identified at the local level were not reported to the state. In one locality, the internal auditor discovered that children from the court services unit were being reclassified from non-mandated to mandated foster care prevention because there were insufficient funds in the locality's non-mandated allocation. This clear violation of the CSA statute's instructions on how funds were to be spent only came to the attention of the state when staff from the General Assembly visited this locality as part of its assessment of CSA (Joint Legislative Audit and Review Commission, 1998).

LEADERSHIP MATTERS

In designing the CSA, considerable attention was given to creating a management structure that respected and reinforced the importance of empowering localities while also providing direction and support to ensure that implementation across the state was equitable and consistent with the core principles of CSA and "best practice." Maintaining this delicate balance between delegating authority to local communities and providing sufficient oversight was largely dependent on the diligent performance of and collaborative interaction among the four management/governance structures established through the CSA legislation: the local FAPT and CPMT teams, and the state-level State Management Team (SMT) and State Executive Council (SEC). A fifth management entity, the Office of Comprehensive Services (OCS), was later added to the Act to manage the core functions of CSA and to assist the SEC. The OCS was staffed by state employees whose sole responsibility was to manage all aspects of this complex system. During the early years however, responsibility for most management function was given to the State Department of Social Services (DSS), which as one of the major agencies charged with caring for at-risk children and families had clear conflicts of interest in this role.

This early strategic decision to entrust DSS with key management functions for CSA has had a significant impact on the development of CSA. The rationale for this decision was that it would be more efficient to use an existing agency rather than create another government entity to perform basic administrative functions. DSS already had in place the capacity to perform fiscal and other administrative functions required to implement the CSA system. On the other side of the argument, critics claimed that embedding CSA management in one of its partner agencies was contrary to the CSA philosophy that all of the child-serving agencies needed to be on equal footing in order to facilitate collaboration. A more pointed criticism of DSS was that this agency had not fully embraced the CSA approach and did not consider CSA a priority. In its review of CSA, JLARC recommended moving the administrative home of OCS from DSS to the Department of Mental Health, Mental Retardation and Substance Abuse (Joint Legislative Audit and Review Committee, 1998). Based on the JLARC report as well as other criticisms of the management structure of CSA, the General Assembly finally enacted legislation in 2000 establishing OCS as the administrative entity for the State Executive Council (Virginia Acts of Assembly, Chapter 937, § 2.1-746.1, April 9, 2000).

Unfortunately, the gubernatorial transition from Governor Wilder to Governor Allen produced not only a diminished institutional memory and understanding of the CSA system but also less investment and attention by the new administration. Whether this loss of interest was due to senior leadership's sense that they inherited CSA and this was not their initiative or was caused by changing priorities that consumed the new administration's attention is not clear. What we do know is that sufficient leadership was not provided to ensure appropriate attention and action needed to actualize this complex fledgling system.

For instance, attendance records at the SEC, the oversight entity comprised of agency heads and other critical stakeholders, indicate that during the first five years the Superintendent of the Department of Education attended only 7 percent of SEC meetings. The attendance record of other agency heads for this period ranged from 55 to 66 percent (Joint Legislative Audit and Review Commission, 1998). Under ideal circumstances it would be challenging to bring together these large bureaucratic entities to craft a collaborative endeavor that would be mirrored at the local level. Without the participation of the chief executives of these state agencies there was little chance they would succeed.

Not unexpectedly, the absence of a role model and the lack of full commitment and participation of members of the highest governing body, the SEC, had ripple effects. In its review of the early years of CSA operation, JLARC concluded that the SMT had not worked effectively with the SEC or the OCS in developing policy, providing technical assistance, coordinating work group efforts, and assessing effectiveness of implementation (Joint Legislative and Audit Review Commission, 1998).

The failure to adequately perform these functions impeded the ability of localities to work through the issues and problems that need to be addressed in order to establish a comprehensive, coordinated system of care. For instance, in its review of CSA, JLARC found that 49 percent of the youth receiving CSA treatment services were given access by local staff without using the multi-agency review process mandated by the legislation. In addition, local CSA staff often inappropriately classified children or "gamed" the system to make them eligible for the statute's mandated service provisions (Joint Legislative Audit and Review Commission, 1998).

The reluctance of localities to adhere to the principles and requirements of the CSA legislation was in part due to the absence of appropriate leadership at the state level. Without clear guidance some localities became frustrated and sometimes disenchanted with CSA.

As the system evolved, it became more apparent that effective execution of the CSA required strong leadership and ongoing support. Over the course of the next 15 years, the governance and management structure of CSA would be carefully scrutinized, and the legislation and policies related to leadership would be amended several times.

OPENING NIGHT REVIEWS

The first three years of CSA yielded mixed results. As noted above, the transition to a new governor and administration interrupted continuity of leadership for this recently established system, which created significant challenges during the early stages of implementation. The most serious problem was the inability to provide the sufficient infrastructure and supports prescribed by the enabling legislation critical to assisting localities to understand the intention and operational requirements of the Act.

On the other side of the ledger, all 138 localities began implementing the CSA structure in July 1993 and continued to operate within the basic parameters of the legislation during this period. Some localities, primarily those that had embraced the system of care philosophy prior to the enactment of CSA, left the starting gate at full throttle. The stakeholders in these communities worked together collaboratively to provide services to at-risk youth and their families in a manner consistent with the values and principles of CSA.

Meaningful quantitative data for this initial period was in short supply. Part of the difficulty was due to an absence of data on a pre-CSA comparison group. Limited data were available on the utilization and cost of youth placed in residential settings. However, prior to CSA most localities did not have a coordinated effort to track services for at-risk youth, making it difficult to establish a baseline for what happened to these young people before the Act became operational. The other major problem was the limited data base available during the initial years of operation.

Several quantitative indicators were, however, tracked for all localities from the beginning. Data were collected on how many youth were served, their eligibility status (i.e., mandated vs. non-mandated), and what type of service they received. Information was also collected on how much services cost.

Limited analysis was conducted on performance during fiscal year (FY) 1993, the year prior to implementation of CSA and FY 1994, CSA's first year of operation. The accuracy of these comparisons may be subject to challenge because different methods were used to gather data prior to the establishment of CSA. The data do, however, provide a rough measure of change during this period.

In the year preceding CSA's initial implementation, FY 1993, youth in Virginia were placed in residential treatment settings using public funds at a total cost of $89 million. The cost of placing young people in residential treatment had been steadily increasing since the late 1980s, at a rate of nearly 20 percent per year (Joint Legislative Audit and Review Commission, 1998). In FY 1994, the first year of operation, CSA served a total of 10,214 youth at a total cost of $104.5 million. Seventy-one percent of these youth were served in residential settings while 81 percent of the expenditures were allocated to residential services (Office of Comprehensive Services, 2013).

A breakdown of the eligibility data indicates that 93 percent of all youth served by CSA in FY 1994 were mandated, and within this group 73 percent received residential services (Office of Comprehensive Services, 2013). The number of children served in each locality was largely proportional to the general population of that jurisdiction with the exception of several urban areas with higher rates of poverty. The City of Richmond, with a population of barely 200,000 served the second highest number of youth, exceeded only by Fairfax/Falls Church in Northern Virginia which had a population of more than 1,000,000. Norfolk and Newport News, also urban localities with high levels of poverty, ranked third and fourth in number of youth served by CSA (Office of Comprehensive Services, 2013).

During the next few years the number of youth served, as well as funds expended by CSA, increased each year. The unduplicated census in FY 1996 was 13,235, an increase of 30 percent from FY 1994, CSA's first year of operation, while the expenditures grew by 43 percent. The cost per child increased by 6 percent from FY 1994 to FY 1996. The state share of total CSA expenditures grew by 40 percent in the same period. The state's contribution represented 61 percent of total cost while localities paid the remainder. Both state and local share grew significantly during the first three years of operation but the proportion of financial burden borne by each of these entities did not change appreciably. Between FY 1994 and FY 1996, the share of total cost paid by localities increased by 1 percent (Office of Comprehensive Services, 2013).

The statistics on distribution of total cost between state and local governments does not tell the entire story. One of the goals of CSA was to provide a rational formula for allocating the cost of services between state and local governments. Before CSA was established, localities were responsible for 44 percent of the cost of services for mandated youth but were not responsible for any costs of non-mandated services. When CSA was enacted the local share for mandated services decreased slightly from 44 to 39 percent while localities' responsibility for non-mandated services rose from 0 to 39 percent. This shift in local fiscal burden appeared to further reduce the incentive of localities to serve non-mandated youth. In 1996, more than 30 localities did not spend any CSA funds on non-mandated youth. Although most of these non-participating localities were poor rural communities, several large, more affluent localities also declined to fund services for non-mandated youth (Joint Legislative Audit and Review Commission, 1998).

It is difficult to ascertain whether increases in caseload and cost were due to growth in the number of youth requiring intensive services or higher visibility and improved outreach of local CSA systems. The JLARC study did, however, analyze factors that may have contributed to growth of caseload and cost. JLARC found evidence of misguided implementation of CSA by localities, but concluded the major forces driving cost escalation beyond the control of local communities. JLARC's research on a sample of CSA participants indicated that increases in caseload could be attributed primarily to factors used as proxy measures for poverty, such as increases in the number of families receiving food stamps, and breakdown in the structure of the family, that is, rising foster care caseloads. For example, among youth participating in CSA in FY 1995, 74 percent were documented to have been abused prior to CSA referral, only 14 percent were living with both parents, and 68 percent came from Medicaid eligible families. More than half of these youth had parents who abused drugs and received Aid to Families with Dependent Children (AFDC), and 35 percent of the parents of youth served by CSA had a criminal record (Joint Legislative Review Commission, 1998).

One of the primary goals of CSA was to reverse the trend of sending youth out of their homes and communities to receive care. The data for the first three years indicate that the reverse was happening. The number of youth served in residential settings increased by 31 percent during this period from FY 1994 to FY 1996 with expenditures rising proportionally. The growth in utilization of residential treatment was not consistent across the state. Some of the localities serving large numbers of youth, such as Fairfax/Falls Church and Richmond had significant growth in the use of residential treatment placements. Interestingly, Hampton and Lynchburg, which are generally considered to be exemplary practitioners of CSA, also showed increase use of residential settings. Other communities viewed as excellent models, such as Chesterfield County in Central Virginia, reduced the number of residential placements during this period. Unfortunately, the absence of meaningful child-specific data within CSA (e.g., degree of risk, level of functioning, and outcomes measures) makes it difficult to understand the impact of changes in residential treatment utilization statewide as well as differences among localities.

Data are also available on the use of non-residential services during the period from FY 1994 to FY 1996. Although residential treatment services consumed the largest share of the CSA budget, the number of youth receiving non-residential services, including day treatment and outpatient therapy, increased 72 percent while expenditures for these community-based services rose by 77 percent. Although total expenditures for non-residential services were considerably less than the cost of residential services, the relative increase in non-residential service utilization and expenditures was considerably larger than the cost for residential services. The rate of growth in use of non-residential services was 2.5 times greater than what occurred in residential care (Office of Comprehensive Services, 2013).

A basic tenet of CSA was the participation and collaboration of all child-serving agencies in the collaborative service planning process. As noted above, more than 90 percent of participants during the early years met the criteria for "mandated" eligibility. Specifically, in FY 1996, 62 percent were referred from local welfare agencies (DSS) and 13 percent came from local school authorities. Referrals also came from CSBs (4 percent), Juvenile Courts (8 percent), and other sources, including self-referral (13 percent).

Problems with state and local managements of CSA, inadequate infrastructure, increased utilization of residential treatment services, and failure to provide services for non-mandated youth during the initial years of implementation were not results that pleased supporters of CSA. On the other side, there were some positive outcomes during this start-up period. More than 70 percent of parents and guardians of youth served through CSA reported that their child's behavior had become stable at home and school, as well as in the community. Localities that employed a multi-agency service planning approach included more than 20 percent of non-mandated youth in their caseload compared to communities that did not use a multi-agency planning approach, where non-mandated youth comprised only 2 percent of their total CSA caseload (Joint Legislative Audit and Review Commission, 1998).

The CSA statute provided localities with considerable leeway on how they could implement this system of care. Therefore it is not surprising to find considerable variation in the manner in which localities approached this Act. In addition to stylistic differences, localities also showed wide disparities in the extent of their fidelity to CSA's core principles and operational guidelines. Although the quantity and quality of the data collected were not sufficient to allow for definitive judgments on the relative effectiveness of specific localities, the limited measures available, as well as anecdotal accounts, provide some basis for assessing the performance of individual localities. From the onset, localities like Lynchburg, Fairfax/Falls Church, and Chesterfield were viewed as exemplary models of CSA practice. In most instances, the localities that performed well during the early years had established strong programs for at-risk youth prior to the enactment of CSA. The key stakeholders in these communities had also supported CSA's vision of a collaborative family-focused, community-based approach to serving at-risk youth and their families.

On the other hand, some of the rural communities as well as large cities with high levels of poverty, had more difficulty adhering to the core tenets of CSA. In some instances, problems were related to an insufficient supply of resources needed to manage a complex system or a particularly challenging caseload. In other localities, there was active resistance to the CSA system and a lack of adequate education and training to prepare the workforce as well as local leaders whose support was essential to ensure effective execution of this interdependent approach.

One of the central questions we attempt to address in this book is how do we account for the wide variation in performance among localities? The CSA legislation spelled out in great detail the programmatic guidelines and operational mechanisms and procedures required for successful implementation of this collaborative system of care. Yet some localities were able to succeed while others did not. In the next two chapters we will provide stories of what happens to at-risk youth and their families when a community fully actualizes the principles, concepts, and operational structures and procedures of CSA, and what factors and forces contribute to establishing and sustaining such a responsive and effective local system of care.

Chapter 6

A New Way

Building a Program Around the Child

WHAT TO DO WITH ANTHONY?

What does the system do with Anthony, a 6-year-old orphan? His mother recently died from the AIDS virus and he was born HIV positive. To make matters worse, he was exhibiting very dangerous behaviors. Foster care seemed like the conventional alternative and most likely the only option. But who is really prepared to parent a child possessing both severe medical and behavioral issues?

The couple that initially fostered Anthony in Hampton, Virginia, had high hopes. Could their love, support, and constant care be enough? Could they tame the wild boy who spit upon and threw his disease-ridden blood on others? For several months the couple persevered through Anthony's tantrums and risky, destructive behaviors. Eventually, they partnered with a private agency in Hampton City to help them solidify the legal adoption of Anthony. In spite of their dedication and determination, both the couple and the agency eventually decided that Anthony could not be adopted. He was too challenging to be safely managed, and subsequently his care was relinquished back to the state of Virginia. Anthony was placed into another foster home.

By the age of 10, Anthony's future was looking dismal. He bounced around from one foster placement to another. Eventually, he was admitted to a state psychiatric residential facility. Unfortunately, Anthony also acted unsafely toward hospital staff and his peers. He was described as "being out of control and wreaking havoc on the unit"—screaming, cursing, cutting himself and throwing blood, spitting, and running out of classrooms (M. Hinson, personal communication, August 20, 2013). Traditional treatment and behavioral interventions were ineffective. Seclusions, restraints, and loss of privileges on the unit were tried but failed to improve Anthony's risky behaviors. However, among the chaos of his everyday life, Anthony would meet someone who would forever change the trajectory of his life.

Meet Mark Hinson

Mark Hinson is a middle-aged, white male with a heavy frame and a constant smile. He speaks quickly and enjoys talking and telling stories. He can carry a conversation all by himself, and typically loses his train of thought several times because he has so much to say. Mark is a humble man who describes himself as "an ordinary guy, just doing the job of a foster care parent" (M. Hinson, personal communication, February 12, 2013). To the untrained eye, Mark indeed appears ordinary. However, Mark is nothing less than extraordinary, and he is definitely more than "just" a foster care parent. He is considered a father and entrusted friend by most of the 100-plus children he has cared for. But these are no ordinary children either. They are considered the most challenging foster youth residing in Hampton, Virginia.

Mark has worked as both a behavior specialist and a foster care parent in the state of Virginia for almost 30 years. Mark reported that he has "seen it all" during his tenor in the mental health field. His initial exposure to children's mental health was in the early 1990s while working at various Virginian psychiatric residential facilities. It was common for children in the 1990s to live at residential units for several years. Subsequently, Mark had the opportunity to develop therapeutic and meaningful relationships with some of these children.

Specifically, Mark recalls in detail his initial impressions of a memorable 10-year-old boy, Anthony. It was 1995 and the residential intake staff was discussing the admission of a little boy who was "hell on wheels." Since Mark had earned the reputation for making connections with challenging children, he was assigned to Anthony for extra support. Even Mark, a seasoned behavior specialist by this time, reported being shocked by Anthony. Mark described him as "a wild and outrageous young boy." Like his encounters with previous hard-to-reach children, Mark eventually connected with Anthony. Because of this connection, he was able to talk Anthony down when engaging in risky and harmful actions. Mark also remembered being a patient advocate for Anthony. He often helped staff members understand Anthony's needs and the likely motivations for his extreme behaviors (M. Hinson, personal communication, August 20, 2013).

Other professionals who have worked with Mark report that he has "magic" with kids. However, Mark attributes his talent to his "good skills at assessing kids and meeting them where they are at" (M. Hinson, personal communication, August 20, 2013). Some children have even told Mark that he is the only adult who has ever listened to them. While it is likely that other adults have indeed listened to them, Mark perhaps has listened to them differently. Anthony was no different and responded well to Mark and his interventions.

Although this therapeutic relationship was meaningful, it was not the end-all cure to Anthony's heartache, mental illness, and dangerous outbursts. Nevertheless, after nine months Anthony showed enough improvement to be discharged to a foster family in Norfolk, Virginia. Mark helped Anthony move his few belongings and luggage to the foster family's house. Mark remembered talking to the foster parents and offering "a few pointers" on how to relate to and intervene with Anthony. He drove away that day thinking he would never see Anthony again. Mark had little understanding that meeting and working with Anthony would significantly change the course of his life.

A Memorable Reunion

Fast forward two years later to 1997. Mark was attending the new employee orientation at a state child psychiatric hospital in Norfolk, Virginia. While walking across the hospital courtyard with the other new staff members, Mark was greeted with a big hug. It was Anthony. After his initial surprise subsided, Mark was not all that surprised to see his former "wild child" still in the care of the state psychiatric system. Deep down Mark had doubts that foster care could actually provide Anthony with what he needed to keep himself and others safe. Unfortunately, Anthony had been admitted to the hospital 14 months ago. And as in past placements, he showed little to no change in his symptoms of outbursts and risky behaviors.

After a month of working at the Norfolk psychiatric hospital, Mark was conversing with staff at the water cooler. Several unit nurses had discovered that Hampton—the Virginia birth city, and the locality ultimately responsible for Anthony—was conducting a nationwide foster care search for Anthony. Mark recalls learning that "a Hampton Judge was screaming down the CSA coordinator's throat to get the kid out of the hospital. But they were having no luck. Nobody was going to take a HIV positive kid throwing blood into their house" (M. Hinson, personal communication, August 20, 2013). And Mark was right. The Hampton CSA director, Mike Terkeltaub was having little to no luck locating a foster care family.

These realistic and complicated obstacles, however, did not deter the judge's ruling. The judge clearly wanted Anthony out of the hospital and told Hampton, "I thought we all believed that children didn't do well in residential treatment when they are there for long periods of time. I'm putting this case back on the docket in 30 days. I want to know what you all have done in 30 days to get Anthony out" (M. Hinson, personal communication, August 20, 2013). Consequently, Hampton CSA had one month to discharge Anthony into a home.

A few minutes after the water cooler conversation, Mark unexpectedly runs into Anthony's social worker. The two of them begin talking about Anthony's foster care search process. Mark had always toyed with the idea of becoming a foster parent. He had been working with children in mental health for over a decade and was ready to try something new. As Mark recalls he said to her, "So what's the deal with this foster care thing?" And she said, 'Really? Are you interested?'" And Mark replied, "I'm interested in being interested." Visibly surprised, she said she would be in touch with him later. Mark thought little of this interaction and went on with his day as usual. However, a few hours later Mark received a call from Mike Terkel-taub at Hampton CSA. A brief conversation took place and ended with Mike saying that he would call Mark back in a few days. Again, Mark thought very little of this day, these conversations, and the ideas brewing over at the Hampton CSA.

Come Wednesday of that same week, just two days later, Mark gets a frantic call at home from Mike Terkeltaub. He explained to Mark that Hampton had located a willing foster care parent. However, she was an older woman and CSA was not totally convinced this was the appropriate placement. The CSA team was concerned that once again Anthony would be set up for failure. The situation had become urgent. The judge notified Hampton CSA to move forward with the discharge plan, even if it was less than satisfactory. Anthony would definitely be released from the hospital in one month.

Mark recalls, "I didn't understand totally what was being said to me. I didn't understand what they [CSA] wanted from me. So when Mike asked if I could meet with him on that Friday, the Friday of Labor Day weekend, I was like 'Yeah, okay.'" Mark said he could barely wrap his head around the conversation. However, one thing was clear, he was the target foster care parent for Anthony.

The House that Hampton Built

Mark appeared at the Hampton CSA on Friday as planned and met with both Mark Terkeltaub and Wanda Rogers. Wanda eventually became the director of Hampton CSA in 2008, but at the time of the meeting with Mark she was a social worker assigned as the Department of Social Services representative on the Family Assessment and Planning Team (FAPT). Mark remembered "instantly liking, and trusting Wanda" from the moment he met her. For several months Wanda had been part of the CSA team trying to figure out a plan for Anthony. Wanda recalls:

> CSA legislation allowed us [Hampton CSA] to be creative and did not tell us
> what we were going to do. So we decided that one of the members of the team

would be assigned Anthony's case and go over to Norfolk Psychiatric every single day, hang out with Anthony, do some additional assessments, and bring back information from that day. And about a week later, this social worker came back and said 'The most amazing thing happened today; I met someone [Mark] that has the best relationship with Anthony that I have seen anyone have in all the months that I have been going to visit him, and now daily that I am going to visit him.' And so you could see Mike and I looking at each other because certainly we were like "bingo", we've got to figure out how to do something with Mark and he's got to be in our plan . . . we didn't know what or how. (W. Rogers, personal communication, August 11, 2010)

During the casual and impromptu meeting, Mike, Wanda, and Mark sat at a table and used a beverage napkin to scratch out details. One of the points discussed was how much it cost per year to have a child in residential treatment. It was over $100,000. Mike and Wanda believed that Hampton could provide a quality service delivery for a lot less than that. They then went on to describe how Hampton CSA wanted to do something radically different. And so they said to Mark, "By now you have probably figured out that we want you in the equation. We would like to know if you would be willing to become a foster parent for the city of Hampton?" (W. Rogers, personal communication, August 11, 2010).

Hampton essentially wanted to build a foster care environment to match Anthony's needs. This meant renting and furnishing a house where Anthony could live and Mark could be the foster parent. It was definitely a profound idea– building a program around a child versus putting a child into an already existing program. Mark said that things were happening fast during the conversation but knew something special and unique was being discussed.

Mark asked exactly what was needed of him. For starters, Mark was living in Norfolk. Mark would be required to move to the city of Hampton. As Wanda phrased it, "We wanted Mark to give up his whole life and come on board" (W. Rogers, personal communication, August 11, 2010). Although Mark was a single person with no children, he reasonably asked why he needed to move. Mike and Wanda told Mark about the culture of collaboration that existed in Hampton and that there would be ongoing meetings with the police officers, judges, and schools. Basically the whole community would be coming together to support this placement. Subsequently, the house needed to be in Hampton. Mike put the situation into terms Mark could understand and appreciate, "If you are in Norfolk and this child runs away, there may not be anybody who even cares about the plan that Hampton has developed with you. And it might not work the way we would like to see it work if there is a problem. So we need you to be in Hampton" (M. Terkeltaub, personal communication, April 2013). Wanda remembers telling Mark:

We believe in full disclosure. We are going to be very candid with you. What we are asking you to do, we have never done before; we are making it up as we go along. The only thing that we could say to you for absolute certain is that if you are willing to come aboard with us we will always be there for you. It does not matter if it is 2:00 am in the morning or 2:00 pm during the day. Whenever you call us we are going to be there, we are absolutely in this with you 100 percent. (W. Rogers, personal communication, August 11, 2010)

Wanda guaranteed that they would locate a house and find the resources to furnish it. Still, this was a life-changing commitment for Mark. The meeting ended by everyone going home over the Labor Day weekend to think it over. Mark remembers it being "so very overwhelming."

Yet, the next morning Wanda received a call from Mark. He told her, "You know what? I have never met anybody who believes in children that passionately, and so I want to be a part of the team." Mark divulged to Wanda later on that her statement of being 100 percent committed to the program sold him on coming on board. But Mark was not going to be a regular foster care parent, he was going to be Hampton's "Specialized Intensive Foster Parent." This meant, Mark could not reject a child placed into his house. In spite of his trepidation, Mark accepted this challenging responsibility and he and the Hampton CSA staff began to put in place a program for Anthony.

Plans had to be rushed. With less than a month until Anthony's discharge, a lot had to happen. Wanda had to file an emergency foster home approval. Mark had to uproot his life in Norfolk and start setting up housekeeping in Hampton. Specifically, he had to buy every individual item necessary to run a household, from toilet paper, to utensils, to bedroom furniture, and lamps. Mark especially remembered going to Wal-Mart on a daily basis filling up cart after cart with home goods.

Alas, even with the community support, dedication of the Hampton CSA team, and Mark's sacrificing efforts, the house was not going to meet Anthony's discharge deadline. Hampton needed just a few more weeks to get everything ready. In the end, the judge ruled that Anthony be discharged into the care of the elderly foster parent and Mark would serve as a respite house as needed.

THE LOST BOYS

All was not lost on Mark and his new house even though Anthony would not live there full-time. Unfortunately, there were many Hampton children similar to Anthony and in need of specialized foster care. However, most of those kids during that time were in residential treatment facilities. Hampton

CSA now had momentum. They also gained community support to get other children out of residential care and placed back safely into the community or home. Most importantly though, Hampton's CSA now had the philosophical belief that residential care was not the answer for their children. Mike Terkeltaub recalls how he and Wanda "became kind of zealous around CSA, the whole systems of care approach, and wrap around services; we really began to think that every kid could come home" (M. Tekletaub, personal communication, May 2013).

Subsequently, several boys were on Hampton's radar as potential children to live with Mark, given that the house was designed to maintain two full-time boys and one part-time respite boy. Mark and Wanda retain fond memories of the first group of boys that resided in the house. These boys' stories capture the severity of their situations, the amazing bond that Mark developed with them, and the passion and values that Hampton CSA embodies.

Doug

Doug was the first full-time child to live in Mark's house. Doug was a 15-year-old white teenager who had been in and out of psychiatric hospitals for five years. By the time he entered Mark's house, he had lived at the same hospital for over a year. He was a tall and hefty boy (about 6'2" and 320 pounds) who had not showered in over a month. Doug thought that if he were dirty the staff would not bother him and make him go to school every morning. When Doug believed he could not control his situation, he would often strip naked to get reactions from peers and staff. Doug was also notorious for punching holes in the walls. Rarely could staff talk him down once he escalated to aggression, and as a result was often restrained or medicated. According to Mark, Doug had a "horrific childhood." Apparently Doug, his parents, and siblings would rob houses together during school hours. Doug was illiterate, suffering from physical health issues, and troubled with mental health problems. Wanda said his "psychiatric diagnoses were all over the place, but most likely he was a manic depressive."

Mark, being a brand new foster parent, was rightfully nervous about meeting Doug. In order to develop some rapport, Mark called Doug each night before their initial meeting. Mark decided to do something unconventional on their first encounter; he arranged to take Doug to the theme park Busch Gardens, which was three miles from the hospital. On the walk over to the car, and within the first 10 minutes, Doug said to Mark, "I'm gonna call you dad." Mark said this comment "freaked" him out. Mark knew that this intimate type of relationship was against hospital policy and could result in an employee being fired. He immediately ran to the phone and called Wanda for advice. Wanda quickly reassured Mark that this relationship was going to be okay. She helped explain to Mark the differences in foster care versus residential hospital roles. Mark knew at that moment this was going to be a different experience for him and these boys.

Naturally, Doug had difficulty adjusting to a stable environment with a reliable adult. For instance, Doug ran away on the first night with Mark. With good foresight, the Hampton team had fortunately developed a plan with Mark for such emergencies. Mark followed protocol, notified the police and then called Mike to let him know Doug had left. Doug eventually came back to the house on his own. He refused to come inside and insisted he would sleep on the driveway instead. It seemed that Doug was "teasing and testing his limits" with Mark, and lay down on the pavement. Mark tried to cajole him back into the house but this only escalated Doug. He soon began threatening to fight Mark. Eventually the police arrived and watched the scene unfold; they were getting concerned. Mike arrived soon after and helped the police understand that Doug was a special needs child, and that Hampton CSA had a plan to deal with such situations. The police were satisfied and left. Doug went inside.

Doug continued to have problems during the first year in Mark's house. He had several encounters with police, including holding a dozen officers at bay with a knife. Although he never hit Mark, Doug did a lot of damage to the house. However, Hampton CSA reinforced to Mark:

> This is the kind of behavior that has gotten him restrained when he was in a residential treatment facility. We are absolutely not going to restrain him. So if he is out of control like that, you do need to call the police but not for the purpose of the police arresting Doug and taking him to jail. It's to help us bring order. He needs to understand that every single time we are going to work with him through this, and you are not going to call us and say he has to be removed from your home. Doug has learned to set it up that way—if I do x, y, and z I'm automatically going to have the social worker show up and I'm going to be removed. Those lessons are going to be some of the first lessons we have to train (W. Rogers, personal communication, August 11, 2010).

Doug frequently refused to attend school. Once the Hampton school recognized Mark as a dedicated parent who was going to be there for Doug, school personnel began collaborating with Mark and the CSA team. Soon special education plans were developed that supported the work Mark was doing in the home. From there, the CSA team started partnering with Doug's therapist, psychiatrist, and in-home counselor. Wanda recalled how "all of it just came together, and all of us were there to support anything that we had not thought of for Doug" (W. Rogers, personal communication, August 10, 2011).

Doug ended up staying with Mark for several years in the house until his social worker developed a plan for him to transition into his adult life. Doug is currently in his early 30s. He was in and out of jail a few times, but has been able to maintain a job. Mark wistfully acknowledges that Doug was his first kid, but is the child that he has the least contact with.

Wayne

Once Mark demonstrated that he could care for Doug in his house, Wanda and Mike decided to add another boy. Wayne was 8 years old when Hampton CSA gained custody of him. His mother was addicted to cocaine and was never able to recover from it. While in Hampton's care, he spent two years in and out of psychiatric facilities and state hospitals. However, the Hampton team was hopeful that Doug and Wayne (now age 10) could share a living space with Mark. Wanda said that Hampton CSA "cringes when they think about Wayne spending his entire childhood in foster care because that is not what they would do now."

Like Doug, Wayne also intimidated others because of his size and the kinds of behaviors he displayed. But that did not deter Mark and the team. When Wanda approached the hospital psychiatrist about discharging Wayne, she was told, "If he is discharged it is against medical advice because there is absolutely no way all his needs can be met in the community. Wayne is someone who needs to be in residential treatment for the rest of his life. In fact, we need to lock him up and throw away the key. He is an animal. A terror."

Wayne was immediately discharged and placed with Mark. And his needs were met. Wayne ended up living with Mark from the age of 10 until he was 18 years old. Mark still keeps in touch with Wayne, who is now a man in his mid-20s. The road has not been smooth, as Wayne has been in and out of jail for minor crimes, but overall Mark said he is doing "fairly well."

Paul

Mark originally agreed to care for 3 children (Doug and Wayne full-time, plus a part-time child, Anthony, as needed for respite). He also signed a one-year lease on the house. However, Mark loved his job and asked for more kids and for a bigger house. Hampton CSA was thrilled that their program was working and wanted to continue transitioning kids back into their community. Mark got a bigger house with that the addition of Paul.

Paul was 16 years old and had been in foster care since he was young. He frequently smoked marijuana and drank alcohol. He bounced around from foster care to residential to substance-abuse treatment programs. Initially, he was going to stay with Mark for a two-day respite. However, he and Mark bonded and stayed for two years. Although he and Mark became close, with Paul calling Mark his "Gramps", he was adamant about leaving foster care when he turned 18. Sure enough, when Paul turned 18 he left the house.

A year later, Mark received a phone call from Paul in the dead of winter. Paul was in Philadelphia and had been robbed. He had no coat, no money, and was asking Mark for help. Mark immediately went to Wanda for advice. They both agreed that Mark needed to help him out even though he was no longer in foster care. Mark bought Paul a bus ticket back to Hampton and got him connected with Job Corp. With Mark's support, Paul earned his GED, learned computer skills, and enlisted in the Army.

Mark had serious concerns about Paul going into the Army. His biggest concern was that Paul's mental health history would prevent him from being accepted. Mark strongly advised Paul not to disclose that he had a history of substance abuse and had been in a psychiatric hospital. Paul listened to Mark and was accepted. However, during boot camp Paul broke down one day while being yelled at by his drill sergeant and revealed his past. Paul was released from camp and told he would not be able to enter the Army. Mark advocated on Paul's behalf and arranged a meeting with the Army base committee; he asked them to reconsider their decision. Mark was turned away and Philip's reentry was denied.

Mark, however, was persistent and would not let up; he was determined to help Paul fulfill his dream of being in the Army. After eight months, Mark finally got an audience with the General and Paul was allowed to reenter boot camp. Mark remembered Paul telling everyone, "My dad is crazy. Look what he did for me." During all that time, Paul lived with Mark at the house and maintained a job.

Paul went away to boot camp again, but was quickly disillusioned. He decided he was quitting because the Army was "mean" to him. Paul was granted approval to quit, but for some reason his base commander said no. The commander informed Paul that he could have his company changed and could start over again in eight weeks, but in no way was he going to be released. Mark laughs when he recalled letters written by Paul during that time. Mark said the letters "were hilarious because Paul was so angry at me. He wanted me to stop encouraging him, and he wanted me to stop telling him that the common denominator for all the problems in his life was him."

Thankfully Mark did not give up on Paul and continued to encourage him. Paul graduated with highest honors from the Army and received a prestigious award out of a class of 500. Mark, of course, flew out to spend the weekend celebrating Paul's graduation achievement. Mark was Paul's guest of honor and went on stage with him during his award ceremonies. After one particular dinner banquet Paul introduced Mark to his boot camp commander. The commander told Mark that he appreciated the letters written to Paul. Evidently, during boot camp the sergeants made a check of Paul's cabinet and found Mark's letters. The commander told Paul, "If you have somebody in your life that cares about you that much, then I'll get you through this boot camp."

Paul is still in the Army today. He has completed several tours in Afghanistan and Iraq and has received several awards for his service. According to Mark, Paul is a successful Army recruiter in south Florida, and has a wife and baby. Mark and Paul are in frequent contact with each other, with Paul calling Mark for advice about life, finances, and much more. Mark gets teary eyed when he talks about Paul. Mark said, "Yeah, him calling me Dad is the real thing."

THE KEY TO MARK'S SUCCESS

There are many other success stories to be told about Mark and his lost boys. Not all of the stories have happy endings, but the fact that the community of Hampton did not give up on these children is in and of itself a real achievement. Hampton was not willing to continue having their children live in residential facilities far away from home. So, how did the Hampton CSA team and Mark foster—and often times reunite with their biological family—over 100 boys considered the most mentally and behaviorally challenged kids?

The "Specialized Intensive Foster Care" program is distinctive in the fact that it does not turn a child away. Mark believes the most important key to their success is making the program child and family specific. Hampton has embraced the CSA philosophy that each child and family is unique with a specific set of needs and goals. "Because of the way CSA is set up, you can do whatever you need as long as it is child specific," said Wanda when describing how CSA gave them the flexibility to create Mark's house. Walt Credle, a former and retired director of the Hampton Community Service Board, recalled the initiation of CSA programming:

> Hampton said, here is the child. What do we do now? Well we build something with this one child. A system of care and make it work in the community. It's planning and implementing at the same time. So we didn't know what it was supposed to look like. We knew what the CSA code said, and knew that we were committed to the values of family-focused and community-based programs . . . but we built it one child at a time not knowing what the outcome was going to be two, three, or five years down the road. But doing it that way I think worked. (W. Credle, personal communication, August 11, 2010)

Another vital strategy implemented with Mark's program was collaboration and relationship building with the greater community. With CSA supporting its mission, Hampton worked diligently with various agencies (e.g., courts, schools, police, hospitals, and social services) in order to provide Mark and the children the support they needed for continued success. Wanda said:

All stakeholder groups are accountable for positive outcomes for children and their families . . . we broke it out of the home and into the school and the community. So if this outcome is not what we expected it to be, it's not you social services, or it's not you court services or it's not you schools that dropped the ball . . . it's all of us. If it fails, we all fail. We don't get to point the fingers. So we just held everybody accountable. We knew that one of our core values was that the child-centered, family-focused, community-based service delivery is the law in Virginia and must be implemented through new practice. Do whatever it takes to support the success of children and families. CSA legislation said that if you do not have it, then develop it. So we began to say, alright, we are going to have to go out there and develop this program through our private providers and our community partners. (W. Rogers, personal communication, August 11, 2010)

However, this program could not have worked with just any foster care parent. Mark Hinson's passion, dedication, and approach with children are much applauded for the program's success. Wanda acknowledged Mark and his commitment by saying, "The thing with Mark's home . . . Mark moved over here and became a full-time foster parent. The rest of our foster parents had jobs and they keep kids like a traditional family structure. Other people wouldn't do that . . . they would say that's not what you are supposed to do." Hampton's appreciation for Mark is clear as they provide him with financial, emotional, and community support around the clock if needed.

Mark believes that his child-centered approach in the house has made a difference with how the boys respond to living with him. Mark is now entering into his sixteenth year in the program. He is in his fourth and largest house, which cares for eight children. Two adults assist him during the day with the boys, but he remains the only adult to live in the house. The focus of the program has also changed over the years. Whereas the initial purpose was to transfer kids out of residential, now it primarily focuses on prevention. The length of stay for the children has also decreased as Hampton has been able to decrease the amount of time a child is in foster care.

Since becoming a foster parent in 1997, Mark believes that he "has never not figured a kid or situation out." When asked specifically what he does to achieve his success, he humbly replied, "I don't know. Magic?" Mark does recognize that he has an uncanny ability to quickly and accurately assess a child's emotional state and then try to meet them where they are at. He is also quick to mention that he does not get into power struggles with his kids. For instance, he never uses the term "bedtime", but instead tells the boys at night that it is "room time." At night the boys are allowed to do whatever they want in their room. The only thing he cares about is if they can get up and attend school in the morning. Typically the boys fall asleep by 9:30pm because there is no fight about bedtime.

Mark also parents with fun and creativity. Mark is responsible for the house's budget and makes sure that the kids have a normal childhood. They have memberships to the YMCA, cell phones, video games, and frequent trips to the movies. Every summer he budgets a "family vacation." Some of the trips have included ten days in Florida or road trips to Michigan. Mark noted that Mike Terkeltaub, although retired from the Hampton CSA, is still dedicated to the program and often joins the vacations as an extra chaperone.

The devotion Mark has towards his foster children does not go unnoticed by the boys. Sometimes the boys catch themselves calling Mark, "Dad" without intentionally doing so. Mark remains in touch with most of the boys after they leave. They frequently call or visit. They "couch surf" a few days when they need a place to stay. They ask for a pair of shoes when they do not have money. They ask him for fatherly advice. Mark knows that these children will come and go. And that is the natural cycle of being a foster parent. But he still has to "steel" himself emotionally each time they leave.

Due to the success of Mark's house, Hampton CSA has replicated this model and now supports several houses within their Specialized Foster Care Project. These homes support children with significant needs and help them to remain in the community, even though they have multiple problems as evidenced by 84 percent of the youth having academic problems, 80 percent of the youth having physical aggression issues, 61 percent of the youth having depressive symptoms, and 30 percent of the youth having suicidal or self-harmful behaviors. The Project has also shown significant success as evidenced by 92 percent of the children in the Project within a 12-month period either remaining in their specialized foster home, moved to a less restrictive home, or became adopted (Triad 2011).

Hampton is not the only Virginian locality to reach success through savvy implementation of the CSA. However, they have been able to achieve something quite special, not only with Mark Hinson's house, but with their entire approach to caring for their youth and families. The next chapter will take a look inside the Hampton community and their collaborative approach to making the CSA a tangible reality and success.

Chapter 7

Putting All of the Pieces Together

A Locality Creates a Comprehensive System of Care

SMALL COMMUNITY WITH BIG ACTION

Hampton, Virginia has a rich history of embracing new legislature, as evidenced by the famous Emancipation Oak—the tree located at Hampton University under which the Virginia Peninsula's Black community gathered to hear the first Southern reading of President Abraham Lincoln's Emancipation Proclamation in 1863. Aside from history buffs and those living in Virginia, few have even heard about the city of Hampton. However, Hampton is well-known and nationally recognized for its best practices in health and human services. The "Hampton Model" has been studied for its lessons and insights within many other counties in Virginia, as well as by other localities in several states (The American Public Human Services Association, APHSA, 2012).

Hampton is a small 136-square mile town. It's located on the southernmost tip of a peninsula southeast of Waynesburg in the Chesapeake Bay. Hampton's homepage describes itself as "a robust waterfront city in southeastern Virginia." According to the 2010 census, the population was a little over 137,000.

Although Hampton is small, it has packed a big punch when it comes to grasping and applying the Comprehensive Service Act (CSA). The city of Hampton has been "lauded as a leader in Systems of Care reform throughout the state of Virginia" (Triad, 2007). Since the law came into place in 1992, the Hampton CSA system has embraced the Systems of Care principles that "all services for children and families should be child centered, family focused, community based, strength based and culturally and linguistically competent" (Triad, 2007). With community support and buy-in, Hampton's CSA office has established a well-deserved reputation. They have been excellent at keeping children and adolescents in the community by delivering child-centered, family-focused, and community-based services for at-risk youth and their families.

This chapter will explore the historical context that provided a foundation for collaboration and success in implementing the CSA within this Virginia locality. Hampton's System of Care service delivery, values, and programs will also be presented with outcomes. Finally, themes that have helped Hampton move away from a child-serving agency system to a community-driven system of care will be outlined.

FORWARD THINKING LEADERS RESPOND TO A FINANCIAL CRISIS

Financial crisis is not often linked with serendipity and a good turn of events. In 1992, the city of Hampton was experiencing a financial crisis like much of Virginia and the rest of the nation. Businesses were downsizing, unemployment rates were rising and revenue to the city government was at a low level. Subsequently, human service agencies were bearing the burden of the social stressors caused by economic hardships. Instead of Hampton's system imploding on itself, the stars were aligned for dramatic growth and restructuring.

Also occurring at this time of fiscal uncertainty, was the inception of the CSA to help reduce costs spent on troubled youth. Retrospectively, Hampton was well prepared to embrace the CSA and a system of care philosophy in the early 1990s.

In the 1980s, the city of Hampton wanted to change the way they were doing business. Subsequently, Hampton reorganized its human service departments into one task force, with the goal of cultivating more flexibility, accountability, and collaboration across multi-disciplinary teams. This atmosphere of collaboration was contagious and soon became the norm among all city agencies. Then in the late 1980s, city leaders and department heads analyzed their economic competiveness. It was evident that Hampton was growing a permanent underclass of youth who had few options in the workforce (Galano et al., 2001). Hampton leaders were determined to turn things around. A group was organized and developed a new mission statement: "To make Hampton the most livable city in Virginia, and a strategic emphasis on creating a globally competitive workforce to attract business investment" (Galano et al., 2001).

Fortunately, Hamptons' leaders were forward thinking and were essential to building a foundation for CSA. Foremost, these city leaders did not choose a quick-fix approach to their financial woes. Instead, they searched for a preventative strategy to boost its economy. As such, they focused their energy towards strategic investment in youth development. A Coalition for Youth was created and together with the city's Citizen Service Task Force, a new initiative was designed and given fiscal support during a time of scarce resources. In 1992, the Hampton Healthy Families Partnership (HFP) was developed as city officials understood the link between strong families, early childhood development, and the creation of a globally competitive workforce. Strong healthy families would provide the foundation for a sturdy economic future.

The time of the inception of CSA was also a time when innovation and best practices were cornerstones of Hampton public policy initiatives (Triad, 2007). Hamptons' city and child-serving agency leaders believed that children have better outcomes when provided supports and services in their homes and communities rather than out of home and out of community in residential treatment placements. Hampton's child-serving agency consulted with national leaders in Systems of Care and the Wraparound model in order to inform their practices. The stars were aligning more as the goals and spirit of CSA were looking quite similar to Hamptons' service delivery and values.

When the CSA was finally enacted in 1993, Hampton understood the promise of CSA and used the new law to improve service delivery. Hampton quickly jumped on the CSA wagon. Hampton organized their Community Policy and Management Team (CPMT) and elected Harry Campbell, the Executive Director of Lutheran Family Services, as the first chairperson. The election of Mr. Campbell signaled the commitment of the city of Hampton to "a true public/private partnership in the development of services for children and families" (Triad, 2007). They also developed a Family Assessment Planning Team (FAPT) dedicated to CSA and co-located at Department of Social Service. The FAPT then created several committees with the purpose of reducing the utilization of residential treatment and developing creative plans for families.

Despite the positive efforts by Hampton's CPMT and FAPT to develop child-centered, family-focused, and community-based services, the utilization of residential treatment continued to be an issue. Robert J. O'Neill, Jr., Hampton's City Manager, sent a memorandum to the CPMT dated October 11, 1994 requesting the development of "local options for providing quality services to our youth but at a more reasonable cost" (Triad, 2007).

In response, Walt Credle, the Hampton Director of Social Services, communicated to the CPMT on October 31, 1994 with a memorandum titled "Reinventing Service Delivery." This memorandum stated, "we have each come from a single-agency, somewhat specialized approach to serving children who are at risk. CSA challenges us to create a new approach, to reinvent the way services are provided." The memorandum included a document entitled *Reinventing Services to At-Risk Children and Families*. This document included the following commentary:

1. The Traditional Single Agency Approach reviews and accepts community-based options at the step before making a residential placement. *The New Collaborative Team Approach creates community-based options for specific children that do not now exist.*
2. The Traditional Single Agency Approach encourages parents to accept residential placements because community-based options are not readily available. *The New Collaborative Team Approach offers parents creative community-based options for their children and commitment to their development.*
3. The Traditional Single Agency Approach continues residential placements beyond the point of significant treatment benefits. *The New Collaborative Team Approach establishes early discharge dates and rigorously pursues step-down plans.*
4. The Traditional Single Agency Approach states that residential placements are driven by statutory and judicial considerations which are external to CSA teams. *The New Collaborative Team Approach states that residential placements are driven by the degree to which we take responsibility for creating alternatives.*

Hampton continues to embrace this 1994 call for services and hold Credle's memorandum as its vision statement and cornerstone. Thanks to innovative leaders who encouraged collaboration and creativity, a financial crisis became a moment of opportunity and paved the way for CSA to be embraced and turned into reality in this small Virginia locality.

UNIQUE AND CREATIVE SERVICE DELIVERY

Hampton has adopted several "Care Core Values and Beliefs", which will be discussed throughout this chapter. One of the primary Core Values is that *child-centered, family-focused, and community-based service delivery is the law in Virginia and must be implemented through new practice models.* Over the past 20 years, Hampton has earned a reputation for developing creative, collaborative, and community-based supports and programs for their children and families. Programs under the "Hampton Model" have been praised by national organizations such as The American Public Human Services Association and the National Alliance on Mental Illness, and highlighted by *The Journal of Primary Prevention* and *The Richmond Times Dispatch*.

A common thread among services are the focus on child-centered, family-focused, community-based, strengths-based, and culturally competent individualized approaches that support children remaining in their homes, schools, and communities. A Hampton CSA document listing the menu of programs under the Hampton System of Care notes that "the success Hampton has had supporting children and young adults remaining with their families and in their neighborhoods and communities has been significantly supported by the array of quality *interdependent and individualized* services provided within our system of care" (B. Clark, personal communication, August 15, 2012). Table 7.1 provides a comprehensive directory of supports and services implemented within the city of Hampton. Two successful programs which capture the spirit of Hampton's programing will be highlighted in the next section.

Hampton Healthy Families Partnership (HFP): Preventative Strategy

As previously mentioned, the Hampton Healthy Families Partnership (HFP) originated during the financial crisis in October 1992. Hampton city leadership was dedicated to their competitive workforce mission statement, and subsequently acknowledged children and families as the most important community resource. City leaders believed that if children were born healthy and ready to learn at an early age, outcomes for children, families, and communities would significantly improve. There was also the belief among Hampton city leaders that there "would never be enough resources to support at-risk children if the issues facing children and families were not mitigated prior to the need for intervention services" (Triad, 2007). The solution? Engage and support families through a community partnership program. All programs would focus on preventive practices and investment in parents.

Hampton leaders moved forward by creating a HFP steering committee, but decided to use a partnership investor model (vs. a traditional stakeholder/community planning model). This investor model brought together a small group of senior staff from local organizations with resources relevant to HFP who all shared the same common passion and mission. Some of the original committee members included representation from the Social Services Department, Mental Health Department, the Housing Authority, schools, libraries, hospitals, and neighborhoods. Together these investors made initial decisions which moved the project from planning to implementation (Galano et al., 2001). The fear was that a more traditional model might delay the new initiative with stakeholders competing for agendas, consensus, and resources. In the spirit of their partnership investor approach, feedback sessions were held through a series of community meetings so that the public (their consumer) might also have a voice in the process.

The Partnership provides a comprehensive array of services from information sharing to intensive home-based services. There are two main Healthy Families program components: Healthy Start and Healthy Community.

Table 7.1 Hampton Service Delivery Programs

Program Name	Program Description
The Hampton Family Assessment and Planning Team (FAPT)	Consists of the agencies serving children and their families and family representatives. The Hampton FAPT is a single team meeting multiple times a week and has staff that devotes a significant part of their work hours to FAPT involvement. All approaches are individualized to the specific needs of children and their families and innovation is supported.
Healthy Families Partnership (HFP)	Supports the link between strong families, early childhood development, and the creation of a globally competitive workforce. The goal of the Partnership is to ensure that every child is born healthy and enters school ready to learn. Program components include Parenting Education, Healthy Stages, Young Family Centers, Healthy Start, Welcome Baby and Child Fair.
Managing Emotions Project (ME)	A partnership between the Center for Child and Family Services and the Hampton Healthy Families Partnership that supports parents increasing parental skills through participation in a variety of group experiences. The primary goal of the project is to insure that parents strengthen their abilities to provide a safe, nurturing environment for their children. The variety of group experiences includes nurturing and parenting; parent anger management; and parent violence anger management.
Pathways to Permanency	A product of the cooperative efforts of the Hampton Department of Human Services, the Hampton Juvenile and Domestic Relations District Court, and other local agencies working to assist foster children and their families in the City of Hampton. Pathway to Permanency is a tool and supportive program designed to reunite children with their biological parents.
Safe Harbor for Kids	Facilitates successful supervised visits between parents and children. This project is part of the Pathways to Permanency project and provides trained professionals to supervise visitation, provide feedback to families as well as feedback to the court and social services. The goal of visits is for children and families to experience love and acceptance as well as provide supervision and support regarding potential safety concerns.
Mediation Project	A component of the Pathways to Permanency project that allows families the opportunity to voluntarily resolve differences to support unified planning and expedite court processes. Mediation offers a strengths base method to open dialogue between family members; an opportunity to find fair and equitable solutions; a focus on the best interest of the children; a confidential forum; and an informal process facilitated by an impartial third party. Family members must voluntarily agree to be involved in the mediation process; agree to ground rules negotiated with the facilitator; and agree to listen to the other family member involved in the mediation process as the mediation moves toward a written agreement between family members.

Best Practices Court Stakeholders Group	A collaborative effort of all child-serving stakeholder organizations led by the Hampton Juvenile and Domestic Relations District Court and the Hampton Department of Social Services. The group has become the forum for an ongoing evaluation of and accountability to progress made by the court and the service providers in achieving better outcomes for children and families. This group emerged as a result of efforts to make improvements to the handling of child dependency issues, service planning and filings, timeliness of hearings and various service delivery issues.
Specialized Intensive Foster Care (SIFC)	Developed as an alternative to residential treatment centers. Professional Parents, with the knowledge and experience to support children and families with the most complex needs, provide 24-hour services, support and housing utilizing an unconditional care approach. SIFC families receive Wraparound supports individualized for each child's specific strengths and needs. SIFC parents connect with the biological family and often serve as mentors to the families and siblings.
Intensive Care Coordination (ICC)	A multi-agency tiered approach to supporting children and families remaining together and avoiding out of home and out of community placements. ICC is provided in family's homes, schools and communities and has been a critical factor in quickly implementing supports and services that reduce the need for residential treatment services.
Specialized Educational Services	Support Hampton's philosophy for children to attend their neighborhood schools and if children need to be placed outside of their home school to support their individualized educational needs; placement at the nearest school is sought. Hampton City Schools was a leader in developing local classrooms for children with autism, intellectual disabilities (ID), and co-occurring behavioral. Hampton City Schools also has a strong vocational program with high school job coaches for children with ID in place for the past 10 years.
Family Stabilization Project	A collaboration between the Hampton Court Services Unit, Hampton Department of Social Services and private child-serving agencies. Children and families involved in the juvenile justice system and at significant risk of removal from their homes and families are provided intensive in-home services including case management, family support, connection to natural and community supports, linkages to an array of community based services, advocacy, and crisis support. Short term out of home stays are available to allow the time for services to be developed as well as an assessment to determine the best possible services and supports for each child and family.
Parent to Parent Support	Provides family mentors to serve as guides and support for families involved in the FAPT process. Parent Partners support families through such diverse activities as IEP meetings, FAPT meetings, mental health and substance abuse appointments, scheduling multiple appointments, social services connections and one to one support based on each family's individualized needs.

(Continued)

Table 7.1 Hampton Service Delivery Programs (Continued)

Program Name	Program Description
Teaching Parent Project	Provides birth parents and other natural supports such as relatives and community members whose children are at imminent risk of removal from their families and communities an array of services and supports including ongoing education and training to support children and families staying together; case management services including behavior management, advocacy, linkages to services and crisis intervention support; ongoing FAPT support and monitoring to insure quality of services; and a monthly stipend to support the goal of children and their families successfully together.
Family Group Conferencing	Provides an active forum for families to make decisions for the best possible placement for children at risk of removal from their homes and families. The Hampton Department of Social Services Foster Care Unit utilizes the New Zealand approach that insures family meetings to develop solutions regarding cases of abuse and neglect. The foster care staff brings together family members and community members identified by the family to develop a family conference. The family is given guidelines to insure safety and meets alone for several hours to develop a strengths based plan and then share this plan with the foster care staff. Hampton has found families can develop real and powerful plans that support children remaining safely in the community.
Specialized Housing Services Project	An option for young adults who have a need for supportive adults in their lives as well as a place to live while transitioning to adulthood. The Supportive Adult serves as a mentor and guide as the young adult travels on his or her journey toward adulthood as well as commits to providing housing and teaching life lessons on the road to independence. Services and supports provided include a place to live, help with house and apartment searches, support mastering independent living skills, coaching and role modeling, career counseling, transportation, educational and vocational support, money management support, volunteerism and development of community supports and activities.
Supervised Independent Transitional Living	Provides apartment living with transitional supports to bridge the gap for young adults over 18 living independently in the community as adults. Services provided include case management, intensive in-home services, independent living skills training, monitoring, supervision and 24-hour crisis support. The young adults are provided with practical and applicable skills development including employment readiness, money management, housekeeping and daily living skills, nutrition and transportation education and support.

Post Adoption Services	Supports adoptive families and reduce the likelihood of adoption dissolutions. Services are provided for families who have adopted children and need additional support; children with complex needs including infants with prenatal drug and/or alcohol exposure; children with physical, emotional or developmental challenges; and children seeking answers regarding their adoption or searching for their birth parents. Services include information and referrals for services, clinical support and general support for the adoptive family and children.
Fatherhood Initiative	Developed to increase the role of fathers in the FAPT process as well as throughout the Hampton children's service delivery system. Fathers attend a 12 week group to provide support and education regarding their child's strengths and complex needs; reduce stressors regarding the role of fathers with their children and families; increase understanding of systems processes and barriers; increasing understanding and access to community based services and supports; and develop each father's skills and abilities to advocate for their child and family.
The Brotherhood	An ongoing group developed to provide a positive outlet for young black men to foster healthy discussions on issues each of them may face day to day. Co-facilitated by a Hampton DSS social worker and a Hampton foster parent.
Fast Forward	A program designed to fit employers with the most qualified employees. Strive to meet each employer's unique requirements by referring only successful Fast Forward graduates who are qualified and ready to perform. Each graduate receives ongoing follow-up counseling in support of continued success on the job. Fast Forward also works with employers to design and deliver special pre- and post-employment training and orientation programs aligned to specific organizational goals. Structured training and apprenticeship programs are part of the Fast Forward program; candidates are carefully screened based on employer requirements with a goal of long-term employment and potential advancement. Training and education dollars are often available to help Fast Forward graduates gain critical skills.
Parents and Children Together (PACT)— Shared Family Care Project	A collaboration of all CPMT/FAPT member agencies, Lutheran Family Services. An individualized approach for families with complex needs to avoid immediate foster care placement and the placement of children and adolescents in residential programs. PACT places entire families together with host families to keep children from entering the foster care system. The plan is for families to remain in the project for up to six months; develop the necessary tools and skills to support their children with complex needs; find employment and housing; and successfully live independently in the community.
Ready by 21	A set of innovative strategies developed by the Forum for Youth Investment that helps communities improve the odds that all children and youth will be ready for college, work, and life.

Source: Clark (2012).

1. Healthy Start is a home-based visitation program available to families at risk of child abuse and neglect who desire to participate (Galano et al., 2007). Participation is voluntary and typically sustained until the child enters elementary school. This program works with children and families to maintain a stable home environment by strengthening parenting skills and by providing intensive support, information, and education. Parents are paired with a Family Support Worker who provides a variety of services, such as effective parenting techniques, home management skills, nutrition counseling, and links to community resources. Each child receives well-baby care, child development screenings, and immunizations.

2. Healthy Community is a set of comprehensive parent education and support programs for Hampton families with children under 19 years of age. A series of parent education classes cover an assortment of parenting issues, such as nutrition, child development, discipline, and Lamaze. The "Welcome Baby" component uses voluntary home visits, while several child fairs provide new parents with support, information, and community resources. The Young Family Center is a special section of the Hampton Public Library which offers books and electronic media to help parents become more effective and nurturing. There is even a series of newsletters that provide the community with child development, age-appropriate activities, immunization schedules, and family-oriented community resources (Galano et al., 2007).

Another goal of the Healthy Families Partnership is to reduce the need for CSA-type intervention services by reducing and eliminating risk factors evident before the child is born and during the early years of the child's life (Triad, 2007). There is evidence suggesting that the development of the HFP has helped decreased the utilization of out-of-home care in Hampton. Outcome reports have been impressive and have noted the following conclusions on HFP Participation in Healthy Start:

- Reduced pregnancy risk status.
- Reduced delivery risk factors and birth complications.
- Families demonstrated more effective parent-child interaction.
- Children are immunized more effectively.
- Families had more adequate home environments and provided increased developmental stimulation to their children.
- Improved child health and physical development.
- Reduced repeat teen births.
- 26.8 percent reduction in the rate of child abuse and neglect between 1992 and 2000 outpacing the region's rate of 3.4 percent.
- 0 percent repeat teen births among Healthy Start mothers versus an average of 30 percent for all teen mothers in Virginia.

- 96 percent immunization rate for 2-year-olds in the Healthy Start program versus 73 percent for all 2-year-olds in Virginia.
- 85 percent of Healthy Start children entered school ready to learn (Galano & Huntington 1999; The Hampton Approach to Systems of Care, 2007).

The Comprehensive Services Academy

The Hampton System of Care launched an innovative program in 2009 that is a quintessential example of interagency collaboration: The Comprehensive Services Academy. The CSA Academy was created by Denise Sterling Gallop, the Deputy Director of the Hampton Department of Human Services. The Academy was particularly inspired by the need to educate Human Services staff about the CSA. It became apparent that most staff members did not understand their role connected to the law and the CSA process. However, the Academy has now become a community-wide effort with community partners attending as well.

This 12-week program ensures that staff and stakeholders support children and families utilizing Hampton's core values and beliefs. The weekly sessions focus on best practices developed by the agency and teach the Systems of Care and Wraparound service philosophies. Each Academy class typically has 10 participants. Participants witness Hampton service delivery in action by attending and observing various CSA components, such as CMPT and FAPT meetings. At the end of the 12th week, participants conclude the Academy with a project. Projects are real-life strategies for integrating the CSA and Hampton philosophies into current work functions.

Highlights of the program include Family and Youth Panels. These two panels are active and fast-moving dialogues that join families and youth with the agency's direct service workers and management in open, honest conversations. Hampton incorporates "lessons learned" from families and youth in its future Academy classes (Triad, 2011). Recent classes have included Department of Social Services staff, Hampton City School leaders, Juvenile Court Judges, Clerk of the Court, Police Department leadership, Community Services Board (mental health) administrators, Recreation (Teen) Center staff, and others. Wanda Rogers, current Director of Hampton CSA, summarized the Academy nicely by saying, "It's just what we believe you need to know in order to understand how to do this work in accordance with the legislation" (Wanda Rogers, personal communication, August 11, 2010).

The Hampton Family Assessment and Planning Team

Not all things are created equal. And this is true of the CSA-mandated Family Assessment and Planning Team (FAPT). Although each locality in Virginia must have at least one FAPT, some FAPTs function better than others. As previously described, the FAPT is responsible for coordinating and managing the provision of services for each eligible child and family. The law was written in such a way that it provides flexibility for each FAPT to design its own procedures to ultimately achieve their required duties and functions. This leeway has pros and cons. Some FAPTs have flourished in their autonomy, while others have floundered. Some have discovered creativity and collaboration, while others have become lost in inefficiency and indifference. The FAPT could be considered the heart and soul of the CSA. If the FAPT is broken, most of the rest of the system will subsequently follow suit.

Hampton's FAPT has been acknowledged as one of the most productive and creative FAPTs in Virginia. Most of their success can be attributed to their core values and beliefs, which emphasize respecting and collaborating with families. Another Core Value of Hampton is that *Families are experts about their families.* Families are referred to as "consumers" and are treated as equal partners during FAPT meetings. The family's culture and personal values systems are honored in such a way that services are based on the family's values.

Betsy Clark, the CSA and FAPT Coordinator of Hampton FAPT since 2011, was emphatic about families having a strong voice. She went as far as saying, "Every child and every family matters that comes through our door. We will not tolerate anyone disrespecting a family. We will kick out a professional or provider out of FAPT if that happens" (B. Clark, personal communication, August 15, 2012). For instance, Mike Terkeltaub, the CSA Coordinator in the 1990s, recalled an early seminal moment when a private agency was "just beating up a family in a significant kind of way" (M. Terkeltaub, personal communication, May 2013). Mike found it frustrating and asked the agency provider to discuss the family's strengths. Unfortunately the provider stated that they could not find any strengths in this family. From that moment on Hampton FAPT decided not to use this agency for their services.

A family served several years ago also illustrates just how Hampton respects families, their expertise, and their distinctive cultures. This family had two adolescent daughters refusing to attend school. The girls would often run away from home and had previously been placed in residential facilities through another locality. No other problems (e.g., drugs, crime, etc.) existed for the girls. After Hampton FAPT worked with the family there became an understanding that no family member for several generations had gone beyond the 7th grade. School was not the priority and focus. The FAPT team worked out a plan for the family which included finding less traditional and academically less rigorous school programs. One of the girls graduated high school and the other received her GED. However, it was not until the system stopped fighting the family and began acknowledging the family's culture that a successful plan was achieved.

Hampton FAPT has also been largely supported by the CPMT leadership to create cross-agency and community collaborations, as evidenced by the Value: *Hampton partners with all who can support children.* Hampton has a strong FAPT support team with consistent representation from the Community Service Board, the Department of Social Services (DSS), the Department of Juvenile Justice, Hampton City Schools, Hampton Benefit's Division, a parent representative, and a private provider from the community. Hampton's FAPT is co-located at the DSS, which allows for easy communication and idea sharing. However, Hampton's FAPT is not opposed to meeting at different locations and in the evenings, which are often more convenient for families.

Hampton has been praised for having the "fabric of the community" bought into their team decision-making and planning (M. Terkeltaub, personal communication, May 2013). Hampton FAPT has reached beyond the traditional child-serving agency network and established relationships and contracts with local retail stores (e.g., Target, Burlington Coat Factory, and local thrift and furniture shops) so that they may purchase basic necessities families often need in order to stay together. They even have contracts with daycare, after-school, and summer camp programs. Hampton will often pay for these programs so that children can receive care and supervision, thereby allowing parents the ability to maintain employment. Hampton FAPT has a niche for tapping into local businesses to create a whole community that responds to ensuring that young people and families succeed.

Leaders interviewed for a 2007 Hampton outcomes report noted that there were "longstanding trust and positive working relationships for all involved with the project" (Triad, 2007). This was clearly evident during a 2013 visit to Hampton during one of their weekly FAPT meetings. It was apparent from the beginning that everyone genuinely seems to like each other. FAPT members sat at a large table, in no particular order, with the consumers (child and parent). Members from the CSA Academy sat to the side observing the meeting and taking notes. One would think from the hugs, handshakes, smiles, and casual dialogue that a group of friends were gathering. FAPT and families spoke openly and informally with one another and frequently brainstormed to solve often emotional and challenging problems. No idea was discarded as being impossible or ridiculous. Families were frequently asked what they wanted most for themselves and their children. Solutions were found, and overall everyone left the table satisfied. Developing strong relationships and trust was critical to helping the meetings run smoothly. After FAPT adjourned, the Hampton team went out to eat at a local restaurant; a tradition started and kept since 1995.

Due to this strong and unified FAPT, Hampton has a history of creating unique programming within the community. Two Hampton Core Values in particular have guided them toward thinking out of the box: (1) D*o whatever it takes to support the success of children and families* and (2) *We begin with outcomes not process.* FAPT and CPMT, each hold meetings to develop innovative programming and this cross-pollination of ideas has led to the development of projects listed in Table 7.1. While new projects are being conceived, two vital goals are kept in mind. Each project must support children and adolescents remaining in the Hampton community and each project must promote the move toward independence and self-sufficiency for children and their families (Triad, 2007).

For instance, during a post-FAPT lunch in the late 1990s, the team discussed concerns for a widowed mother who struggled with psychosis and was caring for her two sons. Besides losing her husband, the mother had lost her job and her home was about to be taken from her. In previous years, the children might have been placed in foster care as the mother struggled to regain employment, housing, and health. However, the FAPT members wanted to keep this family together. Mike Terkeltaub, then Director of Comprehensive Services for Hampton, researched existing programs which might help this family. He discovered the program, Shared Family Care Model, by Richard Barth and Amy Price. This program helps families, by placing parents and children in homes of community members who act as their mentors and work with professionals to help them achieve permanency for their children and move toward self-sufficiency. Hampton decided to move forward with a similar program and created the Parents and Children Coping Together (PACCT). The PACCT host family and PACCT intensive care coordinator supported the aforementioned mother and her two sons. This mother recovered her health, gained employment, and maintained housing and custody of her children thanks to PACCT. Hampton currently has over a dozen "host" families that have allowed families to remain together while keeping children out of foster care.

Hampton FAPT has many success stories due to the constant communication, collaboration, and creativity among staff, partnering agencies, and family members. Specific outcomes of FAPT and the city of Hampton service delivery system will be reviewed below in more detail.

HAMPTON OUTCOMES

The Hampton CSA office has been collecting and utilizing data since the inception of the program in 1993. The CPMT secured the services of Triad Training and Consulting Services to take a leadership role in the development of their outcomes project. Mike Terkeltaub is currently the Executive Director of Triad Training and Consulting Services, and as mentioned earlier, also served as the Director of Comprehensive Services in Hampton, Virginia from 1995 to 1998. Triad conducts an annual Hampton Systems of Care Review and presents these data to the City.

Results of these outcomes reports indicate that Hampton CPMT has consistently and successfully accomplished the original CSA goals. Specifically, Hampton has served children in the community and has provided cost-effective services that supported children and families moving toward self-sufficiency. The results also indicate that Hampton CPMT has continuously designed effective community-based programming to serve children and families.

Take for instance data supporting the accomplishments of Hampton's FAPT. Like most Virginia FAPTs, Hampton's FAPT is not unique in the fact that they serve the community's children with the most complex needs. For instance, a 2008 Triad study found that 88 percent of youth served by the Hampton FAPT had issues with physical/verbal aggression, property destruction, and poor impulse control. However, by embracing the above values and creative tactics, all of these youth were served in their homes (Triad, 2011).

Data from the Triad 2010–2011 Outcomes report captures the success Hampton FAPT has achieved with their "at-hope" (vs. being called "at-risk") children:

- No children placed in residential treatment (since April 2007)
- No children placed in group homes (since September 2008)
- An 85 percent reduction in foster care placements since 2002
- Community-based services account for 99 percent of all services resulting in savings of more than $600,000 in 2010
- 93 percent of foster care youth received a high-school diploma or GED and enrolled in a higher-learning program
- 82 percent of the children coming to Hampton FAPT read at a third grade level or above and 83 percent are attending school everyday
- 71 percent of children supported by Hampton FAPT are earning average or above average grades (Triad, 2011).

Other localities have examined Hampton's numbers and have questioned if the FAPT has manipulated factors (e.g., money, the law, agency relationships) to achieve these outcomes. Betsy Clark repudiates these suspicions:

> We are not breaking the law. We are being creative. We look closely at CSA policy and rules for our framework. CSA gives us the ability within that framework to do what we need to do. Ultimately FAPT's goal is to find a way to work for our families. There is no choice but to figure out a way. (B. Clark, personal communication, August 15, 2012)

Hampton's success may be gauged, in part, by comparing its performance to other communities involved in CSA. Although the number of youth in Virginia placed in residential treatment settings through CSA continues to decline, there were still 1,888 residential placements in 2013 with an average length of stay of 201 days. Yet, Hampton did not have a single child served in residential care during this period, nor has the city had a CSA child placed in a congregate care setting for several years (Office of Comprehensive Services, 2013a). While Hampton served more than 450 youth through CSA in 2011, the average cost per child was $14,961 compared to $19,566 in their region and $20,048 statewide (Office of Comprehensive Services, 2013).

HAMPTON'S THEMES FOR SUCCESS

Whenever you ask Hampton CSA staff and stakeholders what makes them a successful locality, they all give the same response: We focus on family strengths; we do not use a cookie-cutter approach; we have a supportive community; we have developed a unique system of care. The speech goes on and on and begins to sound a little redundant. However, that is what makes Hampton successful. Everyone has bought into, and is passionate about, the same core values and beliefs. Everyone is genuinely together in this CSA project.

What accounts for Hampton's remarkable success in developing community-based services for at-risk children and families? A variety of factors have contributed to the city's effective performance and positive outcomes. Their success is, in large part due their ability to address the multiple programmatic and contextual issues and challenges that impact the development and implementation of a comprehensive System of Care. Consistent with the social ecology paradigm, the Hampton leadership has approached their work in a thoughtful and strategic manner, establishing clear values and goals, creating a collaborative culture, developing a responsive infrastructure, and continually working to improve the systems performance.

In the themes described below, we have attempted to encapsulate some of the key factors that have fueled Hampton's productive efforts to develop and implement an effective system of care for at-risk youth and their families. These themes will be highlighted below by personal stories and quotes from Hampton CSA leaders. While the specific circumstances and actions required to build effective service delivery systems are different for each locality, the themes that characterize Hampton's success have relevance for other localities interested in providing comprehensive, coordinated community-based care.

Leadership and Collaboration

Hampton is consistently praised for having terrific government and community leaders who understand the importance of collaboration. Walter Credle, the former Director of Hampton Social Services and a leader in the development of Hampton's CSA initiatives, noted that "a culture of collaboration began decades ago with the city mayor and manager and is now reinforced by all city agencies" (W. Credle, personal communication, August 11, 2010). Credle believes that Hampton's prior collaborative nature gave Hampton an advantage when CSA originated in the 1990s. Elected officials, city government staff, and child-serving agencies had established strong working relationships. Leaders trusted one other and were ready to continue inter-agency CSA partnerships.

A barrier that many Virginia localities face is overcoming agencies' tendency to be territorial and learning how to share resources. Hampton has successfully overcome "turfism," primarily because of the strong vision and leadership of the city leaders. Hampton's key city department heads have recognized the relevance and urgency of the CSA mission to their departments and the city. Subsequently, they have been willing to share credit and funds in the belief that such efforts will have long-term pay-off (Galano et al., 1999).

An environment of collaboration is enforced and considered the norm. For instance, collaboration is rated on employee evaluations and discussed twice a year in relation to job performance. Hampton has strong commitment, long-standing collaborations, and positive working relationships among city agencies. Regular partnering is common among Hampton's FAPT, Court Service Unit, Community Services Board, School Board, Health Department, Department of Social Services, Public Library, and Police. Wanda Rogers captured the importance of accountability for inter-agency collaborations when she said:

> All stakeholder groups are accountable for positive outcomes for children and their families. We broke it out in the home, in the school and in the community. So if this outcome is not what we expected it to be . . . it's not you social services, or it's not you court services or it's not you schools that dropped the ball. It was all of us. If it fails, we all fail. We do not get to point the fingers. We held everybody accountable. So people would come to the table knowing that we were all being held accountable for those outcomes. (W. Rogers, personal communication, August 11, 2010)

Collaborations extend beyond government agencies. Hampton city leaders recognized that local government cannot, and should not, assume sole responsibility for assisting families in need. Hampton has reached out and connected to community leaders and private providers. Hampton's CPMT and FAPT have partnered with numerous community agencies to develop wraparound services. For instance, Hampton FAPT noticed a deficiency in wraparound programming for families trying to achieve in-home stabilization. FAPT met with local private agencies and asked them to create practical family support services, such as mentoring and coaching parents on basic living skills.

Agencies were more than willing to partner with Hampton CSA and accordingly developed programs to fit the needs of the community.

More importantly, Hampton has developed collaborative relationships with the families they serve. Hampton is well known for hosting open forums where parents and children can voice their strengths, concerns, and ideas. Hampton's FAPT has a reputation for including families in decision-making processes and treating parents as the most important member of the team. Hampton also has the reputation of being up-front and honest with families when barriers arise.

For example, when Hampton's CSA funds for educational programming were decreased from $1 million to $53,000, the CSA office was transparent with parents. Emergency staffing was scheduled with each family impacted by the cut and individual options were explored. Meetings with groups of parents were also held so that potential solutions could surface. Betsy Clark, current CSA and FAPT Coordinator of Hampton, recalled of that particular situation,

> When you are transparent with families they get it. The result was not, 'Why are you doing this to me?' The result was, 'How can we help advocate for ourselves? We know that you guys are doing everything you can for us.' We are not pushing a policy on them; they are part of it. It wasn't us versus them. It was what can we do together? (B. Clark, personal communication, August 15, 2012)

One Child at a Time While Supporting the Family Structure

The most common motto quoted by Hampton staff and the FAPT accountability literature is: *One child at a time* (Casey Strategic Consulting Group, 2008). Hampton exemplifies a system making extensive efforts to treat each child and family as a unique entity. They do not believe in a "one size fits all" formula. What works for one child might not work for another. Each child and family are recognized as having their own distinctive set of strengths, challenges, needs, aspirations and future goals.

The ultimate goal is to keep children and families together. There is a shared belief in the family unit as the structure that must be supported if children are ultimately going to be helped. Hampton has prioritized viewing families as the primary "natural" community resource for children. For instance, Hampton worked with a grandmother who had several teenage grandchildren needing placement in her home in order to avoid foster care. The grandmother's house, however, could not accommodate so many children. Hampton did not want to separate the children. They also did not want to lose the opportunity of a willing family member to care for the children. As a solution, Hampton built an additional bedroom onto the grandmother's house. This story exemplifies how Hampton leaders believe that children have better outcomes served in their family rather than in out-of-home and out-of-community placements.

Hampton has taken risks by developing programs around the needs of one child or one family. The Specialized Foster Care Program led by Mark Hinson, and described in the previous chapter, is a good example of this. Hampton will often create a program for a child, never knowing if another child will use this program in the future. But Hampton team members emphasize the importance of starting with the outcomes wanted for the child versus getting caught up in the processes. Walt Credle talked about this by saying:

> Hampton said, here is the child . . . what do we do now? We build something with this one child. A system of care for this one child and make it work in the community. It's what I call planning and implementing simultaneously. Lots of people get caught up in doing this sequentially. But it's planning and implementing at the same time. And so we didn't know what it was suppose look like. We knew what the CSA code said. We knew that we were committed to the values of family focused and community based. We built it one child at a time not knowing what the outcome was going to be two, three or five years down the road. But doing it that way I think worked. (W. Credle, personal communication, August 11, 2010)

Hampton FAPT does a stellar job creating individual plans. The team starts with a clean slate and develops a plan based on what a child or family has said. Information and resources are pooled and a plan is created that everyone can buy into. And having children stay with their family and in their community is more economical. During fiscal year 2011, Hampton saved almost $700,000 by using individual and community-based services that supported the family.

Betsy Clark summarized the practicalities of creating community programs for one child at a time:

> Community based services are less expensive. When you are not having to pay congregate care expenses, foster parents, or private day placements . . . your money goes farther. If you are paying for services that are more practical in nature, and that are genuinely helping that family because you know what their needs are, it is going to be easier because those services cost less. They just do. (B. Clark, personal communication, August 15, 2012)

Using the Law . . . Creatively

Hampton had a clear focus, from the beginning, on creating innovative community-based services and bringing children home from out-of-community residential treatment centers (Triad, 2007). They also valued how a child-centered, family-focused, community-based service delivery was the law in Virginia and must be implemented through a new practice. The CSA gave Hampton the legal basis to not continue business as usual.

The city of Hampton completely embraced the more proactive, integrated approach to funding and delivering services (Walters, 2010). Officials used the new law to build a system that supported innovative programming and thinking out of the box. For instance, CSA legislation gave localities the freedom to develop programs if they did not exist within the community. Wanda Rogers recalls of the early CSA days:

> We had spent some time reading the code of Virginia and understanding exactly what the law allowed us to do. So we never went outside of what the law allowed. We read the code, and the code said if these programs that you want do not yet exist you have the responsibility to create that. (W. Rogers, personal communication, August 11, 2010)

Creative programming is a definite strength of this locality. Hampton's CPMT and FAPT each hold meetings to develop innovative programming. They also frequently challenge local providers to develop new and innovative service delivery approaches (Triad, 2007). This "cross-pollination" of ideas has led to the development of projects such as those listed in Table 7.1. Innovative programming has supported children and adolescents remaining in the community and supported cost-effective service delivery. Walt Credle believes that "through innovation you could in fact spend less money and get better quality service; they are not mutually exclusive goals" (W. Credle, personal communication, August 11, 2010).

Hampton has dealt with the criticism that their money being spent in a creative manner means that they might be doing something wrong. For example, FAPT once paid for the day-care expenses of six children so that the maternal aunt could purchase a bigger car to transport the children. Hampton's reply? They provide outcome reports that demonstrate their ability to keep families together, stay on budget, and all the while following the CSA law.

The Casey Foundation had the following to say about Hampton's innovation programming:

> Hampton was home to so many good ideas and effective practices that Casey developed and disseminated a micro-case study on Hampton for other Virginia localities. Hampton was not only illustrative of what a high-functioning children and family services system looks like, but it also is proof that transformation is certainly an achievable goal for other Virginia localities. (Walters, 2010).

Chapter 8

Entering an Era of Accountability

Virginia was slow to embrace the trend to control rising health care costs through administrative intervention. Other states had employed a variety of management strategies to alter or limit the delivery of health care. These strategies addressed all facets of health care, including organization, management, delivery, payment, and financing. Managed care approaches employed by government entities ranged from requiring consumers to justify the need for specialty services by obtaining pre-authorization from their insurance carrier to creating health management organizations (HMOs) that did not employ traditional fee-for-service payment methods, but paid insurance carriers a set rate of total payment per enrollee, known as capitation, to incentivize health insurance and service providers to focus on preventive care and limit the use of unnecessary services and procedures. This method of payment allowed HMOs to retain money they saved by not using higher cost procedures. Virginia, with its cautious approach to government intervention and support of an open market philosophy, was reluctant to enter the managed health care arena.

By the mid-1990s the Commonwealth could no longer remain on the sidelines. Health care costs were rising at an average rate of more than 5 percent per year with no sign of easing (Office of National Health Statistics, 2000). The state approved a number of HMOs to serve the Medicaid population and considered other strategies.

During this period the cost of CSA continued to rise. Between 1994 and 1997 the total cost of the CSA program rose 50 percent. Although the caseload also grew by 40 percent in the same period, the cost per child served was increasing and the total cost of the CSA program was attracting the attention of government administrators and legislators (Office of Comprehensive Services, 2011). The State Executive Council (SEC) of CSA decided to examine the growing cost and consider measures to address this trend.

WEIGHING THE OPTIONS

In 1996, the SEC devoted several meetings to the question of how to implement a cost containment strategy that would ensure appropriate services were being provided while also utilizing scarce resources in a prudent manner. They were particularly interested in the use of out-of-home placements, such as residential treatment centers, as this service category accounted for more than 75 percent of total CSA expenditures. The deliberations of the SEC highlighted the contrast among various philosophical and administrative approaches for regarding how to deliver effective, cost-efficient services. These discussions, and the subsequent decisions made by the SEC, also demonstrated the group's commitment to maintaining the core values and principles of CSA while attempting to contain expenditures.

The SEC considered a number of options. The Council was aware of considerable public resistance to managed care health approaches that directly constrained the ability of consumers to choose their health care provider and the services they received. The SEC also did not favor the growing trend to incentivize managed care entities to reduce expenditures by allowing them to retain unexpended funds. They believed that companies rewarded for decreasing costs might be inclined to compromise the quality of services in order to achieve fiscal incentives associated with cost-cutting. Finally, the SEC believed that contracting with a managed care company would likely restrict the ability of localities to make service decisions at the program or individual child level and ran counter to the local empowerment philosophy of CSA. Therefore, the SEC rejected strategies that would employ a central administrative entity to make decisions about which services youth should receive. At the same time, members of the SEC recognized that given rising costs and scarce availability of resources, taking no action was not a viable option (Cohen & Cohen, 2000).

After considerable discussion, the SEC decided to pursue a course of action they hoped would ensure appropriate service planning and management of limited resources by localities, while continuing to adhere to the core principles of CSA. The SEC concluded that the best solution for addressing the multiple challenges confronting CSA was an approach that would provide local decision-makers with accurate information about the needs of children and families referred to CSA as well as allow them to select the most appropriate treatment and service options for each child's situation.

The SEC was interested in exploring whether service decisions made by localities could be enhanced by providing them with an empirically based approach that would enable local decision-makers to assess the needs and strengths of the individuals they were serving while also encouraging them to review how services and resources were being utilized and measure the outcomes that were being produced. By making available useful and reliable tools and data to local Family Assessment Planning Teams (FAPTs) and Community Policy and Management Teams (CPMTs), the SEC hoped that local decision-makers would be better prepared to conduct accurate assessments and match at-risk youth with appropriate treatment and care opportunities. The underlying assumption of this approach was that valid and reliable information is empowering. If localities possessed useful data and guidance on how to analyze and interpret these data, they would be able to serve youth more appropriately and manage resources more effectively.

This data-driven approach for assisting individuals grappling with complex activities and transactions is sometimes referred to as *decision support technology.* The essential components of this approach in clinical settings are the use of a standardized assessment instrument to evaluate the status, needs, and strengths of a participating individual and a set of criteria for evaluating their conditions along with benchmarks indicating appropriate care for various levels of problem and need manifestation. The decision support process also includes development of a data base to store, analyze, and report relevant information along with guidelines for utilizing the assessment data to determine the most appropriate course of treatment and care. Decision support models are intended to be suggestive rather than prescriptive. They generally do not dictate a specific treatment or service based on the assessment results. Rather, they provide guidance to the decision makers, including consideration of mitigating factors that should be taken into account when making a treatment decision.

Although the SEC believed this data-driven approach would allow localities to retain decision-making authority and would also provide the best fit for CSA, they decided to conduct a feasibility study to evaluate whether the use of a decision support model would actually improve utilization of services and resources. They also wanted to assess how key stakeholders perceived the effectiveness of CSA and whether these individuals thought the system could be improved. The SEC decided to procure the services of an organization with expertise in the delivery of services to at-risk youth to conduct this feasibility study.

A TRIAL RUN

In 1997, the SEC contracted with the Virginia Treatment Center for Children (VTCC) of Virginia Commonwealth University to design and implement the utilization management feasibility study. VTCC had been established by the General Assembly in 1962 to provide service, training, and research in child mental health and was widely considered the pre-eminent child psychiatric facility in the Commonwealth. Faculty at VTCC had previous experience with using decision support models to enhance management of behavioral health services. VTCC brought in Dr. John Lyons of Northwestern University as a consultant. Lyons had developed a decision support framework designed specifically to assist decision-makers in matching at-risk youth and their families with appropriate services. His utilization management approach included an assessment tool and critical pathway guidelines which offered an empirical foundation for making placement decisions, assessing utilization patterns, and measuring outcomes. Lyons' approach provided: (a) a rational scheme to support decision-making, (b) a framework for aiding decision-makers in considering the behavioral health needs of a particular child, and (c) a process for reviewing decisions for the purpose of improving the quality of services (Lyons, Howard, O'Mahoney, & Lish, 1997).

The VTCC feasibility study team adopted a modified version of Lyons' Childhood Severity of Psychiatric Illness Scale (CSPI) as the assessment instrument to be used for the CSA project. The adapted version, the Childhood Severity of Behavioral and Emotional Disorders scale (CSBED) was used to generate profiles of youth receiving services from CSA by assessing performance in four domains: symptoms, risk, functioning in various settings, and coexisting needs and problems. Unlike many other child assessment instruments, the CSBED was specifically designed as a tool for determining the level of care needed by a child, rather than a diagnostic scale, or a measure of the number of problem behaviors or degree of pathology exhibited by a child. As such, CSBED was tailor-made to provide data to support utilization management processes focused on ascertaining the most appropriate service level for an at-risk youth (Lyons, Chesler, Shallcross, & Kisiel, 1996). In addition, the Behavioral and Emotional Strengths scale (BES) was administered in order to assess the individual strengths of the children, including their positive or adaptive behaviors in personal domains as well as academic functioning and family involvement (Epstein & Sharms, 1998).

The feasibility study used a multi-method approach to examine the appropriateness of feasibility management strategies for the CSA system. The study employed the following assessment methods to gather data at the local and state levels:

1. A child profiling process was established to develop a baseline description of youth receiving services from CSA. Data collected included demographic and behavioral characteristics of the children, the type of services they were receiving, where the services were provided, and identification of critical factors accounting for placement decisions. At the state level, data were gathered on the 13,000 youth served by CSA in fiscal year (FY) 1996. Twelve localities were selected and agreed to participate in this

phase of the study. The localities were representative of the Common-wealth in size, geographic location, and service and cost trends. Using the CSBED and BES scales to obtain information from case managers and other key informants, profiles were developed for a sample of 270 youth from the participating localities.

2. Statewide data on statewide demographic factors, service utilization, and cost were also analyzed in order to assess the current performance of CSA in relation to its intended purpose.

3. Focus groups were conducted with multiple stakeholders from each of the 12 participating localities, as well as providers and state agency officials to elicit their perceptions of how well CSA was functioning, problems impeding effectiveness, and their suggestions for improving the system.

4. A statewide survey was conducted to elicit attitudes about the application of utilization management principles and strategies to CSA (Cohen, Wiley, Oswald, Eakin, & Best, 1999).

The findings of the feasibility study confirmed that CSA was serving youth with significant behavioral health challenges. Sixty-three percent of the youth who were assessed using the CSBED scale presented recent acute risk of harm to self or others, while 85 percent exhibited high levels of symptomatic behavior. Seventy percent of the children assessed were functioning very poorly in their home, school, and community settings, and the same number had other severe co-morbid problems. Nearly half of the youth in the sample experienced serious caregiver problems and 62 percent had a need for services from three or more agencies.

Although it was apparent that youth served by CSA were experiencing significant problems, it was less clear that these young people were receiving appropriate levels of care. For instance, according to the individual profiles generated by CSBED, 23 percent of the youth living in non-homelike settings had not displayed recent, acute risk behavior and 7 percent of these youth had no history of risk behavior. Since the primary function of these restrictive settings was to reduce risk and ensure safety, the significant proportion of youth being placed in non-homelike settings who had not shown a recent indication of harming self or others, provoked concern about whether youth were receiving appropriate levels of care.

Differences in placement patterns among the localities studied also raised questions about how care decisions were being made. Communities with higher CSA costs per child than the state average placed children in out-of-home settings nearly twice as frequently as communities with lower costs per child, despite the fact that these two groups had children with comparable levels of risk and symptoms. Communities with higher costs per child tended to be more densely populated and have lower levels of poverty. Was the higher

rate of out-of-home placement due to lower tolerance for maintaining youth
with deviant behavior in wealthier communities? Did higher cost communities have better access to out-of home placements? This study was not able
to definitively determine the reason for the level of care discrepancy between
high- and low-cost communities. However, the application of the decision
support methodology made it possible to identify differences in placement
patterns, and provided data that could be used to further understand and
improve how decisions about levels of care are made.

When case managers from all participating localities were asked why
children were placed in non-homelike settings, the most frequently cited factors were: (a) the community did not have resources to provide the necessary
level of supervision, (b) lack of services in the community, and (c) absence of
an appropriate educational program. Conversely, the following factors were
most frequently cited as contributing to a decision to place an individual in
a homelike setting: (a) availability of sufficient in-home support, (b) availability of an appropriate educational program, (c) use of flexible funding for
provision of special services, and (d) availability of appropriate community
services such as day treatment and special foster care.

The findings for the BES scale provided insight into the role of resiliency
and individual/family strengths in how at-risk youth cope and the influence
of strengths on the type of care required to serve them. Youth in the CSA feasibility study who exhibited higher levels of strength were more likely to be
placed in homelike settings than children with lower levels of strengths even
when the two groups had comparable levels of symptoms and risk. Thus,
youth with high levels of symptoms and risk who also had demonstrated high
levels of intrapersonal strength and family involvement were twice as likely
to be placed in homelike settings compared to a youth with similar symp-
tom and risk levels but low levels of family involvement and intrapersonal
strength.

One of the purposes of the feasibility study was to obtain feedback from
key stakeholders on their reactions to the various utilization management
functions and approaches as well as suggestions for improving the effectiveness of CSA. Individuals responding to a statewide survey on the application
of utilization management principles to CSA identified several deficits in the
current utilization management approach. According to respondents, CSA
needed to address the following functions: (a) provide fiscal incentives and
encourage development and delivery of appropriate, cost-effective services;
(b) make available measurement systems for assessing consumer status and
change; (c) ensure the availability of adequate and appropriate data for decisions at the local level; and d) provide funding and technical support for
prevention and early intervention programs. Fifty-two percent of respondents
favored adoption of a utilization management (UM) system that allowed

localities to choose the type of UM system they would use and keep within localities decisions about which services an individual should receive. Only one-quarter of respondents preferred a utilization management approach in which the state or its contractor managed placement of youth in residential care programs.

Participants in focus groups designed to elicit ideas on how to improve overall functioning of CSA strongly encouraged development of an ongoing outcome evaluation by an independent agency. Focus group members also identified the need to (a) conduct and review research on what interventions work for which child, (b) develop data systems for tracking outcomes, (c) provide technical assistance and training, (d) simplify invoices and payments, (e) create a uniform process for contracting with vendors, and (f) develop a process for reviewing utilization of residential placements (Cohen et al., 1999).

The utilization management feasibility study provided useful data for members of the SEC to consider as they began to deliberate on how to enhance the accountability of CSA while retaining the core system of care philosophy and principles upon which the Act had been established. The results of the child profiling assessment study indicated that only 54 percent of children were placed in the level of care recommended by the Decision Support Guidelines. This finding highlighted the discrepancy between actual and recommended placement decisions based upon the severity of the child's risk and symptoms. The focus groups and surveys revealed concern about the shortage of community-based alternatives as well as widespread dissatisfaction with the lack of supportive measures that were being provided by the CSA administration. Respondents wanted access to outcome measurement tools, fiscal incentives for developing innovative services, a pertinent data base, and training/technical assistance.

Survey feedback from providers and local officials indicated there was strong support for incorporating data-based accountability measures in the CSA process. Respondents favored tracking service utilization and evaluating progress. The majority of survey participants favored the use of a decision support approach that allowed localities to retain authority for where youth were placed and provided local decision-makers data and guidance to assist them in making appropriate choices.

CHARTING A COURSE TO ENHANCE ACCOUNTABILITY

During the same time period in which the utilization management feasibility study was being conducted for the SEC, the Joint Legislative and Audit Review Commission (JLARC) was also performing its own review of CSA

(JLARC, 1998). The JLARC study included a specific focus on how localities were addressing the CSA legislation's expressed intent for local agencies to use multi-agency teams to plan, organize, and monitor services. JLARC found that many localities were ignoring the intent of the statute and making unilateral treatment decisions for youth they were serving. The JLARC review revealed that staff in half of the localities in the Commonwealth acknowledged they had altered the eligibility status of youth who did not meet the requirements of the legislation in order to use CSA funds to support services for these individuals.

In a serendipitous coincidence, the JLARC staff utilized the same utilization management decision support methodology that had been employed in the study commissioned by the SEC and essentially reached the same conclusions. JLARC strongly recommended that CSA establish a utilization management review and planning approach in order to ensure that the most cost-effective treatment approaches were being employed. Like the SEC, JLARC recommended that CSA adopt a planning and review model that enabled localities to make service placement decisions based on empirical data and sound treatment guidelines.

The combination of the findings from the VTCC feasibility study and the recommendations from the highly respected JLARC staff persuaded the SEC to move forward with a plan to incorporate a decision support model into the CSA process. A workgroup comprised of the VTCC study team, CSA staff, and other key stakeholders developed a set of guidelines to be used in managing utilization as well as an implementation plan for preparing localities to incorporate decision support strategies into their planning and review process. The Decision Support Guidelines adopted by the SEC provide a framework to assist multi-agency teams assess the needs and strengths of the child and family, using the CSA-endorsed assessment scale as well as other pertinent data.

According to these guidelines, the local team would then identify the desired outcomes, services needed, and recommended level of services needed (e.g., acute inpatient hospitalization, residential treatment, and community-based service). Before making their decision, the team would consider mitigating circumstances such as the child's willingness to cooperate, placement and community safety, family preference, or legal constraints. After the child's service plan was finalized, the team would negotiate with providers to obtain the most appropriate service at a reasonable cost. The negotiation would also be used to clarify expectations for family involvement and the role of the CSA team and the provider in the monitoring process. The plan would then be implemented with periodic review of child and family progress toward treatment goals at designated intervals. Based on the review, the current plan might be continued or changes could be made in the length of time of current service plan, service objectives, aspects of the environment, service provider, treatment modalities, placement, or level of need. The entire decision support process may be repeated to assist in evaluating the current plan, if indicated.

The SEC workgroup also recommended actions for preparing and supporting localities to implement the utilization management (UM) process. These included holding informational meetings with local officials, training all parties involved in the decision-making process, and providing on-going technical assistance to help participants effectively use the UM system.

In 1997, based on recommendations from the Administration as well as its own audit and review division, the General Assembly added a requirement that all CPMTs who wanted to be considered for supplemental funding must incorporate review of how residential placements supported by CSA funding were being utilized.

As they prepared to launch the UM initiative, the CSA leadership worked out the final operational details.

A SMALL BUT SIGNIFICANT LAST-MINUTE ADJUSTMENT

One of the last critical operational decisions the SEC had to make was which assessment instrument would be employed to determine the level of need and strength for children and families served by CSA? It was generally anticipated that Lyons' scale, the CSBED, which had been used during the feasibility study, would be selected. However, that expectation was not fulfilled.

The Chair of the SEC at that time was Dr. Timothy Kelly, a psychologist who served as Commissioner of the Department of Mental Health, Mental Retardation and Substance Abuse Services (DMHMRSAS). The children's mental health division within DMHMRSAS was in the process of developing a uniform method of identifying the behavioral health needs and problems of children and adolescents receiving public mental health services. They had selected a psychometric instrument developed by Dr. Kay Hodges, of Eastern Michigan University as the statewide scale to be used to assess youth seeking services from mental health agencies. Hodges' evaluation instrument, the Child and Adolescent Functional Assessment Scale (CAFAS), was designed to identify the extent to which youth experienced aggression and conduct problems. It was developed in order to assist in assessing the degree of difficulty a child was experiencing and to compare behaviors at different points of time to assess change and measure treatment outcome. The CAFAS was not specifically intended to be used as a tool in utilization management and review processes.

When Dr. Kelly consulted his child mental health division about choosing an instrument for the CSA UM process, he was advised to urge the SEC to select the CAFAS as its statewide assessment scale. The primary reason for promoting adoption of the CAFAS was to ensure consistency in the assessment process for at-risk youth served by DMHMRSAS and CSA. This argument was particularly appealing to Dr. Kelly since DMHMRSAS had already begun preparing staff to use the CAFAS.

Therefore, when the issue of choosing a uniform assessment instrument for the UM initiative was brought to the SEC, Dr. Kelly strongly urged the group to adopt the CAFAS. Given his role as Chair of the SEC, he was able to persuade the members of the SEC, many of whom were not familiar with the technical aspects of assessment tools, to vote in favor of the CAFAS.

Although the CAFAS is a highly respected, methodologically sound assessment instrument, unlike the CSBED, it was not designed to determine the level of service intensity or placement restrictiveness needed by an at-risk youth. The CAFAS was designed as a diagnostic tool, to help service providers understand the degree to which young people manifested specific problems. While the distinction in the stated purposes of these two instruments may not seem perceptible to a lay person, the differences in their intended use is important within the context of performing UM assessments and reviews. The decision support function of the CSA UM process was specifically designed to assist CSA staff, families, and providers to determine the most appropriate level of care for a child and the degree of restrictiveness required to ensure safety. Making this decision requires consideration of the child's symptoms, but most important, must take into account the extent to which a child is at risk for harming him/herself or others, how well he/she is functioning, and whether the current living arrangement is suitable.

Thus, the decision to adopt the CAFAS rather than the CSBED as the official utilization review assessment altered the proposed plan and had a significant impact on the implementation of the decision support process. The designers of the UM system, along with the author of the CAFAs, were able to craft guidelines that correlated to scores on the CAFAs with levels of placement restrictiveness, but since CAFAS was designed as a diagnostic instrument rather than a tool to be used in making placement decisions, it was not as helpful to decision-makers as a scale designed for that purpose.

Despite the mismatch between the intended purpose and actual use of the CAFAS in the UM process, the CAFAS continued to serve as the official CSA assessment instrument for the next 15 years. Whether the longevity of the CAFAS was due to its positive contribution in guiding and reviewing placement decisions or to a lack of understanding of the utilization management process by local and state officials is difficult to discern. What is clear is that as with many other facets of CSA, some localities embraced the UM system and followed it diligently to assist in making appropriate placement decisions and avoid unnecessary expenditures. Other localities paid lip service to the decision support process and the use of a multi-agency collaboration and continued to engage in traditional unilateral, non-evidence-based approaches when deciding where and how at-risk children should be served (Joint Legislative Audit and Review Commission, 2007).

MEDICAID COMES TO CSA

At the same time CSA was rolling out it's UM system, the state became interested in assessing the value of incorporating Medicaid funding into this growing system of care for at-risk youth. With a federal match of approximately 50 percent, state officials estimated that the use of Medicaid funds could produce a savings of roughly $41 million for CSA, with the state receiving 63 percent of the savings and the remaining 37 percent going to localities (Joint Legislative Audit and Review Commission, 1998).

As with the issue of managing utilization, lively discussions ensued within the CSA leadership group, as well as among other state officials, regarding the pros and cons of incorporating Medicaid into CSA. In addition to the Commonwealth's traditional reluctance to become involved in federal funding programs, concerns were expressed about the potentially adverse impact of Medicaid participation on CSA's value- and principle-driven approach to serving children and families. With the growing trend of tightly managing expenditures to reduce rising health care costs, many proponents of CSA worried that the system would shift too far in the direction of ensuring frugality without adequate attention to the most appropriate way of meeting the needs of at-risk youth and their families.

Countering these arguments was a concern expressed about the growing financial burden CSA was placing on state and local budgets, and a sense of urgency for containing the increasing costs of this statewide program. Supporters of Medicaid argued that the proposed CSA UM system was compatible with the manner in which Medicaid was addressing the balance between delivering appropriate services and judiciously spending scarce resources. Backers of incorporating Medicaid offered assurance that System of Care principles were firmly embedded in the management of CSA and there was little risk that the operational philosophy and principles would be compromised by fiscal practices that ignored the child-centered, family-focused, and community-based tenets of this Act.

The opportunity to recoup more than $40 million proved to be compelling and those advocating for including Medicaid prevailed. The State entered into an agreement with the Federal government to expand Medicaid coverage to select services provided to eligible at-risk youth, and in January 2000 CSA began to use this federal funding source to pay for residential treatment and treatment foster care services for eligible children. The incorporation of Medicaid coincided with the launching of CSA's UM system. Given its familiarity with utilization review processes, the Department of Medical Assistance Services (DMAS), the state agency responsible for managing Medicaid, was brought in to assist in developing utilization review and payment support mechanisms for Medicaid and the UM system.

A contract was established with the West Virginia Medical Institute (WVMI), a large quality improvement organization that served the Mid-Atlantic region. WVMI, which had considerable experience in the management and monitoring of federally funded health care services, was hired to facilitate the utilization review process at local and state levels. WVMI provided a range of utilization management services to Virginia. Participation in the WVMI contract was optional for local governments. Those localities that chose to be involved, received a range of services and supports from WVMI. For CSA, WVMI reviewed local requests for funding for individual children in order to assess whether the services requested were consistent with the UM criteria established by DMAS and CSA. If the service request was consistent with state policy and program requirements, WVMI authorized payment. In addition, WVMI provided technical assistance to localities to help them understand and apply utilization management principles and methods.

During the next two years, Medicaid came to play an increasingly important role in CSA as well as the broader behavioral health service system in Virginia. Participation in this federal funding program certainly provided additional funds to provide services for at-risk youth and their families, allowing local decision-makers to stretch available resources. Involvement in Medicaid also increased the influence of state and federal Medicaid officials on CSA policies and practices. Unfortunately, the direction of this influence has not always been consistent with the core values and principles of CSA. Charlotte McNulty, who administered a local CSA program and served as Executive Director of the state Office of Comprehensive Services, contrasts the difference in the perspectives of these two programs:

> Medicaid services are so prescriptive and CSA is, from my perspective, a social needs model of service development. Medicaid is very much a medical model, and so there is a constant conflict between the state saying Medicaid has to be first source of funding considered and CSA is the funding of last resort. But providers say we are not going to take Medicaid because they don't pay enough and we can't do what you want us to do within Medicaid. (C. McNulty, personal communication, August 25, 2011)

Becky China, who served as director of an urban CSA program puts it more bluntly, "Virginia has sold its soul to Medicaid." She explains that in recent years the Commonwealth has incorporated language in the Code of Virginia mandating local CSA officials to consider Medicaid first when seeking services for a child. If Medicaid denies payment for services recommended by the FAPT, CSA still has to abide by Medicaid criteria. Therefore, for a child who is currently receiving a higher level of care, CSA can no longer pay providers at the higher rate associated with this service, regardless of the funding source, because the child has been deemed ineligible for Medicaid. In this case, the locality is forced to either negotiate a lower rate with the provider or move the child to a lower level of care, even if that level is not considered most appropriate to serve the child's needs (B. China, personal communication, July 23, 2012).

Proponents of Medicaid argue that this approach brings a needed element of accountability to this large publically funded endeavor. Cindi Jones, Director of the Virginia DMAS, has been involved with CSA since 1997 when she served as an investigator for JLARC. She is concerned about the lack of uniformity in how localities serve children and the potential for abuse. Jones believes the state has an obligation to ensure that localities spend public funds appropriately. "In the Medicaid program we have checks in the front and back end to make sure people are getting what they are supposed to" (C. Jones, personal communication, April 5, 2012).

Incorporating the UM system and Medicaid into CSA stirred considerable affect and controversy when they were first introduced in the late 1990s. As CSA has evolved, these critical accountability and funding mechanisms have continued to elicit strong reactions from CSA stakeholders and public officials. Even today, administrators and policy makers still look for ways to bring these components into better harmony with the core values and principles of CSA.

ADDITIONAL EFFORTS TO IMPROVE PERFORMANCE AND ENHANCE ACCOUNTABILITY

Having the benefit of several years of experience in implementing this complex System of Care, the CSA leadership as well as state and local officials had a better understanding of what worked and what did not function well. One of the conclusions they drew was that the governance and management structures that had initially been put in place appeared to be inefficient and impractical in many instances. Although most stakeholders did not favor major overhaul, there was strong support for revising and restructuring some of the policies and structures. Spurred on by the JLARC review of CSA published in 1998, the administration introduced several amendments to the CSA statute. The two major amendments are discussed below.

State Executive Council (SEC)

This high-level body is responsible for providing direction and oversight for CSA. Comprised of heads of state child-serving agencies and representatives from local government, service providers and families who are consumers of CSA, the SEC was having a difficult time addressing the large number of issues on its agenda. Part of the problem was the low attendance of members, especially agency heads who had many other responsibilities. The chair of the SEC was elected annually by the members of the Council. The frequent turnover of leadership did not foster continuity. Additionally, representation from localities was not always appropriate. Localities sometimes sent lower-level officials to the SEC meetings. These individuals were often not able to address concerns raised about local participation in CSA. Finally, and perhaps most significantly, state officials recognized that the workload for this complex system of care was too demanding for a large volunteer council to manage.

In order to address these concerns the Governor proposed, and the General Assembly enacted, several amendments to the CSA legislation (Virginia Acts of Assembly, Chapter 800, § 2.1-746, April 6, 1995; Chapter 937, § 2.1-746.1, April 9, 2000). Several new responsibilities were added to the charge for the SEC. Most of these additions were focused on gathering, analyzing and reporting information on key program and fiscal matter, including cost reports, program progress, and recommendations for improving performance of CSA functions. The amendments specified that the local representatives must include a member of the board of supervisors or city council as well as a county administrator or city manager. The Director of DMAS was also added as a member of the SEC. In recognition of the important role played by private service providers, the private representative on the Council was elevated from a nonvoting to a voting member. The minimum requirement for Council meetings was increased from semiannually to quarterly.

Perhaps the most substantive amendment was the enhancement of and establishment in code of the Office of Comprehensive Services (OCS) for At-Risk Youth and Families, which was charged with developing interagency programmatic and fiscal policies as well as managing the core functions associated with the CSA. The OCS was given responsibility for administering the functions previously assigned to the State Management Team. This shift was motivated by concern that expectations for the State Management Team, which was staffed by individuals who had other full-time responsibilities, had proved to be unrealistic. This body was not able to carry out the multiple duties required to effectively manage this complex multi-agency, local-state partnership. CSA had grown to a $200 million endeavor that served nearly 14,000 children per year. As JLARC concluded in its review of CSA:

The most basic elements of an effective management structure—consistent oversight, role clarity among key entities, strong policy guidance, and quality technical assistance—are largely absent from CSA. . . . As the size and complexity of local CSA programs has grown, the emerging oversight, technical assistance, and policy analysis demands cannot be accommodated within the current State structure. . . . It is imperative that a stronger policy development, oversight, and management role be established at the State level. (JLARC, 1998, p. VIII)

State Management Team (SMT)

Having shifted the core responsibilities of the SMT to the OCS, state officials turned their attention to revamping the former structure to better serve the purpose of providing guidance on how to sustain and improve the CSA multi-agency, local-state partnership. The amended legislation changed the name of this group to the State and Local Advisory Team (SLAT) to more accurately reflect the role of this body. The new legislation also modified the powers and duties of previous statute, deleting references to the team's responsibility to "develop and recommend" policies to the SEC and provide support to agencies. The amended legislation replaced these management functions with an advisory role, authorizing SLAT to "advise" the SEC and state and local agencies on matters pertaining to CSA. (Virginia Acts of Assembly, Chapter 937, § 2-1-747, April 9, 2000).

LOOKING TO THE FUTURE

CSA entered the new millennium with a dual sense of caution and hope. There was wide recognition that CSA had fallen short of the lofty ambitions envisioned by its planners and codified in the original legislation. The children and families CSA was serving presented significant needs and problems, and establishing sufficient service capacity, particularly within local communities, was not proceeding as swiftly as planners had hoped. Bringing together the diverse set of stakeholders required to collaboratively implement this intricate partnership had proven to be akin to herding cats. All of the players were still not fully on board and the reaching consensus on critical operational issues was difficult. The sheer volume of the workload required to manage the multiple facets of this comprehensive system of care and often seemed overwhelming. The original structure created to handle these issues was woefully inadequate.

On the other hand, recognition of these problems had spurred corrective action on several fronts. Plans for enhancing accountability had been developed and were in their initial phase of implementation. Local and state agencies had been given tools to help them understand and improve care. Additional financial resources had been identified to support service delivery as well as provide assistance to managers and providers. The General Assembly had taken affirmative steps to address governance and management shortcomings and concerns.

Although significant problems still existed, proponents of CSA had reasons to be guardedly optimistic about the future of this innovative system of care.

Part III

2002–2014

Chapter 9

Moving into the New Millennium
Coming of Age or Arrested Development?

In 2001, Mark Warner, a moderate Democrat, was elected Governor of Virginia. This ended an eight-year reign of Republican leadership, during which the primary focus had been on streamlining government, fiscal austerity, and reducing taxes. George Allen, a conservative Republican, served as Governor from 1994 to 1997. Initially, the Allen administration viewed the CSA as a program to be eliminated, especially when the program was showing a multi-million dollar deficit at the end of his first fiscal year. Over time, as senior officials were educated about the origin and purpose of this system and with the assistance of key legislators, including Delegate Harvey Morgan and staff of the House Appropriations Committee, the Allen administration came to see CSA as a model worth preserving and possibly even replicating. It was during this period that accountability measures such as utilization management and realignment of the governance structure were introduced (A. Saunders, personal communication, December 23, 2013).

The next Governor, Jim Gilmore, a conservative Republican who succeeded Allen in 1998 was only marginally interested in CSA. His primary focus was on reducing the state's car tax. As long as CSA did not require additional funding, generate negative publicity, or impact the car tax initiative, the Gilmore administration tolerated the program. Minor organizational refinements were undertaken but CSA received little attention during Gilmore's term (A. Saunders, personal communication, December 23, 2013).

When Warner took office in 2002, supporters of CSA were optimistic. CSA legislation had been enacted by a Democratic Governor and that party was generally more favorable toward government initiative aimed at enhancing services for vulnerable individuals than the Republicans. In addition, Warner brought on board a number of legislative staff who were familiar with CSA and had been instrumental in supporting the system during its formative years. Bill Murray and Wayne Turnage, who held important staff positions in the Warner administration, had formerly worked with Joint Legislative Audit and Review Commission (JLARC) and been proponents of reform in children's health policy. Steve Harms and Jane Kusiak, who had previously served as key staff members on the Senate Finance and House Appropriations Committees, respectively, were both strong supporters of CSA and played significant roles in Warner's administration.

With the switch from Republican to Democratic leadership in the executive branch, and the involvement of many proponents of improving services for at-risk youth in the new administration, there was a sense that CSA would receive better treatment during Warner's term as governor.

KEEPING SCORE

One of the strongest impetuses for the establishment of CSA had been the Department of Planning and Budget's study of service patterns for at-risk youth in the early 1990s. Their research revealed that large numbers of children were being placed in residential treatment centers, outside of their home communities and often out of state. These placements were putting a significant financial burden on the Commonwealth, with an annual cost approaching $100 million. Therefore, one of the critical goals of CSA, from the outset, was to reduce reliance of out-of-community residential placement.

How well did CSA achieve the goal of reducing the use of residential treatment settings? As CSA entered its second decade of operation, the results appeared to be mixed. On the positive side, more children participating in CSA were receiving community-based services. In 1994, the initial year of CSA operation, 71 percent were placed in residential programs. By 2001, the percentage of residential placements had fallen to 43 percent, and the number of children receiving community-based services had increased to 60 percent since 1994.

The shift of moving children away from institutional care toward treatment which may be more effective within the community was largely promoted after the Substance Abuse and Mental Health Services Administration (SAMHSA) worked in partnership with the National Institute of Mental Health to develop the first Surgeon General's Report on Mental Health (Office of the Surgeon General, 1999). Barbara Burns and colleagues were charged with summarizing the findings of the evidence-based practices (EBP) for children within the Report (Burns, Hoagwood, & Mrazek, 1999). Burns noted that the U.S. Surgeon General Report found concerns about residential care, such as: (a) the lack of a research base to substantiate its effectiveness; (b) out-of-community, often out-of-state, placement were inconsistent with principles of community-based treatment established in the 1980s (Stroul & Friedman,

1986); and (c) the costliness of such services (Friedman & Street, 1985). Attention was given to residential care in the Report because of the use of significant mental health resources, despite an extremely weak evidence base. Subsequently, EBP within the community (e.g., outpatient therapy, partial hospitalization, inpatient treatment, psychopharmacology, case management, home-based treatment, and crisis and support services) were reviewed and explained as alternatives (Burns et al., 1999). Slowly, communities and providers were seeing non-residential EBP as an alternative.

When comparing data from 2001 to 2005, the proportion of children receiving residential services in relation to total children served through CSA had decreased slightly (1%) and the actual number of youth served in their home communities had increased by 13 percent. The total number of youth served by CSA in 2005 had increased to 16,272, a 60 percent growth since its first year of operation and an 11 percent increase since 2001 (Office of Comprehensive Services, 2013).

Progress in controlling expenditures was less clear. As noted previously, both absolute and cost per child had risen during the 1990s. With the addition of Medicaid in the late 1990s the overall expenditures grew significantly. For instance, total CSA costs rose approximately 15 percent during FY 2001. Although overall costs continued to rise, the rate of growth slowed to an average of less than 10 percent per year over the next three years. During the period from 2000 to 2005, total expenditures for CSA grew by 72 percent, with Medicaid funding increasing from $5 million per year to $72 million (JLARC, 2007).

Although much of the increased cost of CSA could be attributed to the growth in the number of youth served, other factors also seemed to contribute to the rise in expenditure levels. The average cost per child served by CSA increased by 31 percent from 2001 to 2005. Some of this increase can be accounted for by general cost of living inflation. However, the consumer price index rose by approximately 11 percent during the same period, indicating that services for CSA participants were becoming more expensive.

In 2005, there were nearly 300 licensed residential facilities in Virginia, an 80 percent increase since the inception of CSA. The number of new facilities was growing each year, with a peak of 49 facilities opening in 2004. Seventy-five percent of the facilities that opened since 2001 identified themselves as for-profit compared to only 16 percent of residential facilities operating prior to that period (JLARC, 2007). These trends suggest that service providers believed there was a strong demand for residential programs for at-risk youth in Virginia.

What do the data about children served tell us about the progress of CSA? The most revealing indicator is the paucity of data available on this subject. Despite extensive discussion about the importance of measuring outcomes and the implementation of the utilization management initiative to provide data-driven decision support processes, little progress had been made in this area. The statewide CSA data base continued to be limited to information about service utilization and expenditures. Although some localities had embraced the utilization management established by CSA, many had not, and there was no statewide data base.

The scant data available do not allow us to draw firm conclusions about the success of CSA, but do provide some insight on how the system was performing. In their evaluation of residential services provided through CSA, JLARC conducted several pertinent analyses (JLARC, 2007). The majority of children served by CSA in fiscal year 2005 came from the foster care system, with the second largest source of referrals being special education. Although 57 percent of all CSA children came from the foster care system, that figure was even higher in relation to residential programs, with foster care youth comprising 75 percent of all CSA participants placed in residential facilities. White males were served more frequently than any other gender/race subgroup. The average age of a child served by CSA was 13, while the youth placed in residential facilities were, on average, two years older. The age of youth serve by CSA had decreased during the past few years. Whether this decrease was due to earlier identification of problems or more severe manifestation of difficulties is unclear.

The primary reasons given for children being referred to CSA were categorized into problems related to their caregivers, such as neglect, abuse, or caregiver incapacity, and problems related to the child's behavior or emotional difficulties. Forty-four percent of children received services due to caregiver-related problems, which indicates that many of the children were living in challenging environments. In 2006, more than 40 percent of children served by CSA had a mental health diagnosis and one-third were receiving psychotropic medication (JLARC, 2007).

The Child and Adolescent Functioning Assessment Scale (CAFAS), which had been chosen somewhat arbitrarily as the standardized assessment instrument for the utilization management process, was used to measure the functioning level of youth receiving CSA services. Despite questions about the appropriateness of this scale, the CAFAS was used to assess change. It provided a rough indication of the extent to which children displayed problem behaviors and was administered periodically. Unfortunately, approximately half of the staff using the CAFAS had not been appropriately trained and most staff believed they were only administering the instrument because it was a requirement and therefore were not devoting sufficient time to ensure the validity of the assessment. JLARC also found that CAFAS was either not administered or scores were not reported for approximately half of the children receiving services through CSA (JLARC, 2007). With these caveats in mind, consider the following findings in relation to changes in functioning for CSA participants over time.

The CAFAS was administered to children receiving residential services through CSA in 2005 at the time of placement and again at a later date. There was an average interval of nine months between the initial and subsequent assessments. Fifty-six percent of the youth receiving residential services were rated as functioning better over time, but 31 percent were doing worse and 13 percent were doing the same as they had at the time of placement (JLARC, 2007).

Case managers surveyed about the progress made by youth receiving residential services reported significant improvement in use of drugs and alcohol, fighting, running away, and/or engaging in illegal activity. However, approximately 20 percent of these youth ran away or were involved in illegal activity more frequently than before their placement. Although the majority of youth showed improvement in school, including behavior, grades, and attendance, nearly 30 percent continued to have significant behavior problems (JLARC, 2007).

Case managers were surveyed about their perceptions of the effectiveness of residential services for children in their care. More than three-quarters stated that providers did a good job of addressing behavioral, emotional, and educational problems of children in their care. Nonetheless, case managers also reported that residential providers were not able to effectively respond to these concerns for 14 percent of children (JLARC, 2007).

As stated earlier, the availability, reliability, and validity of outcome measures for CSA was limited during this period. Certainly none of these results can be viewed as conclusive. For example, even when a positive or negative outcome was found, at best it may be viewed as demonstrating a correlation between the service received and the child's behavior as none of the studies were thorough enough to determine whether the outcome was produced by the service provided or other factors such as the general resilience or vulnerability of the child, or family circumstances that influence the child's outlook and receptivity.

It is interesting to note that the infrastructure of the local CSA program seemed to have an impact on performance and outcome. An underlying tenet of the CSA system is that localities need to invest time and resources to ensure that the collaborative multi-agency process is implemented effectively. Cooperation and creative planning do not come easily and require substantial effort on the part of all stakeholders. One indication of a localities' commitment to the CSA process is whether they are willing to assign a dedicated individual or individuals to perform core CSA planning and management functions. About one-third of localities have employed full-time CSA coordinators to manage their programs. A smaller number of communities have also designated an individual to specifically perform the utilization management/ utilization review (UM/UR) functions to ensure that children receive appropriate care and contain unnecessary costs. Localities that employed a CSA coordinator spent approximately $14,000 per year less per child on residential services. In addition, localities with a CSA coordinator had an average length of stay in residential programs that was 14 days shorter than local government entities that did not have a full-time coordinator. At an average cost of $232 per day for residential services, this translates to an average savings of $3200 per child. Localities with a dedicated UM/UR coordinator had average lengths of stay for youth in residential facilities that were 10 percent shorter than communities without UM/UR staff (JLARC, 2007).

ABSENCE OF VIABLE ALTERNATIVES

Substantial utilization of residential services is often associated with a lack of available community services. Ten years after the inception of CSA, most localities still did not have sufficient services and supports to allow at-risk children to be cared for in less restrictive settings within their home communities. In a survey of local Community Policy and Management Teams (CPMTs), more than three-quarters of respondents identified serious service gaps in their communities in crisis services, family support, and assessment. Respondents also noted a critical need for more outpatient and transportation. The perceived lack of family support services, such as parent and family mentoring and intensive in-home services are troubling in light of the strong emphasis CSA places on involving and supporting families. The shortage of appropriate assessment services is also significant, as it is difficult to determine which services are appropriate for a child without an accurate understanding of the child's needs and strengths. Nearly half of CPMT survey respondents identified the absence of psychiatric assessment as a critical service gap, while 34 percent observed there were insufficient short-term, family-based assessment services available and 18 percent saw a need for behavioral and psychological assessments (JLARC, 2007).

The shortage of child psychiatrists is not unique to Virginia. Child psychiatry has been identified as one of the most understaffed subspecialties in medicine. The current workforce in child and adolescent psychiatrists is unable to meet the needs of American youth, with estimates of their capacity to meet the present demand ranging from 10 to 45 percent. The lack of physicians trained in child psychiatry is especially pronounced in rural and high-poverty areas (Thomas & Holzer, 2006).

The identification of the high prevalence of behavioral health challenges in youth served by CSA, and the lack of appropriate services to respond these needs, underscored a serious problem with Virginia's system of care. At one level, it was apparent that it would be difficult to meet CSA's goal of providing responsive, cost-effective, community-based services without properly trained staff and the availability of services designed to accurately assess and treat mental health disorders. Without appropriate psychosocial and psycho-pharmacological intervention many youth would not be able to sufficiently control their aggressive and impulsive behavior and would thus not be able to function safely in community settings.

The lack of mental health services also highlighted another dilemma for the CSA system. During the establishment and early years of implementation, considerable attention had been given to creating a collaborative inter-agency team approach to planning and providing services for youth and their families. This emphasis made sense in light of the long history of fragmentation and lack of cooperation among child-serving agencies. Much effort was expended to ensure that the perspectives of representatives from social services, education, mental health, and juvenile justice agencies as well as family members were respectfully considered. This attention was necessary in order to create a genuinely collaborative work environment.

With all of the attention being given to establishing a cooperative service planning process, some of the substantive issues involved in serving at-risk youth were overlooked. One of the casualties of this intense focus on developing collaboration was the recognition that many children had specific mental health challenges that required specialized expertise in addition to a coordinated array of general supports. Over time, stakeholders began to pay more attention to the impact mental health challenges on these youth and their families, and how unaddressed behavioral health concerns impeded the ability of CSA to effectively serve these children. Unfortunately, the dearth of child psychiatrists and other qualified mental health providers made it difficult to access appropriate mental health services.

The funding dynamics of CSA further compounded the dilemma of meeting the mental health need of CSA youth. Most of the children and funding for CSA flowed through the Departments of Social Services (DSS) and Education. When the funding contributions were originally established, the Department of Mental Health, Mental Retardation and Substance Abuse (DMHMRSAS), and its local counterparts, the Community Services Boards (CSB), were required to allocate a relatively small amount of money to CSA. In fact, of all of the child-serving agencies, mental health's share was the smallest.

This disparity in funding contributions created several problems. The other child-serving agencies, whose clients were experiencing difficulties stemming from their mental health problems, resented the sparse contribution of resources from the mental health agencies. They believed that DMHMRSAS and the CSBs should be providing more financial assistance. The mental health agencies, in turn, believed that CSA was encroaching on their territory by attempting to serve children with behavioral health disorders. While the intent of the CSA legislation was to integrate funds from all public child-serving agencies, in practice, allocation of funds and provision of care for children with significant behavioral challenges appeared to be fragmented. According to a local mental health administrator:

> Mental health money needs to be carved out of the CSA process. CSA does a fabulous job with DSS and IEP (Individualized Education Plan) kids. But those kids that are Seriously Emotionally Disturbed (SED) are not the population that has been identified by CSA as a population they should be serving. (personal communication, March 2011)

This disconnect regarding how to appropriately respond to the mental health needs of youth, like many other issues impacting the performance of CSA, had its roots in conflicting policy decisions and competing priorities. Given their dual allegiance to the goals of their own departments and those of CSA's multi-agency CSA endeavor, agency officials sometimes had to choose which priority they would support. More often than not, senior staff of partner agencies concluded that endorsing the priorities of their home agency was safer and easier than backing the policies/priorities of CSA. In this instance, the state had viewed the primary mission of DMHMRSAS as ensuring safe and humane care of persons requiring institutional care. Chuck Hall, Executive Director of the Hampton/Newport News CSB, describes why the Department did not make a major investment in CSA:

> The first line in the commissioner's job description is . . . basically to ensure the state facilities run well. There is not much in the commissioner's job description that refers to community-based care except to develop a performance contract with CSB's. And there is nothing in the administrator's job description that says that the Department should develop and promote children's behavioral health except for reference to the commissioner sitting on various state committees. So it was not a surprise to anyone in the CSB system when the CSA started that we were coming to the table empty handed. (C. Hall, personal communication, May 2013)

Hall explains that the legislation that established CSBs neither required nor prohibited local mental health agencies to provide children's services. With the enormous pressure to serve the adult population that had returned to their communities following the deinstitutionalization movement, in the absence of a strong mandate from the state, many CSBs chose not to make a significant investment in serving children.

Administrators, providers, family members, and advocates were becoming increasingly aware of the disparity between the high prevalence of significant mental health challenges for youth served through CSA and the lack of appropriate services for this population. Unfortunately the administrative barriers separating child-serving agencies and the absence of strong leadership at the state level hindered progress in responding to the mental health needs of youth served through CSA, despite enabling the legislation's intent to establish a seamless system of care for eligible youth and their families. Even now, many localities are not able to provide timely, appropriate services for at-risk youth who struggle with mental health issues.

EARLY POLICY DECISIONS CONTINUE TO HAUNT THE SYSTEM

The architects of the enabling legislation for CSA had to make many difficult policy calls. Some of these decisions were made for practical reasons, to ensure sufficient resources for the state funding pool or to obtain sufficient votes for passage of the bill. Although many of these decisions seemed necessary at the time, little effort was made during the 10 years following the enactment of CSA to rectify the negative influence these pragmatically driven policy decisions had on actualizing the original vision and goals of this Act.

The preceding discussion of the difficulty in obtaining appropriate mental health services for CSA participants illustrates the unintended consequences of early policy decisions. The state established a distinction between mandated and non-mandated children in order to obtain a waiver from federal agencies to include entitlement funding for children in foster care, as well as youth eligible for special education. During the first year of operation, 90 percent of the children served were in the mandated category while 10 percent were considered non-mandated. In FY 2005, eleven years later, the proportion of non-mandated youth served had fallen to 7 percent. Even though the total number of children served by CSA had grown by more than 6,000 (a 60 percent increase) during this period, the absolute number of non-mandated children served had increased by only 160 (Office of Comprehensive Services, 2013).

The impact of this two-tiered system on access to mental health services is described by Margaret Crowe, Executive Director for Voices for Virginia's Children, and a strong advocate for children:

> A locality that does not use non-mandated funds and uses strict interpretation of prevention makes it really hard to get kids into the system. It drives a philosophical wedge between social services, education, and the CSB because the kids that are getting the services are going to either be social services or education kids. So then the community-at-large or the mental health system can't get services for their children beyond what they provide if they do not fit into one of those other categories. (M. Nimmo Crowe, personal communication, August 2013)

Speaking directly to the issue of whether CSA has achieved its goal of providing a statewide system for dealing with children's mental health, State Supreme Court Judge William Mims concludes:

Unfortunately, not to the extent that I would like primarily because mental health is not a mandated service. The mandated services being foster care and special education have wound up taking the large bulk of the funding and mental health at worst has been neglected and at best has been under funded. (W. Mims, personal communication, December 13, 2011)

Mims, who previously served as a delegate in the General Assembly and held the top two posts in the Attorney General's office, later played a significant role in removing a significant obstacle for families seeking mental health services for their child.

The impact of the mandated versus non-mandated schism extended beyond the obvious issue of which population received CSA funding. There also were unintended consequences that had not initially been anticipated. This dichotomy also spawned practices that often defied reason and sensibility. One of the most onerous by-products of this two-tiered system involved the requirement for parents to relinquish custody of their children to the state in order to obtain intensive mental services for their child.

The custody relinquishment dilemma was not unique to Virginia. At one time, public agencies in 60 percent of all states required parents to transfer custody in order to obtain residential treatment and other high-end services for children with severe mental health problems (Cohen, Harris, Gottlieb, & Best, 1991). Historically, the rationale for making parents relinquish custody has evolved from a belief that parents caused their children to have psychiatric disorders to a less blaming but equally damaging justification involving administrative requirements associated with the funding source. As noted earlier in Chapter 3, less than 50 years ago, experts such as Bettelhem and Bateson, were definitively declaring that serious behavioral health disorders such as autism and schizophrenia were primarily caused by dysfunctional parenting practices. With such negative attitudes toward parents whose children suffered from severe psychiatric disorders, it was not surprising that many professionals viewed separating these children from their families as therapeutically desirable.

As our culture became more sophisticated about the role of genetics and the complex etiology of mental illness, these parent-blaming theories fell out of favor. However, the custody relinquishment requirement continued to be enforced. Initially, the practice persisted because outdated policies and regulations were still on their books. Despite efforts by advocacy groups and Congress to forbid the use of custody transfer for the purpose of obtaining mental health services, many parents continued to be forced to choose between relinquishing custody of their child and not receiving services for their children.

Analysis of why this practice persisted revealed that the major obstacle to eliminating the custody relinquishment requirement was the nature of the funding sources used to pay for residential treatment and other intensive services for youth with mental health disorders. Virginia, as well as other states, had very limited funds designated specifically for providing high-end mental health services to children with severe emotional and behavioral challenges. The primary source of funding for residential care resided within the foster care divisions in DSS. These funds were supposed to be used to serve children who had experienced abuse or neglect. Because these children's problems were viewed as stemming from inappropriate behavior by their parents, regulations stipulated that the state should assume responsibility for the care of these children, at least until it was determined that the parents were no longer at risk of harming their children.

In the absence of designated funding sources for high-intensity mental health services, families sought help from social services or juvenile justice agencies. These parents were told they would be able to obtain needed services for their child, but in order to qualify they would have to transfer custody of their child to the state. This situation created a dilemma for families: relinquish custody and obtain needed services for their child or keep their family intact and not receive these services. In some instances agency personnel assured parents that this was only a paperwork exercise, that families would still be involved with their children and retain authority. Given the legal nature of the custody relinquishment process, parents did not feel confident about these assurances.

Because of the difficulty in obtaining appropriate services, even the courts participated in this questionable custody transfer process. Demis Stewart, a former DSS official recalls, "The court started bastardizing the system by committing children to the foster care system who really should have been in mental health in order to get a mandated spot" (D. Stewart, personal communication, February 2012). Stewart describes a conversation she had with a group of judges in a rural county in Southwest Virginia:

"They were adamant that they were going to do what they perceived to be the right thing, which was to get this kid care before he got himself in greater trouble and 'screw intent' in terms of what the foster system was supposed to be about" (D. Stewart, personal communication, 2012).

Efforts to bend the original intention of funding sources to obtain services for at-risk youth were fairly common, with more than half of the localities in Virginia reporting that custody relinquishment was the only alternative available when children required residential or longer-term services (JLARC, 2007a). Although the most obvious reason for parents being placed in this predicament was the absence of a mental health services funding source and the existence of the mandated/non-mandated distinction certainly exacerbated the situation. With the lion's share of CSA resources attached to the mandated pool, there were few viable options for families struggling to help their troubled children other than tapping into mandated services funds.

In spite of the heart-wrenching stories of families faced with the custody relinquishment dilemma and the outrage and efforts of CSA stakeholders and government officials, little progress was made in addressing this problem during Governor Warner's administration.

PROGRESSING OR REGRESSING?

CSA continued to grow during the Warner administration (2002–2005). The total number of children served grew by 15 percent while expenditures rose by 29 percent. The increase in children served may be viewed positively in relation to CSA's goal of serving children requiring the services of more than one agency. The rise in cost, while partially attributable to inflation, was not consistent with CSA's goal of cost containment. The number of youth placed in residential treatment facilities increased by 4 percent, a considerably slower rate of growth than for the total number served through CSA. The number of CSA children served in family foster care decreased by 47 percent during this period (Office of Comprehensive Services, 2013). Unfortunately, the lack of progress in developing outcome measures and other performance metrics for CSA makes it difficult to understand the factors affecting these changes and whether the results were consistent with the objectives of the system.

In addition to the continued schism between mandated and non-mandated populations, and the persistence of custody relinquishment practices, there were other indications that CSA infrastructure and performance were not consistent with the vision, guiding principles, and goals of the original legislation. Localities such as Hampton, Fairfax, and Lynchburg continued to build on the CSA philosophy and operational framework, providing comprehensive services and supports for eligible youth and their families. However, many other localities continued to fall short of CSA's collaborative, individualized, family-centered, prescribed approach of serving youth in their home communities. Some localities, reluctance to incorporate the CSA approach may have been due to agencies' perceived loss of power or autonomy under the new system or concern that the state was exerting too much influence on local functioning. Other factors also played a significant role in impeding progress. Officials in localities still did not have a full understanding of the CSA system and those charged with implementing the system at the local level lacked sufficient guidance and appropriate tools.

Many of the supports envisioned by the architects of CSA had either not been developed or, in some instances, had been instituted earlier but then cut back or eliminated. In the late 1990s, the state Department of Social Service (DSS), recognizing that they could capture additional federal Title IV-E funds for training by having a university use their administrative funds as a match for federal dollars, entered into a contract with the School of Social Work at Virginia Commonwealth University (VCU) to provide extensive training for their workers. In 1996, DSS expanded the contract to include policy and practice-related training for staff of CSA. By involving the University, DSS not only enhanced funding support, but also was able to utilize the expertise of School of Social Work, who offered a richer set of knowledge and skills than previous trainers. During its two decades of operation, including ten years in which it provided training for CSA, the DSS-VCU Title IV-E program, which became a national model, offered 150 courses to a total of 80,000 attendees (this is a duplicated count as many individuals took more than one course). At its peak, the training contract had a $19 million yearly budget.

According to Rick Pond, who served as Executive Director of the VCU training institute for most of its ten-year tenure, the program came under scrutiny in 2006 because of its rising cost as well as questions about whether it was appropriate for the University to use indirect cost dollars it was receiving as match funds. The State, which was experiencing significant budget problems during this period, reduced the allocation for the training program to $5 million and in 2010 terminated the contract. Pond believes the decision to close the training institute was not strategic, as CSA and DSS lost valuable expertise and capacity for creating a well-prepared workforce. Unfortunately, the University did not invest much energy in negotiating to retain the contract as the amount of funding it was receiving had been drastically reduced (R. Pond, personal communication, June 20, 2016).

It took several years for CSA to establish another comprehensive training program. The UM initiated during a previous administration was still being implemented in several localities but many local government entities considered this to be another top-down obligation imposed by the state. They did not perceive the value of this process and complied with its requirements only to the extent necessary to receive funding. There was little effort by the state to ensure that localities fulfilled the intent of the UM process.

Support for developing local capacity to serve youth in their home communities also dwindled. The CSA Trust fund, originally established to assist localities in developing, needed early intervention and community-based programs for at-risk youth and received smaller allocations from the state each year. In 1993, the Act's initial year of operation, $4.8 million was appropriated. By 1997 the General Assembly's appropriation to the Trust Fund had been reduced to $2.1 million. The state's contribution was further reduced by using federal funds to replace general state funds. In 1997, state funds appropriated for the Trust Fund had shrunk to $1 million and in 2003 state funds were totally eliminated, the federal funds were transferred to the DSS and the CSA Trust Fund was virtually eliminated (Office of Comprehensive Services,

2003). These reductions were taking place even though localities were able to document significant gaps in service capacity (JLARC, 2007a).

Sufficient oversight to ensure the health and safety of children served through CSA was also lacking. Twelve children placed in residential treatment facilities died during a five-year period and many other serious incidents were discovered, indicating that appropriate monitoring and oversight were not occurring (JLARC, 2007a). Striking an appropriate balance between allowing service providers to function in a free market and the need for government intervention was a challenging task. Reaction against the expanding role of government had been growing throughout the United States as well as in Virginia. At the same time, most stakeholders recognized the importance of protecting the safety and well-being of the vulnerable youth served by CSA and were dissatisfied with the lack of accountability and the licensing agencies' failure to enforce standards and regulations.

By the end of Governor Warner's term CSA had been operational for a dozen years. The limited progress in establishing sufficient infrastructure and meeting the goals of CSA was disappointing, especially in light of the strong cadre of senior officials in the Warner administration who had been involved in the early years of CSA's development and were staunch supporters of the Act. What accounts for the inability to more fully actualize the original vision of CSA?

Certainly, the complexity of the funding and organizational arrangements and ambitious intent of the Act combined with the diverse array of localities in the Commonwealth were limiting factors. Tension between state and local governments and the mistrust generated by this dynamic also impeded progress. The gap between the ideal continuum of care proposed by the CSA legislation and the actual capacity of communities to develop and provide comprehensive services and supports must be considered. Many localities lacked the knowledge and resources required to establish a comprehensive system of care. With the state's diminished role in providing training and technical assistance, as well as funding for establishing community programs, the less developed localities were hampered from moving forward.

A pervasive obstacle to progress was the failure of many localities to understand the full intent of CSA. Greg Peters, CEO of a large not-for-profit service provider and a member of the State Executive Council notes:

> The original purpose of CSA was to go beyond just a funding mechanism and develop a System of Care and I'm not sure we've realized that. We hoped to take down those silos and develop a system where families could enter that system in different places . . . where the CSA would be seen more as a system service provider than a funding mechanism. In my opinion that hasn't happened. (G. Peters, personal communication, January 10, 2012)

The disappointing performance of CSA during an administration that was sympathetic to the Act's philosophy and supportive of its programmatic goals and strategies is puzzling. Some of the failure to strengthen accountability and facilitate progress in less advanced localities may be attributable to the complexity and ambition of the CSA system and the inherent tensions between state and local governments in Virginia. These factors, however, do not fully account for the failure to achieve more progress.

Achieving and sustaining reform requires strong continuous leadership at all levels. The need for ongoing dynamic leadership becomes more important as the intricacy and boldness of the transformation increases. For CSA, the frequent turnover of gubernatorial leadership posed an additional obstacle for ensuring continuity. The Act had survived three changes in the state's top executive, but had never regained the priority status it had enjoyed during the term of Governor Wilder, who established the Act.

In spite of the support of many senior officials within the Warner administration, CSA was not considered significant or urgent enough to warrant the commitment needed to address its shortcomings. The CSA legislation had been amended to give the Secretary of Health and Human Resources greater authority and a more direct role in presiding over the State Executive Council. Jane Woods, who had been appointed to that position by Governor Warner, was a competent administrator and seasoned veteran of the state's political system, having previously served in the state House of Delegates and Senate. Although she invested considerable energy in addressing issues related to CSA, her ability to foster significant change was limited, in part, due to competing priorities within the administration. Governor Warner's top priorities were to alter the state tax code in order to make available additional funds for education. He was successful in enacting the largest budget increase for K-12 education in the state's history, but the effort required for this initiative left little time or resources to support improvement of CSA.

Without a clear mandate or strong support from the top, significant progress was not possible. While this maxim is applicable to most policy and program endeavors, it is particularly pertinent for the Comprehensive Services Act. CSA is an immensely intricate and complicated system. With its multiple facets, including the coordination of planning, service delivery, organizational functioning and funding, and the delicate balance required to promote local empowerment while maintaining accountability at all levels, the system requires considerable attention and guidance from decision-makers at both state and local levels. Absent such intense scrutiny, misunderstanding, and conflict are likely to arise, undermining the foundation of coordination, cooperation, and empowerment upon which CSA is based. For example, senior leaders of localities, who are wary of the state's motivation, are more likely to move toward a more positive stance if they engage in productive dialogue with state leaders who support CSA and understand the benefits it produces for at-risk youth, their families, and local communities. Without a strong commitment from the state, suspicions among local leaders will be heightened and they will continue to be reluctant to fully actualize CSA in their communities.

From its inception, supporters of CSA were aware that bold, visionary leadership was needed to successfully fulfill the mission and goals of this ambitious undertaking. Sustaining this level of governance and guidance is difficult under ordinary circumstances, and is especially difficult when the governor and senior officials turn over every four years. Each new governor wants to establish his/her own unique programmatic focus. Even when a policy or program established under a previous administration is viewed as worthwhile, it will not command the same level of attention as an initiative of the incumbent, unless there is a significant problem or crisis associated with the endeavor carried over from a prior administration.

The level of leadership required to successfully navigate the complex challenges presented by CSA had not been exhibited since the Act had been established. This inadequacy was not due primarily to lack of interest or misguided intentions. Rather, it was the result of a mismatch between the degree of effort needed to effectively address CSA's issues and the lack of will and responsiveness available, given the political priorities of the current administration.

This dilemma frustrated proponents of CSA and left them wondering about its future. They considered several potential scenarios:

- Tall Oak Trees Grow. . . . But Slowly: Given the grand vision and complicated procedures of CSA was it reasonable to expect full implementation, even after a decade of operation? Was CSA a fine wine that needed an extended period of time to reach its peak? Or had the extended lack of nurturance stunted its growth permanently?
- CSA's Reach Exceeded its Grasp: The architects of CSA had spent considerable effort taking into account all of the factors required to build an effective comprehensive system. Even with this diligence they were not able to anticipate future forces that might influence the Act's course of development. Was it possible that the blueprints had been too ambitious? Could one reasonably expect to create and sustain a local-state partnership that required 138 localities adopt an intricate plan of collaboration and flexibility and adapt it to the unique conditions of their local community? Was the changing landscape of the political environment, exacerbated by the term limits of the governor, too fluid to continue to nurture such a complex, interdependent system? Was the inertia of the bureaucracy too strong to

allow child-serving agencies to adapt to a culture that valued cooperation and flexibility?

- An Idea Whose Time Has Come . . . and Passed: Perhaps the unique combination of a large core of committed individuals and a receptive social/ political environment that had fostered the establishment of CSA was also necessary to sustain it. Was it possible that this dynamic was so unique that it was unlikely to endure or recur? Was CSA on a downward spiral that would eventually end in its repeal?

Although each of these scenarios was characterized by varying degrees of pessimism, supporters of CSA remained hopeful. As they prepared for Tim Kaine, to take office as the fifth governor to preside over this system, many proponents continued to believe that with appropriate guidance and support, the system could get back on course to fulfill its mission of serving the at-risk youth in Virginia and their families in a collaborative, caring, and appropriate manner.

Perhaps the most convincing evidence supporting this cautiously optimistic view was CSA's longevity. Concerns by localities about state mandates as well as general concerns about growing costs, failure to meet goals and absence of accountability brought CSA to the attention of the General Assembly every session. Even with these shortcomings and the dissatisfaction of some constituents there were no serious attempts to repeal the Act and its budget continued to grow.

Chapter 10

CSA Reaches Adolescence

Small Signs of Hope

We're trying. We will live on bread and water so our child can have decent care. If I choose to relinquish my parental rights to the state and put my son in the system for treatment, that, to me, is choosing my husband over my child. Or if I choose to get a divorce, I choose my child over my husband. I shouldn't be put in that position. I agonize over that daily. I'm wrestling with the guilt I have either way. People shouldn't have to break up their families to get their children care (Vitanza, Cohen, & Hall, 1999).

Even though policy makers understood the damaging effects of requiring parents to relinquish custody and had attempted to abolish this requirement, when Tim Kaine took office in 2006 as Virginia's 70th governor, this draconian practice was still the only option in the majority of localities for parents seeking residential or long-term services (JLARC, 2007a). The primary obstacle continued to be the shortage of funding for long-term mental health services and the need to draw on other sources, such as foster care funding. During Kaine's term as governor, proactive steps were taken to address the custody relinquishment issue as well as other challenges confronting CSA.

To the surprise of many, government officials were able to find a partial solution to the dilemma of parents seeking intensive services for their children. Progress was also made on other CSA issues, but many of the system's core flaws and deficiencies were not sufficiently addressed, hindering the Act from fulfilling its original promises.

NEW LEADERSHIP FOR CSA

Direct responsibility for administering CSA up to this point had remained fairly consistent. Alan Saunders had served as Director of the Office of

Comprehensive Services (OCS) since 1994. Saunders, whose background was in business and finance, had shepherded CSA through three administrations. In spite of the initial skepticism of many governors and senior officials, he had effectively educated policymakers on the purpose and benefits of the system, and had successfully staved off attempts to dismantle the Act. Although he had not been trained in a human services discipline, he believed in the mission and principles of CSA and worked diligently to attempt to achieve its goal.

Many key stakeholders had become increasingly concerned that CSA was losing its original focus. They felt that too much attention was being paid to fiscal issues at the expense of the broader programmatic mission. One of the major sources of distress was the increased role of Medicaid in funding CSA services. Jane Kusiak, who served as Deputy Director of the House Appropriations Committee when CSA legislation was enacted, reflects on the impact Medicaid had on how the Act was being implemented: "What started out as a very flexible program with the intent being that we were going to wrap services around the client, depending on the client's needs, then felt much more bureaucratic because you had to go through all these hoops to get Medicaid eligibility" (J. Kusiak, personal communication, July 16, 2013).

There was also broad recognition that the current capacity of the OCS was not sufficient to address multiple training, technical assistance, planning, and accountability enhancement challenges CSA was facing.

Toward the end of Governor Warner's term in 2005 the State Executive Council, under the direction of Jane Woods, Secretary of Health and Human Resources decided to restructure the leadership of OCS. In response to the plea for more attention to CSA's programmatic vision, as well as additional guidance and support from the state, they established two leadership posts to replace the single director position that had been in place since CSA's inception. In January, 2005, Kim McGaughey, who had been involved in the Department of Planning and Budget's residential placement study and later served as the chief staff person responsible for creating the CSA legislation, was appointed to the new position of Executive Director of the OCS. Alan Saunders, who had previously been the Director, became the Chief Financial Officer.

Some of the key executive staff from the Warner administration, who had been involved in the establishment of CSA, played an even more prominent role in the Kaine administration. Wayne Turnage, who had been instrumental in the early JLARC study, eventually became Chief of Staff for Governor Kaine. Steve Harms, a social worker who was a strong supporter of CSA when he worked for the Senate Finance Committee, served as Deputy Chief of Staff. Turnage and Harms, along with McGaughey worked diligently to restore the vision and spirit that had fueled the original CSA legislation.

FIRST LADY REDUX

During Governor Baliles' term in the late 1980s, the first lady, Jeannie Baliles, effectively used her position as a bully pulpit to call attention to children's mental health issues and mobilize support for reform. Her efforts, in part, set the stage for the more comprehensive campaign to establish CSA during Governor Wilder's succeeding term (1990–1994). In the following four administrations, none of the first ladies played a comparable role. However, when Governor Kaine took office, the first lady once again became a prominent advocate for children. This time, the first lady brought not only passion for the plight of vulnerable youth, but considerable experience and expertise in addressing the needs of this population.

Anne Holton, the wife of Governor Kaine, graduated from Harvard Law School and served for many years as a judge in the juvenile and family domestic relations regional court in Richmond. During her tenure as judge, she observed first-hand the plight of children placed in foster care. The revolving door process of being moved from one temporary placement to another, and the negative impact this instability had on these children, disturbed her. According to Holton: "The system was totally reactive. We would wait until things were really awful at home, and then we'd remove the children, and maybe we'd find another family for them. Things would fall apart there, and we'd put them in a group home. They'd run away, so we'd lock them up in some institutional setting" (Walters, 2010).

Holton understood that the problems these children experienced were systemic and she wanted to use her position as first lady to change the way the communities served children who were being removed from their homes. As the daughter of Abner Linwood Holton, former Governor of Virginia (1970–1974), Holton was familiar with the political process and intended to use her knowledge of the foster care system, and as well as her political acumen, to improve care for these children. The fact that Virginia ranked last among states for children aging out of foster care without a permanent relationship to family or community provided additional impetus for seeking reform (The Pew Charitable Trusts and Jim Casey Youth Opportunities Initiative, 2007).

In December 2007, Virginia's child-serving agencies, under the leadership of First Lady Anne Holton, launched a comprehensive reform effort known as the Children's Services System Transformation Initiative. The primary goals of the transformation were to: (1) adopt a statewide philosophy supporting family-focused, child-centered, community-based care with an emphasis on permanence for all children; (2) implement a standard practice model focused on permanence in order to increase the number of relative and non-relative foster parents; and (3) utilize relevant outcome measurements to ensure quality and to enhance accountability.

The similarities between the philosophy and goals of the Transformation Initiative and CSA are striking. It is reasonable to ask what the relationship between these two major reform efforts was and what steps were made to coordinate endeavors. These questions will be addressed later in this chapter.

Ray Ratke, Deputy Commissioner of the Department of Behavioral Health and Developmental Services (formerly Department of Mental Health, Mental Retardation and Substance Abuse) was appointed as Special Advisor, responsible for leading the Transformation Initiative. During the next several years he worked closely with Ms. Holton and a leadership team comprised of state and local representatives, as well as outside experts, to implement the transformation. He continued to work on this campaign during the following administration.

Early in the process, a strategic decision was made to engage the Annie Casey Foundation to provide guidance and technical assistance. With the Foundation's extensive experience with child welfare reform and broad array of technical expertise in establishing data bases and tracking outcomes, Casey proved to be a valuable partner.

Virginia's child welfare system was largely administered at the local level with the state providing broad supervision. This structure presented challenges for the Transformation Initiative, as it had for CSA, due to the wide variation in practice among the large number of local government entities. In response to this complex governance dynamic, the transformation leadership chose to proceed with a two-tiered approach, with one group focusing on local issues and the other dealing with state-level policies and procedures.

A group of stakeholders worked with administration officials to determine how state policy, budget, and practice impacted local systems and propose revisions that would facilitate and support improved performance. As a result of these deliberations, several significant changes were put in place. Prior to the Transformation Initiative, the CSA formula for providing state matching funds for foster care placements did not differentiate between residential and family-based placements. Thus, no incentive was provided for utilizing community-based, family-like settings.

The review of how foster care services were funded also revealed that Virginia's reimbursement rates for foster families were significantly below the national average and that more resources needed to be invested in the recruitment and development of foster and kin families as well as adoptive parents. The Virginia General Assembly was already concerned about poor outcomes and high costs in the child welfare system and CSA and was willing to work with the Kaine administration to strengthen the foster care system. The legislators approved budget proposals that:

- Increased foster care reimbursement by 21 percent;
- Provided an additional $2 million for recruitment, training, and support of foster, kin, and adoptive parents caring for children in the system;
- Changed the local match rate that allowed localities to pay 50 percent less to match state funding for community services and 25 percent more in match for non-Medicaid residential services (Walters, 2010).

The second tier of the Transformation Initiative focused on local reform. Thirteen jurisdictions, which served more than half of the foster children in the state, were chosen to serve as change leaders and innovators for improving child welfare system performance in communities in Virginia. The Council on Reform (CORE) was established to work with the identified localities. CORE was comprised of officials from these 13 jurisdictions, along with representatives from statewide advocacy organizations and provider associations. With technical assistance from the Casey Foundation, CORE set out to engage local communities in reforming how youth in the child welfare system were served. Although the early meetings of the group were fraught with tension and mistrust, the group eventually came together to address their charge.

CORE's first challenge was to develop a practice model consistent with the mission and guiding principles of the Transformation Initiative. Once the practice model was in place, the group turned its attention to assisting localities to implement this model. A critical element in this process was the technical assistance and support provided by the Casey Foundation. By establishing key indicators for tracking progress and working with stakeholders to create and utilize pertinent data bases, Casey enabled localities to actualize the principle of "managing by data." The six key indicators selected for the initial tracking system were:

1. Total number of children in foster care
2. The number of children in family-based care, including living with a relative
3. Number of children in congregate care
4. Length of stay in foster care
5. Discharges to permanency, measured by youth being connected to family rather than being allowed to age out of the system without a family connection
6. Number of children returning to the system due to repeat maltreatment (Walters, 2010).

Casey also introduced localities to Team Decision Making (TDM), a process that brought together all of the important individuals in a child's life as a team to understand the child's situation and to examine all of the treatment, service, and options prior to the court hearing (Walters, 2010).

WHAT DID THE TRANSFORMATION ACCOMPLISH?

This intensive effort yielded some positive results. During the initial three years of the Transformation Initiative:

- The percentage of youth in foster care discharged to a permanency increased by 13 percent
- The percentage of foster youth in group care decreased by 40 percent
- The total number of youth under age 18 in foster care decreased by 27 percent (Stewart & Cleary, 2011).

The results in the 13 jurisdictions selected to be change leaders was even more impressive. Between 2007 and 2010, the number of children in foster care decreased by 28 percent in CORE communities compared to a decrease of 17 percent in non-CORE communities. During the same period, the number of children in congregate settings decreased by 54 percent in CORE localities while the reduction in non-CORE localities was 43 percent (Walters, 2010).

Significant cost reductions also occurred during this period, with much of the savings occurring in CSA funding streams. Total expenditures for CSA declined from $380.5 million in 2008, the year prior to the change in the local match rate, to $346.9 million in 2010, a decrease of nearly 9 percent. The cost per child also decreased by nearly 6 percent during this two-year time span. A significant portion of this decrease is attributable to the shift in where children were served. Expenditures for residential treatment services decreased by 14 percent while spending for community services rose by 37 percent during the same period. The change in the local share of CSA expenditures provides further evidence that the Kaine administration's fiscal incentive for local government to shift from residential to community services was having its intended effect. The local share for CSA expenditures decreased by 15 percent from 2008 to 2010, nearly double the reduction in overall CSA costs during that time frame (Office of Comprehensive Services, 2013).

The momentum of the Transformation Initiative continued beyond the Kaine administration. Bob McDonnell, who succeeded Kaine as governor, pledged to support efforts to improve the child welfare system. The number of children in foster care continued to decline. At the end of 2010 there were 5,500 children in foster care, down from 8,000 in 2007. By October 2013 the number of foster children in Virginia had fallen to 4,960. The number of foster care youth placed in congregate care also continued to fall, with slightly fewer than 15 percent residing in group homes or institutions at the end of 2013. The percentage of youth in foster care placed with relative caregivers, which had grown from 4.1 percent in 2007 to 5.61 percent in 2010, declined to slightly by October 2013 (Virginia Department of Social Service, 2014).

While the results of the Transformation Initiative are impressive, it should be noted that the campaign was only partially successful in addressing the problems confronting the Commonwealth's child welfare system. Virginia moved from its previous ranking of 50 among states for the percentage of youth aging out of foster care to a ranking of 49 (Stewart & Cleary, 2011). In Virginia, only 5 percent of foster children are placed with relative caregivers in comparison to approximately 25 percent for most states (McWhinney, 2010).

Racial disparities also continue to afflict Virginia's foster care system. Although Black children comprise 23 percent of the child population in Virginia, 39 percent of foster care youth in Virginia is Black (Stewart & Cleary, 2011). This disparity certainly reflects broader social and economic inequities, beyond the control of social service agencies. Nonetheless, the disparity within the foster care system should be acknowledged and addressed by agency officials as well as policy makers at all levels.

PARALLEL PROCESSES

What accounts for the impressive results of the Transformation Initiative? The Casey Foundation and the Virginia Department of Social Services (DSS) attribute the success of this reform effort to the diligent and sustained reliance on the five "building blocks":

1. Managing by data
2. Engaging families
3. Investing in resource family recruitment, development, and support
4. Creating a continuum of community-based services to support children and families
5. Developing a statewide training system (Virginia Department of Social Services, 2010).

Interestingly, these strategies bear considerable resemblance to the guiding principles of the CSA legislation. Assessments of CSA described earlier, point out the discrepancy between intention and accomplishment in some of these areas (JLARC, 1998; 2007). Specifically, the paucity of pertinent outcome measures as well as other relevant data and the limited investment in training, technical assistance, and infrastructure development, particularly at the local level, were identified as weaknesses in the CSA system.

With the assistance and support of the Casey Foundation, and the strong backing of Governor Kaine and the First Lady Anne Holton, the Transformation effort was able to garner sufficient commitment and resources to engage families and localities by reaching out to these stakeholders and meeting with them frequently to solicit input and provide training. Through these outreach efforts, CORE was able to obtain buy-in on the core principles, goals, and strategies of the Transformation effort. This proactive approach helped reform leaders overcome longstanding skepticism and mistrust. Jane Conlin, Director of Social Services in Roanoke recalls, "I wasn't throwing confetti right away because we'd all seen these kind of things come and go. But the more I got into it, the more impressed I was by the commitment of the state and the knowledge Casey was bringing to the effort" (Walters, 2010, p. 10).

The City of Richmond provides an example of how these strategies were used to produce constructive change. Richmond, who had more children in foster and congregate care than any locality in the state, became the lead pilot for the Transformation. Paul McWhinney, who had recently become the Director of the City's DSS, was interested in modernizing the city's child welfare practices. He explains that through the City's involvement as the lead pilot, "We started implementing all the things we'd only been talking about in Richmond: family engagement, kinship care, in-depth review of our kids in congregate care, and more wrap-around, community-based services, with an overall emphasis on permanence" (Walters, 2010, p. 9).

The City embarked on a series of initiatives to enhance care for vulnerable children. Joining in partnerships with community organizations, they focused on enhancing family engagement, establishing a continuum of community-based services and increasing permanence. Through these efforts they were able to achieve significant reductions in the number of children in foster care as well as a reduction in the percentage of children in foster care who were placed in congregate care settings. The City also increased the proportion of permanency achieved for all children served by DSS (Walters, 2010).

The similarities between the Transformation Initiative and CSA are striking, as are some of the differences. Although the philosophy and guiding principles of these two comprehensive undertakings overlap considerably, the Transformation effort was able to mobilize support and resources to enable local stakeholders to take ownership of the reform endeavor in their community and participate in a locally driven campaign to improve the foster care system. By establishing an infrastructure of training, technical assistance, and outcome tracking the Transformation leaders were able to help localities understand and embrace the reform initiative and empower teams of social service staff, families, providers, and advocates to mount a vigorous campaign to address the child welfare challenges in their home communities.

The persistent involvement and support of the CORE team, state officials, and Casey consultants enabled local participants to develop and implement innovative strategies for reducing foster and congregate care and increasing permanence.

The Transformation campaign not only helped localities put in place new practices and programs; it focused on how the organizational climate of these local social service agencies was impeding staff from effectively serving their clients, and facilitated a fundamental shift to a culture characterized by empowerment, collaboration, and a proactive mind-set. The foster care reform also contributed directly to the improved performance of CSA through its recommendation that the match rate for locality funding be realigned to provide incentives for localities to reduce residential placements and increase use of community-based services.

Although CSA had achieved this level of commitment and collaborative engagement in Hampton and a few other localities, the Transformation Initiative successfully mobilized productive reform processes in most of the participating localities and fostered fundamental changes in the work environment. The success of the Transformation effort is particularly notable, considering the positive results it achieved in the course of a few years, in comparison to the more than 15 years CSA had been operating at that time.

The obvious explanation for this contrast is the Transformation's concerted effort to reach out to local stakeholders and provide them with assistance in the form of training, facilitation, and outcome measures and other data bases. The CSA legislation emphasized the importance of providing infrastructure support and there had been sporadic attempts to offer education and other forms of technical assistance, such as the utilization management project. These efforts, however, were generally not sufficiently intensive to achieve their intended objective and were often short-lived. With the support of the Governor and First Lady, and the assistance of the Casey Foundation, the Transformation Initiative provided considerable resources and assistance to participating localities, giving them the knowledge and tools needed to effectively mobilize a locally driven collaborative reform effort.

Unfortunately, understanding the forces that drive public policy is rarely simple, and in this instance, the obvious explanation is not sufficient. The relatively greater success of the Transformation Initiative in comparison to CSA is in large part attributable to the support of the Kaine administration and the resources it brought to bear on foster care reform. There are, however, some contextual factors that may have contributed to the difference in outcome. The Transformation Initiative was established by First Lady Anne Holton and Governor Kaine, while CSA was created by Governor Wilder and inherited by the Kaine administration. Although both governors were Democrats, there is a tendency for elected officials to support policies and programs that are uniquely identified with their actions. They prefer initiatives they have established or which they have modified to reflect their views. Even though the Transformation Initiative shared many of CSA's values and goals, the foster care reform effort was launched by the First Lady and Governor and was closely identified as belonging to the Kaine administration.

The Transformation Initiative was further accelerated by its association with a problem that had recently received considerable public attention: the last place ranking of Virginia among all states for children aging out of foster care. The same children who were targeted in the child welfare campaign were also being served by CSA and the plight of other CSA youth was often equally dismal. However, the foster care agenda was more visible in the public eye, and thus garnered more attention and outrage.

Paradoxically, one of the criticisms of the Transformation effort grew out of its failure to follow one of the initiative's core principles. The leaders of the foster care reform campaign stressed the importance of understanding the impact of all aspects of the environment on the child's life and engaging individuals and groups from education, mental health, juvenile justice, and other pertinent agencies. Margaret Nimmo Crowe, of Voices for Virginia's Children, recalls that the Transformation Initiative was primarily focused on the foster care system and did not engage the other child-serving systems:

> Unfortunately, at the end of it there were many Community Service Boards (CSBs) and court service units and other education sectors that didn't really know anything about it . . . ideally [the Transformation] needed to continue and have those principles and the practice model be spread to the other child serving systems. (M. Nimmo Crowe, personal communication, August, 2013)

By almost all accounts, the Transformation Initiative was very successful, facilitating significant positive shifts in the culture of social service agencies and producing impressive outcomes in reducing foster care utilization and increasing permanence. Yet, as a public policy undertaking, it fell short of generating comprehensive, all-encompassing reform in the system serving at-risk youth. The campaign by-passed CSA and established a separate course of action for foster children, using many of the same principles and strategies incorporated in the CSA legislation. One can argue that limiting the initiative to the foster care population increased the viability of the effort or that launching a fresh campaign was more likely to generate broad support compared to trying to rejuvenate the already established CSA system. However, the creation of a parallel endeavor introduced a degree of duplication and inefficiency and, as noted above, limited the scope and effectiveness of the reform effort.

MEDICAID: A CHALLENGING PARTNER

By the end of the Kaine administration, Medicaid had become a major funding source for CSA. Medicaid accounted for nearly 25 percent of CSA spending, with nearly $50 million of federal match funds being used to pay for services provided through the Act. As the role of Medicaid in CSA became more prominent, concern was expressed about how compatible this federal health care funding program was with a System of Care approach that considered all aspects of a child's environment to be important and encouraged collaboration among the multiple participants.

Charlotte McNulty, who served as Executive Director of a CSB prior to becoming Director of the OCS in 2009, describes the tension between Medicaid and the private providers who delivered most of the services offered through CSA. At that time, the federal government's contribution to Medicaid payments was greater than 60 percent. According to McNulty, the ability to draw down significant federal funds led the state to prefer billing Medicaid for services whenever possible, and using CSA pool funds only when this option is not available. McNulty explains that the financial incentives for relying on Medicaid are in conflict with the programmatic philosophy of CSA since Medicaid operates on a medical model which prescribes specific treatments for individuals, based on their diagnosis and the severity of the problem. In contrast, CSA's social needs/strengths model encourages localities and providers to deploy a combination of various interventions and supports tailored to the individual needs and strengths of the child and families. The flexible, holistic approach of CSA is often incompatible with Medicaid's rigid, prescriptive model. According to McNulty, "Providers say we are not going to take Medicaid because they don't pay enough and we can't do what you want us to do within Medicaid" (C. McNulty, personal communication, August 25, 2011).

The reluctance of providers to participate in Medicaid posed a dilemma for local CSA administrators. They had to choose between finding another provider, which was often difficult, or pay the preferred provider at the rate they wanted to be reimbursed using state or local funds. McNulty believes that this cumbersome and unorthodox dynamic created an unsustainable situation for state administrators of CSA due to the lack of oversight and accountability in relation to the arrangement between localities and service providers (C. McNulty, personal communication, August 25, 2011).

Medicaid's method of funding services and its apparent incompatibility with CSA's System of Care approach were clearly a source of frustration for proponents of CSA's visionary philosophy. Looking to the future, Margaret Nimmo Crowe says, "As an advocate, one challenge we have is to ensure that CSA doesn't become so focused on Medicaid that it becomes a medical model" (M. Nimmo Crow, personal communication, August, 2013). On the other hand, the resources provided by Medicaid were substantial and the system had come to rely on this payment source to support its array of services. Chuck Hall, Executive Director of the Hampton/Newport Community Service Board recognizes that Medicaid may not view itself as a partner in children's public policy, but it is the largest funder of behavioral health services and the most significant component of state government that is not involved in policy deliberations for youth. Hall warns that "Without recognizing the importance of the Department of Medical Assistance [DMAS; the state agency that administers Medicaid] in Virginia's role with CSA, we could see the whole thing crumble apart" (C. Hall, personal communication, May 2013).

Cindi Jones, Director of DMAS offers another perspective. Jones, who previously worked as an investigator for JLARC when it studied CSA in the late 1990s, notes that CSA has not focused sufficiently on outcome measures and accountability. From her perspective, one of Medicaid's contributions has been to introduce some accountability for service providers. "We have a $7 billion budget and we pay providers, but we also have some checks and balances in the front end and the back end to make sure people are getting what they are supposed to receive" (C. Jones, personal communication, April 5, 2012).

In response to the criticism that Medicaid had become the primary driver of services for behavioral health in general, and CSA specifically, Patrick Finnerty, former Director of DMAS responds, "It almost goes hand-in-hand that the group that is paying such a substantial portion of the costs of these services is probably, just by definition, going to drive a lot of policy because there has to be policy to support the payment" (P. Finnerty, personal communication, June 2013).

The tension between Medicaid and CSA is in some ways emblematic of the shortcomings of leadership in addressing barriers to establishing an authentically collaborative system of care. It is understandable that a major funding source such as Medicaid would want to have influence on how their funds were being used. Ensuring compliance with federal and state regulations, and holding providers accountable are sensible and legitimate functions. In fact, these are goals that DMAS shares with administrators of CSA. The challenge for leadership is how to acknowledge and support these functions while also ensuring that all parties recognize and promote CSA's overarching goals of providing comprehensive, coordinated services tailored to the needs and strengths of the participating child and family.

As with the Transformation Initiative, officials at the highest levels had not exercised sufficient proactive leadership to bring the key players together to identify and resolve obstacles that were impeding CSA from achieving its goals. Eliminating Medicaid as a funding source was not a viable option.

Allowing DMAS to continue its autonomous approach to paying for services would dilute the core values and principles of CSA and compromise its System of Care's ability to achieve its purpose. The potential risk of not addressing the relationship between Medicaid and CSA was significant. Yet, there was little evidence that these issues were being addressed in the collaborative, productive manner that was touted as a hallmark of the CSA model.

A BOLD REACH ACROSS THE AISLE

Despite considerable efforts to remove the onerous requirement for parents, in some instances, to relinquish custody of their child to obtain needed services, this barbaric practice continued in Virginia as well as other states. As noted earlier, this policy was not being perpetuated because policy makers and administrators believed giving up custody of one's child was beneficial. The custody relinquishment perquisite continued because the funding sources being used to pay for services was intended for children who had been abused or neglected rather than young people whose primary issue was a serious behavioral health disorder.

Through a unique confluence of individuals and events, Virginia finally developed a mechanism that allowed most parents to obtain services without transferring custody of their child to the state. The primary actors in this surprising policy reform effort were Governor Tim Kaine, a Democrat, Attorney General Bob McDonnell, a conservative Republican and his Deputy, William Mims, a former state legislator who had become a strong proponent of children's mental health, and Senator Emmett Hanger, a moderate Republican who chaired the state legislature's Joint Subcommittee studying CSA. Important supporting roles were played by the JLARC staff, the Joint Commission on Youth, the State Executive Council of CSA, Kim McGaughey and the staff of the OCS, and a determined group of child advocates, including Voices for Virginia's Children and the National Alliance on Mental Illness in Virginia.

In early 2004, the General Assembly had directed the State Executive Council of CSA (SEC) to investigate the factors leading to the custody relinquishment practice and make policy recommendations on how to abolish this practice and ensure that children had access to appropriate services. The SEC issued its initial report in November 2004, concluding that, "This problem is a direct result of inadequate access to and availability of prevention, early intervention, and intensive mental health and substance abuse treatment services for children and adolescents" (State Executive Council Workgroup, 2004). Based on the Workgroup's further deliberations during 2005, the SEC approved a series of legislative and funding recommendations intended to make it easier for parents to obtain appropriate services without giving up custody of their children.

The custody relinquishment issue continued to garner attention, but not much progress was made in abolishing the practice or establishing viable alternatives. Then, in December 2006, Attorney General McDonnell issued an official advisory opinion that paved the way for significant change. McDonnell addressed four aspects of the code: (1) whether CSA was mandated to provide mental health services, (2) the scope of services included under the definition of foster care services, (3) the statutory definition of a "child in need of services," and (4) how to "interpret and construe" the statutory intent of CSA's stated purpose of "preserving families" and "providing appropriate services in the least restrictive environment." In his opinion, McDonnell found that although the code related to CSA does not mandate the provision of mental health services, the provisions of the statute sections for foster care and child-in-need-of-services clearly reference "treatment" and "community services," which certainly include mental health treatment or services (McDonnell, 2006).

Finally, McDonnell concluded that CSA's expressed legislative intent to *preserve families* and *provide appropriate services in the least restrictive environment* is clear and unambiguous and requires that the state and its localities are obliged to provide sufficient funding to provide appropriate services for children served through CSA (McDonnell, 2006). In a strongly worded opinion, the Attorney General stated that the definitions of foster care and child-in-need-of-services have been interpreted too narrowly and citing the Constitution of the United States as well as the Code of Virginia, affirmed that "the custody, care and nurture resides first in the parents" (Prince v. Massachusetts, 1944). Referring to the Equal Protection Clause of the Constitution, McDonnell argued that "a court could find the statute's differing treatment of children with disabilities to be irrational and the relevant provision of CSA, as presently applied, unconstitutional" (McDonnell, 2006, p. 8). McDonnell concluded that "statutory and constitutional provisions require mandated services pursuant to CSA to be provided to eligible children who are in need of such mental health services without their parents having to relinquish services to local social services agencies" (McDonnell, 2006, p. 9).

The primary internal thrust for the Attorney General's opinion came from William "Bill" Mims who had recently been appointed Chief Deputy by McDonnell. Mims, who had been a member of the House of Delegates and Senate prior to this appointment, had developed a strong interest in children's mental health and had become a strong proponent of improving services for this population. Mims, who became Attorney General in 2009 when McDonnell announced that he was running for Governor, was highly respected by all branches of government as well as members of the children's advocacy community. His involvement in crafting the Attorney General's opinion and working with the executive and legislative branches, as well as groups interested in mental health, facilitated the collaborative effort that occurred after the release of the official advisory opinion.

Shortly after the Attorney General issued his judgment that parents should not be required to relinquish custody to obtain services, the General Assembly acted to ensure that parents would not have to endure this traumatizing experience in order to receive help. Senate Bill 1399, introduced in 2007, expanded the target population of children who could receive state funds. Under this proposed legislation, children requiring mental health services would be able to obtain state-funded treatment without requiring transfer of parental custody if they met the other eligibility requirements for obtaining state pool funding. The stated purpose for adding children requiring mental health services to this funding mechanism was to avoid foster care placement which would be disruptive for the child and family and, in many instances, would increase cost.

This legislation was passed without dissension in the Senate and almost unanimously in the House in March 2007 and Governor Kaine signed it into law in April (Virginia Acts of Assembly, Chapter 840, § 2.2-5212, April 2007). During the remainder of 2007, the SEC considered how to implement the new requirements. The Council established guidelines and procedures ensuring that families could obtain mental health services for their child without relinquishing custody. In December 2007, the SEC adopted "Final Interagency Guidelines on Foster Care Service for Specific Children in Need of Services Funded through the Comprehensive Services Act" (State Executive Council, 2007).

These guidelines defined eligibility and created two types of parental agreements to allow their children to receive needed mental health services without relinquishing custody. The DSS Non-Custodial Foster Care Agreements were between the parent and the local DSS agency. This agreement allowed the child to be in foster care placement, which made him or her eligible to receive mandated funding. The local social service agency had 24-hour supervisory responsibility for the child while the parent retained legal custody. The second mechanism, the CSA Parental Agreement, was intended to be used by agencies other than DSS and allowed the parent or guardian to retain legal custody when the child was placed outside of the home in a treatment setting. This agreement, between the parent and an agency responsible for case management designated by the local Community Policy and Management Team (CPMT), delineated the responsibilities of both the parent and local case management agency when DSS was not the responsible agency.

By 2007, partisan politics and non-productive squabbling among elected officials had escalated in Virginia as well as the rest of the country. Although the extent of this ideologically driven bickering had not reached the level found in the years that followed, cooperation among officials with different political affiliations became rare. Therefore, the constructive response of the Governor's office, as well as the Republican-dominated General Assembly, following the announcement of the Attorney General's opinion on custody relinquishment was unusual and gratifying to proponents of children's mental health and the CSA.

Although the passage of this legislation and the establishment of mechanisms for obtaining services without relinquishing custody was considered groundbreaking and was met with enthusiasm, these actions did not fully address concerns about CSA service limitations. Nimmo Crowe of Voices for Virginia's Children lauds the policy change but points out that parents still have to enter into non-custodial agreements which do not require them to give up full custody, but makes them give up some day-to-day decision-making. "I think we've largely solved the problem," she says, "but I don't think it's totally solved" (M. Nimmo Crowe, personal communication, August, 2013).

Perhaps more troubling is the limited scope of the effort to eliminate the need for parents to relinquish custody of their child to obtain needed services. Because these actions focused primarily on funding related to foster care and to a lesser degree, special education, most families were still forced to rely on funding sources intended to support children eligible for mandated services. Families whose children had severe emotional and behavioral challenges, but were not at risk of being placed in foster care or did not require special education services, were considered to be "non-mandated" in relation to CSA and were unlikely to have access to CSA funds for their mental health treatment needs. In 2007, state and local CSA expenditures for mandated children were $333.1 million compared to only $9.1 million for non-mandated children and more than one-third of localities provided no services to non-mandated children (Office of Comprehensive Services, 2013). While some of the procedural impediments to obtaining intensive treatment services without relinquishing custody had been removed, the issue of having sufficient funds available to meet mental health needs had still not been addressed.

Nearly 15 years after the passage of CSA, despite the strong criticism of advocates and others interested in at-risk youth, a two-tiered system still existed within this system of care. Children who met the criteria for receiving mandated services were assured, by law, that funding for these services would be available. Children considered to be non-mandated had no assurance that they would receive funding, and in many instances received no support through CSA, even when the need for services had been well documented.

SUBSTANTIAL ACHIEVEMENT . . . MISSED OPPORTUNITY

During the Kaine administration, care for at-risk youth improved significantly. The First Lady's Children's Service System Transformation produced positive outcomes in reducing the number of children in foster care and increasing permanent placement for these young people. The Transformation Initiative, with the assistance of the Casey Foundation also brought about profound changes in the culture of local social service agencies and the manner in which they worked with children and families. The First Lady's work even had a direct impact on CSA through its recommendation that financial incentives be created for localities that served youth within their home communities.

By offering localities better match rates for using community-based services, while also providing additional technical assistance to localities, CSA was able to improve outcomes. Localities served more children in their own communities, shifting the balance of resource allocation from out-of-community to locally provided care. This change in locus of care produced a significant reduction in statewide total and per child expenditures for the first time since the inception of CSA.

The CSA leadership also decided to replace the CAFAS, the utilization management assessment instrument that had been unwisely chosen in the late 1990s, with the Child and Adolescent Needs and Strengths (CANS) assessment scale. The CANS, which was created by John Lyons, who helped to create the initial decision support system for CSA, was specifically designed for the purpose of assessing appropriate levels of care for at-risk youth. The adoption of the CANS allowed CSA to begin to develop a functional data base for planning appropriate care and assessing performance of localities and the state in relation to the stated goals of CSA.

The removal of the onerous requirement that families give up custody of their children was also a significant achievement that allowed many parents and children to access much needed mental health care for their children.

Despite these noteworthy achievements, there were instances in which the leadership could have done more to actualize the vision of CSA by enhancing collaboration and facilitating the provision of child-centered, family-friendly care for at-risk youth in their home communities. For example, by limiting the scope of the First Lady's Transformation Initiative to foster care, the leadership created an unnecessary division between the child welfare system and the other partners in CSA's effort to provide comprehensive, integrated care for all at-risk children and their families. The distinct focus of the Transformation Initiative on the foster care system ran counter to the all-inclusive, collaborative philosophy of CSA and resulted in a lost opportunity in improving the entire system.

Likewise, the enhancement of the Medicaid program provided additional resources for serving at-risk youth. However, the failure of leadership to better incorporate and integrate the administrators of Medicaid into the programmatic philosophy and thrust of CSA impeded the system from functioning in the collaborative manner that the founders of CSA had envisioned. As Medicaid became a more powerful funding force for at-risk youth, the difference between the medical model which drove this funding program, and the collaborative, individually tailored program philosophy of CSA became more apparent and had an adverse effect on those receiving care as well as service providers.

Finally, CSA certainly benefited from the progress made in strengthening technical assistance and revamping the utilization management data system. These efforts, however, fell short of providing sufficient infrastructure for enhancing performance and accountability. Many localities still did not have a sufficient grasp of the System of Care approach and were reluctant or unable to fully embrace CSA. The lack of a comprehensive outcome tracking system also served as a deterrent to measuring performance and holding localities and providers accountable.

As eight years of Democratic leadership in the executive branch came to a close, CSA stakeholders anticipated with uncertainty what would happen under Bob McDonnell the new Governor, an avowed conservative Republican. They hoped that McDonnell would offer the same support he showed as Attorney General when he issued the advisory opinion critical of the custody relinquishment. At the same time, they feared that the progress CSA had enjoyed under the Kaine administration might not be sustained or built upon, or worse, could be undone.

Chapter 11

A Surprising Turn of Events

CSA had fared relatively well during the Warner and Kaine administrations. Senior leadership recognized the potential benefit of a comprehensive system of care and allocated time and resources to address administrative, programmatic, and fiscal concerns. Incremental gains were made in improving service delivery and administrative processes and realignment of financial incentives stemming from the First Lady's Transformation Initiative produced positive results. Although performance by localities throughout the state remained uneven and there was still consensus that CSA had failed to fully actualize its original principles and goals, many stakeholders were guardedly optimistic about the direction in which CSA was moving.

So it was not surprising that proponents of CSA were anxious when a conservative Republican was elected Governor of Virginia in November 2009, ending two consecutive terms of Democrat leadership. When Robert McDonnell was sworn in January 2010, individuals and groups associated with CSA did not know what to expect. Their uncertainty was further amplified when McDonnell appointed as Secretary of Health and Human Resources, William Hazel, an orthopedic surgeon whose most prominent credentials were that he served as a team physician for the Washington Redskins and D.C. United soccer teams.

While Dr. Hazel readily admitted that he did not know much about CSA or many other functions his secretariat was responsible for, he proved to be a quick study and after some difficult encounters with key stakeholders, he soon began to focus on a number of significant issues, including improving performance of CSA. Despite his lack of experience with child service systems, Secretary Hazel expressed a keen interest in understanding systems of care, appreciated the need for accountability in delivering health and human services, and was a staunch proponent of data-driven decision-making. After

meeting with a diverse group of stakeholders, he gathered his senior staff and
the leadership of the Office of Comprehensive Services (OCS) and developed
an agenda of issues and concerns related to CSA that needed to be addressed.
True to his first calling as a physician, Hazel was fond of using medical meta-
phors when describing his perspective on CSA. Speaking of the challenge of
addressing the complex children's service issues confronting the Commonwealth, where leadership changes every four years, Hazel says, "This isn't
like the short course of an antibiotic; this is a chronic situation that you have
to manage" (W. Hazel, personal communication, June 26, 2012).

During the next four years, Hazel and his staff tackled many of the items
on that agenda. They began by assessing whether the work profiles of state
agency heads were consonant with the goals of the agency and modifying job
descriptions to bring them in line with the direction in which the state wanted
to move, such as increasing collaboration and accountability. From there,
Hazel and his team developed a detailed plan, describing specific objectives
they wanted to achieve and strategies they would employ to improve social
and behavioral health services.

The response to this proactive approach was mixed, with some groups
favoring the actions that were being taken and others believing the changes
instituted were not needed or in some instances, detrimental. Regardless of
their perspective, all stakeholders seemed to agree that this was an active
period for CSA.

SEEKING TRACTION

Dr. Hazel and other senior official spent much of the first year educating
themselves on the complexities of the behavioral health and children's service
systems as well as responding to crisis such as the lack of accountability for
community service providers. Hazel concluded that the most significant barrier to improving the CSA system was tradition. According to Hazel, "We are
fighting years of institutional culture and a hierarchical approach to delivering
a service in a particular specialty as opposed to an integrated approach across
specialties" (W. Hazel, personal communication, June 26, 2012). Rather than
framing the issue as whether the amount of money allocated is sufficient, Hazel
preferred to ask, "What are we getting for the funding we put in? We probably
suffer from an inability to articulate what a good outcome is" (W. Hazel).

Equipped with this assessment of the organizational culture and a desire to
provide education and tools that enabled stakeholders to engage in evidence-
informed decision-making, Hazel and his team began to work with state,
local, and private entities to identify and implement data-driven processes
for improving performance and accountability. While much of this work was

specifically focused on CSA, they also launched other efforts that impacted the children's system, such as establishing the statewide behavioral health Administrative Services Organization (ASO).

In 2011, Charlotte McNulty, the Director of the OCS retired and Susan Clare, who had previously served as a special education administrator and CSA Coordinator in Central Virginia, assumed that position. Clare recognized the difficulty of effectively implementing a system of care in a state that is administered locally but in which policy and funding are centrally controlled. She considered the CSA vision, principles, and goals to be as salient as when they were codified in 1993, but thought there had not been sufficient attention assisting localities to adapt their administrative and programmatic cultures in order to effectively implement the system. Clare asked, "How do you get back to making this a cultural thing where people understand this is about making good things for kids and families?" (S. Clare, personal communication, November 2, 2012).

Responding to her own question, Clare identified good practice and accountability as critical priorities for her OCS. Believing that simply offering training was not sufficient, Clare and her staff embarked on a systematic effort to work with localities to understand their needs and issues and work with them to address mutually identified concerns and ensure consistent implementation of CSA principles throughout the state. The challenge they faced, according to Clare, was "Putting teeth behind [their efforts] by doing follow-up assessments with communities. . . . To look at what are you actually doing. . . . Are you complying? Do you have things in place that at least meet standards as we define them?" (S. Clare, personal communication, April 25, 2014).

During the next few years, the OCS worked with Secretary Hazel and the State Executive Council to enhance stakeholders' understanding of CSA and System of Care principles and practices, and to assist localities to strengthen their performance, quality of care, and fiscal and programmatic accountability. Consistent with their assessment that more collaboration with local leaders and staff was needed, the strategies they employed relied heavily on hands-on training and technical assistance. These activities were accompanied by efforts to establish metrics and incentives that would encourage localities to improve their performance. The following section describes the major initiatives undertaken during this period.

PREPARING THE WORKFORCE

While CSA had always provided training opportunities for families, providers, and local administrators and staff, the scope of these educational activities was judged to be insufficient to address the complexity of the System of Care and the knowledge and skills required to effectively participate and implement CSA. In 2011, regional and state training offerings were expanded to cover a wide range of topics. Sessions were conducted to increase understanding of how to use the Child and Adolescent Needs and Strengths (CANS), the uniform assessment instrument adopted by CSA and strategies for enhancing family engagement. Training was also offered on subjects related to the specific responsibilities and requirements of participating agencies, including the Virginia Departments of Education, Social Services, and Medical Assistance Service. Local administrators were also provided guidance on obtaining state pool fund reimbursement and managing CSA data sets.

The Executive Director of OCS began conducting regional roundtables to address "hot topic" issues related to CSA that were of interest to local governments. The four technical assistance staff from the OCS traveled to localities across the state, providing guidance on pertinent issues to more than 1,000 participants in more than 100 communities (Office of Comprehensive Services, 2011).

In 2012, a two-day New CSA Coordinator Academy was established to help local coordinators function more effectively and an annual Commonwealth of Virginia CSA Conference was launched. The New CSA Coordinator Academy invited, at the state's expense, CSA coordinators who had been on the job less than 18 months to participate in an intensive training and mentoring experience designed to orient participants to the responsibilities, desired outcomes, funding options, and unique needs of youth served by each of the child-serving agencies involved in the CSA. The training was conducted by members of the CSA State and Local Advisory Team and staff of OCS. The new coordinators received on-going, one-to-one mentoring from volunteer veteran CSA coordinators.

More than 450 individuals attended the First Annual CSA Conference in June 2012. A diverse audience participated in plenary and workshop sessions that focused on enhancing planning, delivery and support of systems of care. Special attention was given to helping participants understand and implement the Wraparound Service and Intensive Care Coordination (ICC) models. State agency staff, private providers, parents, advocates, and local staff from 113 localities participated in the initial three-day conference. Participants who responded to the conference evaluation indicated found the overall experience to be useful. In a three-month follow-up survey, 84 percent of respondents indicated they had evaluated a current CSA practice based on something they had learned at the conference and 64 percent stated they had plans to change CSA practices in their locality (Office of Comprehensive Services, 2012).

In February 2013, with the support of a grant from the Substance Abuse and Mental Health Agency (SAMHSA), OCS established the Virginia

Wraparound Center of Excellence (COE) in order to bring to scale the High Fidelity Wraparound (HFW) Model of Care. Through this four-year federal grant, the OCS, the state behavioral health, social services, and medical assistance departments and the Virginia Family Network work together to implement this individualized, team-based, and care coordination process which has shown to be effective in improving outcomes for youth with severe emotional or behavioral health needs. The COE relies heavily on data-driven training and coaching to ensure adherence to the HFW model throughout the Commonwealth. In its first year of operation, COE trained 21 Community Services Boards and 14 private provider organizations.

While the establishment of COE and its initial accomplishments are laudable, it is reasonable to question why it took so long for the State to launch a concentrated effort to improve adherence to the System of Care principles, which were clearly articulated in the enabling legislation 20 years earlier. It is also noteworthy that a federal grant was required to spur momentum.

In addition to face-to-face training, OCS revamped and upgraded its website and capacity to provide on-line training. An on-line training and certification site was established to allow local caseworkers to be trained and credentialed to use the CANS assessment instrument. In FY 2012, more than 3,400 individuals were certified or recertified on this site (Office of Comprehensive Services, 2012).

The enhanced training activities have allowed participants to gain new knowledge and skills from experts in the field. These sessions have also fostered better communication between state and local staff and provided opportunities for localities to share their experiences with each other. Equally important, offering local consumers, staff, and administrators intense exposure to state-of-the-art practice along with guidance and support, has the added benefit of allowing localities to examine the appropriateness of their own organizational culture. Rather than continuing to view CSA as a state mandated imposition for which they are being forced to fulfill a set of bureaucratic requirements, some localities have begun to grapple with the question of how to adapt these models to their own communities. Increasingly, local FAPTS and CPMTs are trying to "get back to really making this a cultural thing, where you are trying to make good decisions for kids and families" (S. Clare, personal communication, November 2, 2012).

MAKING DATA RELEVANT

Scott Reiner, who was Assistant Director of OCS during that period, believes their CSA efforts to promote wraparound services as an emerging best practice is still slow to be accepted in some places:

New practices are often not fully embraced for a variety of reasons. These reasons include a natural attachment to existing practices and programs that people feel are working, a lack of solid data that might show room for improvement in outcomes, and the challenge of accessing and allocating resources to support the new approach, such as training and ongoing supervision. (S. Reiner, personal communication, April 25, 2014)

Reiner notes that "the evolving field of implementation science speaks powerfully for the need for not only one-shot training sessions, but committed leadership and regular, ongoing coaching to achieve implementation of new programs that have fidelity to the model and achieve the promised results" (S. Reiner, personal communication, April 25, 2014). In order to address these barriers, OCS and the SEC have taken several steps to advance the adoption of wraparound services. These steps include establishing a high bar or target for the use of Intensive Care Coordination (High Fidelity Wraparound) for eligible and appropriate children and families which is hoped to motivate greater acceptance under the concept of "what gets measured is what gets done." This measure is being incorporated into an emerging local CSA outcomes model which will be used to identify high performing localities. Another approach CSA is pursuing is to provide resources to assist localities through ongoing training, establishing a voluntary local wraparound coaches program, an active electronic learning community to share resources and successes, and an updated system of care self-assessment model. Reiner asserts that "together, all of these strategies are hoped to both motivate and enable local CSA programs to achieve the promise of wraparound and other system of care based approaches" (S. Reiner, personal communication, April 25, 2014).

The OCS acknowledged that CSA had not done well in capturing data on traditional outcome measures for at-risk youth, such as improvement in functioning, reduction of problematic behavior, demonstration of resilience, school performance, family stability, and involvement with the juvenile justice system. They also recognized the difficulty in developing a comprehensive outcome data base and the time and resources required to establish a system that would generate meaningful data. While they did not deny the need for such a system, the CSA leadership opted to direct their immediate attention to developing a more modest set of benchmarks that could be established more easily and have a more immediate impact.

One of the first projects they undertook was to create a performance dashboard that contained critical performance indicators derived from core System of Care principles. For each indicator, metrics were chosen to assess the degree of success/compliance, target goals were established, and performance was tracked over time for each locality as well as statewide. For example, the SEC had identified the use of Intensive Care Coordination (ICC) as a key strategy for maintaining children in their home communities rather than placing them in residential treatment facilities. One of the first measures chosen for the dashboard was the percentage of youth receiving ICC against all youth placed in residential settings. A higher percentage of youth receiving ICC compared to those placed in residential settings indicated progress toward compliance with System of Care principles. In the fourth quarter of FY 2013, the percentage of youth statewide enrolled who received ICC compared to those placed in residential treatment was 14.69, compared to 12.51 in the fourth quarter of the previous year. A target goal had not yet been established at the time this book was being written, but the increase of 2.18 percent was noted on the performance dashboard (Office of Comprehensive Services, 2014).

The Department of Social Services (DSS) also chose to participate in the performance dashboard tracking system. One of the initial measures they reported was the percentage of children who move from foster care to a permanent living arrangement. Initially DSS's target goal was set at having 86 percent of youth who leave foster care enter a permanent placement arrangement. In May 2013 they had moved 76 percent of children leaving foster care into a permanent placement, though there had been a decline of 5 percent in the number of successful placements since the previous period (Office of Comprehensive Services, 2014).

Transparency has been an important theme in the development of the performance dashboard. The dashboard data are displayed on the OCS website and are accessible to all CSA stakeholders as well as the general public. At present, only statewide data are posted. However, OCS plans to use dashboard data from localities in the future to assess performance and may consider factoring this information into the process of allocating resources. OCS also plans to expand the number of measures included on the dashboard.

In addition to the performance dashboard, CSA officials have explored the use of other indicators to add to their evolving set of empirical benchmarks. One promising measure is the CANS, the assessment instrument required to be used by all localities to assist in identifying the appropriate level of care for children enrolled in CSA. Although the CANS is not a direct measure of outcome, this utilization assessment tool can provide data on the congruence between recommended and actual levels of placement. CANS also may be used to track changes in a child's needed level of care over time. Although the level of care needed by an individual is not a true outcome measure, as many factors may influence where a child resides, these data may serve as a proxy for how well a community is performing. As a component of a comprehensive set of performance benchmarks, CANS data has the potential of providing useful information on how localities are serving individual consumers as well as how they utilize data in their system-level planning and quality improvement efforts.

APPLYING SYSTEM OF CARE PRINCIPLES
TO THE AUDIT PROCESS

The prospect of being scrutinized by another organization generally evokes considerable anxiety in those who are the target of an audit review. The fear of discovering an unexpected problem and the threat of potential punitive consequences serve as deterrents for staff and officials to view the audit experience as a learning opportunity. For most participants, the audit experience is more like visiting the dentist for a tooth extraction than attending a self-improvement workshop. Given their perception that a traditional audit process would not foster CSA's goal of having localities embrace the System of Care model, the OCS decided to design its own audit process, one that would empower localities to be active participants in identifying and addressing audit targets. By modifying their approach to monitoring programs, as well as administrative and fiscal activities of local FAPTs and CPMTs, the leadership of CSA hoped to alter perceptions of local stakeholders and encourage them to use the process to assess their own strengths and needs and develop a plan for enhancing the system's performance.

Traditionally, audits are conducted to monitor compliance with regulations, policies, procedures and guidelines, assess performance, or address specific problems. Audit recipients typically view this top-down, probing process as serving the needs of the entity conducting the audit rather than the interests of their own organization or constituents. With its emphasis on engaging and empowering families, OCS saw a clear advantage to making use of these values and principles in the new audit process. In developing its audit protocol, OCS relied heavily on System of Care principles such as focusing on strengths as well as deficiencies and involving consumers, in this case, local staff and officials, in identifying goals and developing action plans to address these aims. In fact, one of the core documents of the revised audit process that went into effect in July 2012 is entitled *Empowering Communities to Serve Youth: Self-Assessment Workbook for Locally Administered CSA Programs* (OCS, 2012a). Extensive training on the self-assessment was provided, including offering workshops on program audits at the annual CSA conference.

In the initial phase of the CSA audit process, OCS audit staff meets with members of local CSA personnel to explain the purpose and methods associated with the audit. They emphasize the importance of using this as a period of self-reflection and course adjustment, and describe the technical assistance resources of the OCS that are available, if localities choose to seek help.

At that point, the locality is provided with the self-assessment workbook that addresses seven topics related to CSA. They are:

1. Governance
2. Risk management
3. Internal control
4. Training
5. Compliance
6. Corrective action
7. Certification

Within each topic section, the workbook describes tasks that are relevant to that topic and provides worksheets that list the tasks that must be met to demonstrate compliance/effective implementation of each topic area. The worksheets also provide space for local participants to describe the activities they perform to validate or verify the assessment criteria, and request them to evaluate whether there is evidence to that the criteria have been achieved.

The local CPMT is asked to establish a process for conducting an assessment of the multiple tasks topics and tasks described in the workbook and given time to implement this process. OCS encourages localities to involve all stakeholders in this assessment process and provides advice on the types of data and other information localities may wish to consider during their assessment. Once the self-assessment has been completed, local government officials are asked to review their assessment and identify areas that are critical to the performance of CSA and would benefit from additional developmental or corrective action. Next, the local officials and OCS audit staff reconvene to discuss the findings of the assessment, review the localities self-identified priorities, and develop a plan for addressing these concerns.

The annual audit plan indicates which localities are scheduled for a self-assessment audit. If a locality is on the current audit cycle schedule, their conclusions must be shared with OCS. Cities and counties that voluntarily conduct self-assessments are not required to share their findings with OCS and are not obliged to take corrective action. During FY 2011, CSA conducted 21 onsite audits and 21 audits using the self-assessment process.

Specific examples of how the new audit process has facilitated greater acceptance and adoption of the CSA system of care model include:

• A small city in Central Virginia was relatively uncommitted to the CSA philosophy and operational approach. CPMT meetings rarely drew more than a couple of participants and many of the stakeholder groups mandated by law were not filled. The chair of the CPMT was a private provider who did not bring a broad community perspective to the position. The CSA coordinator basically was responsible for doing everything. She had a good understanding of the clinical and service issues but did not have much support from others. This city was selected as the first city to participate in the new audit process. Through their participation in the self-assessment process, the City Manager and other key leaders recognized the gaps that existed and developed a better understanding of CSA and its benefits for the city and its citizens. Following the audit, the leadership transformed the administrative structure and procedures, bringing them in line with System of Care principles. The CSA Coordinator was promoted to a position of manager and was given additional support to help her implement the system more effectively (S. Clare, personal communication, April 25, 2014).

• Arlington is a suburban county in Northern Virginia with a population of approximately 225,000. When the county's CSA leadership was presented with an invitation to conduct a self-assessment audit in coordination with the state OCS, they responded positively, viewing this as an opportunity to evaluate how well their local policies and practices complied with state policies and procedures. Approaching the self-assessment with a mind-set of full transparency, accountability, and disclosure, the CPMT established an oversight committee comprised of the Special Project Manager, CSA Fiscal Agent, and representatives from the four participating local child-serving agencies. The oversight committee utilized the state's assessment tool that focused on various components of policy and practice. The CPMT also established five "work groups" that used the state's audit tool and case reviews to conduct the assessment. Based on the self-assessment audit, Arlington developed a detailed comprehensive Corrective Action Plan (CAP), including specific policy and practice discrepancies, staff responsible for implementing corrective action, and a schedule for completion. Once approved by the CPMT, the CAP was shared with supervisors of the partner agencies. As a result of the audit, an updated CSA policy manual was developed, areas of violation were immediately reported to staff and supervisors, and an annual CSA training curriculum was established. Outcomes included training all staff of CSA partners using the new curriculum within the first three months of the new fiscal year, achieving 100 percent compliance for staff completing the CANS assessment for all children served, and presenting an Individual Family Service Plan that is aligned with the CANS findings for all children who are being reviewed by the FAPT (H. Stowe & L. Reid, personal communication, July 23, 2014).

CSA administrators readily admit that the progress made in preparing the workforce and using data to monitor and enhance performance is still in early stages of development. While some localities have made significant strides in bringing their programs in line with System of Care principles and goals, many communities continue to lag behind. The scant number of measures currently included on the performance dashboard provide limited information on the performance of local CSA systems and are, at best, proxy rather than direct measures of outcome. Secretary Hazel cautions against seeking simplistic measures of success. "There is a tendency to look for silver bullets in these issues, and unfortunately, since the Lone Ranger isn't here, we don't have a lot of silver bullets" (W. Hazel, personal communication, June 26, 2012). Hazel favors a more systematic practical approach:

> We have to grade what we want the outcome to be and the outcome can't be simple words like permanence. We have to set a target and those targets have to be at a high level, but have to resonate emotionally with people because you don't motivate change with data. Data informs on how you make the change, but you motivate the change on emotional demands. (W. Hazel, personal communication, June 26, 2012)

The SEC and OCS are actively engaged in developing a more comprehensive data system that captures information on performance and outcome measures from all of the participating agencies, including indicators such as changes in a child's score on the CANS assessment instrument, school performance, employment records, juvenile and criminal justice involvement, as well as the social and economic status of their families. The goal of this effort is to be able to track what happens to youth enrolled in CSA over an extended period of time to determine whether the system has an enduring impact on young people and their families (S. Reiner, personal communication, April 25, 2014).

These planning efforts have been spearheaded by Secretary Hazel, who urged planners to establish realistic outcomes, taking into account the baseline status of the children being served. Hazel asks, "How many kids do we have that were born healthy? How many are ready for school?" (W. Hazel, personal communication, June 26, 2012). Hazel also stresses the importance of persevering:

> Once you've established a baseline, you've got to clearly state what you want to accomplish. Define the goals and stick with what you want to accomplish . . . goals gets lost. We are going to measure how we are doing and when we are not meeting [our goals], we are going to stop and see what we're doing that's not working. (W. Hazel, personal communication, June 26, 2012)

THE PUBLIC-PRIVATE PARTNERSHIP
REACHES A CROSSROAD

One of the original goals of CSA was to establish partnerships between government entities responsible for administering the System of Care and private providers who would deliver prescribed services to children enrolled in the system. The rationale for encouraging these public-private partnerships was straightforward. Local government entities are well positioned to identify who is eligible for CSA services, to assess the needs and strengths of these youth and families, and to identify the services and supports that would be most suitable for each situation. Local government and its public child-serving agencies, however, may not be well suited to actually deliver these services and supports. Regulatory and structural constraints often limit the creativity and flexibility required to customize services to the specific situation of each child and families. Private providers, on the other hand, are accustomed to changing market conditions and are able to readily adapt their approach as required. Given the private sector's mobility and flexibility, as well as their familiarity with a business model that links payment with productivity, profit and not-for-profit service providers were considered to be ideal partners for offering timely and appropriate care to CSA clients.

The decision to rely on private providers was also consistent with Virginia's pro-business orientation. Public officials, both Democrats and Republicans, as well as the citizens of the Commonwealth, generally favored limiting the role of government in the direct provision of services. There was a general consensus that private vendors were more efficient and effective and should be employed except in limited circumstances involving public safety and welfare.

Within CSA, each locality contracts with for-profit or not-for-profit vendors to provide services identified in a child/family's individual service plan. Some types of services and facilities are regulated by the state agencies traditionally responsible for those programs. For instance, residential treatment facilities have traditionally been licensed by the Department of Behavioral Health and Disability Services, therapeutic foster care providers are licensed by the Department of Social Services, and the Department of Education is responsible for approving private day schools and other special education placements. In some instances, newer, innovative community-based interventions such as in-home services were not systematically monitored and regulated. In order to assist localities in identifying appropriate service providers, OCS revamped its web-based service directory to make it more interactive. The revised directory allows local CSA staff to identify licensed service providers for children with different needs and conditions. The OCS does not directly advise consumers or localities on which provider it should select. That decision is made on a case-by-case basis at the local level.

As localities were able to reduce reliance on congregate care and develop community-based alternatives, the number of service providers offering intensive in-home and other less restrictive services expanded rapidly. Some of the community-based services were provided by large reputable organizations with a long and proud history of caring for at-risk youth and families. Agencies such as United Methodist Family Services (UMFS) and Elk Hill Farms, Grafton, which had previously provided residential treatment, broadened their scope and began to provide less restrictive community services throughout the state. In addition, well respected in-home service providers such as Family Focus expanded the geographic area they served. At the same time, there was a proliferation of new provider organizations that were offering intensive in-home and other community-based services. Some of these organizations were small and did not have adequately trained service providers or appropriate supervision and oversight mechanisms.

Initially, these community-based providers did not attract much attention. The prevailing pro-private sector sentiment, as well as the political pressure to allow local government to manage its own operations, made state officials reluctant to intervene in the manner in which services were being provided. When speaking of CSA funding, Cindi Jones, Director of the Department of Medical Assistance (DMAS) believes that part of the problem was that local officials often do not view social services and behavioral health as priorities. She states that "The Commonwealth was just putting their wallet on the street and inviting cities and counties to come and get it. . . . some localities are very good at spending money, but it's not a good way to run a mouse trap" (C. Jones, personal communication, April 5, 2012).

During the early years of the McDonnell Administration, the number of new community service providers grew significantly, particularly those offering intensive in-home services (IIH), therapeutic day treatment (TDT), and mental health support services for youth (MHSS). This expansion of services was accompanied by a significant increase in Medicaid expenditures. The total amount of Medicaid funds expended for IIH more than doubled between 2007 and 2010, an increase of more than $100 million. Similar growth occurred in the TDT and the increase in MHSS was proportionally even larger, though the total spent in this area was much less. Expenditures for these three community mental health services in 2010 reached $366 million, more than a four-fold increase from the amount spent in 2007. Overall Medicaid expenditures for behavioral health services in 2012 were $742 million, a 16 percent increase from expenditures in 2009. Despite requiring service authorization, increasing post payment review audits and other measures to control utilization, the number of children receiving these community-based services continued to grow. In 2010 more than 37,000 accessed these services (Ford, 2012; Lawson, 2012).

At the same time these services were becoming more available, reimbursement was being reduced, leading many well-regarded providers to move their practice to services whose reimbursement rates allowed them to cover their expenses. Nominal licensing standards and the ease of obtaining authorization attracted a large number of new service providers, including for-profit providers. While access to these community-based services became easier, there were growing concerns about the quality of care that was being provided. Jean Hovey, a child mental health advocate, describes the dilemma created by this proliferation of IIH service providers:

> Families desperate for some kind of help for their child found the entrepreneurial providers walked families through the bureaucratic maze and were able to provide services; in effect, they ushered families through doors that the families did not know existed. These developments increased access but did not ensure quality service provision, resulting in a rapid increase in public dollars spent on services of uneven quality. (Hovey, 2012)

The dramatic increase in expenditures, and reports of less than adequate service quality as well as unethical or illegal practices, prompted the state to address this troubling situation. The corrective actions that ensued not only impacted the manner in which community services were delivered, but laid the groundwork for a more ambitious effort to coordinate and manage behavioral health care in Virginia utilizing a private managed care administrative entity.

The DMAS took the lead in addressing the immediate concerns and eventually developed a coordinated care model for individuals in need of behavioral health services funded through Medicaid. The first step DMAS took was to establish a screening process to determine the status and needs of all children covered by Medicaid who were seeking community-based behavioral health services in order to determine which services would be most appropriate. Beginning July 2011 all youth under the age of 21 seeking help for behavioral health challenges were required to participate in the Virginia Independent Clinical Assessment Program (VICAP) conducted by a CSB or Behavioral Health Authority (BHA) in order to access IIH, TDT, or MHSS. These assessments were mandated to occur prior to approving all new service authorizations. The assessments could only be conducted by a licensed or license-eligible mental health professional, using a standard assessment format. In addition to determining which services were appropriate for a particular child, DMAS also hoped the new screening process would facilitate coordination of services by making managed care organizations aware of these individuals and their need for other traditional mental health services. Enhanced coordination was deemed to be critical because traditional mental health services for families, such as medication and outpatient therapy were covered through the families' Medicaid-managed care program, but the non-traditional community mental health services were "carved out" of Medicaid-managed care and paid for separately through a fee-for-service system.

As stated earlier, this assessment initiative was also viewed as a precursor to the establishment of a comprehensive effort to coordinate behavioral health services for families enrolled in Medicaid (Department of Medical Assistance, 2011).

In the first year of implementation, CSBs completed more than 28,000 assessments. Based on the assessments, the most frequently recommended services were TDT, outpatient therapy, and psychiatric or medication evaluation, followed by IIT, case management, and MHSS. Less than two percent of assessments resulted in a recommendation that professional services were not needed. Assessments performed for re-authorization or continued care resulted in 2,400 recommendations that the child receive a different level of care (Ford, 2012).

VICAP appeared to have a significant impact on service utilization and cost. In the first year of implementation, there were declines in utilization of IIH (27%), TDT (16%), and MHSS (20%) by youth under the age of 21. For these three targeted services the number of recommended services was fairly comparable to the number of paid claims, suggesting that individuals actually received the services recommended for them. Expenditures for non-traditional community mental health services began to decline following implementation of VICAP, with a decrease of more than 50 percent in monthly expenditures for IIH between July 2011 and June 2012 and more than 30 percent reduction for MHSS during the same period (Ford, 2012).

How has VICAP affected Virginia's system of care and the children and families it serves? The data suggest that the assessment recommendations affirmed that most participating youth needed traditional and non-traditional mental health services and the majority were able to access recommended services. The introduction of a uniform assessment process, administered by qualified mental health professionals provided needed consistency and guidance to a fragmented and often irrational system for determining which services a child and family should receive. Based on service utilization and cost data, the state appears to have achieved its goals of broadening the scope of services an individual receives and reducing general fund expenditures, though how this decrease impacted the quality of care is not clear from available data. Equally unclear is how service outcomes were impacted, as data on changes in child or family functioning and well-being are not available.

One critical question is, how has this initiative impacted the CSA system? Earlier reference has been made to the complex relationship between the CSA and Medicaid programs. Both programs target the same population of at-risk youth and families and are administered through the same secretariat: Health and Human Resources. The OCS and DMAS, the offices responsible for the respective programs interact with each other formally, and informally, to coordinate their efforts. Yet, their culture and methods are not identical and these differences sometimes produce tensions between the two programs. Given the rapid growth in Medicaid behavioral health expenditures for youth in Virginia, DMAS's role in influencing policy and practice has become more prominent. Both programs share the common goal of providing appropriate, high-quality services to youth with mental health needs. As state-sponsored programs, CSA and DMAS are also concerned about controlling costs. While these entities endorse System of Care values, the two programs translate these principles into practice differently. At times, these differences are in conflict, generating confusion and frustration among many of CSA's stakeholders, providers, and consumers.

The manner in which services are authorized provides a good example of the discrepancies in how OCS and DMAS function. Since its inception, CSA has emphasized the importance of tailoring services to the specific needs of each child and family. Localities were encouraged to be creative and flexible in using resources to develop child-centered and family-focused service plans. One of the primary rationales for pooling the funds of the child-serving agencies was to loosen some of the bureaucratic constraints that made it difficult for localities to provide and coordinate child- and family-specific services and supports. The Medicaid program is predicated on a medical model. Services are authorized based on whether the intervention appropriately addresses the specific medical need of the individual. In the case of CSA, there must be a justification that the prescribed service is suitable for their behavioral health condition and needs. Even with CSA's efforts through its CANS assessment process to match children with an appropriate level of care and its focus on controlling expenditures, this system still encourages localities to be flexible in tailoring care to the unique situation of each child and family. The contrast between the prescriptive model of Medicaid and CSA's more elastic approach has not been fully reconciled and continues to pose challenges for families, providers, and administrators attempting to implement this innovative system of care.

Another indicator that the CSA and Medicaid programs are not fully integrated is their choice of assessment methodologies. Even though OCS has chosen the CANS as its statewide tool for assessing which level of care is most appropriate for a child's situation, DMAS did not incorporate the CANS into its VICAP, though DMAS requires a CANS assessment for authorization of specific services such as residential and Therapeutic Foster Care. While DMAS may have decided that the assessment process it selected for VICAP was best suited for the purpose of determining which community services were most appropriate for each child, the decision to not include the CANS has other ramifications. Having parallel assessment protocols operating simultaneously contributes to the fragmentation and confusion that already exists. Additionally, by not including the CANS, the state has missed another opportunity to build a uniform data base of information on how CSA enrollees are functioning that can be used to assess outcomes and guide planning.

In its effort to empower consumers, the designers of VICAP may have produced an unintended consequence. One of the foundational principles of VICAP is to give families freedom of choice in selecting which direct service provider they wish to work with. In addition to being consistent with the philosophical orientation of being family oriented/focused, the family choice policy also protects against conflict-of-interest situations, by preventing individuals or organizations involved in the assessment/service authorization process from referring families to a provider with whom they have a financial or other vested interest. Unfortunately, in attempting to fulfill the family empowerment and conflict-of-interest principles, VICAP did not take into account the complexities of ensuring that children receive appropriate care. This lapse inadvertently created a dilemma for families as well as the broader system of care.

In practice, once the independent VICAP assessor had evaluated the child and made a service recommendation, he or she gave the family a list of all of the qualified providers in their area that offered the recommended service. The family was then asked to select a provider. In cities or large suburban counties the list would contain the names of many providers— in some instances more than 100. Often parents/caregivers did not have knowledge about specific providers and therefore had no basis for deciding which provider would be most suitable for their child or family. Often it was overwhelming, and in some instances caused families to shut down and not seek out services because they did not know how to navigate the first step of choosing a provider.

Given the concerns about conflict of interest, it is understandable that state officials did not want the clinical VICAP assessors to recommend specific providers. However, a closer examination of System of Care principles might reveal a more viable solution to this dilemma. Empowering families is a noble goal, but actualizing this principle requires focused attention and effort. The VICAP process presented an excellent opportunity for furthering this goal without breaching the freedom-of-choice principle. One possible strategy would be to offer families an educational experience in which they would have an opportunity to learn what to look for when selecting an appropriate service provider. Parents/caregivers could be taught to ask questions about the qualifications and experience of the providers. Responses to questions such as whether the provider is licensed, if providers have experience with the specific issues their child is experiencing, and have they worked with families with similar cultural beliefs and backgrounds can help families decide which providers are best suited for their needs. Parents/caregivers might also want to know how the provider engages the child and family in the treatment process. Will they have a voice in determining the best course of action or are they expected to be passive recipients? By coaching parents on what to look for, the system can bolster the family's sense of empowerment while ensuring that freedom-of-choice principles and conflict-of-interest provisions are fulfilled.

The Independent Clinical Assessment experience highlights the contrast between the Medicaid and CSA approaches, and underscores the importance of the responsible agencies working together to resolve issues that may undermine their ability to effectively serve at-risk youth and their families. Each program brings unique strengths to this endeavor. Medicaid has been proactive in using data-driven strategies to match consumers with appropriate services and hold providers accountable. CSA has promoted the provision of care that is child-centered and family-focused. Progress has been made on both fronts, but the Commonwealth had not yet established an appropriate balance and integration among the multiple functions required of a fully functional system of care.

FLIRTING WITH PRIVATE MANAGED CARE . . . AGAIN

Following implementation of the VICAP initiative, the State accelerated its efforts to manage behavioral health services provided through Medicaid.

Virginia, like many other states, had struggled with issues of accountability and cost containment related to the delivery of behavioral health services. From the time he was appointed, Secretary Hazel argued that the CSBs were not adequately managing the public mental health system in their jurisdictions or statewide. This became a source of considerable contention, and when Hazel proposed that the state contract with a private company to administer Medicaid and possibly other publically funded behavioral health services, the Virginia Association of Community Services Boards (VACSB) pushed back vigorously. Hazel persisted, however, and in 2011 the General Assembly directed DMAS to implement a model of coordinated care model for individuals who needed behavioral health services that were not currently being provided through a managed care organization.

In December 2011 the DMAS issued a Request for Proposals (RFP) for a Behavioral Health Services Administrator (BHSA). Two proposals that fulfilled the basic criteria of the RFP were considered. Magellan Health Services, a large managed care company with considerable experience in managing behavioral health services submitted one of the proposals. The other bid was jointly presented by the VACSB and another large health care company with a significant track record in behavioral health management.

Magellan was selected to serve as the state's BHSA, but the other bidder challenged this decision, triggering a prolonged legal appeal. Eventually, the court ruled in favor of the state and on December 1, 2013, Magellan became Virginia's Behavioral Health Services Administrator for behavioral health services not covered under Medicaid/Financial Accounting and Management Information System (FAMIS) Managed Care. For the initial three-year contract, Magellan was contracted to act as an Administrative Services Only (ASO) model. In this capacity, Magellan was tasked with working with DMAS to "improve access to quality behavioral health services and improve the value of behavioral health services purchased by the Commonwealth" (DMAS Fact Sheet, 2013).

In his capacity as BHSA, Magellan was charged with providing comprehensive care coordination, promoting efficient utilization of resources, developing and monitoring progress toward outcomes-based quality measures. Magellan was given responsibility for the following functions:

• Managing a centralized call center to provide eligibility, benefits, referral, and appeal information;
• Recruiting providers;
• Resolving issues;
• Managing networks;
• Training;
• Utilization management;
• Service authorization;
• Claims processing and reimbursement;
• Member outreach, education, and issue resolution.

For CSA, the establishment of a BHSA posed a number of challenges. At a philosophical and conceptual level, this initiative again raised the issue of how to position CSA in relation to managed care. Fifteen years earlier, the SEC had wrestled with this question when they launched the utilization management effort. At that time, leadership had decided that a strong managed care model was not appropriate for CSA's individualized service planning, family-focused systems of care. While they acknowledged the importance of acting assertively to monitor appropriate utilization of services and contain costs, the SEC believed that the traditional managed care approach, with its medical model orientation and cookie-cutter approach to authorizing services, was not compatible with the flexible, multi-agency, ecological orientation of CSA, with its emphasis on resilience and the use of informal supports. These objections were instrumental in shaping the SEC's decision to pursue a less aggressive course. The SEC adopted a data-decision support approach to utilization management, allowing localities to retain authority for managing service delivery while providing them with assessment tools to assist FAPT and CPMT to make sound decisions.

In the time since the SEC's initial encounter with managed care, much had changed. Medicaid was a much stronger player in CSA, with Medicaid payments surpassing $25 million per year, not including Medicaid billings for outpatient behavioral health services for children and families that may have been processed outside of the CSA system. Support for contracting with private care management entities to administer public behavioral health service had also increased significantly in many states during this period. There was even more pressure on public agencies to curtail spending. Becoming a participant in the Magellan BHSA program would increase consistency in how services were authorized and paid for and, in some ways, simplify the administrative process for localities. Joining this managed care effort would also address concerns about CSA's lack of accountability as there was consensus that DMAS had more robust policies and procedures for monitoring programmatic and fiscal performance of vendors and intervened assertively when there was evidence of mismanagement or fraud.

On the other hand, there were compelling reasons to be wary of becoming part of this administrative system. Most managed care entities require pre-authorization of services. Before consumers actually receive care they must obtain approval that the service they are seeking is appropriate for their need and the provider they will be seeing is qualified to deliver these services. This process is typically managed at a central level, with an agent of the managed care organization using a checklist of symptoms to determine the appropriate level of care and selecting a provider from a directory of individuals or facilities that have met credentialing criteria established by the payer and managed care entity. While this process provides some measure of accountability, it also runs the risk of undermining the CSA principles such as empowering local communities and offering services that are family-focused, individually tailored, coordinated among all relevant child-serving agencies, and focus on strengths as well as needs.

Virginia's BHSA, with its exclusive mandate to administer behavioral health services for individuals covered under Medicaid fee-for-service plans, is driven by goals and incentives that are not necessarily compatible with the CSA approach. One risk is that Medicaid relies primarily on a medical model. Although the BHSA is responsible for administering both traditional and non-traditional behavioral health services, CSA is concerned will all domains of a child's life. Taking into account the perspectives and working collaboratively with other child-serving agencies such as education, social services, and juvenile justice may prove to be challenging. Another potential obstacle is provider eligibility. Medicaid requires participating providers to meet a stringent set of licensing and credentialing criteria. These qualifications generally serve a constructive purpose, safeguarding against participation of unqualified providers. Many localities, particularly those in rural areas, are confronted with significant shortages of available providers. Given Medicaid's provider credentialing criteria, finding providers to serve at-risk youth and families in these communities may become even more difficult, especially for non-traditional services. On the other hand, a large central administrative unit such as Magellan is in a better position to negotiate rates and access with providers for an entire region than a small community that only has a few children who need that service.

The longstanding tension between CSA and Medicaid may potentially be exacerbated by the involvement of the new BHSA. The differences in these two system's service authorization, funding, and monitoring approaches already presents challenges to localities engaged in trying to implement a comprehensive, unified service delivery system. The establishment of the BHSA adds another player to the already complex array of agencies that localities have to relate to and further compromises CSA's promise of providing a seamless, integrated system of funding and support. The BHSA, with its targeted goal of improving quality, containing costs, and enhancing accountability for Medicaid fee-for-service behavioral health services, has a specific focus. Although it has been instructed to work collaboratively with all of the CSA entities, the BHSA is not formally designated as a component of CSA and its mission and goals do not extend its responsibilities to the full CSA system and all of the youth and families it serves.

As with First Lady Anne Holton's Child Welfare Transformation Initiative, once again, the Commonwealth has embarked on a course with a noble purpose and good intentions, but has fallen short by failing to recognize the comprehensive scope of its CSA system and fully integrating its new initiative with the state's system of care for at-risk youth and families. This observation is not intended as a criticism of DMAS's effort to enhance services and provider accountability, or to disparage care management approaches. Many localities and states have successfully contracted with organizations to manage children's behavioral health services (Pires, 2010; Stroul & Friedman, 2011). In fact a program called Wraparound Milwaukee, frequently touted as the most effectively managed System of Care program for youth, employs many of the fundamental principles and strategies employed by BHSA and other care management organizations (Kamradt, Gilbertson, & Jefferson, 2008). The differences between Wraparound Milwaukee and Virginia's BHSA initiative, is that the Wisconsin-based system is a county-operated care management entity that is responsible for all expenses and services for all high-cost youth and is financed by a pool funded by all participating agencies. In addition to being a locally based operation, Wraparound Milwaukee's inclusion of all high-risk youth, as well as their blended funding approach, are more similar to the CSA than to the recently established DMAS BHSA model.

The state administrators of CSA have taken a cautious approach to the recent BHSA initiative. Early in term of Governor McDonnell, there was discussion of privatizing the management of the entire CSA operation. As the new administration became more familiar with the complexities and challenges of CSA, immediate interest in privatizing the system diminished, though future consideration of establishing a contractual arrangement cannot be ruled out. As the BHSA contract went into effect in late 2013, the leadership of CSA was content to work with DMAS and Magellan to coordinate the provision of services to at-risk youth and families and monitor how this care management approach plays out (S. Clare, personal communication, April 25, 2014).

One of the key challenges presented by the dual funding streams has been the manner in which localities manipulate the Medicaid and CSA state pool funding criteria to obtain services. Scott Reiner, Assistant Director of the OCS, points out that because Medicaid requires verification that children meet medical or clinical necessity criteria in order to obtain community-based services, such as intensive in-home care, and CSA had not historically required evidence of clinical necessity, local FAPTs tended to use CSA pool funds to pay for this service. Because the CSA pool is funded entirely by state and local contributions and the state receives approximately 50 percent in matching federal funds for services provide through Medicaid, there is a clear fiscal advantage to utilizing Medicaid, when feasible. To rectify the disparity, the SEC approved a policy that required FAPTs to provide evidence that a child meets explicit clinical necessity criteria in order to be eligible for CSA-funded community-based clinical services (S. Reiner, personal communication, April 25, 2014).

In response to local government objection to this policy, the SEC incorporated a process that allowed localities to request an exception based on mitigating circumstances. To date, no locality has requested an exception (S. Clare, personal communication, April 25, 2014).

This example illustrates the delicate balance that exists between adhering to the flexibility and local empowerment principles of CSA and the need to be fiscally and programmatically accountable. As the political and economic landscape has shifted in the direction of exerting greater control over how funds are expended and demanding greater accountability, state and local officials have grappled with how to respond to these growing pressures while maintaining the integrity of the Commonwealth's traditional governance approach and actualizing the programmatic principles and goals of the Comprehensive Services Act. The leadership of CSA viewed the Medicaid BHSA initiative as an opportunity to test this model and examine its impact as well as how these strategies might be applied to the broader CSA System of Care. Susan Clare, Executive Director of OCS, indicates that from the beginning her office made "a pretty conscious decision to do this a bit at a time and see how this works; we are watching it closely" (S. Clare, personal communication, April 25, 2014).

From a slightly more cynical perspective, the state considered another way the BHSA initiative might be useful in promoting their goal of encouraging local officials to pay more attention to and assume greater ownership of the CSA system. By letting localities know that the Medicaid BHSA is able to implement performance improvement and accountability measures statewide and discussing with local administrators the potential benefit of expanding this privatized care management approach to other systems, such as CSA, the state hopes to "help localities step up to the plate and say we need to do a better job of this or something like that [Magellan] is going to happen" (S. Clare, personal communication, April 25, 2004).

REVISITING THE ACCESS DISPARITY ISSUE

The problem of unequal access to services continued to afflict CSA. This dilemma, manifested primarily through the discrepancy in how mandated and non-mandated youth were treated, had been widely discussed, but received little corrective action during the CSAs first 20 years of operation. Toward the end of the McDonnell Administration, the SEC, once again turned its attention to this longstanding problem of disparity. Beginning with the assumption that broad, comprehensive reform was neither politically nor economically feasible, the SEC embarked on a more modest course of incremental improvement. Their goal was to identify strategies for leveling the playing field for youth in the juvenile justice system and other non-mandated children, including finding ways to justify using CSA pool funds to pay for services for these individuals and their families.

For instance, the OCS and SEC worked with the Attorney General's office to find legal justification for expanding the number of at-risk youth eligible for CSA pool funding. The policy they proposed relies on an interpretation that youth who meet the criteria for a child in need of service and are likely to come into the care of social services or juvenile justice or be placed out of their home if they do not receive appropriate community services meet the standard set for the mandated population and therefore should be eligible for state pool funding. With the assistance of the Departments of Social Services and Court Services, the OCS has been able to demonstrate, using existing data, that youth who come into the custody of social services for delinquency or truancy have worse outcomes. Recognizing that the non-mandated population has not had a strong voice at the state executive level, Clare and her colleagues from Social Services and the Supreme Court were "using that data and that voice to kind of come through the back door to say we need to be serving these kids on the front end" (S. Clare, personal communication, April 25, 2014).

Reiner adds, "We need to keep them out of foster care because that is not what they need. They need access to services, and the data show you spend a lot more money in foster care than you would with preventive services . . . and the outcomes for kids in juvenile justice with serious mental health problems are terrible as well" (S. Reiner, personal communication, April 25, 2014).

The SECs initiatives to enable more at-risk youth to access CSA services are laudable, but to date have produced limited results. On an absolute scale, these efforts seem to be proceeding slowly. However, when the SECs recent endeavor to enhance access is compared to the amount of progress made during CSAs first two decades, the leadership deserves credit for its initial pursuit of creative incremental solutions for this longstanding problem.

CSA IN THE MCDONNELL ERA: WINDOW DRESSING OR GENUINE TRANSFORMATION?

There is little doubt that CSA received considerable attention during the period from 2010–2013. Much energy was expended addressing concerns about workforce development and increasing use of standardized data and evidence-based practices (EBP) to guide planning and evaluation. For instance, in 2013 the Virginia General Assembly's Commission on Youth presented the 5th Edition of the *Collection of Evidenced-based Practices for Children and Adolescents with Mental Health and Treatment Needs* (Virginia Commission on Youth, 2013). The 300-plus page *Collection* summarized current research on those mental health EBP that were proven to be effective in treating children and adolescents and was intended to serve a broad readership.

In addition, the SEC and OCS struggled with the challenge of enhancing accountability while continuing to promote System of Care principles such as flexibility and local empowerment. State and local officials also worked to overcome obstacles such as limited engagement of families, inadequate and inappropriate provision of services, and disparity in access to care.

Were these efforts substantive and sufficient or did they fall short of what was needed to put CSA back on track to fulfill its original mission and goals? Secretary Hazel, whose penchant for colorful analogies extends beyond the field of medicine, describes the challenge of trying to transform this large, dynamic system.

It is like trying to work on an engine with the motor running, and you've got this constant turning of kids with needs through the system and you are so busy keeping up with what you are doing today that it almost seems like it would be unethical to deprive these kids of what we think is the best service while we sit back and spend significant resources on programs. You get caught up and you don't step back and say alright, I wish I knew how we are really doing. (W. Hazel, personal communication, June 26, 2012)

In assessing the progress made during Governor McDonnell's term in office, several questions need to be considered, along with the basic issue of whether there was significant improvement in performance and goal attainment for CSA during this period. A realistic assessment requires an understanding of the scope of the issues or problems that were being addressed and the extent of progress that would be feasible to expect within a governor's four-year term. It is also important to take into account the political, economic, social, and technical forces that were prevalent in this timeframe and how they facilitated or impeded efforts to strengthen the system.

Finally, one must ask whether the leadership anticipated what needed to be in place to continue progress during the next gubernatorial term. Secretary Hazel and his staff worked diligently to address issues and concerns related to CSA. They initiated new structures and functions to improve performance and more closely align CSA with its core principles. They established a suitable infrastructure and produced some initial positive results in bolstering workforce preparation, improving performance, and enhancing accountability. For most of these system enhancement endeavors, the CSA leadership laid a foundation and implemented the initial developmental phases of long-term processes that would require many years to become fully actualized. Knowing that their initiatives would be vulnerable when a new administration took office, and that the ability to control the fate of these endeavors was limited, it is still reasonable to expect outgoing officials to take steps to increase the probability of continuity.

Though limited in scope, there are several relevant data sources that can provide useful information in assessing whether there was substantive improvement in CSA performance and goal attainment. The total number of children served through CSA continued to decline during the period McDonnell served as governor. The 17 percent decrease in children receiving CSA services during that time was accompanied by a 6 percent decrease in pool fund expenditures, yielding a 12 percent decrease in the average amount of money spent for each child served. Referrals from the Department of Social Services, which accounted for nearly 60 percent of all referrals to CSA during this timeframe, declined by 14 percent from FY 2010 to FY 2013. The referrals from special education, juvenile justices, and CSBs (mental health) all dropped by slightly more than 20 percent. Only self-referrals from families increased during this period, rising by more than 120 percent, though the actual number of children referred was only 200 (Office of Comprehensive Services, 2013).

Unfortunately limited data are available to assist in explaining the specific reasons for these changes. One of the significant factors in the decrease in expenditures appears to be the decline in the use of residential care, one of the primary goals of CSA. In FY 2013, 1,888 youth were served in residential care through CSA at a total cost of $43.3 million. This represented a 16 percent decrease in the number of youth placed in residential care and a 25 percent reduction in cost in relation to FY 2011. Although the average length of stay increased by 5 percent, which may be attributable to efforts to limit residential placement to youth with more serious behavioral challenges, the average cost per child during this period declined from $23,910 to $22,911, a decrease of 4 percent. The OCS attributed the decreased reliance on residential care to the implementation of the Children's Services System Transformation and the implementation of the incentive match rate system which encouraged localities to develop community-based alternatives by increasing the amount the local government had to pay if youth were placed in residential care rather than served in the community (Office of Comprehensive Services, 2013a).

The quantitative data provided earlier in this chapter, citing how many individuals participated in System of Care training and the number of localities conducting self-assessment audits, also confirms that the CSA leadership was actively pursuing efforts to improve performance and accountability during the McDonnell Administration. Unfortunately, neither this information nor the service utilization and expenditure data address the question of whether the youth served through CSA have demonstrated improvement in how they and their families are functioning. Outcome measures, both short and long term, still do not exist and there is considerable work to be done in order to establish a viable comprehensive evaluation system of assessing the impact of CSA on the needs and strengths of youth and families in the near future.

On balance, the McDonnell Administration deserved good grades on their CSA report card. They acted assertively to address concerns about workforce preparation, family involvement, engagement of localities, and provider and local government accountability. They worked collaboratively with DMAS during the rollout of their statewide behavioral health administration initiative, working to coordinate the Medicaid and CSA-pool-funding systems, but maintaining a cautious stance in regard to fully embracing a centralized managed care approach. The OCS and SEC established the Performance Dashboard as an initial step in measuring effectiveness and began to explore ways to reduce the disparity in access between mandated and non-mandated youth. Secretary Hazel has extended use of the Performance Dashboard to all agencies within the Health and Human Resources secretariat.

Granted, many localities were still not fully engaged in the CSA System of Care approach, access to care remained inconsistent and only marginal progress had been made in establishing data bases and measurement processes for assessing the impact of CSA on youth and families and the performance of providers and localities. However, given the complexity of CSA and the relatively small amount of progress that had occurred in these areas during the previous 20 years, it would be unreasonable to expect dramatic changes in some of these areas during this four-year period. The obstacles to rapid advancement included the steep learning curve for senior officials responsible for CSA, most of whom were newly hired at the beginning of Governor McDonnell's term, and the intractability of the state's bureaucratic system. During that era, Virginia was also impacted by the overall political climate of partisan rancor and legislative inertia, which further impeded the pace of transformation. Finally, some of the improvement efforts, such as strengthening performance and outcome measurement, required sophisticated and expensive technology that was not readily accessible.

In November 2013, the citizens of Virginia elected Terry McAuliffe, a Democrat and long-time aide of President Clinton, as Governor. For the fourth time in CSA's relatively brief history the new occupant of the Executive Mansion came from a different political party than his predecessor. As the inauguration approached, the leadership of the CSA waited anxiously, uncertain of who Governor McAuliffe would appoint to key positions and what the new administration's attitude and approach to CSA would be.

The above chronology of the CSA System of Care was completed before it was possible to assess the McAuliffe administration's position on CSA. However, one of his early decisions broke precedence with the five other governors who had presided during the time CSA had been functioning, and raised a faint glimmer of hope that this administration might be interested in pursuing the same course that had been established during the past four years. In filling his cabinet posts, Governor McAuliffe reappointed Dr. Hazel as Secretary of Health and Human Resources. Shortly after taking office, McAuliffe also established a children's cabinet comprised of leaders from the Commonwealth's child-serving agencies.

Part IV

THE REVIEWS ARRIVE: MAKING SENSE OF CSA's 20-YEAR ODYSSEY

Chapter 12

Percentages, Perceptions, and Profiles

Among the most striking features of CSA are the following: (a) that the Comprehensive Services Act for At-Risk Youth and Families, with its bold and ambitious vision, was actually adopted by a state not always known as a leading force for human service reform and (b) more than 20 years after its inception, this grand exercise in collaboration has survived multiple threats to its existence and is still pursuing its original purpose of serving at-risk youth and their families in a comprehensive and responsive manner. Gail Ledford, who participated in the original planning for the Act, views CSA as "a catalyst that continues to push forward change . . . there has not been one year that the General Assembly has not dealt with CSA; it is being tweaked every year" (G. Ledford, personal communication, August 3, 2010). Chuck Kehoe, a member of the team of state agency directors that established the initial operating procedures for CSA, puts it more succinctly, "Its success can be identified by the fact that it has been in place for 20 years" (C. Kehoe, personal communication, February 10, 2012).

While CSA's perseverance and longevity are noteworthy, its extended duration is not sufficient proof that it has been successful. Views vary on how effectively the Act has achieved its initial goals and there is limited data available to allow definitive conclusions about how well the system has performed. Nonetheless, the perspectives of stakeholders and the data that have been collected during the extended span of the system's operation provide a basis for helping us understand CSA's accomplishments and deficiencies as well as the factors that contributed to these outcomes.

A BROAD BRUSH STROKE ASSESSMENT

As with most other aspects of CSA, it is not possible to condense our evaluation of the Act's performance into a clear-cut conclusion of success or failure. Throughout this book we have attempted to document how the system has not evolved linearly. Some aspects have grown rapidly, while others have improved slowly or failed to thrive. Overall, CSA has experienced phases of positive development as well as periods in which it has been stagnant or has regressed. These stages have not always proceeded as one might have expected.

Even the definition of which goals we use to assess the effectiveness of CSA is subject to debate. Do we measure success by the extent to which the system achieved the goals of the initial legislation? Or, do we benchmark its performance against more recent perceptions of the purpose of the Act, using objectives that have been articulated by policymakers as the system has evolved? There is consensus that initially CSA had two principal goals: (a) improve the manner in which at-risk youth were served through a collaborative, interagency process that individualized each service plan, empowered families to participate and provided services, whenever possible, within the child's home community, and (b) gain better control of spending, diverting funds away from out-of-community residential settings and re-investing the money saved into locally based service programs. CSA continues to view these goals as central, but the priorities have changed and the balance has shifted. Greg Peters, a long-time member of the SEC and director of a leading not-for-profit service agency, believes CSA has moved away from its original intention of establishing an integrated service system and is now more focused on funding and accountability (G. Peters, personal communication, January 10, 2012).

PARTICIPANT'S PERSPECTIVES

In assessing CSA's performance we have tried to take into account its original goals as well as adjustments that have been made over the years as conditions have changed. We will begin with some overall perceptions of individuals who have been involved with the CSA for an extended period of time, in some instances from its inception.

- Former State Senator Edward Houck in response to the question of whether CSA has achieved its goals: "Yes, I do. Because of the dramatic increase in expenditures it has received a lot of unwarranted criticism. . . . I think the bottom line about service delivery is that it was a breakthrough" (E. Houck, personal communication, March 22, 2013).

- Chuck Hall, CSB director: "I do believe CSA has achieved its original policy and fiscal intentions. CSA created the conversation about the priority of children's behavioral health in Virginia. CSA created the active dialogue among human service providers at the state and local levels of human services, court services, education, CSB, health providers, and private providers. . . . In many localities the CSA created some extraordinary financial incentives to, in many cases for the first time, looking at the possibility of not institutionalizing children. I think it was an extraordinary experiment and I think it worked" (C. Hall, personal communication, May 2013).
- Margaret Nimmo Crowe, a prominent advocate for children: "The successes are that funding has gone to provide services for children in need, and particularly those in foster care and special education have been able to benefit from services they would not have gotten from a strictly medical model. In many localities CSA has brought the child serving systems as well as the public and private systems closer together. In places where it is really working, everybody has bought into the System of Care philosophy. On the negative side, it has further categorized children [mandated and non-mandated], making it more complicated for families to figure out how and when they can get help from the system" (M. Nimmo Crowe, personal communication, August 2013).
- Mike Terkletaub, CSA Coordinator for the City of Hampton in the 1990s, in response to the question of whether CSA has achieved its goal as a comprehensive statewide response to child mental health challenges: "Hell no. . . . One of the things we missed here was the family movement; one of the keys to system reform in other states, and that has not happened here. By the way, the state never funded it" (M. Terkletaub, personal communication, March 16, 2011).
- Charlotte McNulty, former Director of the Office of Comprehensive Services (OCS): "From a theoretical perspective it [CSA] is absolutely wonderful . . . magnificent. From a practical perspective, absolutely not. It has done very little to deal with mental health problems because of the mandated versus non-mandated problem. They did not adequately fund CSA to do what it was designed to do and you cannot have that kind of ambitious activity without providing the resources to have it achieve its goals. The one thing that I have been involved with which has been a huge success is the family partnership process that we worked on closely with DSS" (C. McNulty, personal communication, August 25, 2011).
- Director of a Community Services Board in Central Virginia: "Children in Virginia don't access service based on acuity and need. You do not have anyone that is a mental health expert empowered to make mental health decisions. You've got non-clinical people making decisions about how children should be treated. . . . I see social services, who feel they have

a bigger vote because of how much money they put in, put children into residential care just because it's more convenient" (personal communication, March 2011).

- Rebecca China, former service provider, CSA Director, and currently Interim Deputy Director of Richmond Department of Social Services, who has been involved in CSA since its inception: "It is interesting but CSA and the Systems of Care has really just come into its own in the last two years here in Richmond and I am glad to see things happening. We just had our first meeting with the Exceptional Education folks today—everyone involved at FAPT, CPMT, and administration here for a meeting today and ironed out all of the issues that have been between us since I came! It only took one hour and it was amazing how easy it was to deal with issues that no one could tackle successfully before. We have come a long way!" (R. China, personal communication, September 25, 2014).
- Bill Murray, legislative director for Governors Warner and Kaine and lecturer on health policy: "It's [CSA] worked pretty well. It has had some midcourse corrections, which I think have made it work better. . . . On the whole this was a solid B-, which is pretty good for human service work" (W. Murray, personal communication, July 16, 2013).
- Susie Clare, former Director of the OCS: "What's fascinating, here we are 20 years later and nobody is saying we should have tweaked the mission and vision of the Act. Everybody agrees wholeheartedly that community-based care, family involvement, and those principles absolutely exist today . . . it is not outdated" (S. Clare, personal communication, November 2, 2012).
- Amy Atkinson, Executive Director of The Virginia Commission on Youth: "One of the things over the past few years that I think they [CSA] have done real well is to focus on getting the child served in the community and wrap services around the child rather than sending the child off to a residential treatment facility" (A. Atkinson, personal communication, May 2013).
- Greg Peters, Director of a nonprofit program at United Methodist and Family Services of Virginia: "The success of CSA is that it really pushed Virginia to the forefront to try some new things that I think clearly work. Local control is a good thing. There have been a lot of local initiatives that would not have taken place without CSA. FAPT and CPMT created inter-disciplinary teams that were happening in some communities but CSA mandated it statewide" (G. Peters, personal communication, January 10, 2012).
- William Hazel, Secretary of Health and Human Services and orthopedic surgeon, speaking of obstacles to progress: "We are fighting years of cultural institutional culture. There is sort of a hierarchical approach, delivering a service in a particular specialty as opposed to delivering a more integrated approach across specialties. We suffer the same things in

medical care where specialists tend to work independently of each other and pass people from one service to the other. Certainly some would say it's all about the money. There's actually a lot of money being spent today. The question really is what are we getting for the funding we put in? I think we probably suffer from an inability to articulate what a good outcome is" (W. Hazel, personal communication, June 26, 2012).

- A prominent child advocate: "On an individual, case-by-case basis, often it [CSA] has achieved its goal. I'll give you an example of a young woman in Henrico County who was receiving services through CSA. The family had done everything they could possibly do and then when their resources were depleted the FAPT worked with the family to get her a school placement and a comprehensive plan that worked for her. The mother told me one time that the day she had the FAPT meeting was the best day of the year for her. People don't usually look forward to school Individualized Education Plan meetings, but it was the FAPT that created a bridge and helped the young woman move into adult services, and they did a wonderful job of that" (Personal communication, November 22, 2011).

- Kim McGaughey, chief staff person for the CSA planning council and former Director of OCS: "Have we improved outcomes for kids? I think we have made a lot of progress. I think we need to expand creativity, be more flexible, and think out of the box. We need to provide training so people know how to do Systems of Care . . . and how to work across systems. It's heartbreaking when I sit down with CSB folks and they just don't have a clue what System of Care means for any of them" (K. McGaughey, personal communication, November 17, 2011).

CRUNCHING THE NUMBERS

In addition to stakeholder perspectives, quantitative data may also assist us in evaluating the effectiveness of CSA in achieving its stated purposes and goals. Unfortunately, as we have noted previously, one of the areas in which CSA has fallen short is establishing and utilizing data systems to track outcomes and other pertinent performance indicators. Other than several special reports conducted by outside groups, available longitudinal data on CSA is limited to service utilization and expenditure figures by locality, region, and across the state.

One indicator of performance is the number of children served. During 1994, the initial year of operation, slightly more than 10,000 children were served through CSA. The number of youth served increased over the next 13 years, reaching a peak of 18,400 in 2007. During the next six years the total number of youth served decreased steadily each year. In 2013, 14,400 youth were served statewide, roughly the same number served in 2004. Since 2013 the momentum has shifted. During the next two years the total number of youth served increased by nearly 7 percent, reaching 15,600 in 2015 (Office of Comprehensive Services, 2016). From one perspective, the growth in children served may be viewed as a positive indicator that localities recognized the value of the system and chose to enroll youth whose needs required a comprehensive, interagency approach. Regrettably, the absence of meaningful outcome data prevents us from assessing whether the system as a whole effectively served the children enrolled in CSA. Data from the City of Hampton presented in Chapter 7 demonstrates that CSA can provide a vehicle for localities to enhance the functioning of children and families through collaborative community-based care.

Ironically, the decrease in children served through CSA in recent years may be viewed as a positive indicator. The largest factor contributing to this reduction appears to be the drop in the number of children enrolled in foster care associated with the First Lady's child welfare Transformation Initiative. Between 2007 and 2010, the total number of foster care children served by CSA decreased from 6,115 to 3,028, a reduction of 50 percent (Office of Comprehensive Services, 2013a).

One of the driving forces leading to the establishment of CSA was the desire to reduce out-of-community placements in residential treatment facilities and enhance the ability of localities to serve children in their home communities. During the first three years of CSA's operation, 65 percent of all children served through CSA were placed in residential settings and the remaining 35 percent were cared for in non-residential programs. In 2004, 10 years after CSA's initial implementation, the percentage of youth placed in residential facilities had dropped to 41 percent (Office of Comprehensive Services, 2013). According to most recent data, the percentage of CSA youth served in residential facilities in 2015 had declined to 8 percent (Office of Comprehensive Service, 2016). The shift in paradigms from out-of-home-placements to community- and evidenced-based practices was aligning with the System of Care tenets (Farmer, Mustillo, Burns, & Holden, 2008; Farmer, Southerland, Mustillo, & Burns, 2009).

With the dramatic decrease in utilization of residential treatment facilities it is reasonable to ask what happened to the providers of residential care? Many of the smaller providers were forced to close their facilities. Others had to reduce the number of beds they operated, but were able to continue providing residential services through non-CSA funding sources such as Medicaid, which had become a significant funding source for behavioral health care in the Commonwealth, had deemed residential care as an eligible Medicaid service, though each provider was limited to operating no more than 16 residential beds. Some of the stronger programs shifted their focus to offering lower levels of care. For instance, Elk Hill Farms, a highly respected wilderness-based provider in Central Virginia reduced its residential capacity from 72 to 40 beds and developed new community-based programs (M. Farley, personal communication, June 23, 2016).

Lamentably, the schism between mandated and non-mandated children has not improved significantly since the first few years of CSA. In 1994, children eligible for mandated funding comprised nearly 90 percent of those served by CSA. By 2015, the proportion of mandated children served through CSA had risen slightly to 93 percent (Office of Comprehensive Services, 2016). To be fair, CSA administrators have become more creative as CSA has evolved. They have discovered ways to qualify some children who were non-mandated for child welfare entitlement funding from categories such as preventive and CSA parental agreement, which had been created when the custody relinquishment problem was addressed. Although this group accounted for only a small fraction of the total mandated population, it allowed some children who would not have received funding to be served through CSA (K. Reilly-Jones, personal communication, April 27, 2016). Even with this creative "fix," the core systemic problems created by the mandated/non-mandated schism still pose major impediments to access. Despite all of the criticism directed at the disparity in access to care for these two categories of children, the two-tiered system continues to deny care to many children with severe challenges and needs.

Consistent with the increase in children served through CSA, expenditures also rose. Total state pool funds grew from $104 million in 1994 to $350 million in 2015. During this same period, the per child cost increased from $10,000 to $22,000, with most of the increase occurring in the first fourteen years (Office of Comprehensive Services, 2016). Using national per capita healthcare expenditures as a crude proxy for cost of living adjustment, the rise in CSA per child cost since 2008 compares favorably to overall trends in inflation. Since 2008, the per child cost for CSA has risen by less than 5 percent, compared to an increase of 42 percent in per capita health care cost in the United States. This relatively slow cost rate of growth in per child cost may be attributed to the reduction in use of residential placements since CSA's early days of operation, as well as the foster care transformation initiative spearheaded by First Lady Anne Holton during Governor Kaine's term.

Tracking expenditures on a statewide basis is informative, but the variation in spending within the state reveals how local communities have differed in their approach to CSA. As might be expected, Northern Virginia, with its densely populated affluent suburban communities, has CSA per child costs that are 15 percent higher than the state average. In the Central Region, where the cost of living is not as high as Northern Virginia, the cost is even slightly higher. The Western region, which is largely comprised of poor rural localities, has the lowest regional cost per child served, with the average cost running 43 percent lower than the state average (Office of Comprehensive Services, 2013).

Variation within each region is even greater, with average costs per child ranging from just over $2,300 in a small rural county in the Piedmont region to more than $40,000 in a small county in the same region. Many factors might be contributing to this wide variation, including the programmatic approach of the CPMT and FAPT, the availability of services in the locality, and the severity of need of the children served, especially in smaller localities where only a few children may be enrolled. Unfortunately, it is difficult to determine from available data what accounts for these differences. However, it is interesting to note that in localities which reputedly practice in a manner consistent with the core mission and principles of CSA, costs per child are significantly lower than other localities in their region. For example, the average cost per child served in Lynchburg, in the Piedmont Region, is 19 percent lower than the average cost for the region. The average cost per child in the City of Hampton is 30 percent lower than the cost in nearby Newport News, a contiguous city with a relatively similar demographic profile. Prince William County, in Northern Virginia, which has embraced the concept of service utilization management and has established a comprehensive approach to ensuring that children receive services appropriate for their needs, has an average per child expenditure that is less than half of the average cost for their region (Office of Comprehensive Services, 2013).

Data from the Department of Social Services (DSS) are also relevant. Although First Lady Holton's Child Welfare Transformation Initiative during the Kaine Administration did not directly address the Comprehensive Services Act, more youth are referred to CSA from child welfare agencies than any other referral source. Therefore it is worth examining whether the initial success of the Transformation Initiative during the period of 2008–2010 has been sustained. The number of children in foster care has continued to fall statewide, dropping from 5,435 in 2010 to 4,404 in 2013, a decline of 19 percent. The number of children placed in group settings during the same period has been reduced by 10 percent, while there has been a 3 percent increase in the number of children exiting the foster care system into permanency and 5 percent increase in the percentage of family-based placements (McWhinney, 2014).

DSS also tracks safety and permanency indicators for youth involved in the child welfare system and compares performance to national standard. The statewide average of recurrence for children in foster care who have previously been maltreated while in care was 97.3 percent in 2013 compared with the national standard of 94.6 percent. Performance on permanency indicators was not as positive. In Virginia, 26 percent of first-time entrants into foster care were reunified with their parents or relatives within 12 months in comparison to 48 percent nationally. The track record for children who were legally available for adoption actually being adopted also did not compare favorably. Statewide, 20 percent of these young people were adopted, while the national standard was 54 percent. Virginia did compare favorably to the national average on a measure of how many children who had been in foster care for an extended period of time became eligible for adoption. Fifteen percent of children who had been in foster care 17 months or longer in Virginia became available for adoption compared to 11 percent nationally. Finally, Virginia fared comparatively well on measures of how often children in foster care were moved to other placements. Statewide, 36 percent of young persons in foster care for 24 months or longer had two or fewer placements in contrast to 42 percent nationwide (Department of Social Services, 2014).

The child welfare system has continued to make progress on identifying and treating children in care who have behavioral health challenges. DSS has established a benchmark of having a licensed professional assess 100 percent of children with an urgent health, mental health, or substance abuse within 72 hours of entry into foster care. They also plan to conduct periodic CANS assessments for all children who exhibit trauma, mental health, or substance abuse needs in order to determine which services they require and to track whether the needs and strengths change during the course of their placement (Schultze & McWhinney, 2014).

SMALL STEPS TOWARD ENHANCING ACCOUNTABILITY

The recent efforts of the Office of Comprehensive Services (OCS) to educate CSA stakeholders, measure outcomes, and improve performance have yielded modest, but promising results. The Virginia Wraparound Center of Excellence (COE)—designed to train FAPT and CPMT members, as well as staff involved with the Intensive Care Coordination program, in the core values, guiding principles, and practice procedures for the System of Care and the High Fidelity Wraparound Model of Care approaches—has trained 280 participants.

The collaborative audit process, described in the previous chapter, has encouraged localities to take ownership of how their local CSA systems are functioning. Through this empowerment initiative, communities are playing a greater role in ensuring accountability. Over the past several years, an increasing number of localities are becoming engaged in the monitoring system of care performance and addressing identified concerns through quality improvement plans and processes.

In its effort to increase transparency and assess performance, the OCS established a performance dashboard for tracking progress on key indicators. These data are included in reports produced for the SEC, Executive Branch,

General Assembly, and other audiences. The Dashboard is posted on the OCS website and is available to the general public. Initially, five measures were selected for the Performance Dashboard; three measures that directly track OCS performance and two measures specifically linked to DSS functioning. The OCS measures included: (a) the percentage of youth receiving Intensive Care Coordination (ICC) against all youth placed in residential settings, (b) the percentage of youth receiving community-based services out of all youth receiving CSA-funded services, and the (c) the average length of stay per child in residential settings (in days). The DSS measures were: (a) percentage of foster care children in family-based placements and (b) percentage of children who exit from foster care to a permanent living arrangement.

Target outcomes were established for three of the measures. DSS achieved its target goal of placing 80 percent of children in family-based settings, while falling short of achieving its stated objective for the percentage of children who exited foster-care. OCS reached its target goal for increasing the percentage of youth who received community-based services in relation to all youth who received CSA funding. Performance on one of the Dashboard measures improved between FY 2012 and FY 2013, while performance declined on two indicators and remained the same for the other two (Office of Comprehensive Services, 2014).

PROGRESS AT THE LOCAL LEVEL

Bristol City and Washington County

Rural localities face unique challenges in developing an effective system of care. Many of these communities are economically disadvantaged, making it difficult to provide matching local funds. The limited number of residents and lack of population density in rural areas pose additional problems in providing access to services. With a small population base, it is difficult to support an adequate supply of service providers, especially in specialty areas, and therefore families typically do not have ready access to appropriate services.

Located in far Southwest Virginia on the border of Tennessee, Washington County and Bristol City (distinct geopolitical entities) have wrestled with the challenge of actualizing the System of Care philosophy in a rural area and have taken affirmative steps to create a response service system for at-risk youth and families. With a combined population of slightly more than 70,000 residents, these two localities, which are served by a single Community Services Board, have combined their resources and established a single CPMT and six FAPTs to manage their CSA program.

Guided by System of Care principles of family engagement and serving children in the least restrictive setting, local leaders have worked diligently to enhance family participation and collaboration among families and child-serving agencies in planning and delivering appropriate, cost-effective services for CSA enrollees. Family participation in FAPT service planning and review sessions is encouraged by offering multiple time options for meetings and making efforts to accommodate family needs, including funding translation services. The CSA Coordinator often provides pre-FAPT meeting consultation sessions with families and referring agencies, taking a proactive role in dealing with technical and funding issues and helping families prepare for these meetings. Considerable time is devoted to clearly explaining the process and outcomes to FAPT attendees who have limited knowledge of CSA and use an informal consensus-based, decision-making model to develop and modify service plans. The FAPT regularly solicits constructive feedback from all stakeholders, including youth, in order to improve their team process. Recently, the FAPT received feedback indicating that a team member's direct style was offending parents and case managers. The CSA Program Director provided individual consultation to this member and addressed the FAPTSs directly to explain the appropriate way to address guests (A. Richmond, personal communication, July 18, 2014).

Reductions in local funds, decreased incentive to provide local match funds, and narrowing of the special education mandate have exacerbated an already challenging fiscal situation. The shortage of financial resources has been compounded by the significant growth in the number of children placed in foster care, due in large part to increases in poverty and drug-related issues. More than 60 percent of all CSA expenditures in Washington County/Bristol City are currently allocated to children in the custody of the DSS. In response to short supply of financial resources, the CPMT conducted a comprehensive review which resulted in a prioritization of service responsibilities and establishing more prescriptive criteria for preventive programs. All youth placed in residential placements are reviewed by FAPT and CPMT every 90 days, and FAPT has been given a spending threshold to ensure that extensive assessment is conducted to consider placement at a lower level of care (A. Richmond, personal communication, July 18, 2014).

Andre Richmond, the CSA Program Director describes an individual success story:

> We have a boy who originally entered foster care due to severe physical abuse of his two half-siblings (one sibling nearly died and this was the second occurrence for this sibling; the first incident occurred two years prior and resulted in brain damage and partial blindness). This boy and his siblings were also subject to extreme neglect; reported to go days without food and ate inanimate objects.

Upon entering foster care he was initially placed into a TFC program where he presented with extreme behaviors and appeared to enter dissociative states. He was placed into a residential treatment facility less than two months after coming into care where he remained for the next two years . . . his case was reviewed at least every 90 days by FAPT & CPMT during that period where we struggled to identify viable step-down options. He was placed into a TFC-to-adopt home this past January and is doing well by all accounts. (A. Richmond, personal communication, July 18, 2014)

Through their planning efforts, Washington County and the City of Bristol have been able to develop several innovative community-based programs. The CPMT worked with the CSB and local school system to establish a Specialized Education Center day program to serve several children who would have been placed in residential treatment centers at considerably greater cost. The CPMT established procedures for expedited authorization of CSA funds to pay for the CSB's new Crisis Stabilization Program, which has prevented placement in psychiatric hospitals and residential treatment facilities for several youth. The CPMT has collaborated with the CSB to develop child-specific Parent Training programs to help transition youth in their transition from out of home placement back to their family home. When the Therapeutic Foster Care operated by the CSB was reclassified, local CSA expenditures rose due to an increase in the local match rate. The CPMT was able to work with the State Office of Comprehensive Services and the CSB to negotiate a fair rate and new service descriptions and service expectations for the CSB (A. Richmond, personal communication, July 18, 2014).

The number of children and total expenditures for youth placed in congregate care settings remains higher than the leaders in Washington and Bristol would like. However, they have been able to divert several youth to community-based interventions, and have kept the number of children placed in congregate care from rising in recent years. In 2013, 68 percent of foster care youth in Bristol and 80 percent in Washington County were placed with family members (A. Richmond, personal communication, July 18, 2014). The average CSA cost per child in these two localities is approximately $11,000 per year, compared with an average per child cost of $11,500 in the Western Region and $22,000 statewide (Office of Comprehensive Services, 2014a).

Alexandria

Located on the Western bank of the Potomac River, a few miles south of Washington, D.C., this independent city with approximately 150,000 residents is relatively affluent, with an estimated median income of slightly more than $80,000, which is approximately one-third higher than the state average.

The residents of Alexandria are relatively well-educated. Sixty-four percent have a college degree and nearly one-third have obtained a graduate degree. Unemployment is relatively low. Alexandria has a diverse population. Slightly more than 50 percent of the City's residents are Caucasian, with the other half comprised of Black, Hispanic, and Asian residents, in that order. Thirty-five percent of Alexandria's residents were born in another country.

In 2008, the Alexandria Community Policy Management Team (ACPMT) held a retreat to review the performance of CSA, reaffirm its commitment to system of care principles and goals, and establish a goal of bringing and keeping all children home. According to Dawnel White, who has served as CSA Coordinator since 2005, the Alexandria CSA had the appearance and structure of a well-organized system, but was not functioning as it was intended.

> There was a lot of training and coordination with staff and award ceremonies with providers and so a sense of involvement across the community developed. At the same time that these efforts were taking place, there was still a silo structure for individual cases. Cases would be processed through the court service or through DSS or the CSB or the schools and pretty much stay there. They would gather at the FAPT if they needed funding but there wasn't a lot of collaboration across the systems unless there was a direct need of some kind that needed to be addressed. So it wasn't generating the sense of collaboration per say, they were just coming to give service reviews for funding when it wasn't available through the local agencies that the families were involved. (White, 2014)

Ron Lemley, who represented the Court Services Unit on the ACPMT at that time, describes the change that took place within that team:

> I actually was sent to serve on the ACMPT because there was too much in-house fighting and we were accused of non-collaboration and what not. I went in there with a different perspective. I was up front and said hey, listen this is why we've had these problems in the past so I want to be assured that 6 months from now I'm not feeling the same way. I think you have to be bold enough and risky enough to say things like that. Because from there came the strategic goals and the cost containment strategies. (Lemley, 2014)

The retreat coincided with the statewide child welfare transformation initiated by First Lady Anne Holton, and was partially precipitated by the large number of children from Alexandria who were placed in congregate care settings and the newly established local match incentive which required a 27 percent match for community-based services as opposed to a 62 percent match for residential services and a 54 percent match for other services provided outside of City limits (Alexandria Community Policy and Management Team, 2008). The retreat also provided an opportunity for the recently appointed CSB and Court Services directors to become oriented to Alexandria's CSA system and provide input on how to enhance collaboration and service delivery (White, 2014).

The retreat, which was attended by members of the City Council and the City Manager as well as representatives of child-serving agencies and the Northern Virginia Private Providers Association began with a broad review of CSA's purpose and functioning. The meeting evolved into a planning session in which the ACPMT "embarked upon an internal transformation to position ourselves to better meet these needs . . . through the development of family centered policy focusing our resources to prepare our staff to deliver flexible, individualized service in our community" (Alexandria Community Policy and Management Team, 2008). The group established ambitious goals of bringing all children home and preventing children from leaving the community. They also pledged to strengthen existing, and develop new, community resources to achieve their community reunification goals, and to maintain services within their existing budget allocation.

Following the retreat, the group continued to craft the service improvement and cost containment strategic plan, completing their work in November 2008. A detailed set of actions plans was developed to meet each of these goals, including establishing targets for the number of children to be returned from residential care settings and the maximum time that children shall remain in residential facilities (six months). The ACPMT identified the development of crisis stabilization and diagnostic/assessment services as well as day treatment programs as priorities. All children residing in residential facilities were to be referred for Intensive Care Coordination through Alexandria's System of Care project and mechanisms were put in place to ensure that families and children were fully engaged in the process of family permanency and connection. The group committed to developing services to help the large number of undocumented and immigrant children gain family connections, using an international approach. Additionally, the ACPMT promised to continue to strengthen its already effective diversion program to prevent Children in Need of Services (CHINS) from being placed in detention or residential facilities (Alexandria Community Policy and Management Team, 2008).

The plan initiated at the retreat also prescribed extensive training for staff on understanding the ACPMT's goals and commitment to community-based care as well as utilizing available tools for enhancing care, such as using the CANS to assess children's needs based on standards established by the State. Mechanisms were established to ensure prudent use of resources. A commitment was made to cap CSA funding at the current level, audit all Therapeutic Foster Care placements to ensure appropriate levels of placement and mandate the use of Medicaid for all eligible and available services before allowing use of CSA funds. Other fiscal management objectives were adopted to ensure that funding mechanisms which leverage greater-state and federal contributions and providers eligible for reimbursement from these sources were used whenever possible.

Review panels were established to scrutinize frequently used services that consumed a significant portion of allocated resources, such as home-based care, in order to establish caps and time limits for services that are not mandated. Training was conducted for FAPTs to assist them in developing comprehensive service programs for children in congregate care. The plan even addressed enforcing child support payment orders and collecting co-pays from families with financial resources (Alexandria Community Policy and Management Team, 2008).

Once the plan was approved, the CPMT gave it to the CSA Coordinator with instructions to work with agency staff at all levels, from directors to supervisors and case managers to establish specific target objectives and put in place structures and processes needed to implement the plan. As participating staff began to examine how the FAPTs functioned, they realized that the teams were performing both treatment planning and monitoring/management functions, such as utilization review and management. Based on this insight, they restructured the system, incorporating several teams that focused on individual families to ensure that appropriate services and supports were being provided. The new child and family-focused service improvement functions/entities include:

- Family Group Conferences;
- Family Team Meetings;
- Family Finding and Engagement;
- Youth Review Teams;
- Intensive Care Coordination; and
- Wraparound Services.

The FAPT was restructured to focus less on assessing each family and more on examining and synthesizing all of the information that has been gathered at the treatment team meetings that occur prior to the FAPT meeting. Based on this information, the FAPT makes recommendations or approves the service that has been suggested and then monitors over time the activities involved in delivering care less on discussing each case. In addition to these family-specific activities, the FAPT is also responsible for monitoring overall performance of participating agencies and providers as well as the total system to ensure that their actions are consistent with the objectives of the strategic plan (White, 2014).

In restructuring Alexandria's CSA care delivery system, the ACPMT recognized that the original design of FAPT as a venue for bringing together all agency representatives to conduct an in-depth assessment for each child was too cumbersome. They decided it would be more efficient and effective to convene smaller teams comprised of the individuals with a specific interest in the family being assessed. Thus, a child who is at risk of entering foster care may need foster care prevention services. In this situation, the caseworker from the prevention unit may invite the school social worker, a mental health professional and relevant private providers to discuss how to best serve the child. In high-risk situations, where the child's level of disruption may require resources that are not currently available in the community, the high-risk review team may be asked to intervene. This team, which consists of clinical supervisors in the child system, including a child psychologist, is well positioned to assess the child and family's needs and strengths and identify appropriate service resources for the FAPT's consideration (White, 2014).

The revised structure produced several immediate benefits. Clinical staff began to become more involved with each other as the assessment and planning became more targeted and they observed a clear focus on developing a genuine system of care. The participating child agencies also demonstrated greater commitment to the process. In part, this occurred because their staff was more engaged in dealing with issues that were directly relevant to their organization as the assessment/planning process evolved into convening smaller teams focused on the specific service needs of individual children and families. With greater appreciation of the contribution of other agencies and the positive impact of genuine collaboration, participating agencies became more engaged in improving the CSA system (White, 2014).

Ron Lemley, who was the Director of the Alexandria Court Services Unit and Chair of the ACPMT, remembers the agency mentality that existed before the transformation:

> Prior to the time period were talking about, I think this city still struggled agency-wise sitting at the table with our missions, with our individual mission and how could we meet the challenges that we faced in trying to meld so-to-speak those missions. How could we see that the kids coming from DSS, the kids from mental health and the kids from the school for that matter were all of our kids as opposed to having those silos or those barriers between our agencies, our departments? One of the ongoing challenges and quite frankly it probably still is today is trying to understand that . . . try not to put kids in boxes. Try not to categorize them so-to-speak. To see that they are our kids, our community kids and we need to make decisions collectively about those children and try to remove some of the concepts that we have in the past that would separate them. (Lemley, 2014)

How successful has Alexandria been in meeting its service performance and cost containment objectives? One of the indicators of an effective planning process is that the plan has enduring value; that the strategies and goals continue to be relevant beyond the initial period of implementation. By this standard, the ACPMT strategic plan has succeeded. Although the ACPMT has had to make minor adjustments, their commitment to the service improvement and cost containment plan has not wavered. "Every year they revisit the plan," White notes. "They do minor word changes, but if I sent you one from every year, they are not too dissimilar, even though we have had different directors on the CPMT and different people participating" (White, 2014).

The ACPMT reports improvement in several areas of CSA since 2008. Youth remain in residential care for shorter periods of time due to the increased emphasis on using these placements to asses and diagnose the child to support community-based care. The number placed in residential facilities dropped by 72 percent, from 66 in 2008 to 18 in 2014. The percentage of youth discharged from these facilities has increased from 35 percent in 2008 to 83 percent in 2014. Short-term crisis stabilization units and diagnostic facilities have allowed the City to offer stability for children in crisis without placing them in more restrictive settings while wraparound services are being developed and put in place to support the child and family (Alexandria Community Policy and Management Team, 2013—annual report).

Alexandria reduced its annual CSA expenditures by over 2.5 million dollars in five years (FY 08 to FY 14), a 22 percent reduction. By maximizing the use of Medicaid, child support payments, respite funding, procedural reviews, professional training and tightened financial procedures, they have held expenditures below the projected budget targets (Alexandria Community Policy and Management Team, 2013—Annual Report).

What are the factors that have enabled Alexandria to transform CSA into a collaborative, community-based system of care that engages and supports at-risk youth and their families? The leaders of this initiative point to several key driving forces that enabled the City to actualize the vision described in their early planning documents. Dawnel White, the CSA Coordinator, argues that "there has to be the right personalities, the right training, and the right focus to move things along" (White, 2014).

During the early stages of development, there were still members of the CPMT who were ambivalent about the system of care approach that was being proposed. Fortunately, a few members of the Team were already invested and were able to persuade the group to approve the plan. For instance, the Community Services Board (CSB) representative had already been given responsibility for the care coordination component of the system of care, and therefore had a strong stake in working to ensure that the system succeeded. When the CPMT established its goal of reviewing the children placed in congregate care, the CSB staff involved in care coordination was able to bring renewed energy and effective data-driven processes to the Case Review Team, which had previously performed this function in a relatively ineffectual manner. The CSA Coordinator, who had a strong mental health background, provided additional structure and guidance to help the Team utilize data to identify how to best care for participating children and families (White, 2014).

Leadership also provided ongoing education and training to enhance understanding and skill development. In addition to the presentations given to the CPMT during the development of its strategic plan, the City developed an essential training curriculum based on the values and principles of System of Care. The ACPMT established a primary FAPT team, committing the selected staff from the child-serving agencies to work one day a week on the team, thus effectively professionalizing the team by requiring 20 percent of the staff work requirement in participating. FAPT members were required to attend a 10-week training program as well as other periodic continuing education sessions (Corbett et. al., 2014).

Once the ACPMT had established its vision and strategic plan, the organization turned its attention to implementing its aspirations. This required a different type of leadership than was necessary to build consensus on a shared mission and goals. Now they needed the skills and diligent efforts of individual(s) who understood the practical and political aspects of translating a noble vision into an operational system. For Alexandria, that individual was Dawnel White, the CSA Coordinator. Acknowledging that the transformation required the efforts of a team comprised of staff and administrators from all participating partnerships, Ron Lemley, who served as chair of the ACPMT, credits White with being the driving force behind the comprehensive changes that took place in the City's CSA system. According to Lemley, White is a strong, assertive, highly trained, cutting-edge leader who immediately intervenes when she identifies a gap or problem. "If she felt like the schools were losing their focus, she would be out there talking to them trying to set up training, to make sure that they were understanding what we were trying to do" (Lemley, 2014). In addition to the knowledge and skill she possessed, White, who has served as CSA Coordinator since 2005, also provided continuity of leadership during this critical period of implementation.

Finally, Alexandria's relatively prosperous economic status provided an asset that many other localities lack. In most communities in Virginia, the disparity in access to care between mandated and non-mandated children is significant. Because local government in Alexandria was well funded, CSA was able to pay for most children referred for care, regardless of their agency affiliation. The ability to support non-mandated children enabled the City to significantly reduce the access disparity that existed in most localities (Lemley, 2014).

Lynchburg

Even before the CSA legislation was enacted, Lynchburg had a reputation for providing excellent care for children with behavioral health challenges and their families. When asked about what makes Lynchburg's CSA special, John Hughes, refers fondly to the caring culture of this small city located in the foothills of the Blue Ridge Mountains. "Most of the people who work in the human services and school system are just good people," Hughes, the Lynchburg CSA Coordinator says. "And even if they're transplants from somewhere else, there's an overall general desire to help people" (J. Hughes, personal communication, September 17, 2014).

Hughes uses the juvenile detention center to make his point. He explains that in addition to having a formal school and health/mental health program, the community takes added steps to ensure that they do not return to this restrictive setting. The detention center is inundated with church groups and other visitors and volunteer-sponsored programs that "provide uplift for the children and say 'okay you're in this spot, but we can make this better'." Whether they are playing chess or just talking about what is happening in their lives, staff and volunteers recognize that what these young people are lacking is "the human interaction that says I care about you" (J. Hughes, personal communication, September 17, 2014).

According to Hughes, this spirit of caring and community engagement "trickles down from the top." The leadership of Lynchburg's human services programs typically lives and volunteers in the community and serves in ways other than through their employment. These leaders set the tone for CSA, continuously reinforcing the values that the children and families being served are more than numbers, the service providers are more than vendors being paid, and jobs are not just something to be done. "These are people just like we are and I think that's the crucial component of our system here in Lynchburg" (J. Hughes, personal communication, September 17, 2014).

With this person- and community-centered orientation, it is not surprising that when the Lynchburg embarked on a campaign to improve the performance of its CSA, the leadership established two oversight committees, entitled, Coming Home and Keep Them Home. These simple, colloquial labels clearly communicate the focus of the groups, absent bureaucratic nomenclature like "utilization management" and "reduction of congregate care placement" that tend to depersonalize or obscure the real intention of the initiative. The Lynchburg CPMT established these committees to promote the development and improvement of community-based services for at-risk children and families. Local service providers were invited to meet with CPMT members from the schools, social services, juvenile justice, mental health, and the courts to learn more about children who were either currently placed in residential facilities or at risk of being removed from the community. The goal of these two committees was to raise awareness about who these children are and to engage in problem solving discussions aimed at strengthening the continuum of care in Lynchburg.

The Coming Home committee meets twice each month to review children who have been in residential care for an extended period of time and develop a viable transition plan for returning the child to the community. The Intensive Care Coordinator works with members of the child-serving agencies and local service providers to generate creative ideas for putting in place an array of community services and supports for the child and family. Hughes observes that because workers have large caseloads, children in residential facilities are often not a top priority:

> These children are placed on the back burner or are less likely to receive deep thought because they have other fires they are putting out and know that this child in the residential program is safe and sound for the next couple of months. The Coming Home committee process ensures that a couple of different eyes are taking a look at the transition plan, the child's progress and see if there's something else we may be able to do. (J. Hughes, personal communication, September 17, 2014)

These collaborative efforts to enhance understanding and strengthen the community-based continuum of care for children served through CSA in Lynchburg have yielded some positive outcomes. Noteworthy achievements produced by these meetings include:

- Average Length of stay for children residing in residential facilities in Lynchburg was 101 days in 2013 compared to 202 days statewide (Office of Comprehensive Services, 2014).
- The percentage of Lynchburg children receiving community-based services out of all youth receiving CSA services in 2013 was 37 percent compared to 28 percent in 2012 (Office of Comprehensive Services, 2014).
- Per child cost for children served through CSA in Lynchburg increased 1 percent in actual dollars from 2011 to 2014 compared to a 5 percent increase in per child costs statewide during the same period (Office of Comprehensive Services, 2014a).
- Additional community-based services are now available and local service providers are offering more pro bono or discounted services for children and families with financial challenges (J. Hughes, personal communication, September 17, 2014).

Hughes readily acknowledges that Lynchburg is not a rich community. He believes, however, that the "good southern hospitality and strong feeling of home" that pervade the Lynchburg community, compensate for the limited supply of financial resources. The strong sense of commitment that residents feel toward the city and its inhabitants and the large number of people who "want to do good things and are looking for outlets", enhance the CSA and other human service efforts as well as contribute to the revitalization of the physical infrastructure, and the art and historical culture of the city (J. Hughes, personal communication, September 17, 2014).

Metropolitan Richmond Regional Partnership

The City of Richmond, with more than 25 percent of its residents living below the poverty level, is surrounded by two larger, more affluent counties and several smaller localities. This region, with approximately one million residents, is one of the larger population centers in the Commonwealth, surpassed only by Northern Virginia and the Tidewater area in Southeast Virginia. Historically, collaboration among these localities has been hampered by several geographic and political factors. As noted earlier, Virginia is the only state in the nation in which most of its cities are independent and are not embedded within a county structure. In other states, urban cities, with their higher proportion of economic and social challenges are able to obtain support from the counties in which they are embedded due to the contribution of wealthier suburban member communities. Additionally, the actions of the City of Richmond, beginning in the mid-1950s when it participated in Massive Resistance effort opposing integration of schools in the South, created hostility and mistrust from the surrounding counties that has not fully abated. In response to pressure to desegregate the schools in the late 1960s, Richmond annexed 23 square miles of land in Chesterfield County, increasing the City's white population by more than 45,000 residents.

Despite these structural and historical impediments, five local government units (i.e., the cities of Richmond and Colonial Heights, along with Chesterfield, Henrico, and Goochland Counties), three private providers (i.e., United Methodist Family Service, Family Focus, and Elk Hill Farms), and the children's psychiatric hospital of the academic medical center (Virginia Treatment Center for Children) have embarked on an ambitious effort to improve community-based care for youth with serious behavioral challenges and their families in the Richmond metropolitan area. In addition, several other agencies were invited to participate because of their unique perspective and mission. For example, the Office of Multicultural Affairs of the City of Richmond has contributed understanding and access for recently arrived ethnic and cultural groups.

This initiative was largely triggered by a Request for Proposals (RFP) from the State Department of Behavioral Health and Developmental Services to distribute funds from a federal SAMHSA grant designed to bring systems of care to scale in Virginia. Under the leadership of United Methodist Family Services (UMFS), a highly regarded not-for-profit service provider that provides care for at-risk youth and families throughout the Commonwealth, stakeholders from all of the participating entities embarked on an intensive planning effort to design a collaborative system of care in all of the partner localities that employed evidence-based and best practice intervention approaches.

Relying on System of Care philosophy, values, and technology—as well as related research—the planning group selected several strategies for bringing the care delivery system to scale in their region. The primary components they chose for enhancing and institutionalizing care in the five partner localities were:

- Intensive Care Coordination (ICC): a strengths-based, individually focused and community-based process that facilitates the provision of innovative services to children with serious emotional needs and their families in an integrated manner across different systems.
- Parent Support Partners (PSP): Parents with experience navigating systems for their child partner alongside other parents facing similar challenges. They support the parent in developing self-sufficiency and a sense of empowerment in accessing services for their child. PSPs also act as part of the wraparound team, facilitated by the ICC worker. PSP's enhance the family's voice and choice to ensure that both the youth and the family are actively involved in developing the service plan.
- Clinical Coaching: The project manager, also a high-fidelity wraparound trainer and coach, led monthly coaching sessions focusing on clinical skills in ICC, to ensure that actual practice was consistent with the high-fidelity wraparound model. These sessions provided an opportunity for local ICC workers to learn from each other by identifying barriers and challenges, as well as sharing successes. Trained PSP's are also part of these sessions, allowing all members of the ICC workforce to practice skills specific to high fidelity wraparound and the ICC process.
- Community Engagement: Training and support were provided to participating localities, public and private agencies, and involved parents to enable them to increase the availability of professional, paraprofessional, and lay supports for families being served through the SOC partnership program. Partners were encouraged to leverage their relationships in their home communities to identify and engage informal and formal supports.

The partners also sought assistance to improve cultural and linguistic competence for serving the rapidly growing Hispanic population and other ethnic growing groups served through CSA. Finally, planners acknowledged and endorsed the notion that each locality be given discretion in how they tailored services to the unique conditions of each community, as long as they adhered to the basic principles of the model (United Methodist Family Services, 2013).

The planning group engaged in a systematic planning process that required each locality to identify and target substantial impediments to successful implement, develop specific service interventions for their locality, and establish outcome measures. A Steering Committee, comprised of representatives from the partner organizations, including parent representatives, was established to: (a) set the tone for collaboration, (b) represent stakeholders who were concerned with the outcomes of the project but were not members of the steering committee, (c) provide oversight and direction on expenditure of ancillary funds, (d) focus on sustainability of the partnership after funds from the grant were no longer available, and (e) serve as decision-makers on critical policy and implementation issues (United Methodist Family Services, 2013).

Implementation of the SOC grant began in January 2014. Therefore, only limited data are available on how the partnership project has performed. To date, six PSPs have been hired and trained. These support partners have been matched with 24 families participating in the grant's ICC program. A total of 55 families have received ICC services and 18 of these families have been discharged. Based on the Wraparound Fidelity Index (Suter & Bruns, 2009), which has been adopted as a measure of the extent to which SOC providers adhere to principles of the wraparound model by SOC programs in many states, ICC providers participating in the SOC grant had a mean fidelity score of 69 percent, which is 5 percent lower than the national average (S. Nye, personal communication, December 11, 2014).

While it is too early to assess the effectiveness of the Central Virginia SOC enhancement project, the process that led to the establishment of this unique regional partnership may be informative. Why were stakeholders able to successfully actualize this formal partnership among the key localities of the region when previous attempts to forge similar alliances had failed? According to Karen Reilly-Jones, the CSA coordinator for Chesterfield County and City of Colonial Heights: "The central key was that the state offered new funding and we had a private partner [UMFS] that enabled our five local governments to come together quickly and complete an opportunity that required a fast response [five weeks] to a grant request" (K. Reilly-Jones, personal communication, December 22, 2014).

Reilly-Jones observes that the difference between this initiative and previous attempts to encourage regional expansion of SOC was the state's creative funding and flexible programming approach that allowed the partnership to promote strategies tailored to the distinct needs of each of the five participating localities (K. Reilly-Jones, personal communication, December 22, 2014).

Additionally, the establishment of an engaged and active steering committee and the quality of the staff hired by UMFS have enabled the project to develop and establish vision, goals, outcome measures, and capacity in a timely and constructive manner. The involvement of staff from the Virginia chapter of the National Alliance on Mental Illness and a parent representative on the steering committee has provided a strong family voice. Rebecca China, Richmond CSA Coordinator noted the following of the successful collaboration: "There is a strong sense of investment by all, and there are multiple private providers and public agencies sitting at the table for one purpose, but having the flexibility to develop the services at each locality's own pace according to their size, need and financial resources" (R. China, personal communication, December 22, 2014).

RIPPLE EFFECTS

In addition to examining performance within the CSA System of Care, it is also possible to measure the impact the Act has had on other systems. Lelia Hopper, Director of the Court Improvement Program in the office of the Executive Secretary of the Virginia Supreme Court, believes that the court improvement initiative borrowed heavily from CSA's local leadership and collaborative team building approach. Hopper, who now serves on the CSA State Executive Council, credits CSA for providing guidance in assisting juvenile courts to utilize best practices to serve children who fall within their jurisdiction. She describes the extensive, ongoing training process they have employed to develop leadership and build effective teams in local communities. According to Hopper, there are currently 34 active teams, of which 85 percent are good examples of successful transformation. Citing the CSA principle of tailoring services to the unique circumstances of each locality, Hopper emphasizes the importance of allowing localities to determine their own needs and priorities:

> Obviously in Alexandria there are significant issues with immigration and Southwest Virginia has significant issues with drugs like methamphetamine and OxyContin. Everybody needs pretty much the same thing: in-home services, parenting classes. But how they go about doing it and what is successful at the local level and what grabs the passion of the people delivering those services is best determined at the local level. (L. Hopper, personal communication, May 2013)

Although First Lady Anne Holton's child welfare Transformation Initiative was not conducted within the formal structure of CSA, many of the participants had been involved in developing and implementing this system of care. Their exposure to CSA allowed them to acquire knowledge and skills about family involvement and team-based collaboration that were directly applicable to their work with the Transformation Initiative. Margaret Nimmo Crowe discusses the parallels between CSA and the work of the Transformation Initiative. "For many social service agencies there was a shift in thinking. It was much more collaborative, focused on families as partners and bringing in the natural supports and the team members for planning who actually know that child" (M. Nimmo Crowe, personal communication, August 2013).

Leah Hamaker, Senior Policy Analyst for the Virginia Commission on Youth, considers one of CSA's successes to be how it has infiltrated overall policy deliberation in the state. "Youth are not being sent away. There are more services being offered to keep them in their home." Reflecting on how CSA has affected her personally, Hamaker says, "It clicked with me . . . family is family . . . good or bad. CSA has taught me that families and children want to be with their family, and once you recognize that, even when it is not appropriate for kids to be at home, you understand and have empathy" (L. Hamaker, personal communication, May 2013).

Chapter 13

Putting CSA into Perspective

SOCIAL ECOLOGY SQUARED . . . WELL, ALMOST

Given the complexity of CSA and the multiple programmatic, organizational, and fiscal facets of the system, it would be helpful to offer a conceptual framework to guide our assessment. The purpose of this cognitive roadmap is to assist in identifying the critical performance indicators that need to be assessed. In addition, the framework can help us understand how the contextual forces (i.e., political, social, fiscal, and organizational) have influenced CSA's development and effectiveness, and provide a heuristic base for establishing recommendations on how to improve CSA as well as other comprehensive efforts to serve at-risk youth and families.

From its onset, the designers of CSA envisioned a system of care that took into account all aspects of a child's life. They believed that the best way to help at-risk youth was to address the individual child, family, neighborhood, and community factors that might mitigate problems and bolster child and family functioning and resources. Thus, CSA was designed to assess the needs and strengths of the child and family, and identify how the broader environment is currently impacting them. Once this assessment is completed, the Family Assessment Planning Team (FAPT) is responsible for developing and implementing an individualized plan to mobilize resources and supports needed to enhance the functioning and well-being of the child and family.

This multi-dimensional approach is based on a conceptual framework known as the Social Ecology Model (Bronfenbrenner, 1979). The social ecology paradigm posits that effective intervention requires not only taking into consideration the multiple domains of a child's life, but also recognizing the interdependence of these various spheres and the importance of identifying, mobilizing, and coordinating the pertinent individuals and organizations within the neighborhood, school, and community in order to assist the child and family. Once an individual plan is established, it is the responsibility of the FAPT to work collaboratively with all relevant formal and informal support sources to empower and support the child and family. This ecological framework has become increasingly popular within the fields of health and human services (Golden & Earp, 2012; Lounsbury & Mitchell, 2009). See Figure 13.1 for a pictorial representation of Bronfenbrenner's Ecological Systems Model Theory.

Since the Social Ecology Model played a critical role in the development of CSA's program structure, it makes sense to incorporate this framework in our assessment of how well this system of care fulfilled its mission and achieved its goals. The social ecology framework can be used as a template in examining how CSA has addressed each of the domains impacting the child's life as well as how effectively these efforts were integrated. To the extent data are available, we can assess how well localities and the state have addressed the multiple domains in the lives of at-risk youth and whether their

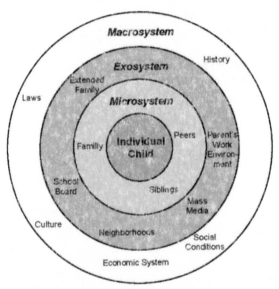

Figure 13.1 Bronfenbrenner's Ecological Systems Model Theory defines complex "layers" of environment, each having an effect on a child's development: (1) Microsystem is the layer closest to the child and contains the structures with which the child has direct contact, (2) Mesosystem provides the connection between the structures of the child's microsystem, (3) Exosystem defines the larger social system in which the child does not function directly, but which impacts children and families, and (4) Macrosystem may be considered the outermost layer in the child's environment and has a cascading influence throughout the interactions of all other layers. *Source*: Bronfenbrenner, U. (1979). *The Ecology of Human Development*. Cambridge, MA: Harvard University Press.

efforts have been coordinated. We can also look at other CSA metrics as well as those of other stakeholders to seek answers to questions such as how many youth were enrolled, where they received services, the cost of these services, as well as resulting outcomes.

Interestingly, the social ecology framework may serve another purpose in the assessment of CSA. Just as this model provides a structure for understanding the needs and strengths of at-risk youth and the roles of the multiple players in the community involved in implementing CSA, the social ecology template may also help us make sense of the macro-level structures and factors that have influenced the programmatic performance of this comprehensive system of care. By replacing the domains that directly impact individual children and families with categories representing the contextual forces that have impacted CSA, we can create a template that will allow us to consider the interplay among the large-scale forces in the environment and the programmatic components of CSA. Using this conceptual tool we can examine how the broader political, social, organizational, and financial forces have impacted the administrative infrastructure responsible for managing CSA and shaped the way localities have provided care for at-risk youth and families enrolled in CSA. Our primary hypothesis is that CSA's success or failure in achieving its goals can be accounted for, in large part, by how these contextual forces have facilitated or impeded the development and implementation of this comprehensive system of care.

THE IMPACT OF POLITICAL FORCES

To some extent, the political affiliation of the incumbent administration has affected how CSA has been able to function and attain its goals. Certainly, the fact that the Act was established during the term of Governor Wilder, a Democrat, is generally consistent with that party's social platform. During the next two administrations, under Republican leadership, CSA was initially subject to considerable scrutiny, but eventually garnered support and constructive efforts were made to enhance the system's infrastructure and improve performance. When the Democrats regained control of the Executive branch, efforts were made to revitalize the core mission and guiding principles of CSA, especially during the Kaine Administration. However, it was under the leadership of a conservative Republican, Governor McDonnell, that the spirit of reform was revived and a comprehensive, proactive campaign was launched to provide the structure and support needed to help localities understand the potential benefits of CSA and how to implement the system effectively, while also introducing measures to hold all participants accountable. The effort made during the McDonnell Administration to actualize the initial vision and mission of CSA was more vigorous and focused than any of the administrations since the initial development activity that occurred when Wilder was governor.

Beyond party affiliation, political ideology has influenced CSA's course of development. This impact has typically not occurred through imposition of dogma at either end of the political spectrum. More often, CSA has struggled with finding an appropriate balance between differing views of the role of government. For example, one of the core premises of the CSA legislation was that services would be best delivered through a strong partnership between the public and private sectors. The vast majority of direct services have been provided through contractual arrangements with profit and not-for-profit service providers. As noted in the previous chapter, many of these organizations have consistently offered excellent treatment and care, responding well to the strengths and needs of the children and their families, and working collaboratively with local FAPTs and CPMTs.

Unfortunately, as the system evolved, one of the other core goals of CSA, to ensure that service providers are held accountable, received less attention. Consistent with the prevailing political thrust to reduce government regulation and oversight, private providers were often given free rein. The lack of appropriate utilization review, regulation, and auditing allowed some providers to deliver services that were not consistent with the principles of CSA. For instance, the use of in-home service providers became popular because they offered services in the child's natural environment and were relatively inexpensive. However, the absence of licensing requirements and lack of monitoring created situations in which the quality of care being provided was suspect. In some communities, large numbers of for-profit, home-based service providers sprung up, using staff that was not adequately trained. Reports of multiple providers serving different children in the same family raised questions about the appropriateness and cost-effectiveness of these arrangements (B. Rafferty, personal communication, February 2011).

In recent years, the state has introduced oversight measures, such as licensing and auditing procedures, to correct these deficiencies. These efforts, which still do not sufficiently address all accountability concerns, may be viewed as an effort to correct the imbalance that existed between the two critical goals of CSA—promoting the use of private providers and ensuring that the performance of these providers is consistent with the aims of CSA as well as government rules and regulations. From a social ecology perspective, continual adjustment is required to ensure an appropriate balance between these core aspirations, as well as among other critical goals and functions within the system. Given the complexity of CSA and the fluid nature of the highly charged political environment, what constitutes an "appropriate balance," is subject to interpretation and is often a moving target.

The most significant political influences on CSA were not those of party affiliation or political ideology. CSA was shaped more by perspectives of various stakeholders on what are the appropriate roles of government bodies, particularly differences among officials at the local and state levels. Views on this issue varied considerably, and the dynamics between local and state entities that ensued often had considerable impact on the extent to which CSA was able to adhere to its core values and goals. The political structure of state government (i.e., one term limit for governor) also affected the continuity of CSA's implementation and its ability to remain faithful to its original mission.

The designers of CSA intended the system to be a collaborative relationship between state and local governments, with the state providing local government with the tools and resources needed to tailor the principles and goals of CSA to the unique conditions of each locality. The CSA legislation delineated clear roles for state government, emphasizing the importance of supplying technical assistance to local CPMTs and FAPTs in addition to providing funding and oversight. Yet, many localities did not trust state government and perceived that they were interested in telling local government how to conduct its business. Alan Saunders, former Director of the Office of Comprehensive Services (OCS), notes that although the new generation of local social services directors is more collaborative, "In terms of state and local politics . . . there is still a level of distrust between the two." Saunders does not believe CSA has made much progress in terms of inter-governmental relations (A. Saunders, personal communication, September 23, 2011).

Gail Ledford of Fairfax County thinks the long-standing adversarial relationship between state and local governments was exacerbated by some provisions of the CSA statute:

> There was an attempt to make one size fit all, recognizing that there needed to be more flexibility in the CSA legislation; yet the areas that needed to be more centralized were too flexible and in areas where it needed to be more centralized, it was too centralized. (G. Ledford, personal communication, August 3, 2010)

Ledford cites the mandated-non-mandated distinction as an example of how the CSA legislation undermined the intent of the system. She notes that some localities perceived the designation of a non-mandated cohort as an option and viewed this as an opportunity to save local dollars by not serving youth in this category. Other jurisdictions, such as Fairfax, worked to find a way to serve non-mandated children. According to Ledford, this is an instance in which the legislation's intention to provide localities flexibility, undermined the Act's core principle of providing appropriate services for all at-risk youth (G. Ledford, personal communication, August 3, 2010).

Former State Senator, Ed Houck, who chaired the Virginia Senate Finance Committee, describes local governments' view of the mandated service requirement more bluntly. "This is just another one of those state mandates they are ramming down our throats . . . we have to pay for it and they're telling us what to do" (E. Houck, personal communication, March 22, 2013).

One of the factors contributing to the distrust of local government has been their perceived lack of inclusion in the state budget process. Jane Kusiak, former Deputy Director for the House Appropriations Committee, observes that when the state goes through budget challenges, "people at the local level aren't feeling heard . . . they often feel they end up bearing the burden of the reduction at the state level". Kusiak does not think the state has "kept up a dialogue as rigid as it should be between the state and local." The issue of dialogue is made more complicated by the fact that "local governments aren't all of one voice and when you talk to people running CSA programs at the local level they may have a very different perspective than the actual lobbyist for local government" (J. Kusiak, personal communication, July 16, 2013).

The considerable variation in how localities have implemented CSA may, in part, be attributed to the tension and mistrust that exist between local and state governments. The CSA legislation, while intending to strike an appropriate balance between empowering localities and providing sufficient oversight, clearly has fallen short of achieving this goal. Some communities saw the benefits of this systemic approach to serving at-risk youth and families, adopted the philosophy, and developed procedures and programs to actualize the CSA vision. Other localities either misread the intention of the Act or conveniently interpreted the ambiguities of the code to serve what they perceived to be the jurisdiction's best interests.

What accounts for CSA's limited success in bringing more localities on board? Charlotte McNulty, former Director of OCS, considers Virginia's governance approach to be consistent with a state-supervised and locality-administered model. She argues that developing a grand policy or law within this model requires adequate resources and "upfront training at the local level for what your expectations are and how there are going to be consequences for not fulfilling these expectations". McNulty believes that without sufficient resources and clear expectations and what consequences will be if expectations are not met, failure is inevitable. She asserts that collaboration cannot be legislated. Instead, it is necessary to:

> Train people on what it means to collaborate and the goals and objectives of that collaboration are . . . what's best for children. If we aren't having an opportunity to really talk about our differing views of what's best for children and come to

some understanding of how we are going to mediate or negotiate around that, it is very difficult to actually do it. (C. McNulty personal communication, August 25, 2011)

Efforts to persuade local government to embrace CSA as a locally driven initiative have been hampered by the dynamic that exists between state and local governments in Virginia. The Commonwealth is a Dillon Rule state, based on a decision by Chief Justice John F. Dillon of the Iowa Supreme Court in 1868 that affirmed an earlier interpretation of the limited authority of local government. The Dillon Rule, which was twice upheld by the United States Supreme Court, limits the discretionary authority of municipalities to engage in activities without the specific sanction of the state. According to the Dillon Rule, there is an assumption that local government does not have power unless it is explicitly granted by the state. Over time, states have been given leeway to determine whether they prefer to function according to the Dillon Rule or wish to allow "home rule", which provides greater authority to local government. Thirty-nine states employ Dillon's rule for all municipalities, while eight states apply this rule for only certain municipalities. Only one state, Florida, predominantly employs home rule. Each state constitution varies in the level of power they grant to local government. Virginia has taken a relatively strict position on the Dillon Rule, requiring the state legislature to approve many bills that directly impact the functioning of local government entities (National League of Cities, 2014).

Gail Ledford, of Fairfax County, again points to the disconnect between the Commonwealth's stated intention to empower localities to administer CSA in a manner consistent with the unique circumstances of their community and the statutory restrictions on local government imposed by the Dillon Rule. Commenting on the subtle impact of this rule on local officials, Ledford says, "It really has created for a local politician an adversarial position, so there is not a grand sense of trust anyway, but along the same lines the state does not fully embrace its responsibility" (G. Ledford, personal communication, August 3, 2010). Given this discrepancy between CSA's encouragement of localities to develop locally driven systems of care and the state's constitutional limits on the authority of municipalities, it is not surprising that some localities have been reluctant to fully embrace CSA.

Within our discussion of political influences on the development of CSA, it is reasonable to conclude that the structure of state government in Virginia has had a major impact on the state's ability to engage local government bodies in adopting and effectively implementing this collaborative system of care. Mounting and sustaining a comprehensive training and technical assistance campaign to support such an ambitious undertaking requires a shared value system and a strong commitment from stakeholders and leaders at all levels. Discussions with staff of the OCS and members of the State Executive Committee (SEC) indicate that there has been a desire to provide assistance and support to localities throughout the more than 20 years that CSA has been in place. On the other hand, recognition of the importance of providing this help as well as holding localities accountable has not always been prevalent among senior leadership in the Commonwealth.

Margaret Nimmo Crowe, Executive Director of Voices for Virginia's "Children, believes: 'The turnover in administration is always a roadblock because you always have to educate a new group of people and I think it's also hindered by the fact that it's led by the Secretary of Health and Human Resources . . . that means there will always be fairly weak representation from schools and public safety'" (M. Nimmo Crowe, personal communication, August 2013).

A local behavioral health administrator from Central Virginia notes that "Virginia is extremely fragmented . . . it [CSA] gets a little energy and then we change governors and just when we are really making strides we start all over again" (personal communication, March 2011). A prominent advocate for children, offers an even more cynical perspective about the discontinuity that occurs when a new administration takes office, "There's the change and then there's also the distrust . . . if the last administration liked it, then we might not like it or we can't like it and support it" (personal communication, November 22, 2011).

The administrative level just beneath the Governor is the Secretariat. In Virginia, there are 12 Secretaries who are responsible for administering state agencies and developing and recommending policies in their areas of responsibility. As noted earlier, CSA has since its inception fallen within the domain of the Secretary of Health and Human Resources. The Departments of Social Services, Behavioral Health, and Health report directly to the Secretary of Health and Human Services. The two other departments that have significant responsibility for children, Education and Juvenile Justice, report to the Secretaries of Education and Public Safety, respectively. Although the three secretaries have, on occasion, worked cooperatively on CSA issues, the divided reporting structure has made it difficult to ensure seamless collaboration among the state's child-serving agencies. The absence of a fully cohesive structure at the state level has impeded coordination and integration at the local level. Governor Terry McAuliffe, elected in 2013, has made efforts to strengthen collaboration among the three secretaries who deal with children's issues, but it is too early to evaluate the effectiveness of this initiative.

Even within the Health and Human Resource Secretariat, collaboration has fallen short of the vision embodied in the CSA legislation. In recent years, there has been increased recognition that CSA needs to pay greater attention to the mental health needs of the youth served by this system. The shortage of child psychiatrists and absence of accessible diagnostic and therapeutic services has been well documented (Office of Comprehensive Services, 2013b). Yet, the Department of Behavioral Health and Developmental Services (DBHDS), the state agency responsible for mental health, continues to play a peripheral role within CSA. According to Chuck Hall, Executive Director of the Hampton-Newport News Community Services Board (CSB), there is not much in the Commissioner's job description that refers to community-based care, except to develop a performance contract with CSBs and there is no indication that the department should develop and promote a children's behavioral health system except for a referenced to the Commissioner sitting on various state committees. Hall laments the state and local behavioral health agencies lack of investment in CSA. "So, it was not a surprise to anyone in the CSB system when the CSA started that our department contributed nothing. CSBs contributed nothing" (C. Hall, personal communication, May 2013).

Advocates have suggested that the fragmented structure of CSA has impeded progress at state and local levels. It is reasonable to assume that with a governance/administrative structure that is less encumbered by the layers of bureaucracy in state government, CSA would be in a stronger position to champion and support an effective, collaborative system of care for children and families. Margaret Nimmo Crowe of Voices for Virginia's Children would like to see the next governor "establish some sort of children's cabinet" to strengthen representation from education and public safety, enhance continuity from one gubernatorial administration to the next, and provide an appropriate balance between ensuring accountability without limiting access to service for children (M. Nimmo Crowe, personal communication, August 2013).

What is the significance of these structural limitations and deficits? How was the effectiveness of CSA impacted by the discontinuity between gubernatorial administrations, the varying degree of commitment from the highest level of state government, and the absence of a more empowered administrative/governance structure in which all sectors of the child-serving system were equally represented?

The simple answer is that CSA is a complex, large-scale system of care whose success is dependent on all of the participants understanding and buying into its underlying philosophy, goals, and guiding principles, and receiving the assistance and support needed to successfully implement this collaborative approach. In addition to needing hard resources, such as funds to provide care and assessment tools and data to track outcomes and enhance accountability, all stakeholders, including families, providers, and CSA personnel need training, technical assistance, and ongoing support to successfully navigate and implement the CSA system. Providing this wide and diverse array of resources and supports requires sustained commitment and support from participants at all levels, but it is especially important that senior officials at the highest level continue to understand the importance of supplying this needed assistance. The hindrances in the political structure described above made it more difficult to maintain the commitment and will be needed to deliver the comprehensive array of information, tools and support required to actualize the CSA vision.

The ongoing issue of mistrust between localities and the state provides a good example of how the political forces described above impeded progress. Using the social ecology paradigm overlay presented earlier in this chapter, it is possible to see the interdependence between the system responsible for providing care for at-risk youth and their families and the administrative superstructure charged with developing and supporting the local systems of care. Localities in which CSA has been effectively implemented generally engage in a process of exploration that allows them to understand and embrace CSA's collaborative approach, develop the processes and procedures needed to execute the system, and monitor and revise their practices as needed. In localities, where mistrust is high and the established service structure is entrenched, additional assistance may be needed to help local leaders understand the benefits of CSA and make a commitment to make it work in their community.

If senior state officials do not share the belief that CSA is a productive and efficient system and are unwilling to commit to provide the infrastructure required to overcome local resistance and make available the tools that allow localities to plan and manage intelligently, the probability of local acceptance and genuine participation is significantly diminished. The absence of sufficient knowledge and support not only impedes local officials from developing the understanding and skills needed to effectively develop and administer their local system. This lack of capacity also allows some of the stakeholders who feel threatened by CSA's collaborative approach to prevail.

One of the strongest barriers to converting to a system of care model is the gravitational forces of bureaucracy that are triggered when faced with the threat of change. At one level, staff in a bureaucratic environment derive some comfort from the stable and predictable nature of their work. There are few surprises, in contrast with the more fluid nature of a collaborative system designed to tailor services to the specific needs of those they are serving. At another level, the rewards and sanctions in a bureaucratic system are generally associated with avoiding mistakes rather than achieving excellence. Agency directors may receive praise for cooperating with other departments. However, in the politically charged milieu of state government, the fallout for an error or omission within one's own agency typically has a greater impact than the benefit that may accrue from any kudos associated with fostering interagency cooperation.

An even more compelling impetus for preserving the status quo is the sense of power some agency personnel experience within the confines of their own organization. By definition, engaging in a collaborative enterprise, such as CSA, requires participants to relinquish a significant degree of autonomy and control. Individuals accustomed to having greater control over decisions may be reluctant to give up this authority in favor of a group-oriented decision-making process. Surrendering power is more difficult when resources which the agency formerly controlled are combined with others and placed in a shared account, such as the State Pool.

The combination of structural shortcomings within state government and the reluctance of agency personnel at the state and local levels to relinquish their autonomous authority and vested interests, proved to be formidable barriers to overcoming localities' mistrust of the state's intentions, and provide the infrastructure supports and resources needed to effectively implement the CSA system of care. Although some localities were able to rise to the task, going into its third decade of operation, CSA was a long way from being able to claim uniform acceptance and actualization across the Commonwealth.

ECONOMIC INFLUENCES ON CSA

The two economic forces that had the most powerful effects on CSA occurred at the time of its inception. The role of the State Department of Planning and Budget (DPB) in dealing with the issue of placing large numbers of at-risk youth in residential treatment facilities was critical in launching and garnering support for the large-scale reform in children's services that became CSA. Bill Murray, commenting on how the CSA was enacted during the tail-end of the last era of almost unified Democratic control of the State, likens the tradition of reform in Virginia to the mandarin tradition of policy and program innovation being managed, for the most part, by apolitical professionals. In contrast to the current lack of political consensus, health and human service reforms in the Commonwealth, including CSA, were driven by the executive branch of government through a series of budget initiatives. At that time, the Secretary of Finance, DPB staff and the legislative budget staff were "by tradition, career professionals who were nonpartisan and operated in that fashion" (W. Murray, personal communication, July 16, 2013).

According to Murray, this group of fiscal administrators recognized the economic and programmatic benefits of the CSA system of care, and worked collaboratively to shepherd the bill through the legislative process. Without this impetus from the budget staff, it is unlikely that CSA would have been enacted. In today's highly charged political environment, it is doubtful that this kind of beneficial fusion of financial and service delivery goals would survive the partisan rancor reaction that most reform initiatives elicit.

The other critical financial factor that had a substantial impact on the course of CSA's development was the decision to create two classes of eligibility: mandated and non-mandated. Early in the planning process, federal agencies responsible for administering foster care and special education informed state officials that the request for a waiver that would allow blending of federal funds with other child service funds would only be granted if Virginia guaranteed that all children authorized to obtain these federal entitlements would continue to receive all services for which they were eligible. Since these funding sources comprised a large portion of the funding for at-risk youth, it is understandable that state officials agreed to these terms. However, the impact of this two-tiered system has had profound negative impact on the provision of services to youth in need of care who do not meet the criteria for mandated eligibility. This dichotomy has created serious problems for localities trying to adhere to the core principles of the Act and has undermined confidence in CSA. The Commonwealth's failure to correct this grave inequity in the twenty-plus years since the enactment of CSA continues to impede the ability of the Act to actualize its original vision, and must be regarded as one of, if not the most significant, shortcomings of the system.

In addition to these early influences, other economic factors have affected the development and performance of CSA. From the perspective of the social ecology paradigm, some of these factors have enhanced the system's capacity to be responsive to the needs of at-risk youth and their families, while other economic forces have hindered CSA's efforts to provide comprehensive, coordinated individually tailored care. The introduction of Medicaid funding in the late 1990s, had both a positive and negative impact on CSA. Although the availability of this federal funding source increased the availability of resources, the manner in which Medicaid authorized and paid for services has also created complications for FAPTs and service providers.

Becky China, a local CSA administrator, is frustrated by how Medicaid has altered how decisions are made to provide services. She references changes to the code which directs localities to use Medicaid funding before other sources due to the comparatively high federal share it offers:

> The language is that you have to seek Medicaid funding first. If Medicaid denies that child, CSA has to follow the policies of all [participating] agencies. So if the child does not qualify for Medicaid, the provider comes to you [CSA] to pay and we say we can't do it because the child doesn't meet the Medicaid criteria, so we're going to have to negotiate a lower rate or step the child down to a lower level of care. (R. China, personal communication, July 23, 2012)

In some instances, China observes, the child may have been in that treatment setting for some time and the program is appropriate for the child. She believes that Medicaid has changed the focus of CSA decision-making from focusing on what is best for the child to being driven primarily by money and politics.

In addition, from shifting the orientation of CSA away from a social needs model to a prescriptive medical model, some proponents of CSA point out that Medicaid has also had a negative impact on the availability of service providers. Charlotte McNulty explains that since localities are required to use CSA as their funding source of last resort, "Providers say we are not going to take Medicaid because they don't pay enough and we can't do what you want us to do within Medicaid" (C. McNulty, personal communication, August 25, 2011). Because Medicaid does not pay for some of the family-based services promoted by CSA, communities have had to use more intensive, more costly services that may not be as suitable for children and families. Susie Clare, former director of the OCS, laments that the absence of appropriate funding has created a regrettable situation for localities: "We have forced our communities into a position where the only services they are offering to kids that are more intensive, and not the family-based training . . . things that are more welfare-based, child safety, family building, family strengthening type of services" (S. Clare, personal communication, November 2, 2012).

Medicaid has also created a fiscal disincentive for localities to use CSA pool funds to pay for services. Since responsibility for funding Medicaid resides primarily with the federal and state governments, cities and counties do not pay a share of the cost of many of the services offered by this entitlement program. Therefore local government entities have a fiscal incentive to use Medicaid rather than the CSA state pool or other sources that require localities to assume part of the cost.

Chuck Hall, the CSB Director for Hampton/Newport News, considers the Medicaid issue to be a critical "crack in the armor" for CSA since almost all children from low-income families have Medicaid, so "wherever possible we augment CSA dollars with Medicaid". Hall contends that Medicaid does not see itself as a partner in children's public policy, even though they are the largest funder of behavioral health services. He asserts that "without recognizing the importance of the role of the Department of Medical Assistance Services (DMAS) in CSA, we could see the whole thing fall apart." Hall rejects claims that too much is spent on Medicaid, and argues that cutting Medicaid spending without addressing the more fundamental public policy of how to integrate Medicaid into the CSA system will be "bracing ourselves for a train wreck . . . a very good public policy at CSA could easily be dismantled without any elected officials even knowing that they are doing this" (C. Hall, personal communication, May 2013).

Confusion about the use of Medicaid may stem, in part, from misunderstanding of the purpose of this program. Funds from this federal program are specifically designated to pay for behavioral health services for children with mental health needs. On occasion, localities have attempted to use Medicaid funds to support children with non-mental health needs. For example, requesting Medicaid to pay for a child to stay in a residential treatment facility for 'child-welfare' rather than 'behavioral health" reasons (S. Clare, personal communication, April 1, 2015).

Although the manner in which Medicaid has functioned in relation to CSA has been problematic, there have been examples of financial policies that have been aligned with CSA's system of care principles and have furthered service goals of the Act. The policy enacted during the Kaine administration to reduce the local share of expenditures for providing community-based services led to increased utilization of less restrictive services and lowered CSA's total and per child costs (Office of Comprehensive Services, 2014a).

At the community level, some localities have been resourceful in establishing fiscal incentives to encourage providers to offer services that are in the best interests of the child. Pat Harris, President of Family Focus, an intensive in-home service provider who sits on the Henrico County FAPT, describes how FAPT responded when they discovered that the majority of money they were spending for therapeutic foster care was going to the agency providing the service rather than the child. "They [Henrico FAPT] decided to offer a stipend to families who were willing to take special needs foster care instead of just regular foster care kids and they launched a campaign to increase their foster families, and train them, and provide supervision" (P. Harris, personal communication, September 26, 2011). Through this effort Henrico was able to triple the number of foster families willing to take children with special needs while also doing a better job of keeping siblings together.

In addition to successfully employing the redirection of funds to improve services, the Henrico campaign also illustrates how a locality is able to employ the community-oriented principles of CSA to improve care. Harris reports that Henrico established a task force to address foster care concerns. They mobilized people from all sectors of the community, including police, fire fighters, Kiwanis, the Lions Club, and multiple agencies, including private providers. "It was an excellent community effort," Harris notes. "They have been real successful and have been able to serve a lot of children that hadn't been served before, and are proud of what they have done." (P. Harris, personal communication, September 26, 2011).

The larger economic climate has also affected CSA's course of development, though it is difficult to pinpoint the precise relationship between these macro forces and Virginia's system of care. The economic recession of 2008 spawned a downward cycle that left many families with fewer resources.

Given the established relationship between financial and emotional stress, it is reasonable to assume that the economic crisis has had a destructive effect on many vulnerable children and families. Increased unemployment and the accompanying economic insecurity, as well as the stress associated with coping with scarce resources, created hardship and instability for many families. There is evidence that family economic insecurity is associated with increased behavioral health problems in children (Dooley & Catalano, 1980; Gutman, McLoyd, & Tokoyawa, 2005; Tobey, Mcauliff, & Rocha, 2013). The number of children living below the poverty level in Virginia increased from 247,000 in 2007 to 278,000 in 2012, an increase of 13 percent (Annie E. Casey Foundation, 2014). Although data are not available to confirm the supposition that higher rate of poverty has placed a greater demand on CSA, it seems likely that the life circumstances of families seeking assistance for their children has intensified the acuity of their needs.

SOCIAL AND CULTURAL FORCES WRIT LARGE . . . AND SMALL

A number of broad societal changes have occurred since the enactment of CSA. The rapid acceleration of digital technology, changes in population demography, and the growth of income inequality have significantly changed the American landscape. The uninterrupted military involvement in Afghanistan and Iraq has directly affected a large number of families in this country as well. These trends have clearly had an impact on CSA.

Information Technology

For the purpose of this assessment, discussion will be limited to a few key social forces. The information technology revolution has reduced the impediments of geographic distance and made it easier for the collaborating partners of CSA, including consumers, to communicate with each other in a timely manner. The internet has provided ready access to information on behavioral health matters, including diagnosis, care and treatment options, and service providers. With a few strokes on the keyboard, consumers, providers, and policy makers can find data on the efficacy of various therapeutic approaches, though there are few controls on the reliability and validity of these studies.

Along with other health and human service programs, CSA has incorporated modern information technology into its operations. On the whole, however, CSA has lagged behind other systems in utilizing these techniques to further program and administrative goals. The lack of accountability and outcome data bases cited earlier is one example of limited progress.

While several localities have made limited use of telemedicine and other electronic communication to provide consultation in rural areas that have scarce behavioral health resources, these strategies have not been systemically incorporated into practice within CSA. At the individual child level, the use of computers and hand-held electronic devices has been shown to enhance communication with children with developmental disabilities who are more comfortable with these modes than face-to-face verbal interaction. Mobile phones have also been used to facilitate efforts to assist at-risk youth to make good choices and avoid engaging in risky behavior (Mason, Ola, Zaharakis, & Zhang, 2015).

Demographic Changes

The demographic profile of children served by CSA has changed in several ways. In 1998, the first year CSA reported demographic data, 49 percent of children served through CSA were Caucasian, while 46 percent were African-American. In 2013, the percentage of Caucasians being served had increased to 57 percent and African-American children in CSA had decreased to 34 percent. Asians represented less than 1 percent of children enrolled in CSA at both points in time. During the same period, the number of Hispanics enrolled in CSA more than doubled, though the proportion of Hispanic youth remained small, increasing from 2.5 percent in 1998 to 5.2 percent in 2013. The ratio of males to females did not change during this time, with boys comprising approximately 60 percent of all children served through CSA (Office of Comprehensive Services, 2014a).

There has been a dramatic increase in the prevalence of children with autism during the past four decades, with estimates ranging from a twenty- to thirty-fold rise. Since the Centers for Disease Control and Prevention began tracking the number of children on the autism spectrum in 2002, the prevalence rate has climbed from 1 in every 150 to 1 in every 68 among children aged 8 years. (Baio, 2014). Although CSA has not collected system-wide historical data on diagnoses, anecdotal evidence strongly suggests that the number of children on the autism spectrum served through CSA has increased significantly. Children with autism typically do not respond well to conventional behavioral health treatment modalities. Therefore planners and providers have had to adapt their service approaches to meet the needs of this population.

Changes in Service Delivery Patterns

General trends in the provision of health care have impacted CSA, though their effect has been less substantive than what has been experienced by other

service delivery systems. The ongoing discussion on balancing local prerogative in providing services with the pressure to enhance accountability has
generated several strategies. The utilization management initiative in the late
1990s provided an external review agency and decision support framework to
assist localities in planning and delivering services. This strategy represented
a compromise between allowing full autonomy and imposing a centralized
decision-making structure on localities. Unfortunately, until recently CSA
has not consistently followed through on supporting or encouraging compliance with this locally driven accountability process.

Medicaid has been more aggressive in pursuing measures to hold providers and localities accountable. The introduction of the Virginia Independent
Clinical Assessment Program (VICAP) was initiated in response to problems
with community-based service vendors not providing appropriate care for
children receiving Medicaid-funded services. VICAP was designed to help
decision-makers choose services appropriate for the needs of at-risk youth.
Although VICAP is not a CSA-initiated effort, the significant role of Medicaid funding ensures that the assessment program will have an impact on CSA.
Regrettably, a narrow interpretation of Medicaid rules prohibiting targeted
referral to specific providers has limited the system's ability to actually facilitate linking children to appropriate services. The results of the assessment
are provided directly to the consumer's family without further instruction on
what to look for in selecting an appropriate provider. By educating families
about what criteria they should look for in selecting a suitable provider and
helping them understand questions they should ask of potential caregivers,
it would be possible to facilitate prudent decision-making without violating
regulations prohibiting direct referral.

In 2013, the state awarded a contract with Magellan Health Services
to serve as the Behavioral Health Services Administrator (BHSA) for the
individuals enrolled in Virginia's Medicaid and Family Access to Medical
Insurance Security (FAMIS), the Commonwealth's program for uninsured
children. The addition of an administrative services organization may bolster
efforts to strengthen accountability. This decision, which drew strong criticism from CSBs, moves the Commonwealth closer to a top-down managed
care approach, which CSA has resisted. While it is too early to know how
the BHSA will impact CSA, the state appears to be moving in the direction
of imposing more uniformity and centralized control within the behavioral
health system. It will be interesting to observe how this thrust will interact
with CSA's goal of promoting locally driven provision of services.

During Governor McDonnell's term, the Secretary of Health and Human
Services and CSA's Office of Comprehensive Services have accelerated
efforts to promote evidence-based decision-making and accountability.
The addition of the Performance Dashboard, comparing state and local

performances on key CSA indicators is a step in the right direction. The proposed initiative to develop a comprehensive cross-agency data base will potentially address longstanding concerns about the lack of outcome and accountability data. This undertaking is clearly consistent with the goal of providing tools that will assist stakeholders in monitoring and improving performance. That it has taken more than 20 years to mount a substantive campaign to address concerns about the absence of outcome measurement and accountability data, is disappointing. The failure of CSA and the state leadership to produce and sustain a comprehensive set of pertinent measures and a functional data base has been a major impediment to advancing the service goals of this large-scale reform effort.

In recent years, the growing recognition of the interdependence of physical and behavioral health has spawned initiatives to integrate these fields. Examples include training primary care physicians to identify and manage behavioral health problems in their patients, co-locating physical and behavioral health services, and incorporating behavioral health strategies into prevention and treatment programs for persons with chronic medical issues (Felker et al., 2006). This coordination of services may increase efficiency and effectiveness. Integrating behavioral health with physical health also enhances the perceived authenticity and importance of mental health challenges in relation to other physical health disorders.

To date, the movement to integrate behavioral and physical health care has not significantly permeated practice within CSA. Further consideration of how to more effectively blend the physical and behavioral health services would be consistent with CSA's holistic mission and might improve outcome. Better integration in CSA could also facilitate identification of at-risk youth and raise awareness among families, practitioners, and policy makers of the importance of appropriately addressing behavioral health concerns.

Stigma

Despite substantial effort to change prejudicial attitudes and behavior, there is still considerable stigma attached to behavioral health and mental illness. The federally enacted Paul Wellstone and Pete Domenici Mental Health Parity and Addiction Equity Act of 2008 forbids group health plans and health insurance issuers that offer mental health and substance abuse benefits from treating these benefits less favorably than other medical or surgical benefits. The Americans for Disabilities Act and other civil rights legislation prohibit discrimination against persons with mental illness. The National Alliance on Mental Illness and other advocacy groups have mounted substantial campaigns to educate the public about mental illness and to reduce stigma. Still, individuals with mental health problems experience prejudice and discrimination, and the recent spate of mass shootings has not made it difficult to foster better understanding among the general population.

Stigma has impacted CSA in several ways. Lack of understanding of the biological and environmental factors that predispose and precipitate behavioral problems has, in some instances contributed to some policy maker's reluctance to support requests to enhance CSA. Misunderstanding has also led to confusion and lack of cohesiveness among child-serving partner agencies. Outdated perceptions that the aberrant behavior of at-risk youth is motivated primarily by willful or manipulative intentions, has led some staff to favor punitive approaches.

Many families still feel embarrassment or shame if their child exhibits problem behaviors. Misinformed views about the causes of their loved ones' behaviors can lead them to feel unduly responsible for their child's condition. These families may worry about how they will be perceived and are reluctant to seek help for their child.

Finally, prejudice and a "not in my back yard" mentality in some communities may make it difficult for localities to pursue CSA's goals of providing services in an appropriate, least restrictive setting in the community. Even with current laws and zoning regulations designed to protect individuals with disabilities, it can be difficult to establish community-based care settings that promote normalized functioning while also ensuring public safety.

It would be unreasonable to hold CSA responsible for reducing stigma. This is a broad societal issue that requires a multi-faceted, long-term response. Given the impact of prejudicial attitudes and behavior, however, it is incumbent upon policy makers and other CSA stakeholders to acknowledge the impact of stigma on the system, and contribute, in some fashion, to the public education campaign to increase understanding and acceptance of the challenges faced by at-risk youth and their families.

Culture Counts

Philosophical and spiritual beliefs as well as ethnic and religious customs may impact a system of care in many ways. For the purpose of this assessment, the focus will be confined to a specific aspect of culture: the way in which personal and organizational beliefs and values have influenced the evolution and performance of CSA.

In examining the factors that have affected the development of CSA, it soon becomes apparent that all of the multiple political, economic, social, and technical forces described earlier have, to some extent, facilitated or impeded the Act from achieving its goals. While all of these elements have had some impact, it appears that none has been more influential than the organizational culture at the state and local levels, and the manner in which these entities have responded to the core principles and goals of CSA. Simply stated, the success of localities, as well the system as a whole, has been largely dependent upon whether the stakeholders involved have integrated the basic values underpinning CSA into their work ethic.

In Hampton, CSA evolved from a strong tradition of collaboration and teamwork established by Robert O'Neil, the visionary administrator who served as the city manager between 1984 and 1997. The Hampton CSA leadership, including judges and agency director, as well as line staff, came together for the primary purpose of figuring out how to best serve at-risk children and their families. They did not allow vested interests, agency politics, or bureaucratic boundaries to interfere with their collaborative efforts to develop innovate, individually tailored, family-focused, and community-based service strategies. From the highest levels of local government to the direct care staff, individuals involved with Hampton's system of care embraced the values of working together creatively and collaboratively to keep children in their home communities and incorporated these beliefs and principles in their day-to-day work. Even when the players changed, the work ethic remained the same.

Other localities, including Alexandria, Lynchburg, Fairfax, Chesterfield, Portsmouth, and Bristol-Washington, have been able to develop and sustain systems of care that have been faithful to the vision and mission of the CSA legislation. Their success is due, in large part, to the commitment of upper echelon leadership to the core values and principles of CSA and their ability to distill this commitment to all parties involved in this collaborative enterprise. The leaders in these communities have understood the importance of providing comprehensive, coordinated services to children and families, and have been able to move beyond the traditional intra- and inter-organizational barriers to forge a common purpose and work cooperatively on behalf of the at-risk children and families in their communities. Their willingness to refrain from traditional silo-like behavior should not be viewed as an indication that CSA stakeholders in these localities are conflict avoidant. On the contrary, when there are disagreements within the local systems, or between local and state governments, participants confront the issues directly and work proactively to achieve resolution that is in the best interest of children and the community.

In some other localities, the principal stakeholders have not been able to overcome their suspicions and fears and move beyond the long-standing conflicts between local and state government, as well as the organizational barriers that have existed within their own communities. In these cities and counties, convenience and habit have trumped cooperation and creativity. These communities have not been able to fully actualize CSA and have fallen short of serving the best interests of at-risk youth and their families.

This assessment of how organizational culture may impede development of effective local systems of care should not be taken as an endorsement of the position that localities bear sole responsibility for these shortcomings. In many instances the action or inaction of state government has contributed significantly to localities being ill prepared to appropriately implement their systems of care. The same causal link is applicable to the influence of the federal government on the ability of state and local governments to develop seamless systems of care.

The Commonwealth's failure to provide sufficient infrastructure to localities has been a major stumbling block. Moving from traditional agency-based functioning to a more flexible interagency approach represented a significant change in how many localities operated. The original blueprint for CSA prescribed a number of supports that would be needed to assist localities in working through this transformation. The requisite supports included providing training to all stakeholders to enable them to understand the core principles and goals and acquire the knowledge and skills needed to successfully develop, implement, and sustain a collaborative interagency system of care. The CSA legislation also authorized the provision of administrative support and fiscal incentives to assist in establishing comprehensive local systems, ongoing technical assistance, and guidance and information needed to plan, implement, and monitor operations at the local level. CSA also promised to provide tools to aid localities to manage utilization, measure outcomes, and improve performance.

Many of these functions have been addressed by senior state officials, the General Assembly, and the OCS over the course of CSA's existence. However, the attention has not been consistent, fluctuating from one administration to the next. And rarely has the effort to provide appropriate support been sufficiently comprehensive or intense to achieve its intended goal. With the exception of Howard Cullum and Bill Hazel, Secretaries of Health and Human Resources during the Wilder and McDonnell administrations, and to some extent, Marilyn Tavenner, who oversaw the First Lady's child welfare transformation initiate when Tim Kaine was governor, officials at the highest levels of the Executive Branch have not given the attention required to significantly enable CSA to achieve its original goals. This is not to imply that other administrations did not appreciate the benefits of CSA or support efforts to improve the system. Productive leadership was provided by senior officials during these periods. Unfortunately, given competing priorities that demanded much of their time, these leaders were not able to provide the considerable attention and resources required to overcome the historically rooted tensions between local and state government and the entrenched practices at all levels. Without such an extraordinary effort, it would be unrealistic to expect that the participating agencies and organizations would be able to successfully transform themselves from a silo-oriented to a collaborative-oriented culture.

Stated more simply, changing organizational culture requires steadfast commitment and a willingness to provide the resources and other supports needed by the participants to effectively engage in this transformation. CSA leaders in several localities embraced the system's vision and managed to develop effective programs without the full complement of supports promised by the CSA legislation. Other communities became stalled because they did not have sufficient comprehension or resources. Whether all of these localities would have adopted more favorable attitudes toward CSA and established more robust systems if they had more assistance from the state is difficult to determine. However, it is reasonable to infer that given more support, many localities would now have more evolved systems of care. Commenting on the State's inadequate leadership role in relation to CSA, Charlotte McNulty believes that the state did not initiate "the upfront effort to help localities really understand what was being expected of them" (C. McNulty, personal communication, August, 25, 2011). She acknowledges that such an effort would have been very ambitious, but also believes it may have resulted in a better understanding.

In addition to initiating training and dialogue, McNulty also contends that the state failed to hold localities accountable for their lack of compliance with the legislation's provision for cooperation. Surmising how a local leader might view this situation, McNulty says, "Just because the law says we should be collaborative doesn't mean I am going to behave collaboratively, especially because there are no consequences for not collaborating" (C. McNulty, personal communication, August 25, 2011).

Among the forces that have influenced the development and performance of CSA, organizational or system culture may seem less palpable than political, economic, or technical factors. The core beliefs and values of the Act and how these are transmitted and promoted have, however, been crucial in establishing and sustaining effective systems of care. When leaders understand the importance of education and infrastructure, and are willing to commit the effort and resources to assure that these supports are available, success is more likely. Over the course of its history, CSA has had varying degrees of commitment. Notable achievements at local and state levels have generally been associated with strong commitment by leadership to ensure that stakeholders understand and practice collaboration and have the tools needed to manage the system in line with the principles and goals of the Act.

Conversely, in areas where CSA has fallen short, there has inevitably been an absence of proactive, sustained leadership. At the state level, these deficits have impeded effective collaboration among state entities as well as led to lapses in attention to key policy issues. The continuing absence of synchrony between Medicaid and CSA and the inability to address the access problems created by the two-tiered mandated/non-mandated eligibility criteria are examples of state-level leadership deficiencies. Insufficient leadership has also contributed to shortcomings at the local level. As noted earlier, the state's inadequate effort to help localities understand and manage CSA has fueled local resistance and impeded CPMTs and FAPTs from functioning optimally. Susie Clare observes that many localities still view the CSA legislation as just another state-imposed mandate:

> So instead of understanding it as a philosophy and coming to it from that perspective, it becomes, how do you comply with that? [The state] needs to return to getting people to understand that CSA was developed to give flexibility to communities . . . to make good decisions for kids and families. (S. Clare, personal communication, November 2, 2012)

THE ELUSIVE QUEST FOR BALANCE

The social ecology paradigm, cited earlier, may be useful in understanding CSA's successes as well as its shortcomings. The extent to which CSA achieved its programmatic goals can be traced, to a large extent to the influence of the macro-level political, economic, technological, and social culture forces. When the proactive efforts of leadership, or in some cases, serendipity, aligned with the core principles and goals of the Act, good things happened. For example, the CSA legislation most likely would not have been enacted if the DPB had not seen the potential financial benefits of replacing residential treatment with less costly community-based alternatives. Likewise, the proposed law's provision that most decision-making would take place at the local level, with localities working in partnership with private service providers, swayed some conservative legislators to support the Act. And when Governor Kaine and Attorney General McDonnell put aside party affiliation in the interest of addressing a serious threat to family integrity, they were able to find an effective alternative to the long-standing practice of requiring parents to relinquish custody in order to obtain intensive mental health treatment for their child.

On the other hand, when the Commonwealth's economy was weak, more attention was given to cutting the cost of the program rather than promoting the service goals of the system. The reluctance of some communities to embrace and promote the system of care principles has its roots in the long-standing local-state struggle over where the locus of control should reside. This inability to overcome this resistance in certain localities was not helped by the lack of continuity of leadership at the state level caused by the one-term limit for the governor.

Organizational and system culture have clearly affected performance within CSA. For instance, the tradition of team-based, inter-departmental cooperation provided a firm foundation for establishing Hampton's collaborative system. In other localities, entrenched bureaucratic boundaries and a tradition of agency autonomy made it difficult to implement system of care principles.

At a less linear level, the interplay of the domains of the service system and broader spheres of influence can be best understood using a core principle of ecology. A basic tenet of all ecological systems is that functioning is optimal when all domains or subsystems are interacting in a harmonious, balanced manner. This principle applies to individual biological systems in which the organs of the body are supporting each other, and is also pertinent to complex ecosystems where smaller subsystems are nested within each other and each subsystem is an integrated whole as well as part of a larger system. According to the ecological paradigm, systems require continual flow of energy to enable them to grow and adapt. Recognizing that change in nature as well as in communities is continuous, ecological theorists acknowledge the importance of maintaining a dynamic balance within systems and understand that these systems will be contend with cycles within individual systems as well as in the broader environment (Center for Ecoliteracy, 2014).

How are these ecological principles applicable to our assessment of CSA? We have already noted how the individual domains of the larger ecosystem have influenced performance at the service delivery/program level. We may also use these general ecological principals to gain a better understanding of the complex interplay among the multiple macro and micro components of the system of care and the impact of these interactions on CSA's ability to achieve its goals. For example, ecological theory emphasizes the importance of maintaining a dynamic balance among components of a system. The architects of CSA recognized that they were working in a complex social and political environment. They understood that passage, and ultimately the success of the Act, was dependent on being responsive to a diverse set of values and interests, and attempted to take these into account as they crafted the legislation.

One of the core issues planners had to deal with was the tension between support for privatization and interest in ensuring accountability. The designers of CSA were sensitive to the increasing concern about the role of government, particularly pertaining to the direct provision of services. In response, they incorporated language calling for a strong private-public partnership, with for-profit and not-for-profit organizations contracting with local government entities to provide services to children and families who are eligible. Recognizing that considerable public funding would be allocated to pay for services for this vulnerable population, planners also included goals and mechanisms for holding these private providers accountable.

AS CSA evolved, more attention was given to identifying and recruiting service providers. This was often challenging, particularly in rural areas where there was a scarcity of community-based providers. Some effort was made to introduce accountability measures, such as the utilization management initiative in the late 1990s and Medicaid's attempts to establish checks and balances to ensure that children are receiving appropriate services. However, it was not until the in-home service providers proliferated at the end of the first decade of this century that policy makers took serious notice of the imbalance between the emphasis on privatization and need for holding service providers accountable. Even when the mandatory assessment process was introduced for families seeking community-based services paid for by Medicaid (i.e., VICAP), the effort fell short of assuring that families would receive services that were most appropriate for their situation. Recent efforts to strengthen the CSA audit process, increase training of FAPT and CPMT members, and develop uniform assessment and outcome measures are consistent with CSA's oversight goals. However, considerable work still must be done to put in place a comprehensive and responsive accountability system.

At one level, it can be argued that the imbalance between promotion of privatization and local control versus efforts to hold service providers and localities accountable represents a clear failure on the part of state officials and CSA administrators. Reflecting on how CSA has managed this issue, Greg Peters says, "One of my frustrations is we need to have local control, but I think there are times when the state needs to move in and set some bottom lines and say you've got to have outcomes" (G. Peters, personal communication, January 10, 2012).

Viewing the issue of balance through an ecological lens, however, provides a different perspective. From an ecological viewpoint, maintaining a dynamic balance among components is a complex process. The broad prevailing forces in an environment may create an imbalance that is resistant to change. Often, realignment of the polar ends of a continuum, such as a free versus regulated market takes a long time, as predominant political and social do not usually shift quickly. The current anti-government sentiment has been evolving for several decades and it is difficult to predict when it will begin to swing in the other direction.

Within CSA, what constitutes an appropriate balance among these seemingly conflicting orientations? Should there be an equal emphasis on encouraging free market activity and providing oversight to ensure accountability? Or do we need to acknowledge the significant role political and social forces play in shaping the interplay of domains within a specific ecosystem, such as CSA, and ascertain what constitutes equilibrium in relation to how these forces facilitate or constrain the influence of free market or regulatory approaches? Using this latter perspective, a dynamic balance would be defined within the context of the limitations created by broader forces. Rather than assuming that equilibrium is achieved when privatization and regulation are given equal weight, we might conclude that given public sentiment against government involvement, the current system can be considered to be in dynamic balance when free market influences are stronger than the thrust for accountability.

The purpose of offering an ecological perspective that takes into account broader environmental influences is not to rationalize CSA's inadequacies in achieving its service and accountability goals. There is no doubt that CSA has fallen short of its original purpose in several ways. More could have and should be done to strengthen the system's ability to respond to the dire circumstances of at-risk youth and their families.

Rather than justifying the status quo, this framework is intended to heighten awareness of the limitations imposed by prevailing sociopolitical trends and to encourage those interested in transforming or improving service systems to factor these influences into their strategic efforts to affect change. For example, knowing prevailing attitudes toward misuse of public funds and understanding how accountability measures can be enacted in a manner consistent with the collaborative goals of CSA may assist policy makers and administrators in moving the oversight functions closer to the center of the free market-regulatory continuum. Consider the recent efforts of the OCS to work collaboratively with localities to establish targets and conduct quality improvement reviews and remediation activities. By tailoring their approach to the popular themes of locally driven enterprise and efficacious use of public resources, the OCS has been able to strengthen their audit and oversight functions without incurring the wrath of conservative politicians and constituents.

Understanding the cyclical nature of ecosystems also helps strategists gain perspective on the fluid nature of large systems such as CSA. Systems do not remain inert. Domains of a system that are currently considered to be dynamically balanced may move to a state of disequilibrium if the alignment of broader forces changes. When prevailing attitudes toward privatization and local control may have swung too far to the right, public sentiment will inevitably swing in the opposite direction. When that happens, the balance between free market and oversight government will become realigned, making it easier to introduce accountability measures.

The changes that have occurred in the governance structure of CSA since its inception provide another example of how contextual factors may impact equilibrium and functioning of the system. The enabling legislation of CSA established the State Executive Council (SEC) to oversee the administration of the Act. The initial composition of the SEC called for six members, including the heads of the major child-serving agency and a parent representative to be appointed by the Governor. The individuals who crafted this legislation recognized that successful implementation of such a complex would require significant effort and collaboration by the leaders of these agencies. The role of the parent representative was to ensure that a family perspective was included in their deliberations. Thus, the SEC was conceptualized as a small working group that would work cooperatively to develop and implement a collaborative system driven by the core system of care values and principles. The SEC was expected to assess the limitations and problems of the previous arrangement, in which agencies functioned in a largely autonomous manner, and work through the specific details of what would be required to develop and sustain a cooperative interagency approach that was responsive to the needs and strengths of at-risk youth and their families.

As CSA evolved over the next 20 years, legislative amendments added representatives from the General assembly, other relevant state agencies, local government, and private service providers to the SEC. Currently, there are 19 members on the SEC and the Council operates quite differently from the way the designers of CSA envisioned. Rather than functioning as a small deliberative body of state leaders engaged in figuring out how their agencies can work more collaboratively to serve children, the Council is now a very large body of members with diverse areas of primary interest and responsibility. The structure of the Council is more formal and the members typically view themselves as representing the vested interests of their constituent groups rather than as a cohesive board committed to advancing a common agenda for effectively serving children and families through CSA (S. Clare, personal communication, April 25, 2014).

From one perspective, the change in composition and role of the SEC is understandable. As CSA has evolved, the need for greater inclusion and attention to administrative detail has led to a growth in membership and more structured decision-making. On the other hand, these shifts have resulted in a loss of the collaborative spirit that characterized early efforts and has weakened the ability of the Council to influence the attitudes and behavior of key players in relation to CSA. The lack of buy-in from many localities still represents a serious impediment and the presence of five representatives from localities on the SEC does not seem to have improved local understanding or acceptance of the CSA systems of care approach.

Interestingly, one of the key issues Governor McAuliffe is addressing at the beginning of his term in 2014 is how to enhance the integration and responsiveness of services for all children. He has established a Children's Cabinet (Meola, 2014). The Cabinet will be comprised of high-level state officials responsible for matters related to children and families empowered to improve care for children and families. The new oversight body, which is reminiscent of the original SEC, may be viewed as an attempt to move away from a fragmented policy structure toward a more interactive and collaborative approach to shaping policy in line with core system of care principles and goals. From an ecological perspective, the structure that has evolved within the SEC in response to a perceived need to increase stakeholder representation and attention to administrative procedures is no longer responsive to the current demands of the system. The movement toward more substantive engagement at the policy level can be viewed as an effort to correct the current imbalance and establish a more harmonious equilibrium among the multiple forces that currently affect how children are served.

Taken to an extreme, the complexity and relativity of the ecological paradigm can be mind-numbing. The constructs and principles are, however, useful in understanding and assessing comprehensive reform efforts, such as CSA. The designers of the system set a high bar in relation to what they expected CSA to achieve. Fortunately, they took into account some of the critical contextual forces that needed to be addressed to ensure successful implementation of the service goals. From the beginning, proponents of CSA have acknowledged the importance of being fiscally prudent, respecting the differences among localities and giving local government latitude in designing and implementing systems responsive to the unique circumstances of their communities.

Planners have also recognized the need for uniformity, consistency, and oversight in order to ensure that at-risk youth throughout the Commonwealth were treated equitably. The enabling legislation stressed the importance of establishing collaborative partnerships among stakeholders from local and state government as well as the private sector and consumers served by CSA. Through these partnerships they hoped to address all of the goals of the Act while maintaining an appropriate balance among all domains and sectors of the system.

To date, the CSA endeavor has produced mixed results. As the preceding assessment has shown, there have been some successes as well as areas in which CSA has fallen short of its aspirations. In situations where CSA has remained faithful to its original mission and made progress toward achieving its goals, at both state and local levels, effective leadership has almost always been a key ingredient. These leaders typically share the common attributes of being passionate about pursuing the best interests of children and families and having a good understanding of the intricate relationship among the macro and micro factors that impact care for young people as well as the strategies required to align these forces with system of care objectives. Successful leaders have also been willing to step outside of their comfort zone, leave the security of their insulated organization or group, and engage collaboratively and creatively with individuals with different perspective and backgrounds to enhance policy and practice for at-risk youth and their families.

The future of CSA is largely dependent on the ability of the system to identify, educate, and mobilize individuals with these leadership attributes. Although it sounds overly simplistic, the extent to which the Act's original vision will be actualized hinges on whether CSA can replicate the spirit, savvy, and determination of the original planners. These early champions forged a broad coalition of diverse stakeholders who worked collaboratively to establish the CSA system of care. Through education and persuasion they were able to garner sufficient support for the passage of this visionary legislation.

Many of the successes that have followed, at both the local and state level, can be attributed to efforts by small groups of individuals who possess the same willingness to work cooperatively to identify creative approaches to serving at-risk youth and their families. The innovative local systems of care established in Alexandria, Bristol-Washington, Fairfax, Hampton, Lynchburg, Portsmouth and other localities have their roots in community leaders with the personal convictions and political will to replace traditional service arrangements with more flexible interagency team approaches. The same spirit and resolve fueled the First Lady's Child Welfare Transformation Initiative, and the unlikely alliance of Democratic Governor Kaine and Republican Attorney General McDonnell who worked together to remove the onerous requirement for parents to relinquish custody of their children to obtain services. And in recent years, Secretary Hazel and the staff of the OCS have displayed the same sense of shared purpose and commitment to promoting system of care principles as they have guided the effort to establish accountability measures and other infrastructure components needed to revitalize CSA and enable localities to align their systems of goals with the principles and goals promulgated in the original legislation.

Returning to the ecological paradigm described earlier in this chapter, it is clear that further progress for CSA will require appropriate attention to the forces that directly impact the well-being of children and families as well as the impact of broader contextual forces on the system of care. Future success will require strong leaders at the state and local level, who understand the interdependence of these micro and macro forces and are willing to act creatively and assertively to ensure that all of the infrastructure elements, including training, technical assistance, data systems, and financial incentives, are in place. If state officials can mobilize these resources and convince their local counterparts that the Commonwealth is serious about supporting efforts to develop locally driven systems of care, CSA will continue to evolve in a positive direction. Without appropriate leadership at all levels, progress will be curtailed and recent gains may even recede.

Part V

OTHER VENUES, AND LESSONS FOR THOSE WHO ASPIRE TO ACT ON THE STAGE OF REFORM

Chapter 14

Systems of Care in Other States

Much has happened since the concept of a comprehensive system of care for at-risk youth was first put forward in the mid-1980s. National consumer-based organizations along with their state and local chapters, such as the Federation of Families for Children's Mental Health and the National Alliance on Mental Illness (NAMI), have advocated in support of this service model. Federal agencies, particularly the Substance Abuse and Mental Health Administration (SAMHSA), and the Administration for Children and Families of the U.S. Department of Health and Human Services have allocated resources to improve the quality and availability of wraparound and system of care services through training, technical assistance, program development and evaluation, and other infrastructure development. Two important federal systems of care initiatives have been The Child and Adolescent Service System Program (CASSP), which began in 1983, and the Comprehensive Community Health Services for Children and their Families Program, created by Congress in 1992. Both of these programs have provided significant funding and technical assistance to assist states and localities develop comprehensive systems of care for youth with mental health challenges and their families.

Federal agencies have also engaged in partnerships with organizations interested in improving services for children and families, including the child divisions of the National Association of State Mental Health Program Directors and the American Public Health Association to promote the use of evidence-based practice in collaborative efforts to serve children and their families.

In addition, Foundations such as Annie E. Casey, Lucile Packard, and Robert Wood Johnson have provided grants and other financial support to foster improved care for children with behavioral health challenges. State- and University-sponsored training and technical assistance efforts supported system of care development. Since the mid-1980s, the Louis de la Parte Florida Mental Health Institute, located at the University of South Florida and the Portland State University Research and Training Center for Family Support have conducted high-impact training and research to improve the quality of life for young people with mental health challenges and their families. The National Technical Assistance Center for Children's Mental Health, located at the Georgetown University Child Development Center, has also been a significant contributor to promoting best practice for serving at-risk youth and families. Working in partnership with families and leaders from a variety of sectors concerned about the well-being of children and families, funded by SAMHSA, the Annie E. Casey Foundation and other public and private entities, the Georgetown-based Center has become the pre-eminent source of information, training, technical assistance for individuals, organizations, and government entities interested in developing and improving systems of care for children and families.

In this chapter, we will review some of the exemplary and promising efforts to develop and sustain systems of care efforts at the state and local levels. Given the apparent absence of a fully actualized comprehensive state-wide system for at-risk youth and families, we will highlight state-level efforts that have excelled in select domains and describe local programs where there appear to be examples of more fully developed approaches. Whenever applicable, the achievements of CSA will be assessed in relation to these highly evolved systems.

A SYSTEM IS THE SUM OF ITS PARTS . . . AND MORE

It should be apparent by now that a key defining characteristic of effective systems of care is complexity. Providing comprehensive services in a collaborative and responsive fashion requires involvement of multiple stakeholders working together cooperatively to identify needs and strengths, and developed innovative strategies consistent with the core values and principles of wraparound and systems of care approaches. These efforts must also take into account the multiple social, cultural, fiscal, and political contextual forces that impact care.

When assessing the performance of systems of care, it is therefore necessary to examine how each effort addresses the multiple factors and components required to meet the stated goals of that system. Effective efforts typically take into account the various facets of the system and manage these intricacies in a systematic and coordinated manner. As we observed earlier, when CSA neglected significant aspects of the Act's core principles, such as accountability and infrastructure development, performance suffered.

Sheila Pires, generally considered to be the leading national authority on practical operational mechanics and strategies for developing systems of care for children and families, has provided a useful framework and guidelines to assist individuals and groups interested in the practical challenges of establishing and sustaining effective systems of care. In her workbook, *Building Systems of Care: A Primer* (Pires, 2010), Pires offers a template of the requisite functions of a system of care along with the structural components needed to support these functions. She also describes the core elements of an effective system-building process. Finally, Pires identifies and defines how to establish the three non-negotiable elements of successful system-building processes and structures: (a) strong family partnerships, (b) youth partnerships, and (c) cultural and linguistic competence.

Although space limitations do not allow us to do justice to the detailed guidance Pires provides, the following list of core elements provides a useful framework for assessing the system of care efforts described in this chapter and how they compare to Virginia's CSA system of care.

System of Care Functions Requiring Structure

- Planning (i.e., the planning process itself requires structure)
- Decision-Making and Oversight at the Policy Level (e.g., governance)
- System Management (i.e., day-to-day management decisions)
- Outreach, Engagement, and Referral
- System Entry/Access (i.e., referred to as intake; how children, youth, and their families enter the system and what happens when the get there)
- Screening and Service Planning
- Care Management and Service Coordination, Including Use of Care Management Entities
- Crisis Management at the Service Delivery and System Levels
- Benefit Design/Service Array (i.e., define types of services and supports that are allowable and under what conditions within the system of care)
- Evidence-Based and Effective Practices
- Prevention and Early Intervention
- Provider Network (i.e., network of services and supports)
- Purchasing and Contracting
- Provider Payment Rates
- Billing and Claims Processing
- Utilization Management
- Financing
- Human Resource Development
- External and Internal Communication and Social Marketing
- Quality Management, Continuous Quality Improvement, and Evaluation

- Information and Communication Technology
- Protecting Privacy
- Ensuring Rights
- Transportation
- System Exit (i.e., how families leave the system and what happens when they leave)
- Technical Assistance and Training (Pires, 2010).

Pires also defines the core elements of an effective system-building process. She organizes these elements under the following system development priorities:

- *The importance of leadership and constituency building.* Key elements include: (a) establishing a core leadership group that contains key stakeholders including youth and families, (b) ensuring collaboration and cultural and linguistic competence, and (c) connecting to neighborhood resources and natural helpers. The leadership process also needs to give consideration to ensuring that the interests of stakeholders at all levels are aligned, effective communication processes are put in place, and mechanisms for conflict resolution, mediation, and team building are established.
- *The importance of being strategic.* System-building should proceed with a strategic mind-set and a shared vision based on common values and principles. The process should be informed by a clear focus on which population will be served, shared outcomes, an understanding of community strengths and needs as well as traditional and de facto systems and providers and the major funding streams. System-builders should have clear goals, objectives and benchmarks, and allow adequate time to assess and address opportunities and barriers.
- *The importance of an orientation to sustainability.* In order to ensure that systems will function effectively after initial implementation, leaders must strive to infuse system of care into traditional system policies, operations and practices, and cultivate leaders and champions. Attention should also be given to establishing partnerships between states and localities, and state and tribes. It is critical to develop long-term financing strategies and sound data systems to track performance and outcomes. Training, coaching and capacity building needs to be conducted on an ongoing basis and systematic effort should be directed at generating broad support and an advocacy base (Pires, 2010).

Beth Stroul and Robert Friedman (1986), who wrote the original monograph on Systems of Care described in Chapter 1, and are widely acclaimed as the "parents" of system of care also recognize the importance of addressing philosophical and infrastructure concerns when developing or expanding systems of care. In their report of the national evaluation of the federal Comprehensive Community Mental Health Services for Children and their Families Program, Stroul and Friedman identify five broad categories of expansion strategies that states should consider when developing or expanding systems of care. They acknowledge the importance of leaders tailoring their approaches to the unique conditions of their own state, but emphasize that success is more likely if they take into account all of the domains addressed by these strategies when evaluating, developing, or expanding their systems:

1. Implementing policy, administrative, and regulatory changes
2. Developing or expanding services and supports based on the system of care philosophy and approach
3. Creating or improving financing strategies
4. Providing training, technical assistance, and coaching
5. Generating support for the system of care approach (Stroul & Friedman, 2011).

EXAMPLES OF STATE-LEVEL SYSTEMS OF CARE

Systems of Care need to be tailored to the unique configuration of each state. When deciding on the specifications for a particular state, the geographic, demographic, political and social configuration and inclination of that entity needs to be considered. For example, Virginia, with its Dillon Rule statesupervised and locally administered governance structure, is still struggling to find an appropriate balance between encouraging local empowerment, and ensuring that children and families are treated equally in all parts of the state and holding localities accountable for complying with the principles, regulations, and statutes for CSA.

The states highlighted in this section have taken different approaches to developing systems of care. Their success, in part, has been due to their recognition of what structures and processes are most compatible with their local circumstances. The following examples have been selected to illustrate how states with varying characteristics and cultures have employed strategies to establish and improve comprehensive systems of care for at-risk youth and their families. While each state has demonstrated diligence, strategic thinking, and creativity in planning and implementing their system, there is no state, at the present time, that has wholly actualized the values, principles, and goals embodies in the systems of care approach.

It should be noted that the states described below are not the only states that have made significant investments. Recent research has identified, Maine, Maryland, Michigan, Oklahoma, and Rhode Island as examples of states that have successfully expanded their systems of care and others are engaged in improving their care systems for at-risk youth and their families (Stroul & Friedman, 2011).

New Jersey

The Garden State has one of the most fully actualized systems of care in the nation. With its nearly nine million residents living in a fairly small geographic area, it is the most densely populated state in the United States, with clusters of urban and suburban communities. Caucasians comprise slightly less than 70 percent of the population, while the rapidly growing Latino/Hispanic population now ranks second with 17 percent, and African-Americans representing 13 percent of the population. Even within its small geographic area, there are still rural communities in New Jersey (U.S Census Bureau, 2014).

Upon receiving a federal Children and Adolescent Service System Program (CASSP) grant for Burlington County, the state embarked on a comprehensive planning process to improve services for children and adolescents throughout the state. With a focus on implementing systems of care statewide, they undertook an ambitious process to incrementally establish systems of care in each county or cluster of small counties. Over the next five years the state rolled out fully operational systems of care for all of its 21 counties, as well as state policies and governance/management structures to support effective implementation (Guenzel & Hancock, 2010).

This comprehensive endeavor was aided by several factors. Families played a critical role in developing and garnering support for a concept paper that laid the foundation for the broader initiative. Family advocacy also helped government officials become aware of the benefits of a system of care approach. The support from the governor's office and other state officials was critical in mounting and sustaining the system of care expansion. Initially referred to as the Children's System of Care Initiative, responsibility for administering the system was subsequently given to the Division of Child Behavioral Health Services, within the Department of Children and Families. An interagency committee provided coordination and guidance.

New Jersey has, in large part, been able to successfully implement the systems of care approach at the county level because of the state's ability to create a single integrated system of behavioral health care that serves children and families who rely on public funding. The system spans all child-serving agencies and is supported through a pool of funds that blends mental health, child welfare, and Medicaid resources (Stroul & Friedman, 2011).

System of care development was aided by a succession of assertive administrative decisions. In 2000, the state restructured its funding system in order to enable the state to obtain additional federal funding through the Medicaid

Rehabilitation option. Building on its managed care experience in physical health, New Jersey established a series of infrastructure mechanisms designed to enhance care delivery and accountability. Beginning in 2002, the state contracted with a commercial behavioral health manage care organization to serve as the statewide Administrative Services Organization (ASO) and private, nonprofit agencies at the local level to management care for youth with serious and complex behavioral health challenges. The local Care Management Organizations (CMO) were mandated to work in partnership with Family-run Support Organizations (FSO) in order to ensure comprehensive, coordinated care for these youth and their families. The CMOs contracted are responsible for developing individualized care plans, providing intensive care management and contracting with providers to deliver services prescribed in each child's plan (Gruenzel & Hancock, 2010).

Through the ASO, utilization review and care coordination were provided, and a statewide management information system was established. New Jersey adopted the Child Assessment of Need and Strengths (CANS) as the required assessment instrument to be used for all children served through this system. The CANS, which is the same measure currently used in Virginia's CSA, provided child-specific data to be used for service planning, evaluating care outcomes, and provider/system performance. During this same period, a statewide training and technical assistance program was established.

In 2006, the Department of Children and Families became an independent cabinet-level department. This elevated status gave administrators of the SOC greater authority and enhanced visibility of the system. The Division of Child Behavioral Health Services was subsequently reconfigured, and is now called the Children's System of Care, and reports directly to the Commissioner.

Outcomes associated with New Jersey's system of care efforts include the following:

- Children served in community-based programs, excluding outpatient services reimbursed by Medicaid, has increased by more than 300 percent since 2002.
- Percentage of youth receiving residential care has decreased from 35 percent in 2002 to 10 percent in 2010.
- The length of stay in residential care has decreased by 14 percent between 2003 and 2010.
- The average CANS score at admission to residential treatment centers increased from 25 in 2003 to 37 in 2010 (i.e., higher CANS scores indicate greater need for placement in a restrictive setting).
- The percentage of children under the age of 14 who are enrolled in system of care programs increased from 40 percent in 2003 to 60 percent in 2010.

- Readmission to acute inpatient care within 30 days of discharge decreased by more than 50 percent between 2002 and 2010.
- Six of the nine largest counties had a statistically significant decrease in admissions to juvenile justice following implementation of systems.
- Family satisfaction with their participation in treatment increased from 62 percent in 2004 to 78 percent in 2009 (Gruenzel & Hancock, 2010).

New Jersey has been able to develop and sustain a relatively comprehensive and mature system of care. Several key factors have contributed to their success. The assertive advocacy of family members captured the attention and interest of the governor's office and other high-level officials, leading them to establish the Children's System of Care initiative. The establishment of the state- and local-level administrative and coordinating entities, coupled with family-based support organizations provided a sound locally managed, state-guided system. The state's prior involvement with similar strategies for managing health care facilitated the development and acceptance of these structures.

The strategic decision to implement systems of care incrementally, focusing on a small number of counties each year over a five-year span proved to be effective. In contrast to the Virginia CSA experience, New Jersey utilized a locality specific approach, devoting considerable time and resources to the development of each local program. This approach gave each county an opportunity to address and work through their concerns with the state prior to full implementation. The state was also able to apply lessons learned from the initial rollout to subsequent local development efforts. Development also was enhanced by the introduction of data-driven decision support processes and the continuous provision of an array of training and technical resources.

Several other differences between New Jersey and Virginia also influenced the evolution of their systems of care approaches. Although there were several outspoken parents involved in the creation of the CSA legislation, in recent years, family-driven advocacy has not been a significant factor in Virginia. In contrast, parents of children with behavioral health challenges were a key driving force in developing a statewide system of care approach in New Jersey and FSOs are currently an essential component of each local system.

In New Jersey, the governor may be elected for two consecutive terms, providing greater opportunity for continuity of leadership than in Virginia, with its one-term limit for governors. Although senior state officials do not always serve for two complete terms, the potential for fully developing policies and programs developed under their watch is definitely greater. Virginia also faces additional challenges from its local government structure. Unlike other states, Virginia's cities are not embedded in or coterminous with county government units. For example, in New Jersey, the city of Newark has its own governance structure, but also is part of Essex County. In Virginia, cities and counties are independent of each other. One implication of this arrangement is that urban areas, which often have a higher proportion of economically disadvantaged residents, cannot rely on the surrounding county, with its more affluent suburban population base, to support core services such as health and human services. In addition to the economic handicap of having cities that do not receive financial support from wealthier counties, Virginia's large number of local entities poses another challenge. Transforming a complex conceptual paradigm, such as systems of care, into effective local programs, is more challenging in a state like Virginia, with its 39 independent cities and 95 counties than it is in New Jersey, which has to deal with only 15 counties.

Finally, the Systems of Care philosophy is generally more consonant with a liberal political orientation that is more supportive of human service and safety net goals. Many of the states that have embraced the systems of care approach are in the northeast region, which is typically more liberal in its political outlook than the rest of the country. In spite of the strong bi-partisan support that CSA has received in Virginia, it is reasonable to conclude that a comprehensive approach to serving children and families would receive a warmer reception in a more progressive-oriented state like New Jersey.

Ohio

There is a long history of commitment and support for children's services in Ohio. In 1984, Governor Richard Celeste launched an initiative requiring each county to establish an interagency group to work collaboratively to plan services for children with complex service needs and who are served by multiple agencies. Through an executive order, Governor Celeste created Children's Clusters in each of Ohio's 88 counties. Recognizing that the Children's Clusters functioned primarily at a clinical level, Governor George Voinovich, in 1993, successfully urged the legislature to establish Family and Children First Councils (FCFC) in each county. The Councils were given responsibility for strengthening system-level collaboration in order to support child and family specific efforts (Stark, 1999).

Since the inception of FCFCs, there have been several legislative efforts to enhance the authority and accountability of these local councils. In 2006, House Bill (HB) 289 required localities to establish a process to select priorities, track progress in meeting these priorities using indicators determined by the FCFC, and create an annual plan for identifying inter-agency efforts to enhance child well-being in the county. Each FCFC was required to report progress to a statewide Ohio Family and Children's First Cabinet Council (OFCF) as well as their county commissioners. In 2010, the children's planning legislation was modified to reduce duplication and enhance coordination. Under the new Share Plan Model, each county FCFC is no longer required to develop a separate plan. Instead, counties are required to align local plans focused on priorities for children and families. These shared plans build on data-informed efforts that already exist in local communities and are required to include specific details and progress on shared priorities, outcomes, indicators, and strategies. The plans for each county are readily available on the Ohio Family and Children First website (Ohio Family and Children First, 2014).

OFCF serves as the Governor's Children's Cabinet and is charged with streamlining and coordinating services for all of Ohio's children and families. The Cabinet is comprised of the directors of 11 state agencies and the Governor's Office. In addition to the traditional child-serving agencies, the Office of Budget and Management and the Rehabilitation Services Commission also participate in the Children's Cabinet. The Deputy Directors of these agencies serve on a group that assists in supporting and making operational the work related to the four core functions of the OFCF displayed in Figure 14.1.

Ohio has 11.5 million residents, making it the 7th largest state in the United States. With Caucasians comprising 80 percent of its population, African-American's 17 percent, and Hispanic/Latinos 5 percent, Ohio is less diverse racially and ethnically than Virginia, New Jersey, or Hawaii. However, a significant proportion of Ohio's population is poor. Although Ohio's per capita

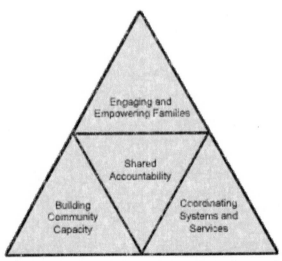

Figure 14.1 Ohio Family and Children First Councils (OFCF) Are Mandated to Perform Four Core Functions as Illustrated in the Triangle. *Source*: From Ohio Family and Children First (n.d.). Retrieved May 7, 2015, from http://www.fcf.ohio.gov/. Reprinted with permission of the author.

personal income is slightly below the national average (ranks 31st in per capita income), several cities are considered to be among the poorest in the country. While much of the state's population resides in densely populated metropolitan areas such as Cleveland, Cincinnati, and Columbus, Ohio has a sizable rural population (22%) (U.S. Department of Commerce, 2013).

Not surprisingly, a significant driving force in the development of Ohio's system of care for children and families has been the realignment of how services were paid for. Like other successful systems cited earlier, Ohio undertook a review of its funding practices and concluded that there was a disconnect between the stated goal of providing care for individuals with serious behavioral health challenges in the community and the disproportionate amount of money that was being allocated to congregate care. Beginning in the early 1990s, Ohio established a series of strategies to offer incentive to localities that developed and utilized community-based services. The initial legislation redirected funds from state psychiatric hospital care and provided new funding, making available an additional $30 million to support development of community services for individuals with serious mental illness. More than 80 percent of local mental health boards chose to take advantage of the enhanced availability of community funding. Although this legislation was primarily directed at serving adults, it established a precedent for encouraging localities to modify their programmatic efforts by providing financial incentives (Hogan, 1992).

Efforts to promote collaborative, community-based services for at-risk youth and families in Ohio include establishing the Ohio Children's Trust Fund and the creation of a flexible funding pool to give localities greater latitude for serving children and families. The Trust Fund, established in 1984, serves as a catalyst for preventing child abuse and neglect by funding a variety of primary and secondary prevention activities at the local and state levels, including strategies designed to strengthen families. A flexible funding pool mechanism was established as part of the systems of care initiative in order to enable communities to pool funding from various state accounts to enhance services for children, families, and adults. Improvements to the flexible funding strategy were designed by an OFCF workgroup in 2010 and codified by the state legislature through HB153. The new legislation allows local public agencies to transfer certain state general revenue funds to the local flexible funding pools administered by the OCFC. Previously, even when state funds were "pooled," local agencies had to fulfill the requirements attached to the original state funding source. Now, all of these state requirements are waived and localities can use pooled funds as they see fit for prevention, early intervention, and treatment efforts on behalf of children, families, and adults. Localities have access to family-centered services and support resources for the specific purpose of providing non-clinical, community-based services to keep children and youth with identified multiple systemic needs in their own homes (Ohio Family and Children First, 2014a).

One of Ohio's strengths has been its systematic focus on establishing and supporting evidence-based practices. Under the leadership of Michael Hogan, Director of the Ohio Department of Mental Health from 1991–2007, a systematic campaign was undertaken to introduce mental health services and other practices that had been shown to be effective using empirical data. Using state funds, five regionally based university centers of excellence were established to provide training and technical assistance to localities to promote adoption and appropriate utilization of these evidence-based approaches (Svendsen et al., 2005). Included among these evidence-based approaches were several strategies targeted to address mental health challenges for children and families. Since that time, these centers have expanded into seven Coordinating Centers of Excellence (CCOE) that work with all of the stakeholders participating in systems of care for children and families. Each Center focuses on a specific practice, employing training, consultation, fidelity assessment, and/or outcome evaluation. Practices related to systems of care that have been supported through extensive training and technical assistance include high-fidelity wraparound services, family engagement, local service coordination, and treatment modalities and approaches such as trauma-informed care and treatment for individuals with co-occurring substance-abuse and mental health challenges. The Centers are comprised of a wide range of stakeholders, including consumer and family advocacy groups and local mental health boards, as well as clinicians and researchers (Ohio Mental Health and Addiction Services, 2014).

Another positive feature of the Ohio system is the systematic use of data- and protocol-driven processes and their transparency throughout the state. Considerable attention has been given to establishing indicators and guidelines that can be adapted by local communities and counties for their own purposes. Consistent with their highly publicized core value of *shared accountability*, reports of local metrics and procedures are readily available on the OFCF website and groups are encouraged to share information (OFCF, 2014).

Ohio continues to pursue efforts to improve its system of care. In 2013, the state received a four-year Systems of Care Expansion grant from the Substance Abuse and Mental Health Services Administration to increase wraparound services for youth and young adults statewide. The OFCF Family Engagement Steering Committee has been working to align, coordinate, and consolidate parent/family engagement resources, policies, services, and efforts among OFCF cabinet agencies. The Parent Advocacy Connection, overseen by the National Alliance on Mental Illness of Ohio, and funded by the state, provides trained volunteer advocates to assist families involved in the Families and Children First (FCF) Service Coordination process. These advocates provide education and support to families, helping them to understand the systems of care process and encouraging parents to speak on behalf of their children. When appropriate, advocates will accompany parents to Individual Education Plan (IEP) meetings, juvenile court hearings, and other treatment planning and review meetings (Ohio Families and Children First, 2014).

One of the obvious similarities between the Ohio and Virginia interagency efforts on behalf of children and families is that both have been operating for a long time. It has been more than 30 years since Governor Celeste issued his executive order to establish Children's Clusters in each county. Initial efforts to establish CSA in Virginia began in the mid-1980s and culminated with passage of the Act in 1993. The manner in which these two comprehensive systems have evolved is quite different. CSA was enacted as a comprehensive reform, requiring significant changes in funding, governance, and program operations. The Ohio system has evolved more gradually, establishing key system components over time and improving these functions incrementally. The Children's Clusters were replaced in 1993 with county-based Families and Children First Councils, which had stronger legislatively mandated responsibilities and authority. Improved planning and flexible funding strategies have been adopted in Ohio every few years.

Are the differences in development and performance trajectories for the systems of care in these two relatively large states attributable to the contrast in how they were established? Given the multiple factors that contribute to how major transformation initiatives play out, it would be difficult to verify whether the incremental approach in Ohio led to greater acceptance and buy-in from key stakeholders than sweeping all-at-once reform legislative package that was enacted in Virginia. Nonetheless, it is a hypothesis worth considering. Is it possible that Virginia attempted to do too much, too soon? Would a more gradual transformation have yielded better results? Conversely, would anything less than a total reform initiative have precluded the possibility of further enhancement at a later time? Did the planners of CSA take advantage of a unique window of opportunity in Virginia in the early 1990s to achieve major reform? If they had not taken full advantage of that period of receptivity, is it possible that legislators might not have been willing in the future to consider enacting such a bold, comprehensive approach?

The Ohio system had several contextual advantages and benefited from strategic decisions that established a strong, central leadership cadre within the governor's office. In contrast to Virginia, governors in Ohio are eligible to serve two consecutive terms. Governor's Celeste and Voinovich, both of whom were supportive of integrating children's services at the local and state levels, were in office for more than one term. Having the chief executive officer of the state in place for eight years provided continuity of leadership and allowed senior officials to more fully implement their reform efforts. Additionally, the Children's Cabinet housed in the governor's office with participation from state agency leaders and the support of the deputy director's workgroup provided an excellent vehicle for establishing and enhancing children's policy and programs. With these governance assets, Ohio has been able to create and maintain the strong, comprehensive infrastructure needed to support viable systems of care for children and families at the local and state levels. Unlike Virginia, Ohio has been successful in establishing and sustaining, data-driven planning, training and technical assistance, outcome indicators, and other measures that facilitate effective service delivery and promote accountability.

Another difference between the two states is that the Ohio Department of Mental Health and Substance Abuse Services and its local mental health boards have been strong leaders in the systems of care development process since its inception. Similar to other states with effective systems of care, Ohio has recognized the critical role mental health plays in functioning of at-risk youth and families, and has assigned specific responsibilities for providing services and supports for assessing and treating these challenges. In Virginia, the role of the state behavioral health authority and local Community Service Boards (CSBs) within CSA has been less prominent and their involvement has varied considerably across localities.

A final advantage of the Ohio system is that they have been able to integrate all of their child and family activities, including prevention, early intervention, and treatment into a single set of state and local structures. The Ohio Families and Children First Cabinet Council and its local counterparts are charged with addressing all issues that impact the well-being of young people and their families and are responsible for integrating these efforts, whenever possible. In Virginia, the system of care structure for at-risk youth and families is still primarily focused on children with complex behavioral challenges who require the services of multiple agencies.

Louisiana

Unlike Virginia and New Jersey, which are among the most prosperous states in the nation, Louisiana ranks 29th in per capita income (U.S. Department of Commerce, 2013) and has the 2nd highest percentage of persons living below the poverty level (U.S. Bureau of Census, 2014). Although the state's economic situation has improved considerably since the early part of the twenty-first century, when it ranked 45th in income level, the state faced considerable challenges in serving its residents. Louisiana has not fully recovered from the devastating effects of Hurricane Katrina and consistently ranks in the bottom

10 percent in educational performance and health status. The state has one of the highest rates of poverty and fares poorly on key indices such as spending on social welfare and health systems performance (Commonwealth Fund, 2014; Sauter, Hess, Weighly, & Allen, 2012). In the midst of their economic and post-hurricane recovery challenges, Bobby Jindal, Louisiana's politically conservative Republican governor, decided to launch a bold initiative to address the problems of how at-risk youth were being served.

Similar to other states, the initial trigger for transforming Louisiana's behavioral health system for young people was the heavy reliance on hospitalization and out-of-home placement for youth and the high cost of these residential services. Both the child welfare and juvenile justice systems used out-of-home placement as an intervention as there was an absence of appropriate community services. Leadership from the core child-serving agencies began to meet to explore how to improve the service system. Based on their research and consultation with experts in the field, this group developed a plan to organize and provide a coordinated network of broad, effective services for a segment of Louisiana's at-risk children and youth. In March 2012, the State initiated a managed care project to provide comprehensive and coordinated wraparound care to 1200 at-risk youth in five of Louisiana's nine service regions.

As part of this work, Governor Jindal, who was interested in improving outcomes and reducing the state's cost of providing services, issued an executive order to establish a formal governance structure within the Louisiana Department of Health and Hospitals (DHHS). The order directed DHHS to work with other relevant state agencies to establish a Coordinated System of Care (CSoC) Governance Board. The Board, composed of nine members including senior leadership from the state's child-serving agencies, two family and one youth representatives, and a representative from the advocacy community, was charged with overseeing Louisiana's comprehensive service system for youth with significant behavioral challenges and their families who required intensive services. The CSoC had three primary objectives: (1) to improve the overall outcomes of these youth and their caretakers; (2) reduce the state's cost of providing services by leveraging Medicaid and other funding sources as well as enhancing service effectiveness and reducing duplication among agencies; and (3) reduce out-of-home placements for children and youth with significant behavioral challenges or co-occurring disorders (Jindal, 2011).

Using state funds pooled from the child-serving agencies, the state applied for and received a Medicaid waiver from the federal Center for Medical Services. Since Louisiana was eligible for a federal match rate of 62 percent, each state dollar was able to leverage more than $1.60 of federal aid, significantly increasing the funds available to pay for services (Henry J Kaiser Foundation, 2014).

The initial planning of behavioral health-managed care was focused on children. However, the scope quickly broadened to include behavioral health care for all individuals in the state eligible for Medicaid. On March 1, 2012, Louisiana launched a statewide-managed behavioral health care system as well as implementation of CSoC. Since the adult population consumes most of the attention and resources of the mental health system, the prominent role of children's services in Louisiana's behavioral health reform initiative merits acknowledgment.

The Louisiana Behavioral Health Partnership (LBHP) was established to develop and manage a comprehensive statewide system of care for Medicaid and non-Medicaid adults and children with significant behavioral health needs who are in or at risk of out-of-home placement and require specialized services. A Request for Proposals (RFP) was issued by the State for the purpose of contracting with a Behavioral Health State Management Organization (SMO) to operate the prepaid behavioral health plan and manage the essential functions of this system. The SMO was responsible for managing access to services, management of care, utilization management, quality management, development and maintenance of a provider network, and other critical operational functions (Office of Behavioral Health, 2011). In 2012, Magellan was selected to serve as the SMO for the LBHP.

The SMO reports to the Office of Behavioral Health (OBH) and receives oversight from OBH with support from the other child-serving agencies. The SMO is responsible for assisting the LBHP in achieving the following goals:

1. Foster individual, youth, and family-driven behavioral health services.
2. Increase access to a wider array of evidence-based home- and community-based services that promote hope, recovery, and resilience.
3. Improve quality by establishing and measuring outcomes.
4. Manage costs through effective utilization of State, federal, and local resources.
5. Foster reliance on natural supports that sustain individuals and families in homes and communities (Office of Behavioral Health, 2011).

Within the statewide-managed children's behavioral health care system, CSoC services are organized regionally. Each of the nine participating regions is required to make available the following five specialty system of care services as well as general behavioral health services:

1. Parent support and training
2. Youth support and training
3. Short-term respite care
4. Independent living and skills building
5. Crisis stabilization

The service process is initiated when a referral is made to the SMO, currently Magellan of Louisiana. Referrals can be initiated by the family, or a child-serving provider/agency. For youth with complex behavioral health needs who evidence a certain level of need according to a brief screening process, Magellan refers the child to a designated local Wraparound Agency which conducts an assessment, using the Child and Adolescent Needs and Strengths measure. Based on this assessment, the Wraparound Agency meets with the family and develops a service plan for their child and the family. The Wraparound agency then assists the family in accessing and navigating appropriate services and supports.

Implementation of the CSoC began in 2012. Therefore, at this time, only limited data are available to assess how the system is functioning. However, the monthly reports produced by the SMO for the CSoC Governance Board provide some indication of how this managed behavioral health approach is performing. The number of youth enrolled in second quarter of 2014 had more than doubled since the initial report covering the second quarter of 2012. The 1,016 youth enrolled represented 45 percent of the initial target of 2,400 youth who would require CSoC services. Considerable progress had been made in recruiting appropriate agencies for the provider network in the area of independent living/skill-building, but shortages still existed in finding respite care and crisis stabilization service providers. The percentage of youth placed in restrictive placements following their enrollment in a Wraparound Agency (18%) was lower than the percentage residing in restrictive placements prior to enrollment in a Wraparound Agency (31%). Other changes in functioning and performance reported by Magellan include:

- Continued improvement in functioning demonstrated through the Child and Adolescent Needs and Strengths (CANS) assessment scores over time.
- Continued decrease in school suspension over the last quarter.
- Continued downward trend in number of inpatient psychiatric hospital admissions.
- Increased use of Home and Community-Based Services (Magellan of Louisiana, 2014).

Louisiana's comprehensive program for young people with significant behavioral health needs is still in the early stages of development. The CSoC incorporates the core values and principles of the nationally recognized system of care models. The leadership of the state has taken into account the social, political, and economic norms of the state and methodically established a governance and management structure that is sensitive to the needs of the youth and families, the fiscal aspects of the service delivery system, and the geopolitical dynamics of the state. In addition to tracking the programmatic and financial performance over time, it will be important to monitor how this highly privatized endeavor to assess whether it remains faithful to its stated principles and goals. Will the CSoC continue to adhere to its individually tailored, family-driven, collaborative care philosophy? Will the system be able to maintain an appropriate balance between promoting this entrepreneurial approach and ensuring accountability at all levels.

There are several significant similarities as well as differences between Louisiana's CSoC and Virginia's CSA. Both efforts were initiated by a dual interest in improving care for at-risk youth and containing rising costs. The systems established in these state are statewide and are governed by formally established boards comprised of senior officials from the state's child-serving agencies as well as other key stakeholder groups. In addition to promoting a spirit of cooperation among child-serving agencies and local government entities, the leadership in Louisiana and Virginia required agencies to pool funds and provided other fiscal requirements and incentives designed to enhance collaboration. Both states use the CANS assessment instrument, though there are differences in the manner in which this measurement scale is utilized. Louisiana requires the CANS to be administered by an independent, licensed professional whose assessment is a mandated requirement for determining which services will be offered as well as a tool for measuring progress over time. Virginia allows greater flexibility in how the CANS is used.

The differences between Louisiana's and Virginia's approaches are indicative of the contrast in the respective political/governance dynamics within these states as other contextual forces. In this instance, the prevailing attitudes toward health care delivery approaches such as managed care accounts for some of the variance. The contrast in the roles of state and local government sectors in Virginia and Louisiana is critical in understanding how their systems of care evolved. Specifically, in Virginia, although the services are considered to be the responsibility of the state, cities and counties fiercely advocate to retain control of how their locality functions and how to adapt the mandates of the state and federal governments to the unique conditions of their municipality. In contrast, there is considerably less tension between local and state governments in Louisiana in relation to the question of who is in charge of how services are delivered. In Louisiana, public behavioral health services as well as most other services for-at-risk individuals are largely driven and funded by the state, with local government having a less prominent role. This dynamic allowed the Governor Jindal to move swiftly to establish the new system of care. Because this service system was being paid for by funds that had previously been allocated to the state's child-serving agencies, no further action was required from the Louisiana legislature. Since the system of care initiative did not require legislative approval, the time period from design to implementation was reduced even further. The agency leaders began their planning in 2010 and the initial operation of the coordinated system began in 2012.

Several other factors have influenced the sometimes divergent courses these states have pursued. While the population of Virginia is less than twice as large as Louisiana's, the number of children and adolescents enrolled in Virginia's CSA is fourteen-fold greater than those served by the CSoC. Some of this discrepancy may be due to differences in maturity of the systems. CSA has been serving at-risk youth for more than 20 years, while Louisiana's CSoC has been functioning for less than three years. However, even in its first year of operation, more than 10,000 youth were enrolled in CSA compared to slightly more than 1,000 enrollees in CSoC during its second year of implementation. These differences may be partially due to the manner in which the states chose to put their systems into operation. CSA was implemented statewide from its inception, while Louisiana chose a more gradual roll-out process, allowing regions to decide when they were ready to opt-in. Louisiana also identified a smaller potential population of focus, possibly because their system initially focused on youth enrolled in Medicaid or receiving other forms of public assistance, while CSA chose to focus on a broader group of at-risk youth. Regardless of why the two states have significant differences in the numbers of youth enrolled, it seems reasonable to conclude that managing a service system with 1,000 enrollees is less challenging than dealing with 14,000 participants.

The developmental path of these two systems has also been shaped by the period in which they were conceived and the prevailing attitude of each state regarding the best way to manage the delivery of health care services. In 2011, when CSoC was introduced, there was broader acceptance of the utility of contracting with private entities to manage care than during the early 1990s when CSA was established. Granted, Virginia has made adjustments to CSA to accommodate the increased demands for accountability and fiscal control and continues to modify its policies and procedures. However, it is generally more difficult to restructure complex systems once they are operational than incorporating contemporary features during the design phase, prior to implementation. In addition, in spite of its generally pro-business, limited government orientation, Virginia has been reluctant to move quickly to privatize CSA.

In this chapter we have described how New Jersey, Ohio, and Louisiana have voluntarily pursued reform of services for children and families with multiple stressors. The similarities and differences among efforts of these states and Virginia are in large part driven by the political, economic, and social dynamics of each of these jurisdictions. How services were previously provided as well as governance issues such as the role of state and local governments and private entities in the delivery of care for youth and families played a significant role in determining the pathway for developing comprehensive systems of care. In the next chapter we will examine what happens when states are mandated to improve care as a result of litigation precipitated by problems and deficiencies in the existing service delivery system.

Chapter 15

When States Are Ordered to Reform

HAWAII

In contrast to New Jersey, where systems of care development were driven largely by family members who were able to convince the governor's office of the value of this approach, in Hawaii, the legal system served as the primary impetus for pursuing this model. In 1994, Hawaii entered into the Felix Consent Decree, as part of a settlement to a class-action lawsuit alleging that the state was not providing adequate education and related mental health services to children with disabilities. As part of the settlement, the state was mandated to develop and provide a statewide system of care based on the Child and Adolescent Service System Program (CASSP) principles (Stroul & Friedman, 1986). Initially, most of the leadership for this initiative came from the federally appointed Court Monitor and a group of external experts who provided technical assistance. Although the consent decree was established on the basis of federal education law, in the early stages, the leadership from the education sector of the state was only peripherally involved. Consistent with other externally imposed changes, the consent decree was able to establish changes in policies, programs, and procedures that are rarely possible in self-governing systems (Chorpita & Donkervoet, 2005). Not surprisingly, as often happens when change is instigated from outside, some of the key stakeholders, particularly the state education system, resisted these new initiatives.

Hawaii has a population that is more diverse than any other state and a unique geographic configuration and history. Caucasians are in the minority (25 percent), while Asians are the largest subgroup (39 percent), Native Hawaiian and other Pacific Islanders comprise 20 percent of the population and 20 percent of the population identify as being of two or more races (U.S. Census Bureau, 2014). Approximately three-quarters of the state's 1.4 million residents live in Oahu while the remainder live on seven other islands or sparsely inhabited islets. More than one-in-five residents are under the age of 18.

In addition to its diverse population and being located more than two thousand miles from the mainland, Hawaii has a long history of colonialism and externally dominated commercial development. Therefore, it is not surprising that the court-imposed changes were greeted with skepticism and resistance (Chorpita & Donkervort, 2005). In fact, the court's supervision remained in effect for 12 years, with the consent decree finally being terminated in 2005. According to Ivor Groves, the court-appointed monitor for the Felix Consent Decree, "I think the whole special powers issues triggered some of the political sacred cows . . . or traditions. . . . All of that went counter to the kind of traditional way business has been done" (Kua, 2002).

With the assistance of experts from the mainland, Hawaii was able to establish key components of a system of care that offered identification, assessment, and treatment in school settings and intensive treatment coordination provided by seven Family Guidance Centers across the state. In an effort to tailor the CASSP system of care to the values and needs of Hawaii, including language, culture, and geography, a technical assistance council was formed to work with a broad array of local stakeholders. A series of 17 community forums was held to educate family members, educators, community leaders, and others on the core system of care principles and obtain input on how to modify these guidelines to be compatible with local circumstances. Community Children's Councils, comprised of a broad array of stakeholders, were established in 1995 to guide the development of local service systems. Subsequently, a partnership was formed with Hawaii Families, a statewide family organization in order to jointly design manage, implement, and evaluate services at all levels. Each Family Guidance Center employed a parent of a youth with mental health challenges as outreach workers responsible for assisting families and professionals to understand and access the system of care (Chorpita & Donkervoet, 2005; Hodges, Ferreria, Israel, & Mazza, 2006).

Initially, the Child and Adolescent Mental Health Division (CAMHD) of the Hawaii Department of Health was responsible for most of the service delivery across the state. Beginning in 1999, the Hawaii Department of Education became more involved. While considerable progress was made during the first five years, the increasing size and cost of the system drew attention and criticism. Costs had risen from $30 million in 1995 to $81 million in 1999, with little evidence that functional outcomes were improving and a significant number of youth were still being served out of state. The rising costs, slow development of community capacity, and lack of attention spurred the state legislature to act, and in 1999, CAMHD launched a strategic initiative to assess the empirical evidence supporting the services being provided through the system of care.

This endeavor, which also engaged a diverse group of key stakeholders to identify promising approaches that had empirical support, set a foundation for developing an ongoing array of data-driven activities designed to improve services and system of care performance. These activities include a systematic quality improvement operation, ongoing training and technical assistance, and utilization management efforts that use data to ensure that youth are receiving appropriate services. An Evidence Based Services Committee (EBS) was established to facilitate efforts to incorporate evidence-based decision into systems of care functioning at the local level. The EBS has been instrumental in encouraging development of several salient initiatives, including adoption of multi-systemic therapy (MST; i.e., an evidence-based treatment approach for youth with serious behavioral problems), a performance monitoring system that provides data on how individual therapists employ practices with an evidence base, and incorporation of specific evidence-based interventions for families of children with conduct disorders (Chorpita & Donkervoet, 2005; Hodges, Ferreira, Israel, & Mazza, 2006).

Although the Hawaii system of care development effort encountered significant obstacles during its early years, much progress has been made, and in some respects, has become an exemplary state model. Having been released from the consent decree in 2005, 12 years after it was instituted, Hawaii has continued to actively work to improve care for at-risk youth and their families. Hawaii's system of care leadership has demonstrated that spending time to educate and obtain input from community stakeholders, incorporating data-driven decision-making, and holding participants accountable for producing results may be labor intensive, but produces positive results. This state has also made effective use of strategic partnerships and has shown the value of developing operational plans and service infrastructure. Initially, the majority of services were being provided through the state's CAMHD. After the Department of Education became engaged in the late 1990s, an integrated service model was established, in which mental health services were combined with school programs. Hawaii's devotion to transparency and inclusive and open management has allowed the state to overcome strong resistance and continue to expand and improve a comprehensive system that is responsive to youth and families as well as the communities where they live (Hodges, Ferreira, Israel, & Mazza, 2006; Stroul & Friedman, 2011).

The demographic, geographic, and governance for Hawaii and Virginia are quite different, making direct comparison difficult. Service delivery in Hawaii is primarily directed by the state, whereas responsibility for provision of services is divided in Virginia, with localities playing a stronger role. The governance structure in Hawaii is also less complex, with the state having only three counties, compared with more than 130 local entities in Virginia. Hawaii's diverse population and its geographically isolated island structure indeed pose significant challenges for implementing a statewide system of care. Although Virginia has always been strongly influenced by history and tradition, making it reluctant to embrace change, the colonial history of Hawaii and the resulting suspicion of its residents to externally imposed ideas have presented formidable obstacles for system of care proponents to overcome.

Given the emphasis placed on cultural competency in the systems of care philosophy, it is interesting to speculate on how the cultural values and history of these states have been taken into account in developing and transforming their systems of care. In Virginia, planners were sensitive to the seemingly incongruous traditions of tradition and change, and harmony and conflict during the initial development as well as subsequent refinement of CSA (Wallentstein, 2007). It is not surprising that the federally imposed consent decree took so long to gain acceptance in Hawaii. Even with the assertive efforts made to engage stakeholders at all levels, there was considerable resistance. Whether there were additional culturally based strategies that could have been employed to facilitate acceptance of these changes is difficult to ascertain.

MASSACHUSETTS

The Commonwealth of Massachusetts has a long-standing reputation as being at the forefront of social innovation. In recent years the state has revamped its "Taxachusetts" image as a free-spending state. Massachusetts currently ranks in the middle in terms of state and local tax burdens on taxpayers (Kiernan, 2014) and has elected three Republican governors since the late 1990s. Nevertheless, the Commonwealth continues to be viewed as a socially progressive state, as evidenced by the leading role it played in comprehensive health care reform during the period when Mitt Romney served as governor. While Massachusetts has the highest rate of health insurance coverage in the country, it also had the highest rate of state debt, with the debt comprising 131 percent of the Commonwealth's revenue compared to an average of 50 percent for all states (Sauter, Frohlich, Hess, & Allen, 2013).

Several key contextual factors shaped the state's readiness to establish a statewide system of care for young people with behavioral health needs. Massachusetts was one of the early adopters of managed health care. The Commonwealth began to manage its Medicaid program in the early 1990s. The experience of operating a comprehensive statewide managed health care system for individuals requiring public assistance accelerated the learning curve of state officials when they turned their attention to developing a system of care for children with serious emotional disturbance in 1998 (Sherwood & Simons, 2014).

The Rosie D class-action lawsuit, filed in 2001, also propelled the development of Massachusetts' comprehensive behavioral health care system for children and youth. This lawsuit, initiated by the Center for Public Representation, was filed on behalf of Rosie D and eight other Medicaid-eligible children who were hospitalized or at risk of being hospitalized due to an absence of home-based services. The plaintiff claimed that MassHealth, the State's Medicaid agency, was not complying with the "reasonable promptness" and Early Periodic Screening, Diagnosis and Treatment (ESPDT) provisions of federal Medicaid law (Center for Public Representation, 2009; Massachusetts Executive Office of Health and Human Services, 2012). Although the State was not pleased to be the subject of a class-action claim, senior officials had already expressed an interest in improving care for children with significant behavioral challenges and were taking constructive action to develop a comprehensive behavioral health system of care.

In January 2006 the US District Court found that the Commonwealth had violated the EPSDT mandate and ordered the state to develop an array of home-based services including comprehensive assessment, case management, behavior supports, and mobile crisis services. A remedial plan was approved in 2007 and a Court Monitor was appointed to oversee implementation, mediate disputes between the parties and determine whether the state was in compliance (Center for Public Representation, 2009). The Court's ruling and the subsequent remedial plan forced the state to invest heavily in the evolving system of care. Emily Sherwood, who directs Massachusetts' Children's Behavioral Health Interagency Initiative, attributes the substantial growth in children's behavioral health services to the Rosie D lawsuit. Prior to the complaint, Massachusetts spent approximately $500 million in Medicaid funds for behavioral health care for approximately 1,000,000 adult and child recipients. Following the Court's decision, the state increased funding by 40 percent to cover the cost of the new services. Sherwood notes that in this era of fiscal austerity, "no governor is going to be able to say, gee, I want to spend $200 million on 25,000 kids" (Sherwood & Simons, 2014).

One of the defining characteristics of Massachusetts' system of care initiative is the manner in which pilot programs and incremental implementation were employed. In 1998, the Commonwealth used a Mental Health Services Program for Youth (MHSPY) grant from the Robert Wood Johnson Foundation to develop a pilot program to serve a small group of Medicaid-eligible children with significant behavioral health, employing a managed care approach in which behavioral and physical health were integrated. The pilot program, managed by Harvard Pilgrim Health Care, provided care for 80 children across six towns in one geographic area. The children were offered a full array of community-based services using a wraparound model (Sherwood & Simons, 2014). Prior to initiating the Rosie D class-action suit, the Center for Public Representation met with state officials to request that the MHSPY pilot be expanded to the entire state. Although it was not feasible to implement the systems of care initiative statewide at that time, at least voluntarily, the state agreed to extend the MHSPY pilot to four other cities. The expanded Medicaid behavioral health effort was renamed the Coordinated Family Focused Care and management of these programs was assigned to the Massachusetts Behavioral Health Partnership, the State's behavioral health Medicaid management entity, which at the time was administered by Value Options (Sherwood & Simons, 2014).

Shifting management of the systems of care initiative from a management structure in which physical and behavioral health care were integrated to a carve-out organization that focused exclusively on behavioral health triggered discussion about the relative benefits of an integrated health plan versus a carve-out management approach. The emerging focus on the impact of physical and behavioral health on each other and the growing trend to co-locate primary care and mental health services suggested that an integrated management structure was preferable. On the other side, proponents of a carve-out approach argued that behavioral health typically received lower priority than physical health in the allocation of limited financial resources, and adults consumed the majority of resources within the mental health system. Sherwood suggests that the State's decision to adopt a behavioral health carve-out model reflected the general trend of health care policy in Massachusetts. "It's not mental health that drives Medicaid program thinking about structural, strategic issues," Sherwood says, "but we, of course, are influenced by those decisions" (Sherwood & Simons, 2014).

When the court issued its decision on the Rosie D case and the State moved forward with implementation of the remedial plan, the efforts to establish a statewide system of care were aided by the knowledge gained from the pilot and expansion initiatives of the past seven years. Previous experience with the wraparound approach and involvement with families as partners in the delivery of care proved particularly helpful in expanding the scope of services and geographic area covered. The MBHP-managed care organization and clinical provider community's familiarity with these core strategies reduced the amount of time required to orient stakeholders to the systems of care approach and facilitated bringing this comprehensive family-driven system to scale (Sherwood & Simons, 2014).

Although the remedial plan provided a brief explanation of the services to be provided through the new statewide system, further work was required to develop a detailed description of the expanded community-based services as well as to define the performance specifications and medical necessity criteria that would guide the service delivery system. The Court Monitor, with approval from the plaintiffs, hired nationally recognized system of care experts to assist in this design process. The plaintiffs were intimately involved, reviewing the proposed services and specifications line by line. The service design process, which began in Fall 2006, prior to the court's final judgment in 2007, took nearly three years to complete, with initial implementation commencing in June 2009 and all services becoming operational by October 2009.

The Rosie D remedy, known as the Child Behavioral Health Initiative (CBHI), called for the provision of seven home and community-based services, in addition to other existing services:

- Intensive Care Coordination (ICC) (Wraparound)
- Family Support & Training (FS&T) (Family Partners)
- In-Home Therapy (IHT)
- In-Home Behavioral Services (IHBS)
- Therapeutic Mentoring (TM)
- Mobile Crisis Intervention (MCI)
- Crisis Stabilization (CS) (Massachusetts Executive Office of Health and Human Services, 2012).

Massachusetts submitted amendments to its Medicaid State Plan to the Center for Medical Services (CMS) to allow the state to bill Medicaid for these new services. Although some of these services such as family support and training and therapeutic mentoring have not traditionally been paid for by health insurance, the amended State Plan was approved for all but crisis-stabilization. Obtaining permission to expend federal resources for the new services allowed Massachusetts to move forward with its comprehensive remediation plan. Parenthetically, the inability to procure approval for crisis stabilization services continues to hamper Massachusetts' ability to create sufficient crisis response capacity and has prevented the state from offering a full continuum of community-based services in many communities (The Children's Behavioral Health Advisory Council, 2013).

In this new system, Massachusetts took a strong position on adhering to the core principle that services would be family-driven. Families enrolled in Medicaid's children's behavioral health care program are issued an insurance card and are able to choose the service provider they would like their child to work with. Families are able to directly access specific services without referral or prior authorization. Once they select a service provider, a clinical assessment is conducted to determine whether their child meets medical/clinical necessity criteria and whether other services are needed. However, the family is able to choose the initial service they think is most appropriate and plays a significant role in the process of deciding which services they should receive. Access to services is organized around three entry "hubs", described in Figure 15.1.

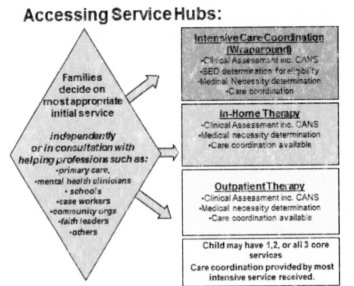

Accessing Service Hubs:

Families decide on most appropriate initial service

independently or in consultation with helping professions such as:
- *primary care,*
- *mental health clinicians*
- *schools*
- *case workers*
- *community orgs*
- *faith leaders*
- *others*

Intensive Care Coordination (Wraparound)
- Clinical Assessment inc. CANS
- SED determination for eligibility
- Medical Necessity determination
- Care coordination

In-Home Therapy
- Clinical Assessment inc. CANS
- Medical necessity determination
- Care coordination available

Outpatient Therapy
- Clinical Assessment inc. CANS
- Medical necessity determination
- Care coordination available

Child may have 1,2, or all 3 core services
Care coordination provided by most intensive service received.

Figure 15.1   Massachusetts's Family-driven Access to Care Allowed Families to Enter the System Through Various "Hubs" Such As: Wraparound, In-home Therapy, Outpatient Therapy, or Care Coordination. *Source:* Massachusetts Executive Office of Health & Human Services (2012). How to Build a Statewide System of Care. Presented at Training Institutes 2012, National Technical Assistance Center for Children's Mental Health, Georgetown University, in Orlando, Florida.

One of the other defining features of Massachusetts's full-scale statewide implementation of the remedial plan, known as the Children's Behavioral Health Initiative (CBHI), is its emphasis on screening and assessment. Under the terms of the Court's final judgment, all primary care medical providers in the Commonwealth are required to conduct standardized behavioral health screening for children seen in their practice. Pediatricians and other primary care providers are required to discuss concerns identified with the family along with how they might want to address these issues. Primary care physicians are reimbursed $10 for conducting these screenings with Medicaid-eligible children. A comprehensive campaign was conducted prior to implementation to obtain physician buy-in and train providers on the behavioral screening process. By the third year of CBHI's implementation, more than 300,000 children were receiving behavioral health screenings by primary care physicians. This represents 70 percent of all children between the ages of six months and 17 years of age seen by primary care physicians. Approximately 8 percent of children screened were identified as having behavioral health needs (Massachusetts Executive Office of Health and Human Services, 2012; The Children's Behavioral Health Advisory Council, 2011).

The other significant child evaluation process prescribed by the CBHI was use of the Child and Adolescent Needs and Strengths (CANS) tool to ensure uniform, comprehensive assessment of child needs and strengths. The CBHI required administration of the CANS in order to assist in deciding which services were appropriate for each child and to track progress at the individual, program/organization, and system levels. It has been noted earlier that many states have used the CANS to as an assessment and decision-support tool. Massachusetts, however, has surpassed these states in the ways in which it utilizes the CANS and the extent to which it has integrated this comprehensive, multifaceted assessment tool into the core functions of its system. The State has offered many face-to-face and online training opportunities to assist providers and other stakeholders in understanding and using the CANS. Ongoing training is still being provided (Executive Office of Health and Human Services, 2012).

Administratively, CBHI is housed in the Executive Office of Health and Human Services. Oversight is provided by the CBHI Executive Committee in conjunction with the Children's Behavioral Health Advisory Council, and assistance is furnished by the CBHI Interagency Implementation Team. CBHI works in close partnership with the MassHealth (Massachusetts' Medicaid program) Office of Behavioral Health which manages MassHealth's contracts with the six managed care entities (MCE) who deliver health care services across the state. The MCEs are responsible for performing the customary functions performed by care management organizations, including:

• Work with OBH to ensure oversight of providers;
• Ensure that services are delivered according to specifications;
• Provide technical assistance, quality management, and a systematic data feedback loop to providers to promote continuous quality improvement and management of outliers (Massachusetts Executive Office of Health and Human Services, 2012).

In contrast to Virginia, in Massachusetts, local government does not have a formal role in administering the system of care for children. The service system is administered by the state with assistance from the six MCEs. This structure has some advantages, including the ease of establishing uniform performance standard and procedures throughout the state and the reduced impediments to implementation caused by conflict between state and local officials in their respective roles in relation to governing and supporting the system of care. The absence of a formal role for cities or counties does not mean that local government is a silent partner. Massachusetts has a well-deserved reputation for citizen participation, including lively town meetings in which community issues are addressed with intensity and passion. The fact that the State, which is responsible for managing the Massachusetts Medicaid program, was therefore responsible for implementing the Court's remedial order also allowed Massachusetts to move more quickly to carry out corrective action (Sherwood & Simons, 2014).

The absence of a significant formal role for cities and counties also poses some challenges. One of the primary goals of the systems of care model is to maintain children in their home communities, whenever possible. Achieving this objective requires active support and involvement of multiple stakeholders within the community. The notion that "it takes a village to raise a child" is, in part dependent on communities embracing this vision and committing to provide leadership and resources needed to actualize this intention. When local government does not have a formal role in the system of care, it can be difficult to marshal the broad support, both formal and informal, required to develop an effective community-based system of care.

How has Massachusetts' CBHI fared? Like other statewide initiatives, there is a paucity of convincing longitudinal outcome data. There have however, been systematic efforts to track adherence to the principles and objectives of the Rosie D remedy plan as well as collecting data on the utilization and impact of the service system.

Massachusetts has collected data on various aspects of CBHI service utilization since full implementation began in 2009. In the initial year of operation, 18,473 members of MassHealth, which represented 3.54 percent of all youth eligible for MassHealth services, received one or more CBHI services, with slightly more than half of these individuals receiving Youth Mobile Crisis Intervention (MCI). Four years later. The number of youth served had risen to 34,577, an increase of 53 percent. The percentage of MassHealth youth enrollees served increased by 70 percent to 6.03 percent of the total youth membership. The locus of service also changed significantly with slightly more than 50 percent of participating youth receiving In-Home Therapy (IHT), with equal numbers of youth receiving Therapeutic Mentoring (TM) (36%) and Mobile Crisis Intervention (37%) (MassHealth, 2014).

Clearly, the CBHI is reaching more at-risk youth. While it is difficult to draw definitive conclusions from these data, one possible hypothesis is that the relative increase in utilization of home-based therapy and intensive mentoring are indicative of enhanced community capacity to provide appropriate services for youth, thus reducing the over-reliance on crisis services. This conjecture is speculative and will require further evidence to verify or negate its validity. It should also be noted, that while the relative prominence of crisis intervention in the service utilization hierarchy declined, the absolute number of youth as well of the percentage of all eligible members receiving this service actually rose. Once again, it is difficult to determine whether this growth in utilization reflects an increase in capacity, a shift away from more restrictive traditional crisis responses or some other factors. Changes in several utilization figures provide modest support for the interpretation that greater availability of mobile crisis responders and increased community capacity has produced positive effects. Specifically, the number of encounters with MCI resulting in inpatient psychiatric admissions has decreased by 25 percent and the total use of inpatient bed days by MassHealth enrollees under 19 years of age has decreased by approximately one-third since the inception of CBHI in 2009 (Massachusetts Executive Office of Health and Human Services, 2012).

An increasingly popular strategy for assessing system of care performance is to measure the extent to which a program is adhering to the underlying values and tenets of the system of care model. By evaluating the degree to which a service or program complies with core principles such as ensuring that planning for care is individualized, recognizing the importance of child and family strengths as well as needs, and incorporating the family's voice and values, it is possible to assess the extent to which providers comply with the System of Care model. Additionally, whether services are outcome-based, culturally competent and delivered in a collaborative, team-based approach are taken into account. This strategy for evaluating the fit between principles and practice, commonly referred to as fidelity assessment has practical implications. Research has shown a correlation between services and programs that have attained high fidelity scores and enhanced outcomes for youth being served, including improved functioning in school and community, increased resilience and quality of life, and improved mental health outcomes (Suter & Burns, 2009; Effland, McIntyre, & Walton, 2010).

Fidelity assessment measures include ratings by trained independent raters and structured interviews conducted with consumers. Massachusetts instituted a fidelity assessment system during the initial implementation of CBHI. Based on the rationale that assessing fidelity lays the groundwork for measuring outcomes, the state adapted several nationally used fidelity assessment instruments for use in Massachusetts. During the first year of operation, they measured the extent to which all of the new services conformed to their intended purpose as gauged by their adherence to the core principles. Although there was variation in how well providers performed, overall most services achieved high fidelity scores. For example, Intensive Care Coordination, also known as Wraparound Services, is the primary hub for children with significant behavioral health need and plays an instrumental role in how well the system of care performs. Based on responses to the Wraparound Fidelity Index, which asks caregivers to rate how well service providers followed 10 core principles, the statewide average score on the Index was 78 percent, which was four percentage points higher than the national average. In comparison to states that did not provide wraparound services, Massachusetts's scores on the same instrument were 20 percent higher. On the Team Observation Measure, which utilizes the ratings of independent raters, Massachusetts achieved an average score of 83, six points above the national average (King, 2010).

The state also periodically evaluates the quality of care being provided to youth served through the CBHI. Using the System of Care Practice Review (SCOPR) process developed at the University of South Florida, teams of trained reviewers assess the extent to which providers are applying system of care (SOC) principles in their practice. Based on reviews of a youth's treatment record and interviews with providers, caregivers, and youth guided by the SCOPR, reviewers rate the degree to which the young person's care is consistent with system of care values in four domains:

1. Child-Centered and Family-Focused
2. Community-Based
3. Culturally Competent
4. Impact

The findings of these reviews, which usually involve examining multiple cases in a specific region of the state, are used to identify opportunities for improvement and are used to inform efforts to build upon strengths and improve quality through in-service training, staff supervision or incorporated into a provider's quality assurance processes. A recent review of Intensive Care Coordination (ICC) and In-Home Therapy (IHT) in the Central Region found that SOCPR average scores for these services ranged from 4.91 to 6.13, with scores from 1 to 3 representing low implementation of SOC principles, scores in the 5 range associated with good implementation, and scores in the 6–7 range indicating enhanced implementation. When all cases were combined, the overall mean score was 5.41. Forty-one percent of the 22 cases examined scored in the 6 range and 13 percent were in the 3 or 2 range, indicating poor performance. In the Central region review, providers performed best in the domain of Community-Based care as a measure by the SCOPR process. Providers received the second highest scores in Culturally Competent, Child-Centered and Family-Focused and Impact. The report concluded that providers of ICC and IHT in the Central region were generally following SOC principles in planning and delivering services, and have opportunities to improve in the following areas:

- Service plans should better incorporate child and family strengths into goals, and both service plans and the planning process should be better integrated across providers and agencies.

- Service planning should be inclusive of both formal and informal providers, with more intentional inclusion of informal and natural supports in both the service planning and delivery processes.
- A smoother and more seamless process is needed for connecting youth and families with additional services and supports (Arienti, English & Horton, 2014).

As reported earlier, Massachusetts has chosen the Child and Adolescent Strengths and Needs (CANS) scale as its primary tool for assessing the functional status of youth and assisting to determine which services are appropriate for their care. As of August 2012 CANS data had been collected on 67,000 youth enrolled in the MassHealth CBHI program. More than 90 percent of the youth assessed by CANS met the SAMHSA criteria for serious emotional disturbance (SED) and 82 percent met the federal Individuals with Disabilities Education Act (IDEA) criteria. Data have been collected and reported on life domain functioning, child emotional/behavioral needs, and child risk behaviors. CBHI also tracks CANS scores on child strengths, family needs and resources, and transition to adulthood. Forty percent of the 67,000 youth assessed using CANS scored at a level indicating they needed intervention for emotional control, while 32 percent demonstrated a need for intervention for depression. In the domain of transition to adulthood, 26 percent of older youth scored at a level indicating a need for intervention related to independent living skill and 28 percent needed assistance with financial resources. The CANS identified a high percentage of youth with usable strengths. More than 60 percent of the total number of youth assessed had scores indicating they had usable strengths in the areas of interpersonal skills, optimism, education, talents and interests, and resiliency. Thirty-six percent of families were rated as needing intervention to help them deal with stress associated with parenting (Simons, 2013).

Data on how youth and families' performance on CANS has changed during their involvement with CBHI is limited, but some preliminary findings are available. For instance, higher scores on the Depression item of the CANS indicate a child requires action or intervention while a lower score suggests that no action is required. When CBHI compared initial Depression scores for children receiving IHT at the time of intake with the fourth administration of the CANS, typically conducted after nine months of enrollment, they found a 48 percent drop in the number of youth requiring intervention, 13 percent of the children whose CANS scores indicated a need for intervention for depression at intake were rated as needing intervention for depression at the fourth administration of the CANS. The evaluators caution that changes in scores may be due to better understanding of the problem or the quality of information used in the assessment as well as actual changes in the level of depression (Simons, 2013a).

COMPARING VIRGINIA'S CSA AND
OTHER STATE INITIATIVES

What are the key similarities and differences between CSA and the system of care efforts of other states? Like Virginia, the states cited above, as well as others that have developed statewide service systems for at-risk youth, have acknowledged that children with significant behavioral health challenges and their families have multiple needs and require a comprehensive, coordinated effort by multiple stakeholders. All of these states have made an effort to engage families as well as representatives of all of the major public child-serving agencies and private providers. States have consistently incorporated the nationally recognized system of care principles into their programs. State and local officials have consistently educated and encouraged all stakeholders on the importance of individually tailoring services to the specific needs and strengths of the child and family, enhancing community capacity to provide care in appropriate, least restrictive settings, and providing families a strong voice in matters related to the care of their children.

Virginia and the other states that have embarked on transforming care for at-risk youth and their families have also recognized the importance of addressing cost, accountability, organizational dynamics, and other issues that impact the delivery of care. Leaders have given careful attention to ensuring that costs are reasonable, utilization and performance are tracked, providers are held accountable, and infrastructure needed to support and sustain these systems of care is developed. In addition, training and quality improvement have been given priority status by exemplary programs. Attention has also been directed at measuring outcomes, though to date, progress in this area has been limited in most states.

There have also been differences in how states have approached the challenge of developing comprehensive systems of care for at-risk youth and their families. Specifically, the impetus for reform, the eligibility criteria, and the manner in which delivery of services has been structured vary among states. Many of these differences have been driven by local conditions and dynamics. For example, major deficits leading to court mandates played a major role in propelling the establishment of the Hawaii and Massachusetts systems. In New Jersey, family advocates were instrumental in facilitating the development of their system of care.

One of the areas in which Virginia has lagged behind is engaging youth and families. Early in the process of developing CSA the statewide Parent and Children Coping Together (PACCT) family advocacy/support organization and its local chapters played a significant role in shaping the system of care. However, in recent years, the family voice has not been as strong and family members have not been consistently involved at the direct service, program management, or system oversight levels. There are fledgling efforts to prepare and engage youth in leadership roles within CSA, but to date these efforts have not had a substantial statewide impact.

In contrast, other states have made considerable progress in realizing the goal of engaging youth and families at all levels of system of care activity. Arizona has contracted with the Family Involvement Center, a family-run organization, as a service provider as well as to assist in expanding the system of care. The Center has become a Medicaid provider and provides family support services. In Rhode Island, the state has a contract with the Parent Support Network (PSN), also a family-driven organization to offer family leadership development services at a regional level as well as to provide family input at the policy and system levels. There is strong consumer representation on Rhode Island's family-consumer advisory board, with youth and families comprising 51 percent of the membership of this body (Stroul & Friedman, 2011).

In recent years, increasing widespread attention has been given to involving youth in shaping their own care. Youth M.O.V.E. National (YMN), a youth-led advocacy and support organization, has been instrumental in promoting youth engagement at local, state, and national levels. In 2013, YMN had grown to 70 chapters across 34 states and has as its mission to:

> Work as a diverse collective to unite the voices and causes of youth while raising awareness around youth issues. We will advocate for youth rights and voice in mental health and the other systems that serve them, for the purpose of empowering youth to be equal partners in the process of change. (Youth MOVE National, 2013)

While a chapter of M.O.V.E. was recently established in Virginia, the Commonwealth has been slow to embrace the trend to formally support articulation of the youth voice.

Maryland has incorporated peer-to-peer youth support as a billable service in its Psychiatric Residential Treatment Facility Medicaid Waiver. In New Jersey, where a Family Support Organization (FSO) is attached to every Care Management Organization, each FSO contains and supports a youth partnership entity. In addition to promoting peer-to-peer support, several states, including Michigan and Rhode Island have promulgated policies requiring youth guidance in the planning, delivery, and coordination of wraparound services (Stroul & Friedman, 2011).

The manner in which states have managed the delivery of public health care services, particularly those supported by public funds, has also influenced funding and oversight of these comprehensive behavioral health initiatives. In New Jersey, Massachusetts, and Louisiana, managed health care was either a strong presence or an emerging priority. For these states, it made sense to incorporate their system of care efforts into existing or parallel care management structures, typically administered by one or more large managed health care companies. Virginia, where CSA was established prior to the introduction of significant managed care approaches in the Commonwealth, has taken a more cautious approach. The Virginia State Executive Council has been wary of turning over administration of CSA to a managed care entity. This reluctance has been fueled primarily by a fear that some of the core underlying principles of the Act, such as individualizing care plans, might be compromised under a traditional managed care structure. In recent years, there has been increased momentum to enhance accountability and efficiency of behavioral health services and greater acceptance of incorporating managed care strategies in Virginia. It will be interesting to observe how this trend will affect CSA in the future, particularly in light of the Department of Medical Assistance Services recent contractual agreement with Magellan to serve as the Behavioral Health Services Administrator for all Medicaid-funded behavioral health services in Virginia.

The role of state and local governments in administering behavioral health services and the relationship between these government entities also have shaped to some extent the way in which these systems developed and evolved. In states such as Louisiana, Hawaii, and Massachusetts, where there is a clear understanding that the state is primarily responsible for administering public behavior health services, there is less tension between levels of government and therefore fewer governance issues that may potentially impede implementation of a system of care approach. In small states like Hawaii, which has only three counties, there are fewer government entities involved, reducing the complexity and probability of conflict. In Virginia and other states where there are multiple local government units, each of which believes it should have a significant voice in determining how services are provided in their localities, there is greater likelihood for disagreement and tension between state and local governments, which may slow progress in actualizing system of care approaches.

Other differences between Virginia and the states cited earlier include term limits for the governor and the oversight structure for children's services within the executive branch of the state. The other states described earlier allowed for the governor to seek at least one additional term. Furthermore, Virginia has been disadvantaged by having a more fragmented, less centralized structure for planning and governance of children's services. In contrast, New Jersey and Ohio have created cabinet-level councils responsible for policy development and oversight for all children's services. Having these high-level coordinating bodies facilitates cross-agency collaboration and integration of services. Recognizing the potential benefits of a high-level coordinating body for all children services, Terry McAuliffe, who took office as Governor of Virginia in 2014, early in his term established a Children's Cabinet in the Commonwealth. The Cabinet will be co-chaired by the Secretaries of Health and Human Services and Education. According to Governor McAuliffe, the Cabinet will "develop and implement a policy agenda related to health, poverty, safety, education, nutrition, and housing to advocate and to educate on behalf of all Virginia's children" (Meola, 2014, p. 1).

Perhaps the most striking differences between Virginia and other states are the scope of the Commonwealth's reform effort and the relatively small role played by the agencies responsible for behavioral health services, particularly the State Department of Behavioral Health and Developmental Services (DBHDS), formerly known as the Department of Mental Health, Mental Retardation and Substance Abuse Services (DMHMRSAS). Many states with commendable systems of care have focused their attention primarily on Medicaid eligible and other low-income youth and families. From its inception, CSA has been all-inclusive, assuming responsibility for all youth with complex challenges, regardless of income or agency affiliation. While Virginia has experienced disparities in access to care for children who do not meet the mandate service eligibility criteria, the state continues to attempt to serve a broad range of children who require the assistance of more than one child-serving agency. Including at-risk youth from all socioeconomic strata adds complexity to implementation and creates additional challenges for policy makers, administrators, and providers. Despite these difficulties, this aspiration to be fully inclusive continues to be a unique and laudable defining characteristic of Virginia's CSA, especially in an era in which contraction of services and narrowing of eligibility criteria seem to be in vogue.

The other conspicuous difference between Virginia and other states is the minor role public mental health agencies have played in CSA. Although Howard Cullum, the Secretary of Health and Human Services during the Wilder administration, was the leading force behind the establishment of CSA and had previously served as Commissioner of that agency, the state's behavioral health authority has not played a significant leadership role during most of the Act's 20-plus years of operation. Initially, DMHRSAS contributed fewer financial resources to the state funds pool than any of the child-serving agencies. Despite the growing awareness of the importance of appropriately responding to the behavioral health needs of children served by CSA, DBHDS and many of the local CSBs have not provided assertive leadership in caring for these youth. By contrast, most of the states with exemplary systems of care have assigned primary administrative responsibility for these initiatives to their state behavioral health agency and these departments have provided strong leadership in developing and enhancing care. The absence of significant involvement of the public mental health agencies has impeded the Commonwealth's ability to address the serious behavioral health challenges of youth being served through CSA.

Overall, Virginia appears to have implemented CSA in adherence with generally accepted core system of care principles. The strategies employed by the Commonwealth also seem to be consistent with those utilized by other states that have developed promising systems. There are, however, differences between Virginia's system of care for at-risk youth and those developed by these other states. While Virginia's CSA is broader in scope than the comparison states' systems and has been operating longer than most of these programs, it has not performed as well in some areas. Virginia has lagged behind some states in collecting and utilizing performance and outcome data as well as taking other measures to ensure accountability. Other systems have also been more effective in engaging and empowering youth and families. Many of these states have provided comprehensive training and technical assistance to assist stakeholders to understand system of care principles and evidence-based/informed practice. Although Virginia has recently made progress in this area, workforce development remains a critical priority for CSA and the Commonwealth could benefit from considering the innovative strategies employed by other states.

Comparing the performance of CSA with other states systems of care is made more complicated by differences in when initiatives were established and how long they have been operating. Systems that have been established in recent years have been able to take advantage of new research and technology to create better processes and services. While systems like CSA, which have been functioning for an extended period of time, may also utilize these innovative approaches, it is generally more difficult to modify an existing program than to incorporate them into a new initiative. On the other hand, new programs often have considerable momentum and support, and are therefore able to produce immediate results. The question is whether these fledging initiatives are able to sustain and improve their positive performance. The efficacy of any complex system is impacted by changes in the broader political, economic, and social environments as well as within the immediate system of care programs. As we observed in reviewing the CSA experience, performance has fluctuated over time. The fact that CSA has demonstrated improvement in recent years is a positive testament for the adaptability and durability of this system of care. The passage of time will reveal whether more recently established initiatives are able to sustain and build upon their early successes.

Borrowing from Wall Street

As system of care developers have become more sophisticated in employing technology and data to enhance service delivery and oversight, advances have been made in measuring performance and outcome. These measures have been used to monitor progress, improve performance, and justify the systems of care approach to policy makers. Recently, administrators and advocates have turned to the corporate sector for assistance in making their case.

The system of care enterprises in Virginia and most other states and localities were initially driven by both programmatic and fiscal factors. In addition to being motivated by a desire to reduce placement of at-risk youth in residential settings and enhance care in their communities, local and state leaders were also concerned about the rising cost of caring for these young people. For many years, reducing the cost of services has been a primary goal of these systems for many years. In some instances, the focus has been on lowering how much is spent for each child. Some elected officials have also been concerned about reducing the total amount allocated for the care of these children and their families. This desire to lower overall cost has posed problems for many communities in light of the significant amount of unmet need and limited resources appropriated for serving at-risk youth and families.

Recently, researchers and administrators have relied on metrics produced by the financial sector to generate new ways to assess the effectiveness of systems of care. Recognizing the potential interest in the financial productivity of programs serving children with behavioral health challenges, as well the impact of these systems on functioning and well-being on those they serve, leaders in the field have begun to examine the broader economic impact of these enterprises, employing the concept of Return on Investment (ROI). Stroul and her colleagues have provided a useful monograph describing economic benefits produced by systems of care, including case examples of how data on ROI have been gathered and applied and recommendations on how states and communities can produce and use return on investment information for the benefit of the youth and families they serve (Stroul, Pires, Boyce, Krivelyova, & Walrath, 2014).

Most ROI analyses have limited their focus to assessing the extent to which system of care efforts have yielded reductions in current spending. The problems associated with this narrow approach include an innate bias against finding economic benefit because short-term expenditures will rise due to increased allocations for these behavioral health interventions. Focusing exclusively on immediate cost savings also fails to recognize other potential economic benefits deriving from having healthier, better functioning youth, such as increased productivity, earnings and tax revenues, and reduced use of future social and behavioral health services as well as juvenile and criminal justice systems. Although many of these indicators are difficult to measure, there is ample justification for encouraging development of a more comprehensive set of societal benefits, including those that cannot be readily converted to monetary terms. There are currently some promising efforts to translate these less tangible cost savings and productivity outcomes into ROI indicators (Stroul, Pires, Boyce, Krivelyova, & Walrath, 2014).

Earlier in this book we cited examples of cost savings metrics reported by Virginia's CSA and other state and local systems of care. Being able to demonstrate that their services have helped to reduce per child costs has helped the leaders of New Jersey's Children's System of Care, Massachusetts's Children's Behavioral Health Initiative, and Wraparound Milwaukee continue to obtain support needed to sustain their programs. Oklahoma compared the cost of serving youth through a system of care approach with a comparable group that did not receive care management, and found a 41 percent reduction in the cost of behavioral health services compared to a 17 percent reduction for the comparison group. When behavioral and medical costs were combined, the reduction in total average charges for youth receiving care management was 35 percent versus a decrease of 15 percent for youth in the comparison group (Strech, Harris, & Vetter, 2011). Similar reductions have occurred in other states in areas such as utilization of inpatient psychiatric hospitalization, residential treatment, and juvenile justice facilities, as well as Medicaid and state custody costs (Stroul, Pires, Boyce, Krivelyova, & Walrath, 2014).

In a multi-state analysis of the Children's Mental Health Initiative (CMHI), researchers found a number of cost savings and productivity outcomes that impacted the child welfare, juvenile justice, and education systems as well as the health and mental health systems. Reductions in visits to the Emergency Room (ER) from six months prior to enrollment in a CMHI-funded system of care to a 12-month follow-up yielded a 57 percent decrease in the average cost per child for ER visits. The estimated savings related to ER costs for all children enrolled in a CMHI-funded system over a five-year period was $15 million. Similarly, the 42 percent reduction in utilization of psychiatric inpatient services as measured across the same pre-enrollment and follow-up timeframe produced an estimated savings of $37 million from 2006 to 2013 (ICF International, 2013).

Stroul and colleagues describe another multi-site cost savings finding. The Centers for Medicare and Medicaid Services (CMS) offered a Medicaid demonstration program that provided waivers to states interested in instituting and evaluating home- and community-based services to children and adolescents with serious mental health challenges. All nine states that participated, using a system of care approach, achieved substantial savings, with an average per child savings of $35–40,000 in relation to previous costs. Expenditures for waiver services were on average only 32 percent of the cost of providing services in psychiatric residential treatment facilities, the most common treatment option prior to the establishment of the waiver program (Stroul et al., 2014).

Return on investment findings for children enrolled in system of care efforts include a significant reduction in the number of youth who had to repeat a grade after 12 months of enrollment in a system of care (6.3% vs. national average of 9.6 percent for children in the general public) or dropped out of school (8.6% vs. national average of 20 percent for high school students with mental health challenges). Taking into account the direct cost of education services as well as gains in average annual and lifetime earnings, the researchers estimated a $3.3 million cost savings associated with the decrease in repeating a grade and $380 million in savings and potential economic gain for all participants in the multi-site CMHI systems of care. They also found that caregivers of children participating in CMHI missed fewer days of work and were 21 percent more likely to be employed at the 12 month interview compared to six months prior to enrollment. The reduction in missed work days was estimated to equate to a 39 percent decrease in the average cost associated with lost productivity (ICF International, 2013).

In a meta-analysis of youth participating in the wraparound process, Suter and Bruns (2009) found economic benefits associated with the juvenile justice system. A group participating in the wraparound process spent 58 percent fewer days in juvenile detention and had lower recidivism rates than a comparison group that were given traditional mental health services, producing immediate savings for the community. When the researchers extrapolated these findings to potential lifetime savings for a single youth who might avoid a life of crime through this approach, they calculated a cost savings of approximately $1.5 million, which would be enough to pay for wraparound services for 164 youth for a full year (Suter & Bruns).

Most studies have focused on the immediate direct cost savings associated with enrollment in systems of care. While these data may be helpful in educating policy makers, administrators, and citizens about the benefits of the system of care approach, the potential impact of this approach is limited. In the current political environment, there is considerable interest in reducing expenditures, but less enthusiasm for investing additional funds to build new programs, even when there is a high probability that these initiatives will produce savings over time. Persuading policymakers to provide greater flexibility in how current funding is utilized to support children's services or investing resources in developing improved infrastructure will require ingenuity.

Making a stronger case for the material, as well as human benefits of the system of care approach is a promising strategy for seeking greater support for collaborative, family-driven community-based initiatives. The return on investment concept resonates with elected officials and the general public. While there are technical challenges associated with expanding the way in which ROI is calculated and reported, several prominent foundations, including The Pew Charitable Trusts and the MacArthur Foundation are supporting efforts to develop ROI indicators that measure long-term productivity benefits as well as direct cost savings. These efforts are addressing the positive social benefits of system of care as well as returns that are more easily translated into monetary terms (Stroul, Pires, Boyce, Krivelyova, & Walrath, 2014).

Looking toward the future, proponents of systems of care in Virginia and other states will need to continue to justify the financial and administrative assistance they are currently receiving and, in many instances, may have to seek additional support. The probability of obtaining ongoing approval will be dependent on the performance of their systems as well as broader political, social, and economic factors. Those systems that can report accurate consumer, provider, and fiscal outcome data have a better chance of succeeding. Being able to convince policymakers that the investment they are making in the system of care approach is producing beneficial child and family, societal, and fiscal results will bolster their ability to sustain and improve systems of care for at-risk youth and their families.

Chapter 16

Local Systems of Care

Virginia's experience with CSA demonstrated that there may be wide varia-tion in the manner in which localities implement a statewide system of care for at-risk youth. Some cities and counties have embraced the philosophy and have taken assertive action to develop collaborative, community-based service systems consistent with nationally recognized principles and goals. Other communities, for a variety of reasons including mistrust of the state, insufficient knowledge or leadership and lack of resources, have moved more slowly. Similarly, there are considerable differences within other states. In fact, some of the most fully evolved local systems of care are located in states that do not have well developed statewide programs.

Deborah Stark has chronicled the efforts of six unique and diverse commu-nities that have been working to establish collaborative working partnerships among three main groups: (a) families, (b) child welfare, and (c) children's mental health agencies and staff. These communities participated in a joint national initiative involving national organizations representing the three par-ticipating stakeholder groups known as A Partnership for Action. Stark has identified principles that have been helpful in guiding collaboration such as building and maintaining trust, agreeing on core values and common goals, respecting the knowledge and experience of each participant, recognizing strengths, limitations and needs, and sharing decision-making, risk-taking and accountability. From her research she also pinpointed interrelated ele-ments that characterized effective collaboration. These elements build upon the guiding principles described above as well as systems of care, and include strong relationships and trust, meaningful involvement of families/other caregivers, cultural competence, a focused work plan, and commitment with measurable goals, clear decision-making processes, and an understanding of the political environment (Stark, 1999).

Each site addressed a target issue that was germane to its community and engaged partners that had a stake in the issue. Each community was at a different developmental stage, with some sites already having strong family and/ or longstanding relationships between key agency personnel, while others had less fully developed infrastructures. In Sedgwick County, Kansas, which had recently privatized child welfare services, the parent advocacy program of the Mental Health Association worked with the private foster care contractor, the community health center, and the State Department of Social and Rehabilitative Services to strengthen the development of individualized plans of care for children with serious emotional disturbance and provide training for contractor staff on how to involve families. The collaborators utilized the strategy of co-locating child welfare staff with staff from the community mental health center by sharing office space, holding joint meetings, and celebrating special events together. Participants perceived that the co-location strategy produced strong personal and work relationships and led to improvement in care plans and more rapid access to appropriate services for children and families (Stark, 1999).

In Maryland, where separate reform efforts were taking place in welfare, child welfare, education, health and mental health, interested family members, and representatives from the child-serving agencies as well as clergy, labor, transportation, and local universities worked to determine the individual and collective effects of the multiple reform initiatives and decide how these various efforts could support and reinforce each other. Regional efforts were encouraged and the East Baltimore Mental Health Partnership (EBMHP) was established to coordinate reform efforts. Because key leaders within the child-serving system already had established relationships with each other, the partners were better able to listen and understand their issues, be responsive when partners asked for assistance, and act quickly and constructively to address challenges and problems.

Based on input from interviews conducted by family and community members, as well as an administrator from EBMHP, Neighborhood Liaisons were employed to act as a bridge to the program and the community to ensure that the services were meeting the needs of families. The Neighborhood Liaisons were chosen by family and community members and were required to live in the communities they work with. They performed a variety of functions to support families including serving as an aide in school when a child was experiencing difficulties, managing a tutoring program, assisting families to obtain clothing and household items, and arranging recreational activities. The Liaisons also needed to understand the importance of the mental health issues confronting the family and worked collaboratively with clinicians to assist the children and families. Supervisory staff was responsible for ensuring that the Neighborhood Liaisons and clinicians respected each other's roles and interacted in a mutually supportive manner (Stark, 1999).

Research on the EBMHP found that a majority of the 203 children served through this system of care showed significant improvement in functioning after six months compared to performance just prior to receiving services. Based on performance on the Child and Adolescent Functioning Assessment Scale (CAFAS), the scores of 60 percent of participants improved significantly, while 15 percent had the same scores after six months, and 25 percent showed a decline in functioning. Interestingly, improvement in functioning for these children appeared to be unrelated to key personal attributes, including age, gender, referral source, diagnosis, and risk level (Walrath, Mandell, & Leaf, 2001).

The EBMMHP employed a vertical systems integration management strategy. Careful attention was given to ensuring that collaboration was supported and reinforced at the three levels of their partnership: (a) the EBMHP Board, (b) the Multi-Agency Case Coordinating Committee, and (c) the service programs. This emphasis on collaboration assisted families and staff at all levels of the agency to become involved and focus on their own clearly delineated roles as well as the broader mission of the partnership. The director of the EBMHP cited the vertical systems integration management approach as a critical element of the program's success (Stark, 1990).

Developing effective child mental health programs in Native American communities poses unique challenges. The Sacred Child Program, which began as collaboration among four tribal entities and three affiliated tribes in North Dakota, offers a wraparound approach that addresses 12 life domain areas including spirituality, legal, and financial matters as well as traditional mental health issues. The Sacred Child Program, operated by the Turtle Mountain Band of Chippewa Indians, utilizes a team of five to ten people from the child's extended family, school, and community to provide a 'supportive web' for the children with mental health challenges and their families. The goal of the team, which often includes spiritual people in addition to institutional representatives, is to integrate community resources, cultural protective factors and natural support systems. Team meetings frequently occur in the family's home. The team employs a positive, strengths-focused approached to empower the child and family by convening people the family trusts who are able to offer positive support. The project coordinator describes a wraparound team meeting in which a boy, who was sitting outside of the group in a rolling chair, rolled his chair back to the table after hearing encouraging and hopeful comments and visions from members of the team. Eighty percent of children who have been temporarily removed from their homes in Turtle Mountain have been reunited with their families. In most instances where parents have terminated their parental rights, nearly all of the children have been placed with members of their extended family (Roundtree, 2010).

Other innovative Native American wraparound programs include the Mille Lacs Band of Ojibwe Family Services program in Onamia, Minnesota, which is entirely family-driven, and the Rosebud Sioux Tribe Sicangu Child and Family Service, which has adapted from a family-driven approach that originated with the Maori people in New Zealand. Families in the Mille Lacs Band choose the members of the wraparound team and identify child and family strengths and develop an individualized care plan. Foster care placement has decreased from 49 percent to 7 percent since the inception of this program. On the Rosebud reservation, Lakota philosophy, principles, and practice are integrated with conventional clinical approaches. Family members are encouraged to include cultural teaching, natural laws, and ceremonies in the preparation of their individualized family plan. For example, family engagement meetings borrow from the New Zealand Maori format by starting with the traditional practice of welcoming participants and offering words of wisdom. As the meeting proceeds, family members continue to acknowledge each other and state their relationship to the child (Rountree, 2010).

WRAPAROUND MILWAUKEE: THE GOLD STANDARD

I came into Wraparound on October 3, 2011. In my head I was thinking it was going to be a bad thing to do, that it wasn't going to work for me. But once I got into it, it was one of the best experiences I've had in my life. Even though it had me telling my feelings I realized it was going to help me get close to my family and open my leadership skills that are going to help me in the future. The family events, team meetings, and all the programs help you stay close to your family. Doing the talent show was one of the most fun things I ever did, and the Youth Council was a great place to have fun and eat. And my Care Coordinator was so good at helping me with stuff I didn't know. So you ask me how was my time in Wraparound? I will say it was one of the greatest times of my life and made me the person that successfully made it through Wraparound! (Wraparound Milwaukee, 2013, p. 5).

Wraparound Milwaukee (WM), established in 1995, has received many accolades, including being selected as an exemplary program by the President's New Freedom Mental Health Commission and receiving the Harvard Kennedy School 2009 Innovations in American Government Award in 2009. Frequently cited as a model system of care, WM has been a source of inspiration and guidance for many systems of care planners and administrators (Pires, 2010; President's New Freedom Commission on Mental Health, 2003; Sood & Cohen, 2014; Stroul, Pires, Boyce, Krivelyova, & Walrath, 2014).

What makes WM such a unique and emulated system? And how does WM maintain diligence in thoughtfully and methodically managing all of the elements of system of care philosophy and practice? The Milwaukee program has employed a comprehensive ecological approach to successfully incorporate the core system of care principles and goals into the direct service, program, organization, and overall system levels (Kamradt, 2000). In light of the strong trend toward privatizing services and the decision of most states to contract with managed care organizations to provide administrative services for their system of care programs, it is noteworthy that the County's Behavioral Health Division continues to serve as the care management entity for WM.

Initially funded by a six year, $15 million grant from the Center for Mental Health Services, Wraparound Milwaukee has grown into a comprehensive system of care and publicly operated managed care entity (i.e., HMO) serving families of children with severe emotional disturbance. With a budget of $48 million per year, including $28 million from Medicaid, WM provides care coordination for more than 1,500 children/families per year as well as direct services for more than 4,000 young people through its Mobile Urgent Treatment Team (MUTT) and other service programs for adolescents and youth transitioning to adulthood (Wraparound Milwaukee, 2013). The stated purpose of WM is to serve "children/adolescents with serious emotional and mental health needs and their families across child servicing systems including mental health, child welfare, juvenile justice, and special education" (Wraparound Milwaukee, 2013a, p.1).

According to Bruce Kamradt, who has directed Wraparound Milwaukee since its inception in the mid-1990s, several major situations converged simultaneously in Milwaukee to generate a "perfect storm" that spawned the establishment of this unique program. As many as 375 children from the county resided in high cost residential treatment facilities on any given day. The cost of paying for these placements had caused the child welfare and juvenile justice to add local funds to their budgets for several years, and the County Executive was annoyed about the rising expenditures and lack of creative solutions. At the same time, the Planning Council of Milwaukee had conducted studies showing poor outcomes for children discharged from these residential facilities. Wisconsin Medicaid was concerned about the growing number of children being admitted to psychiatric hospitals and the proliferation of private psychiatric hospitals in the region. Psychiatric hospitalization for children represented the fastest growing segment of the Medicaid budget. There was strong motivation to reduce the use of residential treatment facilities and inpatient psychiatric care as well as to improve the manner in which emergency rooms were being used to provide care for children with serious emotional disturbance (B. Kamradt, personal communication, August 13, 2014).

Serendipitously, Milwaukee was selected as one of the first 10 recipients of the federal Substance Abuse and Mental Health Services Administration (SAMHSA) grants to develop the relatively new system of care model. The SAMHSA funding provided an opportunity to address the concerns of the county administrators by testing the system of care approach. They began by developing a pilot project to return to their home community a select number of children who had previously been placed in residential treatment facilities and were not deemed as appropriate for discharge. These pilot projects, known as the "25 Kid Projects," gave Milwaukee an opportunity to work on developing the wraparound services, structures, and processes that would enable the county the ability to maintain child safely in the community while serving them at a considerably lower cost. In order to avoid skewing the pilots in favor of children with less severe problems and risks, they accepted the first 25 children referred, regardless of their level of symptoms or functioning. The first pilot project took six months to plan and two weeks to return the children and enroll them in the new community system. After conducting a series of these pilot initiatives, the leadership decided it was ready to go live, and decided to enroll the remaining 350 children over an 18 month period. (B. Kamradt, personal communication, August 13, 2014).

The core elements of WM's mission—treating youth and families with respect and dignity while supporting them to remain safely in their homes and community, collaborating with other agencies to create one plan for a better life, delivering culturally responsive quality care, and providing leadership to create lasting resources for families in their communities—resonate clearly with generally recognized system of care principles. Through a series of well-designed programs and administrative processes, the staff of WM, under the adroit leadership of Bruce Kamradt, has been able to largely fulfill this mission.

Through its managed care entity, WM contracts with eight community agencies that provide more than 100 case coordinators. These coordinators play a key role in assisting families to obtain needed services and supports using a wraparound approach that is strengths-based and highly individualized. WM has also organized and manages a network of more than 200 agency and individual service providers that deliver approximately 80 different services to children and families. Children and families often use three or four different services during their enrollment, with crisis stabilization, in-home therapy, transportation supports, individual/family therapy, and residential care representing the most frequently utilized services. Services are paid for through a fee-for-service approach, allowing families to have a wide choice of providers while providing oversight to ensure that all participants in the provider network meet uniform performance expectations. Families also are able to access flexible, discretionary funds to meet a specific need or enhance a plan of care on a one-time or emergency basis (Wraparound Milwaukee, 2014).

Wraparound Milwaukee employs a variety of care management strategies and techniques to ensure that services are provided in a manner consistent with the principles and goals of the system. Performance of providers is monitored through periodic utilization reviews, evaluations, and audits. A comprehensive data base is maintained to provide information on process, structure, and outcome indicators. Data are collected on who is being served and which services are being utilized, as well as whether planning of care is conducted according to system of care principles such as family and community-based service delivery and collaboration. Information on the cost and impact of services is also gathered and monitored. Outcome is evaluated using standardized assessment instruments that measure how the child and family are functioning, where the youth is living, how he or she is performing in school, and how satisfied the youth and family are satisfied with the care they are receiving. A high priority is placed on stakeholder development and performance enhancement through ongoing training and quality improvement programs and projects (Erdman, 2014).

In addition to its care management functions, WM has also established specific programs and structures to serve and support families. Responding to an unmet community need, a Mobile Urgent Treatment Team, comprised of teams of psychologists, social workers, nurses, case managers, and a consulting physician are available 24 hours per day to provide crisis intervention services to youth enrolled in the WM Program. Specific services programs also serve families with high-risk children with multiple challenges and young people with serious emotional or mental health needs who are transitioning to adulthood. WM also sponsors or has partnership with family and youth advocacy groups, including Families United of Milwaukee, which provides family advocacy and support service, and MOVE Wisconsin, a youth-run group (Wraparound Milwaukee, 2014a).

A notable strength of the WM program is the large amount and range of data it collects and makes available on a wide range of performance and outcome indicators. A recent report revealed that 70 percent of enrollees were African-American, with 12 percent Caucasian, and 10 percent Hispanic. Approximately twice as many boys are enrolled, though the number of girls served has increased by 5 percent during the past couple of years. The average age of enrollees is 14 years. Sixty-five percent of enrollees in WM were court ordered, with the majority of these youth having a Delinquency order and approximate one-third referred through a Children in Need of Protective Service order. The most frequent diagnoses were conduct disorder, ADHD and mood disorder. The top three presenting issues for youth for WM were school/community concerns, severe aggressiveness, and attention problems. The family issues most often presented were family emotional/mental illness, single/no parent in the home, and alcohol/drug abuse in the home (Wraparound Milwaukee, 2013; Erdman, 2014).

The principal evaluation tools used for measuring function levels of youth enrolled in WM programs are the Child Behavior Checklist (CBCL), completed by the parent/caregiver, and the companion Youth Self-Report (YSR), completed by the adolescent (Achenbach, 2009). Measurements are taken at intake, six months, one year, annually, and at the time of discharge. The CBCL and YSR provide data on the child's internal functioning such as mood and thought processing and external functioning as indicated by social and interpersonal interactions and behavior in the community. The total scores on the Internal and External scales of both instruments indicate the youth's level of function in that domain, and are categorized according to where they fall within three levels of functioning: (a) normal, (b) borderline, and (c) clinical. Youth whose total scores place them within the clinical range typically are in need of clinical intervention. Youth discharged in 2013 showed an improvement in total External scores on the CBCL, moving them from the higher end of the clinical range at intake to just outside of the borderline range at the time of discharge. On the Internal scale of the CBCL, youth moved on average from the high end of the borderline range at enrollment into the normal range at discharge. Improvement in functioning was slightly more pronounced for youth enrolled in the REACH program, a specific program designed for high-risk youth with more complex challenges. Youth reporting on the YSR viewed their level of functioning as less impaired than their parents/caregiver on the External scale at time of intake, but the degree of reported improvement at discharge closely mirrored parent/caregiver reports (Erdman, 2014).

One of the primary goals of the WM program is to help youth remain in the least restrictive environment and limit the number of times a young person changes placements. In 2013, 77 percent of WM youth achieved permanency at the time they left the program as defined by residing at home with their parents, being adopted, living with a relative or subsidized guardianship, or living independently. Another indicator of success is improved attendance at school. During 2013, school attendance exceeded the 85 percent benchmark for both WM and REACH enrollees (Erdman, 2014).

As previously mentioned, youth and family satisfaction surveys are administered one month after the family is enrolled, at six months, at one year, and each subsequent year and at the time the youth leaves the program. Youth and families are asked to rate their satisfaction with Care Coordination and Provider Network Services on a variety of indicators. For Care Coordinators, families are asked to assess how respectful the Coordinator has been, whether meetings are held at convenient times and places, and if information and service options are explained clearly. On a 5-point rating scale, with 1 meaning strongly disagree and 5 representing strongly agree, the average overall scores in 2013 for families rating their Care Coordinator at various time periods ranged from 4.80 after one month to 4.14 at the time of disenrollment.

Youth surveyed at the time of their disenrollment had an average overall satisfaction score of 3.99 (Erdman, 2014).

Family satisfaction with the Provider Network Services they received was also measured during the 4th and 9th months of enrollment. Average overall scores at 4-months were 4.59 and 4.69 at 9-months. It should be noted that the percentage of families that returned surveys was relatively small, except for family responses to Care Coordinators at time of disenrollment, which yielded an 80 percent return rate for youth and families asked to complete these surveys. The average rate of return for Care Coordinator Services prior to disenrollment was approximately 14 percent, while 6 percent of families completed Provider Network Services surveys (Erdman, 2014).

The average cost per year/per youth is $40,800. Although this is not a small sum, it compares favorably with the cost of other traditional service settings for these youth. The average yearly cost in the Milwaukee area of placing a youth in residential care is $108,000; for a corrections facility the approximate cost is $106,000 per year, and group home care averages $70,000 (Erdman, 2014). In comparison, the average cost per year/per youth in Virginia's CSA is slightly less than $23,000 per year (Office of Comprehensive Services, 2014). Comparing program costs for different geographic areas is difficult. Available data do not allow for ascertaining whether the populations served by different states are comparable, and cost of living and other local state and locality-specific factors may influence the cost of services. However, the costs of living for Wisconsin and Virginia are fairly comparable and Milwaukee is an urban county, indicating that the WM program has been relatively effective in containing costs for serving high-risk youth.

WM also tracks several process and structure indicators in order to evaluate and improve performance of the core functions of the system of care. For instance, developing and implementing a family- and needs-driven plan of care provides a strong foundation for providing appropriate services. Families are asked to rate the degree to which progress is being made in meeting identified needs using a 1–5 rating scale for which 1 represents minimal progress on a particular area of need and 5 indicates the need has been successfully met. In the most recent quality assurance/quality improvement report, the average overall rating for progress related to needs was 3.41. This score represented a 9 percent improvement over last year's ratings, but fell short of the 3.75 target score established as a threshold of desired performance (Erdman, 2014).

The agency also uses audits, surveys, evaluation data, and other outcome measures to monitor the quality of care and compliance with policies and practice. The results of these reviews often form the basis for corrective action and performance improvement initiatives. A recent audit of seven crisis stabilization agencies found overall compliance scores of more than

97 percent for compliance with quality of care criteria and agency/provider compliance with administrative and fiscal expectations. The most recent Performance Improvement Project (PIP) examined how to enhance planning for the transition to adulthood. The specific question addressed by the PIP was whether "targeted transition training focusing on the growth and development of youth, increase the knowledge and skill of Care Coordinators as it relates to transitional planning?" The agency hopes to use the results of a pre-post training test to determine whether increased knowledge of transition planning following training will improve compliance in completing the transition summary for enrolled youth age 16 and above, and will enhance transitional planning for young people moving into adulthood (Erdman, 2014).

In addition to focusing on process and outcome, the WM program places a strong emphasis on structure. The program's director, Bruce Kamradt asserts that:

> A lot of the failures I see, and there have been many failures of programs, have been around the structure and organization. So we created a very tight model, with Wraparound Milwaukee functioning as what we call a care management entity that would oversee all provision of services to children with serious emotional and mental health needs across all systems. (B. Kamradt, personal communication, August 13, 2014)

The administrative team of WM tracks progress and initiates corrective action to ensure that Care Coordinators and Child and Family Teams (CFT) are functioning in accordance to stated expectations and objectives. For instance, WM established an 85 percent threshold for Care Coordinators documenting in their progress notes that a CFT has been held each month. For 2013, compliance for this indicator was 90 percent. Attention is also given to how the Provider Network is educated. An assessment of WM's training program revealed that Care Coordinators were not receiving critical information on a timely basis. Based on this finding, the team responsible for training modified the presentation schedule to present training modules more frequently, resulting in smaller classes that allowed for greater personal interaction and more expedient provision of educational material (Erdman, 2014).

The Wraparound Management Team and Quality Assurance/ Quality Improvement Department review all functions of the system to assess performance and identify opportunities for improvement. Even procedures for registering formal grievances and complaints are scrutinized. The agency tracks the number and source of grievances, complaints and concerns, as well as their disposition. WM reported that family members or enrollees did not file any grievances in 2013 and of the 33 written and verbal complaints about service providers that were received, approximately 50 percent were substantiated or partially substantiated (Erdman, 2014).

Periodic evaluations are conducted to address critical issues. Concern about the extent to which delinquent behavior of enrollees was being reduced prompted WM to conduct a recidivism study to assess the extent to which youth who were referred to wraparound because of a delinquent offense have committed subsequent offenses during their enrollment. Data were analyzed for youth enrolling in WM between October 1, 2009 and July 31, 2010. Of the 411 youth whose enrollment had been prompted by delinquent behavior during this time frame, 46 youth, or 11 percent of all WM youth committed a subsequent offense (Goldfarb, 2010). In contrast, the researchers of other states reported juvenile crime recidivism rates ranging from 30 to 50 percent. Analysis of when youth reoffended revealed that delinquent behaviors were significantly more likely to occur within the first three months of enrollment and continued to taper off during the two subsequent three-month periods included in the study (Goldfarb, 2010). This finding prompted the leadership of WM to focus more attention on addressing risk factors associated with reoffending at the beginning of the at-risk youth's enrollment.

Wraparound Milwaukee has a proud 20-year history of effectively serving families of children with severe emotional disturbance. The numerous accolades and positive reviews it has received, along with the impressive results it has produced, affirm its reputation as an exemplary local system of care. The leadership of WM has successfully incorporated all of the philosophical, programmatic, technical, organizational, and financial components prescribed by the system of care model, along with its supporting research in its continuous efforts to establish, sustain and improve their comprehensive, collaborative, family-driven managed care entity and array of community-based services for more than two decades. While the outcomes it has produced are laudable, the attention given to improving and evolving the system is equally impressive. WM is indeed a complete package.

What accounts for the enduring effectiveness of Wraparound Milwaukee? How does this Wisconsin-based program compare with Virginia's CSA? Clearly, the designers and administrators of WM have worked diligently to ensure that their efforts are faithful to the core tenets of the system of care model. In addition to addressing all elements of this comprehensive ecological framework, they have painstakingly striven to establish and maintain appropriate balance among the critical factors and forces within the system. Knowing that large complex service systems are susceptible to rapid expansion of procedures, routine, and other self-insulating organizational forces, Kamradt and his colleagues have continued to make sure that families have a strong voice at the direct service, program, and system governance levels. While a high priority is placed on service provider accountability, WM management staff recognizes the importance of adequately preparing and supporting those who are providing care. Thus, efforts have been made to continuously offer training on evidence-based and practice informed approaches and have developed strategies for making it easy for providers to electronically document service notes and obtain payment in a timely manner (B. Kamradt, personal communication, August 13, 2014).

The leadership of WM acknowledges the importance of investing energy to ensure that all key stakeholders embrace a shared vision, guiding principles, and goals. They also realized that simply having a sound wraparound philosophy was not enough. They credit the success of WM to the attention that has been paid to working through the administrative and operational issues and details that could facilitate or hinder effective implementation.

Initially, it was important to understand the unique political structure of Milwaukee's child-service system. In Wisconsin, the county generally operates juvenile justice, education, and mental health services. However, Milwaukee County has a hybrid system in which child welfare, Medicaid, and other funding sources are state operated. A high priority for the MW leadership was to establish strong collaborative relationships with these child-serving agencies and establish mechanisms for pooling funds from multiple sources to create a single payer in order to provide flexibility and leverage financial resources. These relationships have been enhanced by attention to detail. WM has written contracts with all of its partners and Kamradt explains the importance of having these written agreements. "They spell out roles and duties, so you know who does what, who pays for what and what is everyone's role" (B. Kamradt, personal communication, August 13, 2014). Kamradt also credits WM's good relationship with the courts:

> The judicial system has supported us because Milwaukee Care Coordinators have legal standing in court the same way as child welfare and juvenile probation workers so we go to court . . . we present our reports in court, our recommendations, we have screeners in court, we have care coordinators, read court reports, we confirm the plan reviews for the justice kids, so we do a lot of the things but the court legitimizes that authority by saying technically in a way there are three systems in Milwaukee county: child welfare, juvenile justice, and wrap around. Those are the three systems and wraparound is the system for severely emotionally disabled kids across all other systems. So, I think the court helped us legitimize all of those processes. (B. Kamradt, personal communication, August 13, 2014)

The establishment of a single, comprehensive data system has also contributed to the cohesion and effectiveness of WM. By 2000 they had created one of the country's first electronic health records for a behavioral health system of care. All partners, including care coordinators and service providers participate in the information system and have access to the data generated. Information on performance and outcomes is shared and utilized in order to ensure that practice is consistent with system of care and Wraparound principles and for other quality assurance/improvement purposes. Providers can get authorization and submit claims through the electronic information system as well and record their progress notes. Providers appreciate the systems efficiency as they are often paid within five to six days of submitting their online bill. The information system also facilitates connecting families with a strong family organization (i.e., Families United) that is a useful vehicle for providing training to caregivers (B. Kamradt, personal communication, August 13, 2014).

When asked to identify the core elements that have enabled WM to sustain its effective level of performance for nearly 20 years, Kamradt responds, "A key to our success has been that the principal leaders and managers have stayed from the start of the program" (B. Kamradt, personal communication, August 13, 2014). Kamradt estimates that 75 percent of the original administrative staff still works in the program. Although, there has been more turnover at the direct care and administrative structures of partner agencies, many of the individuals who leave their positions continue to work in the mental health field (B. Kamradt, personal communication, August 13, 2014).

As noted earlier, strong, continuous leadership at the highest level, is a critical factor in developing and sustaining effective systems of care. Kamradt has been at the helm of the WM program since its early stages of planning. Prior to leading WM, Kamradt served as an administrator in child welfare and juvenile justice court agencies and worked as a hospital administrator in a children's mental health facility. In addition to having knowledge about the practices and cultures of these child-serving systems, he has always had an orientation toward community-based care and brought to this endeavor a perspective that:

> It was a little strange that our approach was fundamentally kind of separate, with the separate systems addressing their own kids and families and not really coordinating well and thinking about the advantages of doing this in a single system with a single approach. (B. Kamradt, personal communication, August 13, 2014)

Finally, Kamradt confesses to liking the business side of children's services, which led him to focus on developing managed care system. "I wanted to do it [WM] as a health insurance model and surrounded myself with people who were likeminded and had expertise we could utilize" (B. Kamradt, personal communication, August 13, 2014). In response to a question regarding expressed concerns about managed care entities being more concerned about

bottom-line profit than the quality of care, Kamradt responds, "From a philosophical and value basis, this strength-based, family-drive, family-involved
model is really easy to get behind and support; it's not the money because
I work for the government" (B. Kamradt).

Parenthetically, in Wisconsin, as in Virginia, support for this large-scale
transformation endeavor has not always followed party-lines. One of the
strongest advocates for WM was Scott Walker, the Governor of Wisconsin,
who led the controversial effort to downsize state government. Prior to serving as governor, Walker served as County Executive for Milwaukee County
from 2002 to 2010.

Through a unique blend of visionary planning, innovative program
development, and sound business practice, Kamradt and the diverse set of
committed stakeholders in Milwaukee, have been able to create an effective
comprehensive System of Care for children and adolescents with serious
emotional and mental health needs and their families. Over the past 20 years,
they have developed and sustained a system that is responsive to the unique
conditions of their locality, including the political and economic dynamics of
the area, while remaining faithful to the CORE SOC principles. In the next
and final chapter, we will attempt to synthesize the efforts of Wraparound
Milwaukee, Virginia, and other states and localities that have launched ambitious initiatives to transform services for children and families with multiple
stressors. Drawing upon the experiences of these bold pioneers, we will highlight the factors that contributed to successful outcomes as well as those that
seemed to impede progress. We will describe the tensions inherent to such
a complex system and strategies for trying to establish an appropriate balance among these sometimes competing forces. Finally we will offer lessons
learned and provide guidance for those interested in embarking on complex
system reform endeavors.

Chapter 17

Walking a High Wire on a Windy Day

Lessons from the Field

Establishing a System of Care (SOC) is not for the faint of heart. The challenge of sustaining and enhancing a coordinated, comprehensive, child-centered, family-driven program of community-based services and supports for at-risk youth is equally daunting. Assembling the multiple components required to operate a High Fidelity Wraparound program requires ingenuity and patience. Traditional attitudes and practices, which include a view of service consumers as passive recipients and a silo mentality regarding agency functioning, are often deeply entrenched. These ideological biases and bureaucratic tendencies are in direct conflict with SOC values and principles. Considerable dialogue and education are needed to actualize principles of child and family engagement and interdisciplinary collaboration.

There are also multiple technical issues that have to be dealt with, including creating a functional data system for recording, monitoring, and evaluating performance, establishing operating policies and protocols as well as management structures that support the principles and goals of the system. It is also necessary to put in place quality assurance/improvement measures to ensure that the programs are functioning effectively. In addition to focusing on the specific elements of the system, attention must also be given to less tangible aspects of this multi-faceted, collaborative endeavor. Successful SOC endeavors have diligently promoted good communication among all stakeholders and have been able to maintain an appropriate balance among potential competing interests and goals. Each of these internal SOC priorities needs to be addressed: empowering individuals and organizations, providing quality care, controlling costs, and holding partners accountable. Equally important is the need to educate key community stakeholders and the general public as well as attend to the multiple factors outside of the immediate system that may impact its programs.

Beyond ensuring that the structures and processes within the SOC are operating effectively, planners and administrators also have to be cognizant of the influence of broader contextual forces. How will prevailing political interests and ideology impact support for the SOC approach? What effect will overall economic conditions and specific fiscal policies have on the program? Are there social, cultural, or technological factors that leadership needs to take into account in planning and modifying their local or state SOC?

Just as the tightrope performer has to take into account multiple factors that may impact his/her immediate journey, including how taut the wire is and the strength and direction of the wind, proponents of system reform are constantly gauging the effect of internal and external forces as they delicately navigate the precarious course leading to successful transformation. For both participants in these high-risk endeavors, balance is imperative.

Having already acknowledged that each community and state is distinctive and that SOC design efforts must take into account unique conditions of their specific geographic area, there is opportunity to benefit from the experience of others. There are lessons that can be learned from the efforts of families, policy makers, administrators, providers, and advocates who have wrestled with the complex issues inherent in developing and managing these community-based systems. In this chapter, the successful strategies that have been employed as well as the false starts and unintended consequences that have occurred in Virginia and other states that have established comprehensive SOC are presented. This material has been synthesized into a series of guidelines and suggestions intended to assist those engaged in reform initiative.

These guidelines are not intended to be directly prescriptive; rather, their purpose is to heighten awareness and stimulate thinking about approaches and strategies that are relevant for individuals and organizations involved in transforming services for children and families. Hopefully these suggestions will resonate with policy makers, administrators, advocates, and others who are grappling with the multi-faceted challenge of system reform, who can adapt these guidelines to the unique characteristics and conditions of their localities or states. The first set of guidelines pertains to transformation efforts in general. These universal suggestions are followed by recommendations specifically focused on SOC reform and management initiatives.

UNIVERSAL GUIDANCE FOR PROMOTING SERVICE SYSTEM REFORM

Having a Shared Belief System is Necessary

Significant transformation of longstanding policies and practice requires all stakeholders to adopt a common vision of what they are trying to produce and the core values and principles that will guide their reform efforts. One of the defining characteristics of the successful state and local SOC examples cited earlier was the strength and consistency of stakeholders' commitment to SOC tenets. The state and local leaders in Virginia, Massachusetts, New Jersey, and other states invested considerable time and resources to ensure that participants at all levels understood the importance of engaging and empowering families, focusing on strengths as well as needs, individually tailoring programming, and developing community-based service opportunities. Government officials, child agency staff, service providers, and families were educated on the importance of genuine collaboration in providing holistic care and achieving positive outcomes. Ongoing training in these fundamental principles was provided and stakeholders were continually and incentivized to incorporate this way of thinking into their behavior and actions.

In local communities and states where reform is effectively implemented and sustained, the underlying belief system becomes an organic component of how service is provided and, in fact, transforms the culture of the environment of the workplace. Simply paying lip service to a set of high-sounding platitudes may propel short term momentum, but establishing and maintaining genuine reform requires ongoing commitment from all stakeholders. Translating philosophical principles into practice is not easy, especially when previous work routines were convenient and offered staff protection from external threats. Successful transformation leaders recognize the value of establishing a shared belief system, as well as the difficulty of helping stakeholders change traditional patterns of behavior. These officials, administrators, and advocates take into account the resources and energy needed to nurture and sustain fidelity to the basic tenets of the reform when developing their implementation plans.

. . . But a Common Set of Values and Principles Is Not Sufficient to Actualize an Effective Reform

While establishing a common philosophy and vision are critical components of major change efforts, considerable attention must also be given to creating a sound infrastructure and functional operating procedures to support implementation of the reform. Bruce Kamradt, the Director of the nationally acclaimed Wraparound Milwaukee Program stresses the importance of organizational structure, noting that "building a very tight organization has been a key to making and sustaining what we have been doing over time" (B. Kamradt, personal communication, August 13, 2014).

The quality of service provision is affected by a variety of factors. The knowledge and skill of individuals delivering the service, as well as their access to state-of-the art technology is obviously important. The ways in which these services are organized and the supports required to ensure that they achieve the intended results are also critical. Pires (2010) identifies 24 functions that need to be organized in a defined manner to ensure that care is provided in a manner consistent with the core values and principles of the SOC. These functions include, but are not limited to planning, day-to-day system management, and financial functions, such as financing, purchasing, contracting, and billing, and claims processing. Pires also lists planning and management for individual consumers and service programs, workforce development, utilization management, and quality management/improvement as critical functions that require appropriate structure. Finally, she notes the importance of having in place suitable mechanisms for protecting the privacy and ensuring the rights of consumers.

Building an appropriate infrastructure for a comprehensive service system requires considerable diligence. Continuous effort and attention to detail are needed to develop each of the many structural and procedural components associated with these complex systems. Beyond attending to each function or structure, it is also important to ensure that the individual elements are properly aligned and coordinated with each other as well as the broader mission of the service system. Efforts to establish effective and efficient programs and operating systems must focus on both micro and macro levels. A strong local infrastructure will not function optimally without sufficient support and direction from state and federal levels. Likewise, the quality of a central system is dependent upon performance at the community level.

The following examples from SOC described earlier in this book illustrate the importance of developing sound organizational structure to support service delivery transformation.

- Recognizing the importance of having a well-prepared child mental health workforce, Ohio established seven university-based Coordinating Centers of Excellence to provide training, technical assistance, and other forms of support. Each Center focuses on a specific service system practice, working with all stakeholders to ensure that their participation is guided by the best available empirical evidence in that practice domain. These Centers address a range of critical child and family service issues, including high-fidelity wraparound services, family engagement, local service coordination, and treatment modalities and approaches such as trauma-informed care and treatment for individuals with co-occurring substance as abuse and mental health challenges.
- The state of New Jersey recognized that while engaging families was an important component of an effective system of care, overcoming traditional negative attitudes and behaviors toward families of children with serious behavioral health issues would not be easy. In response to this challenge,

the state established a statewide network of family-run Family Support Organizations (FSO) to work with local Care Management Organizations. The FSOs are funded to provide family-to-family assistance to engage and empower families with children participating in the state's SOC.

- Concerned about rising costs, relatively high numbers of children placed in congregate care settings, and a lack of substantive collaboration among child-serving agencies involved in the Comprehensive Services Act for At Risk Youth (CSA), The City of Alexandria in Virginia launched a strategic planning initiative. A diverse group of stakeholders, including senior city officials, child agency representatives, private service agencies, and family members developed a strategic plan to address these concerns. In the year following the establishment of the plan, the number of children placed in congregate care declined significantly, expenditures were reduced and collaborative participation increased. The strategic plan continues to serve as a guide for managing Alexandria's SOC. The plan is formally reviewed each year and the City continues to demonstrate improvement in the areas addressed by the plan.

- In establishing their system of care, Massachusetts wanted to ensure that children received services that were responsive to the needs and strengths of the child and family. Considerable attention was given to developing and implementing appropriate clinical screening and assessment measures and putting in place mechanisms for matching consumers with suitable services. In addition to providing extensive initial and ongoing training on these assessment procedures, the Executive Office of Health and Human Services, which is responsible for administering the children's behavioral health initiative, also evaluates child outcomes. Using the Child and Adolescent Needs and Strengths (CANS) instrument, procedures have been established for monitoring the extent to which practice adheres to the stated principles and goals of the system. Using an empirically validated scale, evaluators routinely measure the degree of fidelity between practice and principle in areas such as whether care is individualized, strength-based, and culturally competent, as well as whether service is provided in a collaborative, team-based manner, allowing for families to have a voice and exercise choice in determining how care is delivered. These data are compared to the performance of other states and are incorporated into performance improvement initiatives.

- The leadership of Wraparound Milwaukee (WM) was familiar with the difficulties associated with attaining genuine collaboration among organizations and agencies. In developing agreements between service provider organizations and WM, the Milwaukee county administrators took affirmative steps to promote clarity among participants and establish customer-friendly transaction procedures. Contracts with service providers spell out the specific roles and duties of the parties, defining in detail the precise responsibilities and rights of all parties. WM has also established an efficient, internet-based billing system that allows service providers to easily submit claims and receive payment in a timely manner.

Sustaining a Successful Reform Requires Continuous Vigilance

As President George W. Bush painfully learned when he prematurely congratulated the Director of the Federal Emergency Management Agency during Hurricane Katrina, there are risks associated with declaring victory too soon. While the enactment and initial implementation of a significant change initiative or major reform is cause for celebration, the hard work of ensuring that the transformation continues to fulfill its intended purpose should not be underestimated. In *Who Killed Change? Solving the Mystery of Leading People Through Change,* Blanchard and his colleagues present a clever dramatic depiction of the reasons 60–70 percent of organizational change initiatives do not succeed (Blanchard, Britt, Hoekstra, & Zigarmi, 2009). They identify 13 critical organizational functions that change agents often fail to adequately address once the change initiative has been launched.

These core functions, which Blanchard and associates consider essential to sustaining organizational reform, include the culture of the organization, the willingness of members of the organization to engage in new behavior demanded by the change, and communication between change leaders and individual's being asked to change. They also cite the importance of having an active change leadership team that speaks with a single voice, resolves concerns expressed by those being asked to change, and reinforces the sense of urgency by continually explaining why the change is needed and the importance of implementing the new practices immediately. Mirroring the experience of SOC proponents, Blanchard also stresses that organizations need to have a clear and compelling vision of what the future will look like after the change has been successfully integrated, along with a realistic implementation plan and a viable effort to define and create an infrastructure to support the change. Finally, the authors of *Who Killed Change?*, point out that many change initiatives fail because sufficient attention is not given to training participants to acquire skills needed to succeed, offering appropriate incentives to reinforce desired behaviors and results, managing performance by providing appropriate structure and support, and holding staff and leaders accountable by ensuring that their actions and results are consistent with the intentions and goals of the change initiative (Blanchard, Britt, Hoekstra, & Zigarmi, 2009).

As the authors of *Who Killed Change?* expose readers to the potential suspects, it soon becomes apparent that all of these organizational functions need to be adequately addressed to ensure effective, ongoing implementation. If even one of the core functions is neglected, the risk of failure is significant. System of care leaders in localities such as Hampton and Alexandria, Virginia, and Milwaukee, Wisconsin as well as state officials in Virginia and other states that have engaged in comprehensive transformation of services for at-risk children and families have recognized the important role these functions play in establishing and maintaining effective service systems. They also acknowledge the difficulty of devoting sufficient resources and attention to all of these critical areas, and maintaining an appropriate balance between encouraging stakeholders to take initiative and providing structure, guidance, and at times, sanctions to make sure stakeholders' actions are consistent with the principles and goals of the reform initiative.

The Race Is Not Always to the Swift

Mobilizing a major reform campaign requires considerable energy, commitment, and a belief that the proposed changes will produce significant positive outcomes. Reform leaders need to convince concerned stakeholders as well as government officials that if enacted, the proposed policies will lead to significant improvement. Unfortunately, the need to garner support sometimes leads reform proponents to promise too much. When this occurs, unrealistic expectations are set and post enactment performance is bound to be disappointing.

Lyons (2004) encourages public sector leaders to follow a course of 'planned incrementalism' in order to mitigate disappointment stemming from the discrepancy between anticipated and actual progress. By establishing a timetable that prescribes a logical sequence of developmental objectives and activities leading to the overall goal of the proposed transformation, it may be possible to reduce frustration and even increase support for the change effort. Lyons acknowledges that progressing by taking small steps is not very "sexy," but is more likely to enhance the credibility and success of the initiative.

New Jersey and Massachusetts, both of which have sustained effective SOC approaches over an extended period of time, developed their programs incrementally. In New Jersey, officials first restructured the funding system and developed a comprehensive plan for implementing SOC. During the next six years, the state systematically implemented systems of care in 15 service areas, focusing on several geographic areas each year. New Jersey also added critical support components such as training, utilization review, care coordination, and data support processes during this same period. Massachusetts, which was under a federal court order to remediate problems with its child behavioral health system, also employed a planned incremental implementation approach, including conducting pilot projects in discrete geo-graphic areas in order to evaluate and refine their SOC model.

UNINTENDED CONSEQUENCES HAPPEN

Despite the best efforts of reform proponents and planners, comprehensive change initiative will always produce unexpected outcomes. While some of these results may be harmless or benevolent, more often the unintended con-sequences are problematic.

Although it is not possible to completely prevent unintended consequences, recognizing that reform efforts are likely to produce unforeseen after-effects may assist in reducing their occurrence. In the early stages of initiation, planners should study similar reform efforts in order to identify unexpected outcomes that arose following enactment. With this knowledge, it may be possible for policy makers and administrators to anticipate potential problems and incorporate provisions or safeguards that will diminish the likelihood of unintended results.

Having a perspective on how reform efforts evolve may also assist plan-ners to anticipate future problems. The United States has been focused on reforming government since shortly after the ink was dry on the first version of the U.S. Constitution. While reform is inherent to the democratic system of government, the focus of reform efforts change periodically. Paul Light has described the tides of reform as they applied to making government work better. He observes that unlike ocean tides which simultaneously erode and reshape the shore, tides of reform are accumulative, adding administrative sediments such as new rules, statutes, paperwork, and administrative hier-archy. Because these tides are accumulative they may inadvertently create things they hope to eliminate (Light, 1997).

Typically, these tides take the shape of comprehensive statutes rather than an experiment with the single agency. Even when pilot initiatives are under taken the full force of implementation usually takes place regardless of the outcome of the pilot. Light also observes that tides are often at cross pur-poses. For example, striving to open government to make it more transparent to the public, sometimes closes other curtains in veils of secrecy. At one time programs are zealous about putting more inspectors in the field to monitor and regulate behavior, while in the next year these same programs may leash them back.

According to Light, these tides of reform seem to be accelerating. The time between reforms is shrinking, they occur more frequently and seem to change directions more quickly (Light, 1997). Although it is not possible to control these tides, planners and administrators who understand these cycles may be able to prepare more effectively for shifts in public sentiment.

For example, the movement toward privatization has spawned significant growth in the number of for-profit and not-for-profit service providers. It is not likely that this trend will be reversed in the near future, but policy makers and administrators have become aware of potential problems associated with having large numbers of private service providers. This knowledge has led to enhanced efforts to monitor the performance of these organizations and provide safeguards in order to reduce risks. Although current public sentiment does not generally favor government intervention, increased regulation has been deemed acceptable when significant problems or abuses have been discovered. In addition to strengthening regulatory functions, there are other less controlling approaches that may be employed to protect consumers, and improve performance and compliance. These strategies include providing feedback using performance data, encouraging private providers to participate in performance and quality improvement initiatives, and offering training on appropriate and evidence-based practices.

Could the original developers of Virginia's CSA have anticipated that establishing an eligibility distinction between mandated children who received federal entitlement benefits and non-mandated children would produce problems? Probably. Were they able to envision the extent to which the mandated versus non-mandated division would create a two-tiered system that severely limited access to services for those without mandated benefits? Probably not. And even if the CSA developers were aware of the future difficulties that would ensue, it is unlikely that they would have been able to address the concerns of federal agencies that wanted guarantees that children entitled to federal benefits would be served by the new CSA, while also finding a viable way to serve all children and families who needed this level of care.

However, the long-term detrimental impact of this two-tiered eligibility system could have been ameliorated. Once policy makers became aware of the extent to which non-mandated children with severe behavioral health challenges were being denied appropriate care, corrective action could have taken place if there had been stronger external advocacy pressure and greater awareness of the problem and commitment to the CSA system from senior officials.

This criticism is not intended as glib second-guessing. Sustaining a complex reform effort, given the multiple political, social, economic, and technological forces that may impact such an initiative is a demanding undertaking. Ensuring that the transformation continues to be faithful to its initial values and guiding principles adds additional degrees of difficulty. Yet, as the bipartisan effort in Virginia to eliminate the onerous requirement that forced parents to relinquish custody of their child in order to obtain services demonstrates, with sufficient will and persistence, unintended consequences can be remediated.

GUIDANCE FOR ESTABLISHING AND
SUSTAINING EFFECTIVE SYSTEMS OF CARE

The universal transformation principles and strategies described above are relevant for individuals and organizations interested in developing and improving system of care policy and practice. The following guidance, while also germane to other types of health and human service reform, is more specifically tailored to the issue of providing comprehensive care for vulnerable children and their families.

Be Sensitive to Culture . . . at Multiple Levels

System of care principles highlight the importance of taking into account and being responsive to the ethnic, religious, and other cultural beliefs and practices of the families being served. Given the diversity of contemporary communities, this is a formidable challenge. Addressing culture, however, is central to SOC in other ways. Longstanding misperceptions about behavioral health and mental illness have permeated the attitudes and behaviors of policy makers and practitioners as well as the general public. Overgeneralized fear about all children with emotional difficulties being prone to violent behavior has often spawned overly restrictive placement decisions. Unfounded perceptions that parents are the primary source of their children's problems have fostered attitudes of mistrust and blame in some child-serving staff. This parent-blaming orientation, which is manifested in covert as well as overt ways, is detrimental to the family engagement and empowerment principles of SOC. Changing these entrenched beliefs, or replacing staff who are unable to alter their views, takes time and requires considerable training as well as other administrative intervention and support.

Effective implementation of the SOC paradigm also requires a significant change in the organizational culture and practice of participating child-serving agencies. Agency personnel have traditionally functioned within a silo-oriented environment in which the internal priorities of the organization are addressed through a linear management hierarchy, and emphasis is placed on protecting the agency from external threats. The political pressures that public agencies experience often produce a risk-adverse work environment. Actualizing SOC principles, such as team work, collaboration, and child/family engagement requires a substantial shift in mind-set, a different array of workplace behaviors, and a drastic change in organizational culture.

Altering entrenched organizational patterns begins with a commitment and accompanying supportive actions from the highest level of leadership. Within the child-serving system, this involves obtaining buy-in from cabinet members and elected officials as well as agency heads. In addition to blessing the

SOC collaborative approach, leadership must also realign incentives. Senior officials and agency directors need to recognize the value of cross-agency cooperation, and devise strategies for rewarding innovative, interdisciplinary teamwork, and other proactive practices consistent with the SOC philosophy. These changes must occur at all levels of the organization, with agency directors working with senior managers, who in turn work with unit directors and line supervisors to ensure that everyone understands and embraces these new practices.

Too often, senior administrators think it is sufficient to issue a proclamation informing staff of the proposed changes in practice without taking the actions needed to ensure successful adoption and implementation of the collaborative approach. When this occurs, line-level staff are often left to function in a vacuum, lacking the support of their supervisors and the agency. In these instances, staff typically feels scapegoated and reverts to safer, bureaucratic practices.

Exemplary SOC endeavors such as Hampton and Alexandria in Virginia and Wraparound Milwaukee at the local level and efforts in states like Massachusetts have acknowledged the importance of addressing the organizational culture and practices needed to effectively implement the SOC paradigm. The leadership of these systems has invested considerable resources in training participating stakeholders and continually monitoring and refining performance to ensure that actual practice conforms to stated principles.

Well-Targeted Incentives Leverage Desired Change

When Virginia modified its CSA funding policy to provide a higher state match rate for community-based services, localities accelerated their efforts to reduce placement of at-risk youth in residential settings for which they would receive proportionally less reimbursement from the state. Wraparound Milwaukee, recognizing that many service providers were reluctant to participate in the child service system because the billing and payment were cumbersome, redesigned its payment system to be more efficient and provider-friendly. In order to enhance the role of families in their system of care, New Jersey created a funding mechanism as well as a statewide network of family-run support organizations that enabled veteran families to assist families with children currently being served to understand and participate as partners in their child's care process.

These examples of providing incentives to encourage practice consistent with the SOC paradigm illustrate how well-targeted inducements may facilitate transformation efforts. In some instances these incentives may add additional costs. These expenses are often offset by long-term savings produced by improved performance. Even when reimbursement rates are increased, as in the case of Virginia increasing its state match rate for community-based services, the net effect may be cost neutral or even produce decreased total expenditure due to reductions in placing children in more expensive congregate care settings.

Deciding which incentives will have the most beneficial impact requires a careful cost/benefit analysis as well as a good understanding of the driving forces that influence the individuals or organizations one wishes to influence. For instance, in Virginia, where both local and state government play a significant role in managing and funding services for children, it is important that the inducement offered does not conflict with other political, fiscal, or social priorities of the locality. If local officials or their constituents had perceived that the intervention of the state was intended to strengthen state control over service delivery rather than enhance local government's ability to function effectively, the state match policy change might not have been well received. In states where local government does not view itself as having as much direct responsibility for managing and supporting children's services, establishing funding strategies that facilitate achieving SOC goals would pose different, and perhaps, fewer challenges.

Policy makers and administrators need to realize that incentives should not be limited to offering financial inducements. Realigning payments to encourage use of less restrictive alternatives and providing bonuses for exceptional performance certainly facilitate goal-congruent behavior. However, there are other strategies that should be considered by those interested in enhancing productivity and encouraging practice consistent with the SOC paradigm. For instance, agency staff accustomed to more traditional approaches may feel uncomfortable or unprepared to function within the collaborative SOC framework. Providing sufficient training and enhanced supervision will likely assist workers in making this transition. Recognition of progress, in the form of awards or targeted praise will likely be appreciated. CSA programs in Virginia and SOC programs in other states have established mechanisms for acknowledging teamwork, cooperation among stakeholders, and other practices consistent with SOC principles and goals. Offering opportunities for staff to provide input on how to improve work processes and performance as well as workplace satisfaction may also promote a sense of empowerment and boost morale.

Good Data Facilitates Sound Decision-Making

One of the hallmarks of successful state and local SOC efforts has been their ability to effectively establish and utilize data to inform planning, implementation, and modification of policy and practice. Given the complexity of the transactions they are dealing with and the diversity of perspectives among the multiple participating stakeholders, these SOCs recognized the need to create a firm empirical foundation to guide their work. The data bases created by programs like Milwaukee and Massachusetts are comprehensive and functional. They address all aspects of system performance, beginning with the initial assessment of the needs and strengths of the child and family being served and concluding with measurement of outcomes, including child and family functioning and disposition and cost of care. In between the intake and outcome components, these systems also track performance that is incorporated into intermediate processes and functions such as utilization management, quality assurance, and continuous quality improvement.

These data are used at the individual child and family levels as well as aggregate program or system level, where the progress of multiple children is monitored. For example, the CANS assessment has been used as a tool for assessing the level of service required for an individual child. The CANS has also been employed to measure outcomes for each child. In addition to its use as a functional assessment instrument for individual consumers, aggregate CANS data have been used by administrators and policy makers to evaluate program performance, make decisions about allocating resources, and guide modify/improve system structures and processes (Simons, 2013).

Other outcome measures have been utilized to assess recipient and program outcomes and assist in improving the performance of SOCs. In addition to the CAFAS discussed earlier, self-report instruments such as the Achenbach System of Empirically Based Assessment, the Behavior and Emotion Rating Scale and the Strengths and Difficulties Scale have been employed to evaluate the impact of children's services and systems (Deighton, et al., 2014). Other widely outcome measures for at-risk youth and families include functional status scales such as the Children's Global Assessment Scale (CGAS0 and the Residential Living Environment and Placement Stability Scale, and family functioning instruments such as the Family Adaptability and Cohesion Scale. There are also consumer satisfaction scales such as the Client Satisfaction Survey (CSQ) and Family Empowerment Scale that have been used to assess the impact of SOCs on children and families (Pumariega et al., 1998).

John Lyons (2004), who developed the CANS and the Total clinical Outcomes Management Approach, asserts that traditional outcome measurement methodologies are not well suited for the System of Care model. They are typically too narrow in scope and are not compatible with SOC principles, including family empowerment and the provision of individually tailored comprehensive service plans delivered in a collaborative manner. He advocates for a communication model for measuring outcomes. In addition to selecting measures that can easily and accurately communicate results, Lyons believes that all partners in the service-delivery system, including consumers, must participate in developing measures and deciding how they are used;

measures should be clear, concise, and relevant; each item should be directly translatable into action steps that inform the treatment planning process; and the measures should be comprehensive, addressing all levels and aspects of the SOC.

In addition to being comprehensive, the most useful data systems have been embedded into the day-to-day work activities of line-level personnel as well as supervisors, administrators, and governing bodies. These personnel have learned the value of incorporating data into their decision-making processes and, in many instances, seek information beyond that which is readily available to enhance their understanding. Exemplary SOC programs have also fashioned their use of data to be consistent with SOC principles. For example, traditional access to individual and aggregate performance data has been limited to staff. Consistent with the SOC guiding principles emphasis on engagement and empowerment of children and families, it makes sense to share these data with families and seek their input on how to best use this information.

Virginia's refinement of the audit process provides an example of how the use of data can be tailored to SOC values and principles at the administrative/governance level. Program and fiscal audits have traditionally been conducted in a hierarchical manner, with an external local, state, or federal agency swooping in with short notice to review an organization's records. While this approach may provide a necessary safeguard for detecting improper practices, it is more effective in engendering fear in those who are being audited than encouraging staff to be proactive in addressing potential problems. By inviting localities to become partners in identifying and studying concerns and areas of desired improvement, Virginia's CSA has facilitated empowerment of local government, one of its stated goals, and fostered a more collaborative, proactive approach for improving performance (S. Clare, personal communication, April 25, 2014).

The take-home lesson from how SOCs have utilized information systems is that data are not only relevant for assessing performance and guiding decisions at the individual consumer and program levels, but when utilized appropriately may enhance performance and facilitate development of an organizational culture that is consistent with SOC principles and goals.

Town-Gown Partnerships Yield Benefits

Academic institutions have played a significant role in the development and enhancement of the SOC movement. With support from federal, state, and local governments, university personnel have helped SOC programs to plan, implement, evaluate, and improve services to at-risk youth and families. Through collaborative arrangements with local and state government entities, faculty have identified best practices, including evidence-based and evidence-informed approaches, assisted in developing functional assessment and program evaluation strategies, conducted training, and provided other forms of technical assistance.

The National Technical Assistance Center for Children's Mental Health at Georgetown University has been a major player in helping localities and states establish and sustain effective comprehensive data-driven systems that provide collaborative, family-focused, community-based care for children with severe behavioral challenges. The Center offers multiple training opportunities, provides consultation, and produces and disseminates written materials that offer guidance and describe recent advances in the field. The University of South Florida and Portland State University have also had a significant nationwide impact on the development of SOCs since the inception of the reform movement.

Many successful local and state SOCs have benefited from partnerships with university personnel. Maryland and Ohio have contracted with universities in their states to serve as academic centers of excellence that provide assistance to local programs. These academic centers provide training, program development, and evaluation of targeted evidence-based practice as well as other aspects of SOC functioning. Numerous SOCs have adopted assessment instruments such as the CANS and Child Behavior Checklist (CBCL), and call on their university-based developers to assist them. Academic personnel have also worked with state and local SOCs to design and implement utilization management, program evaluation, and other data-based strategies.

Developing collaborative relationships between agencies responsible for managing service delivery and academic institutions often requires considerable effort by both parties. The orientation and cultures of these organizations are quite different and sometimes appear to be in conflict. However, those academic organizations that have been able to work through the issues that may impede collaboration have found that the benefit derived from these partnerships justifies the energy expended to establish the relationship.

Effective Programs Seize the Moment

In their study of effective strategies for expanding the SOC approach, Stroul and Friedman (2014) concluded that while it is helpful to establish a strategic plan with multiple strategies, it is also important to capitalize on opportunities that could not have been anticipated. They cite the example of states leveraging new grant programs and pursuing Medicaid waivers that provide greater flexibility in funding community-based services and state and local governments to recoup enhanced federal revenue. States like Hawaii and Massachusetts, faced with class-action law suits, viewed this as an opportunity to improve services. Taking an affirmative stance, leaders in these states developed comprehensive SOC programs to serve youth and families included in the litigation as well as others with similar challenges.

Staying Aloft on the Tightrope Requires Flexibility and More

A central theme of ecological theory is that a system's survival is dependent on its component organisms remaining in dynamic equilibrium. While this principle is usually applied to biological ecosystems, it is also relevant for social ecological phenomena, such as SOC for children. For SOCs to thrive, leaders must not only strengthen the individual parts of the system. They also must address the relationship that exists between its integral elements, ensuring that an appropriate balance is maintained among the stakeholders, and functions as well as across the micro and macro levels of the system.

Lyons (2004) observes that the children's public mental health system is fraught with tensions that arise from competing or incompatible goal. Lyons identifies system, program, and child-family-level tensions and argues that establishing and sustaining an effective children's public mental health system is dependent on exercising constant vigilance in order to maintain an appropriate balance among these conflicting forces. Examples of the types of tensions that require attention are:

- System Level Tensions
  - Central versus Local Control
  - Budget Silos versus Blended Funding
  - Differences in Service Area Boundaries for Participating Child-Serving Agencies
- Program Level Tensions
  - Business Model versus Clinical Model
  - Accountability versus Quality Improvement
  - Liability versus Learning Culture Environment
- Child and Family Tensions
- Parents versus Professionals: Who Cares More?
- What Youth Want versus What Others Want for Them
- Child Focus versus Family focus (Lyons, 2004).

The competing elements within a system are neither good or bad, nor right or wrong. Like the organisms within a biological ecosystem, each component of an SOC has an important functional role. Achieving an appropriate balance is difficult because the multiple elements that comprise and impact the system interact in complexity and sometimes unpredictable ways. The task of maintaining balance within an SOC is made more difficult by the fact that these systems are not static. The dynamics within and between programmatic and administrative entities at the local, state, and federal levels are continuously changing. What constitutes a suitable equilibrium at one point in time may no longer be appropriate due to new imbalances caused by shifts in influence among conflicting elements as well as changes in broader political, economic and social forces.

Proponents of effective systems of care have demonstrated a unique ability to reconcile the multiple perspectives and interests of participating stakeholders. These successful change agents have shown ingenuity, flexibility, patience, persistence, and a knack for anticipating how the changes they make will impact the other components of the system and potentially create new sources of disequilibrium.

Unfortunately, traditional policy and regulatory mechanisms are not generally appropriate vehicles for dealing with the complex array of tensions and conflictual relationships that exist within Systems of Care. Enacting legislation and issuing policy directives are effective instruments for setting a course of reform and providing structure and resources to support transformation. Dealing with the nuances and tensions that affect the performance of collaborative SOC demands continual scanning and monitoring, using both quantitative and qualitative data.

Each entity participating in the SOC is motivated to promote the interests and sustain the viability of its own organization as well as support the principles and goals of the overall system. Aligning the functioning of these entities with the SOC objectives without threatening the integrity of their own organizations is not an easy task. Effort needs to be directed at ensuring cooperation and adherence to the overarching principles and goals of the system. However, it is also important to understand the responsibilities and mandates of the member groups and the tensions that exist between their own goals and those of the system. Although some of the interests of participating organizations are strictly self-serving, these organizations also have legitimate mission-based concerns that must be addressed. Successful resolution of the conflicts that may arise between individual organization and system goals requires the diverse group of participating stakeholders to be willing to participate in negotiation and problem solving processes that may, at times, be stressful and frustrating.

The following issues are illustrative, but not exhaustive of important tensions that arise within systems of care approaches and must be addressed to maintain equilibrium among the multiple components of the system and ensure effective functioning:

Funding

A major aim of the SOC approach is to find better ways to pay for services. Traditionally, each child-serving agency had discrete categories of service it supported as well as specific eligibility criteria. Many of the children with multiple needs fell through the cracks because this silo-like approach to funding made it difficult, if not impossible to obtain and coordinate the array of supports and services required to effectively care for these young people. In spite of initial resistance from some agencies, SOCs have been able to alter this dynamic through enhanced coordination of funding streams and better alignment of reimbursement in order to support the services needed by each child and family. These strategies have proven to be more efficacious than traditional approaches which tried to shoehorn children into fixed categories of service with narrow eligibility criteria.

Some systems of care have developed strategies for coordinating or braiding funds in order to obtain the desired mix of services. This approach has enhanced their ability to provide an individually tailored set of services in a more integrated manner, while not requiring agencies to drastically restructure their funding systems.

When the CSA was enacted in Virginia, the state opted for an even more ambitious approach. They transferred funds from the jurisdiction of the participating child-serving agencies and placed them in a common pool, which was distributed proportionally to localities. This strategy, known as blending, theoretically offered even greater flexibility to FAPTs responsible for developing individual service plans for children served through CSA. Some of the agencies who lost their ability to control funds previously allocated to them, reacted negatively to this encroachment. They believed, with some justification, that they retained the same responsibility for caring for youth, but now had diminished resources for meeting these obligations. In the case of juvenile justice, whose children were not mandated to receive federal entitlement benefits, and therefore not considered to be high-priority candidates for CSA funding, these concerns were certainly valid. Departments of Social Services also felt hampered by their loss of direct control over the resources previously allocated to their agency.

In response to this perceived disparity between responsibility and authority, many agencies, particularly at the local level, did not fully embrace CSA, making it difficult to achieve the degree of cooperation needed to function effectively. More than 20 years after its inception, there are still pockets of resistance, raising the question of whether the more radical approach of blending funds created significant unintended consequences. Did the drastic alteration of funding streams within individual child-serving agencies organizations have a significant negative impact on their structure and functioning? Did the difficulties created by changes in the funding formula make individual agencies more reluctant to fully engage in the collaborative CSA endeavor? Currently, within CSA there is considerable discussion of the relative merits of employing braiding approaches to funding, which have a less severe impact on agencies, versus blending strategies, which are more seamless, but also more disruptive of individual departments (S. Clare, personal correspondence, April 25, 2014).

Empowerment versus Accountability

In addition to being responsible for ensuring that services are available and funded, governmental agencies are also obligated to regulate these activities and transactions. Local, state, and government officials are charged with making sure that the actions of participating agencies and providers are being performed in accordance with applicable policy and rules. Oversight responsibilities include monitoring how funds are expended and whether the services are being delivered appropriately.

Historically, the balance between free market and government oversight forces has been significantly influenced by the prevailing political orientation. During periods in which conservatives are in control, private sector entrepreneurial activity is promoted and government intervention is discouraged. When more liberal political views prevail, there is greater emphasis on government regulation. Officials in states that have adopted an SOC approach are faced with additional challenges as they seek to create a harmonious balance between these sometimes competing orientations. The concept of empowerment finds support on both sides of the aisle, depending on how it is framed. With its strong emphasis on fostering flexibility and innovation, SOC leadership has struggled with achieving an appropriate balance between promoting empowerment and ensuring accountability.

In its effort to enhance the availability of community-based care, Virginia encouraged localities to develop relationships with private for-profit and not-for-profit service providers. When it became apparent that some of these organizations were not employing qualified staff and were not delivering appropriate services, the state strengthened licensing and credentialing requirements and increased monitoring activities. The state also recognized that localities were not consistently utilizing evidence-based practices, another priority of the CSA, and began to provide additional training and other supports to enhance adoption of empirically validated assessment and intervention strategies.

Localities and states have also found ways to incorporate an empowerment focus into traditional monitoring functions. Chapter 12 provides a description of how the administrators of Virginia's CSA adopted an empowerment-oriented approach to auditing by inviting localities to play a proactive role in identifying and working through SOC performance concerns. By integrating the principle of enhancing local competence and control into their performance and fiscal review process, state officials were able to obtain greater involvement and acceptance of the SOC approach by participating local governments.

Other states have been able to reconcile the potential conflict between promoting use of best practices and encouraging local control by introducing decision support methodologies. By helping localities to understand and employ data-driven processes for assessing and planning activities at the individual child/family, program, and system levels, these states have been able to increase adherence to SOC service goals while also enhancing local engagement.

Enhancing Growth versus Ensuring Safety

The most frequently cited goal of the SOC approach is to improve functioning of children with serious behavior health challenges through a process that recognizes the strengths of the children and families and empowering them to act on their own behalf. A fundamental guiding principle of SOC is that at-risk youth are best served in the least restrictive, appropriate setting. This least restrictive orientation is driven by the conviction and supporting evidence that at-risk young people are best able to acquire and generalize appropriate coping skills in an environment that is similar to their natural community setting. Belief in the least restrictive philosophy is further bolstered by evidence demonstrating that placing these children in congregate settings with other youth with significant problems increases the likelihood that they will learn deviant behaviors from their association with these peers (Burns & Hoagwood, 2002; Dishion, McCord, & Poulin, 1999).

A less publicized but equally important goal of the system is to keep the child, family, and community safe. Children enter SOCs through a variety of pathways. Some youth are brought directly to the SOC by their families, while many are referred by agencies that are already serving them. Each agency has a unique mandate and goals. The primary focus of the juvenile justice system is public safety. This agency attempts to rehabilitate youth who have been placed by the court and also has a responsibility for making sure youth do not harm other youth or the community. Child protective service units in social service agencies are responsible for protecting children who have been neglected or abused and strive to find a safe environment for the child. These units work with the parents to address the problems that precipitated the removal of the child. If the child cannot be returned to the original home setting, the agency is responsible for finding a safe and suitable permanent placement for the child. Mental health agencies have a treatment focus, but also are responsible for ensuring that children at imminent risk of harming themselves or others are kept safe.

Thus, all of the participating child-serving agencies have an interest in maintaining safety, though the focus of each agency's concern is different. The challenge for SOCs is to establish a prudent balance between the desired goal of providing youth with opportunities to learn and function in normalized, community settings while also protecting the youth they serve, as well as members of the community. Unfortunately there are no foolproof methods for preventing violence. Achieving and maintaining an appropriate balance between the potentially conflictual program goals of serving youth in least restrictive settings and keeping everyone safe requires good planning and constant vigilance.

Effective SOCs have employed several strategies to ensure safety within this community-oriented model. Empirically validated assessment instruments are administered upon enrollment and throughout the course of care to accurately assess risk and functioning in order to determine which treatment and safety measures are most appropriate. By individualizing service plans and continually monitoring risk and progress, these systems have been able to avoid over- or under-reacting to the actual threat of harm. Additionally, many localities have developed alternatives to traditional institutional approaches to serving youth in crisis. While the level of risk for some youth still necessitates placement in an acute psychiatric facility, many systems have been able to avert many admissions to highly restrictive settings through evidence-based programs such as mobile crisis teams and community-based crisis stabilization units.

Consensus versus Specialized Planning

Teamwork and collaboration are core tenets of the SOC approach. Agency personnel and families are encouraged to work together to identify strengths and needs and develop responsive service plans. This collaborative approach is intended to remediate the problems of the traditional silo-like, fragmented service delivery model as well as facilitate family-driven service planning. Much effort goes into developing good communication among participating stakeholders.

The benefits of this collective approach are considerable. Team-based deliberation permits sharing of multiple perspectives and generates a broader range of information and ideas. Group-driven decision-making also has some limitations and potential shortcomings.

Some youth served through SOCs present issues that require specialized treatment. For instance, many youth present with complex behavioral health challenges that significantly impacts their ability to function. In order to provide appropriate care, these individuals require a thorough assessment by a qualified professional and access to therapeutic interventions tailored to their specific situation. While family assessment and planning teams and other interdisciplinary service planning teams are capable of incorporating expert input into their deliberations, they require the involvement of qualified professionals to help them understand what the child needs. Unfortunately, child psychiatrists are in short supply nationally, and communities often have difficulty identifying other licensed mental health professionals who are willing to work with public child-serving programs.

It is not coincidental that most states with effective SOCs have placed behavioral health agencies in prominent leadership roles at both state and local levels. States such as New Jersey and Louisiana contract with private behavioral health care companies to manage provision of SOC services and funding statewide. Interestingly, in Virginia, where the CSA has been operating for more than 20 years, the Department of Behavioral Health and Developmental Services has not played a prominent leadership role in this system. Not surprisingly, the Commonwealth has struggled with providing adequate mental health services for youth with severe behavioral health challenges.

LOOKING BACK FROM THE FAR SIDE OF THE WIRE

The Systems of Care movement has made considerable progress in the nearly 30 years since Stroul and Friedman first articulated their vision of a comprehensive community-based strategy for working with children with severe emotional and behavioral challenges and their families. SOC's are currently functioning in communities in all 50 states. Many states have adopted the SOC paradigm as their official statewide service delivery system for at-risk youth and families and others are moving in this direction. With federal assistance from SAMHSA and Medicaid and Administration for Children and Family Title IV-E Waiver projects, states are expanding their capacity to provide a coordinated continuum of child-centered, family-driven, community-based care.

During this period, we have gained a better understanding of what triggers the emotional and behavioral reactions of children in care and how to best respond to these vulnerable young people and their families. A prominent example of the shift in the service system's thinking is the growing awareness of the impact of traumatic experience on children and families. The high prevalence of post-traumatic stress in children as well as military personnel, police, and other adults has led to the development of a range of trauma-informed treatment approaches. Overall, the evidence base of SOCs has increased substantially. Advances in psychosocial therapeutic interventions and psychotropic medication have yielded more positive outcomes. Treatment and service modalities that have undergone rigorous clinical trials are now standard practices in most SOC programs and a number of localities and states are requiring service providers to utilize practices that have demonstrated positive outcomes, whenever empirical validation is available. Increasingly, states and localities are reporting that SOC efforts are producing significant improvement in shifting care from residential to community settings and enhanced functioning of participating children and families (Burns & Hoagwood, 2002; Pires, 2010; Stroul & Friedman, 2011).

Systems of Care have also yielded immediate and long-term financial benefits. States and localities have reported increased return on investment (ROI) as measured by reductions in per child service costs as care has moved from congregate to community settings, and have projected future gains associated with increased productivity and cost avoidance. Children with serious behavioral challenges who receive appropriate care are more likely, in the future, to earn more and less likely to become involved in the criminal justice or other costly service systems than those who do not receive timely treatment (Stroul, Pires, Boyce, Krivelyova & Walrath, 2014).

The use of empirical evidence is playing a more significant role in the operation of SOC initiatives in other ways. Standardized assessment instruments are commonly used to measure baseline and change in functioning of individual clients as well as program and system performance. The exemplary systems described earlier share a strong commitment to ensuring that decisions at all levels are informed and driven by pertinent, reliable data. Having a comprehensive data base that can be employed in clinical assessment and decision-making, continuous quality improvement, utilization management, outcome measurement, and other critical performance functions has become widely accepted as a requisite for effective SOCs and system leaders are increasingly incorporating these data-based processes to fuel performance improvement and accountability efforts (Suter & Bruns, 2009; Lyons, 2004).

The fact that political leaders at all levels continue to support adoption and expansion of SOC efforts during difficult economic times is also testimony to the progress that has been made in gaining widespread acceptance of this unique comprehensive, community-based approach.

These positive attributes and accomplishment of the SOC movement are laudable, but there are still considerable challenges that need be addressed before declaring victory. At the broad societal level, progress has been made in raising public awareness about issues such as mental illness, and the difficulties experienced by families with multiple stressors, including raising a child with serious behavioral challenges. Grassroots, family-led advocacy groups such as the National Federation of Families for Children's Mental Health and the National Alliance on Mental Illness and their local affiliates have assisted families trying to navigate the service system, educated the general public, and helped to shape federal and state policies on caring for children with behavioral health challenges. These advocacy efforts have been bolstered by collaborative partnerships with professionals and concerned citizens, most notably through the Children's Mental Health Network. Although stigma has abated to some extent, considerable misconception and prejudice still exist. Families are reluctant to acknowledge that their child has problems, fearing that they will be blamed for causing these difficulties. In the current political climate, with pervasive mistrust of government intervention, there is reluctance to expand support for public mental health and other human service programs.

Since the economic downturn in 2008, many families have experienced significant financial stress, which has created further insecurity and instability. In some instances, these added stressors have precipitated serious emotional and behavioral difficulties for vulnerable youth. To make matters worse, in the face of increased demand, many child-serving agencies have experienced substantial reductions in funding.

At the program level, communities and states continue to have difficulty attending to the multiple facets of the complex SOC paradigm, especially in areas such as collaboration among child-serving agencies and ensuring that all participating stakeholders incorporate the core principles and evidence-informed strategies into their daily practice. Entrenched work attitudes and habits are difficult to change. Broader political, economic, and administrative entities in which SOC initiatives are embedded do not always understand or provide incentives or support for these innovative approaches. Prevention and early intervention, which are highly valued by child mental health advocates, have only been marginally addressed by current SOC programs.

Given the intricacy of this ecological model and its ambitious vision and goals, full actualization of an SOC initiative may take several years, and sustaining effective performance requires diligence and persistence. Even those localities and states that have achieved successful implementation are wary of unanticipated negative forces and continue to expend considerable energy to maintain fidelity and optimal functioning.

The fluctuations in how Virginia's CSA has functioned during its more than 20 years of operation provide convincing evidence that SOCs are not static. Changes in leadership, shifts in political, economic, and social priorities, and evolving program technologies have influenced the magnitude and direction of resources and other forms of support the Act has received. In some instances, such as when the General Assembly mandated cost-cutting measures be taken when overall expenditures rose sharply, the shift was predictable. At other times, including the bi-partisan alliance between a Democratic Governor and Republican Attorney General, the Commonwealth was able to achieve a practical resolution for removing longstanding impediment of forcing parents to relinquish custody in order to obtain intensive services for their child. It is also noteworthy that the recent revitalization of CSA occurred during the administration of a conservative Republican governor. Although Governor McDonnell was not directly involved in managing the efforts to increase CSA's adherence to its original mission and goals, and enhance infrastructure and performance, the individuals who provided leadership for these improvement efforts were hired by and served under the Commonwealth's Chief Executive Officer.

It is premature to conclude that the SOC movement has achieved all or even most its goals. Significant progress has been made in expanding the number of SOC initiatives, as well as the quality of care they are delivering. However, some states and many localities have not yet adopted an SOC approach and there are many children and families with multiple stressors who are not receiving comprehensive care, even in areas where good systems are being implemented. Additionally, many of the current programs are still in the early stages of development and have not yet demonstrated that they can withstand the political, economic, and social forces that may potentially threaten even exemplary efforts.

Overall, champions of the SOC reform movement have effectively educated policy makers, administrators, and practitioners about the rationale, goals, and benefits of this complex innovative approach and have provided the tools and data that enable local and state officials to develop and implement viable systems. The compassion, commitment, ingenuity, tenacity, and skill of SOC stakeholders have been admirable. They have persisted in the face of multiple political, economic, cultural, and technical obstacles. Their ability to combine a clear and convincing philosophical and conceptual framework with evidence-informed intervention strategies, and planning and decision-making approaches that are data driven have enabled SOC supporters to gain support for and effectively actualize their bold vision.

As SOC proponents look to the future, they would do well to borrow from the guidance they employ in designing and providing care for the children and families they serve. The SOC approach emphasizes the importance of tailoring services to the unique strengths as well as the needs of each child and family, and addressing the multiple direct and contextual factors that impact their lives. Considerable importance is attached to being creative and flexible, using informal as well as formal supports, and adapting to the constantly changing conditions of the environment. Finally, engagement and empowerment of children and family are viewed as essential tenets of the SOC design.

These same attitudes and strategies are equally relevant at the macro level, as supporters of this comprehensive approach face the challenges of expanding and sustaining effective care for vulnerable children and families in a continuously changing, sometimes unfriendly environment. The best practices of today may be replaced by more effective strategies as research generates more precise diagnostic instruments and intervention tools. Advances in genetic investigation may provide more accurate information on the biological aspects of etiology and lead to better targeted therapeutic modalities. Increased understanding of the relationship between brain structure and functioning and environmental stressors such as trauma will produce more effective treatment approaches. The current trend toward integrating physical and behavioral health has had some impact on SOC operations, but in most instances, has not had a significant effect on how services are organized and delivered.

The SOC principles that inform service design and implementation are also applicable to initiatives to promote policy reform and system development initiatives. Enlisting the assistance of informal sources of support is critical to localities interested in expanding the community resources available to bolster the strengths and meet the needs of vulnerable children and families (e.g., increasing the availability of mentors, recruiting foster parents, and creating job training apprenticeship opportunities). Advocates also recognize the importance of broadening the base of support for SOC policy and budget initiatives. Garnering the support of civic groups and others interested in the welfare of children increases the likelihood that elected officials will act favorably on proposals that enhance care for children participating in SOC programs.

Successful leaders have also incorporated the SOC principles of engagement and empowerment in their efforts to encourage localities and states to adopt and expand the SOC approach. The federal government has recognized the importance of allowing each state to tailor its SOC initiatives to the unique conditions of their jurisdiction. Federal grants and demonstration programs have typically asked applicants to submit a plan describing how they will configure their service delivery program to align with the geopolitical situation of the state or locality while also meeting the criteria and goals of the funding source. Likewise, many states have allowed localities to adapt their service systems to the specific structure, dynamics, and needs of their community. The strategy of promoting local input not only increases the probability that the service system will be responsive to local needs, but also makes it more likely that local officials and other important stakeholders will embrace the SOC approach since they have had an opportunity to shape the program.

The future of the SOC movement will in large part be determined by its ability to continue to be faithful to its core values and principles. Sustaining and expanding SOC initiatives at all levels will require proponents to be vigilant in applying the social ecology paradigm and its correlates to the broader policy and program development efforts as well as to provision of care to children and families in local communities.

The experiences of Virginia and other jurisdictions in developing and implementing comprehensive SOC have further reinforced the conventional wisdom that there are no "magic bullets" or simple formulas. Transforming policy and practice for serving vulnerable children and families is a complex endeavor that requires a multi-pronged approach and leaders that are willing to quickly adapt their strategy in response to rapidly changing dynamics and conditions. The social ecology paradigm, which is central to the SOC service design, also provides a useful framework for viewing the reform process. Understanding the multiple forces that impact the shaping of policy and establishment and maintenance of comprehensive, community-based service systems enables SOC proponents to incorporate a broad array of strategies and tools into their reform efforts. This multi-layered template also heightens stakeholders' awareness of the need to be flexible and tempers their expectation that a complete and permanent solution will be found. Even the most effective SOC initiatives have been unable to effectively respond to all of the issues and challenges they were designed to address. SOC supporters have learned through experience that even good programs may be threatened by broader political, economic, and social forces that are beyond their control.

Viewed through the prism of the dynamic, multi-tiered ecological paradigm, Virginia's CSA has effectively navigated many of the requisite SOC challenges and fallen short in addressing others. The Act continues to be plagued by several significant shortcomings, including the failure to resolve the disparity in access to care created by the mandated versus non-mandated distinction, and large gaps in practice capacity for providing evidenced-informed care in many localities. The Commonwealth also has not yet effectively addressed the lack of access to child psychiatrists and other specialized behavioral health services and has not fully actualized the principles of youth and family engagement/empowerment. While the state has recently made progress in developing and implementing a responsive data system, much work needs to be done to establish an infrastructure and processes to support empirically based planning and decision-making.

On the other side of the ledger, CSA has persisted in the face of significant threats and obstacles. This comprehensive, community-based SOC, established by the innovative groundbreaking legislation in the early 1990s, has proven to be resilient, continuing to function through the administrations of seven governors who were almost equally divided between both political parties. CSA continues to pool funds from multiple sources, promote inter-agency collaboration at all levels, and endorse delivery of child-centered, family-focused, community-based care. Although it has not fully resolved the tensions between state and local governments, officials continue to grapple with the challenge of maintaining an appropriate balance between encouraging local empowerment while maintaining accountability.

One of the most impressive achievements of this ambitious reform endeavor is that it has avoided becoming static or calcified during its 20-plus years of operation. The performance of CSA has fluctuated during the course of its existence, but the system has consistently engaged in self-assessment and improvement activities. The recent surge in efforts to increase fidelity to SOC principles and enhance evidence-informed practice is indicative of CSA's capacity to respond proactively to the intricate array of internal and external challenges and forces that affect its performance. While there is no course of action that will ensure continued success or even survival of such a multifaceted endeavor, CSA's recognition of the complex, interdependent environment in which it functions and its willingness to engage with the multiple stakeholders involved have contributed to the Act's longevity and bode well for the system's ability to effectively confront future challenges.

References

Achenbach, T. M. (2009). *The Achenbach System of Empirically Based Assessment (ASEBA): Development, findings, theory, and applications.* Burlington, VT: University of Vermont Research Center for Children, Youth, & Families.

Adams, E. J. (2010). *Healing invisible wounds: Why investing in trauma informed care for children makes sense.* Retrieved from https://www.ncjrs.gov/App/Publications/abstract.aspx?ID=257744.

Alexandria Community Policy and Management Team (2008). *CSA service improvement and cost containment strategies from the ACPMT.* Alexandria, VA: Department of Community and Human Services.

Alexandria Community Policy and Management Team (2014). *FY14 annual report.* Alexandria, VA: Department of Community and Human Services.

Annie E. Casey Foundation Kids Count Data Center (2014). *Children living below the poverty threshold by family nativity.* Retrieved from http://datacenter.kidscount. org/data/tables/117-children-living-below-the-poverty-threshold-by-family-nativit y?loc=1&loct=2#detailed/2/2–52/false/868,867,133,38,35/78,79/449,450.

American Psychiatric Association (2013). Diagnostic and statistical manual of mental disorders (5th ed.). Washington, DC: Author.

Apter, S. J., Apter, D. S., Trief, P. M., Cohen, N., Woodlock, D., & Harootunian, B. (1978). *The bridge program: Comprehensive psychoeducational services for troubled children and families.* Syracuse, NY: Author.

Arienti, F., English, K., & Horton, A. (2014). *System of care practice review: Regional report of findings, central region.* Boston, MA: Executive Office of Health and Human Services, Commonwealth of Massachusetts.

Atkinson, F. (2006). *Virginia in the Vanguard: Political leadership in the 400-year-old cradle of American democracy, 1981 - 2006.* Lanham, MD: Rowman & Littlefield Publishers.

Baio, J. (2014). Prevalence of autism spectrum disorder among children aged 8 years autism and developmental disabilities monitoring network, 11 sites, United States, 2010. *Surveillance Summaries, CDC Morbidity &Mortality Weekly Summaries, 63,* 1–21.

Bateson, G., Jackson, D. D., Haley, J., & Weakland, J. (1956). Toward a theory of schizophrenia. *Behavioural Science, 1,* 251–54.

Battle, C. L., Shea, M. T., Johnson, D. M., Yen, X., Zlotnick, C., Zanarini, M. C., & Morey, L. C. (2004). Childhood maltreatment associated with adult personality disorders: findings from the Collaborative Longitudinal Personality Disorders Study. *Journal of Personality Disorders, 18,* 193–211.

Bettelheim, B. (1967). *The empty fortress: Infantile autism and the birth of the self.* New York: The Free Press.

Blanchard, K., Britt, J., Hoekstra, J., & Zigarmi, P. (2009). *Who killed change? Solving the mystery of leading people through change.* New York: Wayne Morrow.

Bloom, S. L. (2000). Our hearts and our hopes are turned to peace: Origins of the ISTSS. In A., Shalev, R. Yehuda, & A. S. McFarlane (Eds.). *International handbook of human response trauma.* New York: Plenum.

Bloom, S. L. (2005). The sanctuary model of organizational change for children's residential treatment: Therapeutic community. *The International Journal for Therapeutic and Supportive Organizations, 26(1),* 65–81.

Bloom, S. L., & Sreedhar, S. Y. (2008). The sanctuary model of trauma-informed organizational change. *Reclaiming Children and Youth: From Trauma to Trust, 17(3),* 48–53.

Bremner, J. D. (2006). Traumatic stress: effects on the brain. *Dialogues in Clinical Neuroscience, 8(4),* 445–61.

Bronfenbrenner, U. (1979). *The Ecology of Human Development.* Cambridge, MA: Harvard University Press.

Burchard, J. D., Bruns, E. J., & Burchard, S. N. (2002). In B. J. Burns & K. E. Hoagwood (Eds.), *Community Treatment for Youth* (pp. 125–54). Oxford: Oxford University Press.

Burns, B. J., & Hoagwood, K. H. (2002). *Community treatment for youth: Evidence-based interventions for severe emotional and behavioral disorder.* New York: Oxford University Press.

Burns, B. J., Hoagwood, K. E., & Mrazek, P. J. (1999). Effective treatment for mental disorders in children and adolescents. *Clinical Child & Family Psychology Review, 2(4),* 199–254.

Casey Strategic Consulting Group (2008). *Getting the most out of CSA: A guide to Hampton, V.A. best practices.* Retrieved September 22, 2015 from http://www.pccyfs.org/dpw_ocyfs/NGA-2009/HamptonCSAGuide(8'15'08)FINAL.pdf.

Center for Ecoliteracy. (2014). *Ecological principles.* Retrieved from http://www.ecoliteracy.org/essays/ecological-principles.

Center for Public Representation (2009). *About Rosie D.* Retrieved from http://www.rosied.org/page-67061.

Chamberlain, P. (2002). Treatment foster care. In B. J. Burns, B. J. & K. E. Hoagwood (Eds.). *Community treatment for youth: Evidence-based interventions for severe emotional and behavioral disorders* (pp. 117–38). New York: Oxford University Press.

Children's Behavioral Health Advisory Council (2011). *Annual report 2011.* Boston, MA: Executive Office of Health and Human Services, Commonwealth of Massachusetts.

Children's Behavioral Health Advisory Council. (2013). *Annual report 2013.* Boston, MA: Executive Office of Health and Human Services, Commonwealth of Massachusetts.

Chorpita, B. F., & Donkervoet, C. (2005). Implementation of the Felix Consent Decree in Hawaii. In R. G. Stele & M. C. Roberts (Eds.). *Handbook of mental health services for children, adolescents & families: Issues in clinical child psychology* (pp. 317–32). New York: Kluwer Academic/Plenum Publishers.

Clark, B. (2012). *Hampton System of Care: Directory of Services.* Hampton, VA: Hampton Community Services Board.

Cohen, R., Harris, R., Gottlieb, S., & Best, A. M. (1991). States' use of transfer of custody as a requirement for providing services to emotionally disturbed children. *Hospital & Community Psychiatry, 42(5),* 526–30.

Cohen, R., Wiley, S., Oswald, D., Eakin, K., & Best, A. (1999). Applying utilization management principles to a comprehensive service system for children with emotional and behavior disorders and their families: A feasibility study. *Journal of Child and Family Studies, 8(4),* 463–76.

Cohen, R., Preiser, L., Gottlieb, S., Harris, R., Baker, J., & Sonenklar, N. (1993). Relinquishing custody as a requisite for receiving services for children with serious emotional disorders: A review. *Law and Human Behavior, 17,* 121–34.

Commonwealth Fund. (2014). *Aiming higher: Results from a scorecard on state health system performance 2014.* New York, NY: Author.

Corbett, J., McAllister, A., Sheads, L., Wright, T., O'Beirne, E., Lewis, J., White, D., & Chapman, J. (2014, March). *Strengthening team development and rapport: A FAPT perspective.* Presented at the 3rd Annual CSA Conference, Roanoke, VA.

Costello, E. J., Angold, A., Burns, B. J., Erkanli, A., Stangl, D. K., & Tweed, D. L. (1996). The Great Smoky Mountains study of youth functional impairment and serious emotional disturbance. *Arch Gen Psychiatry, 53(12),* 1137–43.

Deighton, J., Croudace, T., Fonagy, P., Brown, J., Patalay, P., & Wolpert, M. (2014) Measuring mental health and wellbeing outcomes for children and adolescents to inform practice and policy: A review of child self-report measures. *Child and Adolescent Psychiatry and Mental Health, 8(14).*

Department of Medical Assistance. (2011, June). Children's community mental health services: Independent clinical assessments for intensive in-home services, therapeutic day treatment, mental health support services, and levels A and B residential services. *Presented to State Interagency Management Team* in Richmond, VA.

Department of Social Services. (2014). *OASIS child and family services review performance indicators monthly report, April 2014.* Richmond, VA: Author.

Dodge, K. A., Kupersmidt, J. B., Fontaine, R. G. (2000). *Willie M: Legacy of legal, social, and policy change on behalf of children.* Report to the State of North Carolina, Division of Mental Health, Developmental Disabilities and Substance Abuse Services. Retrieved from http://dukespace.lib.duke.edu/dspace/handle/10161/7489.

Dooley, D., & Catalano, R. (1980). Economic change as a cause of mental disorder. *Psychological Bulletin, 87,* 450–68.

Effland, V., Walton, B., & McIntyre, J. (2011). Connecting the dots: Stages of implementation, wraparound fidelity and youth outcomes. *Journal of Child and Family Studies, 20(6),* 736–46.

Epstein, M. H, & Sharma, J. (1998). *Behavior and Emotion Rating Scale.* Austin Texas: PRO-ED Publishers.

Erdman, P. (2014). *Wraparound Milwaukee 2013 quality assurance/quality improvement annual report.* Milwaukee, WI:Wraparound Milwaukee.

Farmer, E. M. Z., Mustillo, S., Burns, B. J., & Holden, E. W. (2008). Use and predictors of out-of-home placements within systems of care. *Journal of Emotional and Behavioral Disorders, 16(1),* 5–14.

Farmer, E. M. Z., Southerland, D. G., Mustillo, S. A., & Burns, B. J. (2009). Returning home in systems of care: Rates, predictors, and stability. *Journal of Emotional and Behavioral Disorders, 17,* 133–46.

Farmer, E. M. Z., Wagner, H., Burns, B. J., & Richards, J. T. (2003). Treatment foster care in a system of care: Sequences and correlates of residential placements. *Journal of Child and Family Studies, 12,* 11–25.

Felker, B. L., Chaney, E., Rubenstein, L. V., Bonner, L. M., Yano, E. M., Parker, L. E., Worley, L. M., Sherman, S. E., & Ober, S. (2006). Developing effective collaboration between primary care & mental health providers. *Primary Care Companion to the Journal of Clinical Psychiatry, 8(1),* 12–16.

Ford, S. (2012, October). Independent clinical assessments and care coordination model update. *Presented to House Appropriations Subcommittee on Health & Human Resources* in Richmond, VA.

Friedman, R. M., & Street, S. (1985). Admission and discharge criteria for children's mental health services: A review of the issues. *Journal of Clinical Child Psychology, 14,* 229–35.

Golden, S. D., & Earp, J. L. (2012). Social ecological approaches to individuals and their contexts. *Health Education and Behavior, 39(3),* 364–72.

Galano, J., & Huntington, L. (1999). *Evaluation of the Hampton, Virginia healthy families partnership: 1992–1998.* Waynesburg, VA: Center for Public Policy Research, The Thomas Jefferson Program in Public Policy, The College of Wayne & Mary.

Galano, J., Credle, W., Perry, D., Berg, S. W., Huntington, L., & Stief, E. (2001). Developing and sustaining a successful community prevention initiative: The Hampton healthy families partnership. *The Journal of Primary Prevention, 21(4),* 495–509.

Goldman, P. (2010). *Understanding wraparound: A Study in recidivism.* Milwaukee, WI: Wraparound Milwaukee.

Gruenzel, J. J., & Hancock, B. (2010). *10 years of system of care implementation: Letting the data tell the story.* Trenton, NJ: Division of Child Behavioral Health Services, New Jersey Department of Children and Families.

Gutman, L. M., McLoyd, V. C., & Tokoyawa, T. (2005). Financial strain, neighborhood stress, parenting behaviors and adolescent adjustment in African American families. *Journal of Research on Adolescence, 25(4),* 425–49.

Henry J. Kaiser Family Foundation. (2014). *Federal medical assistance percentage (FMAP) for Medicaid and Multiplier.* Retrieved from http://kff.org/medicaid/state-indicator/federal-matching-rate-and-multiplier/.

Hodges, S., Ferreira, K., Israel, N., & Mazza, J. (2006). *Leveraging change in the Hawaii system of care, child and adolescent mental health division, Hawaii Department of Health: Site report for case studies of system implementation.* Tampa, FL: The Research and Training Center for Children's Mental Health, University of South Florida.

Hogan, M. F. (1992). New futures for mental health care: The case of Ohio. *Health Affairs, 11(3),* 69–83. Retrieved from www.sprc.org/library/college_sp_whitepaper.pdf

Hovey, J. (2012). *Intensive in-home services for children's mental health in Virginia: Time to focus on quality.* Richmond, VA: Voices for Virginia's Children.

Hyman, S. (Ed.). (2001). *Autism: The science of mental health.* New York: Routledge.

ICF International. (2013). *Avoided costs of system of care-related outcomes: 2005–2010 communities funded by the federal children's mental health initiative.* Atlanta, GA: Author.

Jindal, B. (2011). *Executive order no. BJ 2011 – 5: Coordinated system of care governance board.* Baton Rouge, LA: Executive Department, State of Louisiana.

Joint Legislative Audit and Review Commission. (1998). *Review of the comprehensive services act.* Richmond, VA: Author.

Joint Legislative Audit and Review Commission. (2007). *Evaluation of children's residential services delivered through the comprehensive services act.* Richmond, VA: Author.

Joint Legislative Audit and Review Commission. (2007a). *Follow-up report: Custody relinquishment and the comprehensive services act.* Richmond, VA: Author.

Kamradt, B. (2000). Wraparound Milwaukee: Aiding youth with mental health needs. *Juvenile Justice- Youth with Mental Health Disorders: Issues and Emerging Responses, 7(1),* 14–23.

Kamradt, B., Gilbertson, S. A., & Jefferson, M. (2008). Services for high-risk populations in systems of care. *The system of care handbook: Transforming mental health services for children, youth, and families,* 469–90.

Kanner, L. (1949). Problems of nosology and psychodynamics in early childhood autism. *American Journal of Orthopsychiatry, 19(3),* 416–26.

Kendler, K. S., Prescott, C. A., Myers, J., & Neale, M. C. (2003). The structure of genetic and environmental risk factors for common psychiatric and substance abuse disorders in men and women. *Arch Gen Psychiatry, 60(9),* 929–37.

Kiernan, J. S. (2014, March) Best & worst states to be a taxpayer. *Wallet Hub.* Retrieved from wallethub.com/edu/best-worst-states-to-be—a-taxpayer/2416.

King, M. A. (2010, July 16). *MA Wraparound fidelity assessment system: Promoting positive outcomes through fidelity monitoring.* Presented at Managed Care Entity/ Community Service Agency Statewide Meeting, Marlboro, MA.

Knitzer, J. (1982). *Unclaimed children: The failure of public responsibility to children and adolescents in need of mental health services.* New York: Children's Defense Fund.

Kua, C. (2002). Felix monitor says DOE resists change. *Honolulu Star-Bulletin.* Retrieved August 7, 2015 from: http://archives.starbulletin.com/2002/08/07/news/story8.html.

Lawson, K (2012, February). *BHSA overview*. Presented to the Virginia Health Care Foundation, Richmond, VA.

Light, P. C. (1997). *The tides of reform: Making government work, 1945–1995*. New Haven: Yale University Press.

Lounsbury, D. L., & Gwin Mitchell, S. (2009). Introduction to special issue on social ecological approach to community health research and action. *American Journal of Community Psychology, 44(3/4)*, 213–20.

Lyons, J. S. (2004). *Redressing the emperor: Improving our children's public mental health system*. Westport, CT: Praeger Publishers.

Lyons, J. S., Chesler, P., Shallcross, H., & Kiesel, C. (1996). The childhood severity of psychiatric illness: A tool for needs-based decision making and support. *Family Matters* (special issue), 1–10.

Magellan of Louisiana. (2014). *Coordinated system of care: Report to the governance board*. Baton Rouge, LA: Author.

Mason, M., Ola, B., Zaharakis, N., & Zhang, J. (2015). Text message interventions for adolescent and young adult substance abuse: A meta-analysis. *Prevention Science, 16*, 181–88.

Massachusetts Executive Office of Health & Human Services. (2012). *How to build a statewide system of care*. Presented at Training Institutes 2012, National Technical Assistance Center for Children's Mental Health, Georgetown University, Orlando, Florida.

Masshealth. (2010). *Number and percent of Massachuseets members Under 21 who received CBHI services at any point between July 1, 2009, through June 30, 2010*. Boston, MA: Massachusetts Executive Offices of health and Human Services, Commonwealth of Massachusetts.

Masshealth. (2014). *CBHI service utilization FY 2013*. Boston, MA: Massachusetts Executive Offices of Health and Human Services, Commonwealth of Massachusetts.

McWhinney, P. D. (2010). *Improving permanency outcomes for youth in Virginia's foster care system: Making a case for kinship care custody assistance*. Richmond, VA: Virginia Department of Social Services.

McWhinney, P. D. (2014). *Virginia plan to safely reduce the number of youth in foster care: report to delegate Chris Peace*. Richmond, VA: Virginia Department of Social Services.

Meola, O. (2014). *McAuliffe sets up children's cabinet to aid youth*. Retrieved August 11, 2014 from: http://www.timesdispatch.com/news/state-regional/mcau-liffe-sets-up-children-s-cabinet-to-aid-youth/article_7c7982d6–218b-11e4–9f15–0017a43b2370.html.

National League of Cities. (2014). *Local government authority*. Retrieved from: http://www.nlc.org/build-skills-and-networks/resources/cities-101/city-powers/local-government-authority.

Office of Behavioral Health. (2011). *Request for proposals: Statewide management organization for Louisiana behavioral health partnership*. Baton Rouge, LA: Department of Health and Hospitals, State of Louisiana.

Office of Comprehensive Services. (2011). *Annual report to the general assembly: Regional and statewide training regarding the comprehensive services act*. Henrico, VA: Author.

Office of Comprehensive Services. (2012). *Annual report to the general assembly: Regional and statewide training regarding the comprehensive services act.* Henrico, VA: Author.

Office of Comprehensive Services. (2012a). *Empowering communities to serve youth: Self-assessment workbook for locally administered CSA programs.* Henrico, VA: Author.

Office of Comprehensive Services. (2013). *CSA statewide statistics.* Henrico, VA: Author.

Office of Comprehensive Services. (2013a). *Utilization of residential care under CSA: Annual report to the governor and general assembly.* Henrico, VA: Author.

Office of Comprehensive Services. (2013b). *FY 12 CSA critical service gaps.* Henrico, VA: Author.

Office of Comprehensive Services. (2014). *Performance dashboard.* Henrico, VA: Author.

Office of Comprehensive Services. (2014a). *CSA statewide statistics.* Henrico, VA: Author.

Office of Comprehensive Services. (2016). *CSA Statewide statistics.* Henrico, VA: Author.

Office of National Health Statistics, Office of the Actuary. (1996). National health expenditures, 1994. *Health Care Financing Review, 17(3).*

Office of the Surgeon General Center for Mental Health Services National Institute of Mental Health. (1999). *Mental health: A report of the surgeon general.* Retrieved from https://profiles.nlm.nih.gov/ps/retrieve/ResourceMetadata/NNBBHS.

Ohio Family & Children First. (2014). *FCFC shared plan model (HP 289).* Retrieved from http://www.fcf.ohio.gov/BuildingCapacity/FCFCSharedPlanHB289.aspx.

Ohio Family & Children First. (2014a). *Flexible funding.* Retrieved from http://fcf.ohio.gov/Initiatives/FlexibleFunding.aspx.

Ohio Mental Health & Addiction Services. (2014). *Ohio's coordinating centers of excellence.* Retrieved from http://mha.ohio.gov/Default.aspx?tabid=135.

Pumariega, A., Diamond, J., Dominguez, E., Fallon, T., Grimes, K., Hanson, G., & Solnit, A. (1998). *Best principles for measuring outcomes in managed care Medicaid programs.* Washington, DC: American Academy of Child and Adolescent Psychiatry.

Pires, S. A. (2010). *Building systems of care: A primer (2nd Ed.).* Washington, DC: National Technical Assistance Center for Children's Mental Health, Georgetown University Center for Child and Human Development.

President's New Freedom Commission on Mental Health. (2003). *Achieving the promise: Transforming mental health care in America: Final report.* Retrieved from http://govinfo.library.unt.edu/mentalhealthcommission/reports/reports.htm.

Reddy, L. A., & Pfeiffer, S. I. (1997). Effectiveness of treatment foster care with children and adolescents: A review of outcome studies. *Journal of the American Academy of Child and Adolescent Psychiatry, 36(5),* 581–88.

Roundtree, J. (2010). *Exemplary programs in Indian child welfare: Profiles of tribal and urban programs.* Iowa City, IA: National Resource Center for In-Home Services.

Sauter, M. B., Frohlich, T. C., Hess, A. E., & Allen, A. C. (2013). *The best and worst run states in America: A survey of all 50.* Retrieved from http://247wallst.com/special-report/2013/11/21/the-best-and-worst-run-states-in-america-survey-of-all-50–2/#ixzz37eoKkS5w.

Schultze, M., & McWhinney, P. D. (2014, June). *Virginia's three branch initiative: Sustaining well-being of families in foster care.* Presented at Transformation in Action, 2014 AHSA National Policy Forum, Washington, DC.

Simons, J. (2013). What we've learned about the CANS population. *CANS News, 4(1),* 2–4.

Simons, J. (2013a). *Assessing child outcomes with the CANS.* Retrieved from http://www.mass.gov/eohhs/docs/masshealth/cbhi/cans-assessing-child-outcomes.pdf.

Soler, M., & Warboys, L. (1990). Services for violent and severely disturbed children: The Willie M. litigation. In S. Dicker (Ed.), *Stepping stones: Successful advocacy for children* (pp. 61–112). New York: The Foundation for Child Development.

State Executive Council. (December, 2007). *Final interagency guidelines on foster care services for specific children in need of services funded through the comprehensive services act.* Richmond, VA: Office of Comprehensive Services.

Stark, D. (1999). *Collaboration basics: A companion guide – Strategies from six communities engaged in collaborative efforts among families, child welfare and children's mental health.* Washington, DC: National Technical Assistance Center for Children's Mental Health, Georgetown University Center for Child and Human Development.

Stein, L. I., & Santos, A. B. (1998). *Assertive community treatment of persons with severe mental illness.* New York: W. W. Norton.

Stewart, M. D., & Cleary, H. (2011). *A portrait of Virginia's child welfare system.* Richmond, VA: Voices for Virginia's Children.

Stone, M. (2014). *Ecological principles.* Retrieved from: http://www.ecoliteracy.org/essays/ecological-principles.

Strech, G., Harris, B., & Vetter, J. (2011). *Evaluation of the care management oversight project.* Norman, OK: University of Oklahoma, College of Continuing Education.

Stroul, B. A., & Friedman, R. M. (1986). *A system of care for children and youth with severe emotional disturbances.* Washington, DC: CASSP Technical Assistance Center.

Stroul. B. A., & Friedman, R. M. (2011). *Effective strategies for expanding the system of care approach: A report on the study of strategies for expanding systems of care.* Washington, DC: National Technical Assistance Center for Children's Mental Health, Georgetown University Center for Child and Human Development.

Stroul, B. A., Pires, S. A., Boyce, S., Krivelyova, M. A., & Walrath, C. (2014). *Return on investment in systems of care for children with behavioral health challenges.* Washington, DC: National Technical Assistance Center for Children's Mental Health, Georgetown University Center for Child and Human Development.

Substance Abuse and Mental Health Services Administration. (2016). *National Child Traumatic Stress Initiative.* Retrieved May 31, 2016, from http://www.samhsa.gov/child-trauma.

Suter, J., & Bruns, E. (2009). Effectiveness of the wraparound process for children with emotional and behavioral disorders: A meta-analysis. *Clinical Child and Family Review, 12,* 336–51.

Svendson, D. P., Cutler, D. L., Ronis, R. J., Herman, L. C., Morrison, A., Smith, M. K., & Munetz, M. (2005). The professor of public psychiatry model in Ohio:

The impact on training, program innovation, and the quality of mental health care. *Community Mental Health Journal, 41(6),* 775–84.

The American Public Human Services Association. (2012). *The Hampton model.* Retrieved January 27, 2014 from: http://www.aphsa.org/content/APHSA/en/home.html.

The Hampton Approach to Systems of Care. (2007, November). *Hampton Virginia comprehensive services community policy and management team.* Retrieved June 6, 2015 from http://dls.virginia.gov/GROUPS/CSA/meetings/112007/hamptonsystem.pdf.

The Pew Charitable Trusts & Jim Casey Youth Initiative. (2007). *Time for reform: Aging out and on their own.* Retrieved from: http://www.pewtrusts.org/uploaded-Files/wwwpewtrustsorg/Reports/Foster_Care_reform/Kids_are_Waiting_Timefor-Reform0307.pdf.

Thomas, T. R., & Holzer, C. E. (2006). The continuing shortage of child and adolescent psychiatrists. *Journal of the Academy of Child and Adolescent Psychiatry, 45(9),* 1023–31.

Tobey, T., Mcauliff, K., & Rocha, C. (2013). Parental employment status and symptoms of children abused during a recession. *Journal of Child Sexual Abuse, 22(4),* 416–28.

Triad Training and Consulting Services. (2007). *Historical perspective, data, outcomes and practice improvement project: Hampton, Virginia comprehensive services act community policy and management team.* Norfolk, VA: Author.

Triad Training and Consulting Services. (2011). *Building a sustainable child and family service system: Hampton, Virginia systems of care in review: 2010–2011.* Norfolk, VA: Author.

U.S. Bureau of Census. (2014). *State rankings: Persons below the poverty level.* Retrieved from http://www.census.gov/compendia/statab/2011/ranks/rank34.html.

U.S. Department of Commerce. (2013). *Per capita personal income by state.* Retrieved from http://bber.unm.edu/econ/us-pci.htm.

Uttaro, T., & Mechanic, D. (1994). The NAMI consumer service analysis of unmet needs. *Psychiatric Services, 45(4),* 372–74.

Virginia Department of Social Services. (2014). *Performance indicator monthly report.* Richmond, VA: Author.

Virginia Acts of Assembly, Chapter 837, §§ 2.1–745–759, April 15, 1992.

Virginia Acts of Assembly, Chapter 800, § 2.1–746, April 6, 1995.

Virginia Acts of Assembly, Chapter 800, Chapter 937, § 2.1–746.1, April 9, 2000.

Virginia Acts of Assembly, Chapter 840, § 2.2–5212, April 2007.

Virginia Commission on Youth. (2013). *Collection of evidenced-based practices for children and adolescents with mental health and treatment needs* (5th Ed.). (House Document No.7). Richmond, VA: Government Printing Office.

Vitanza, S., Cohen, R., & Hall, L. L. (1999). *Families on the brink: The impact of ignoring children with serious mental illness.* Arlington, VA: National Alliance on Mental Illness.

Wallenstein, P. (2007). *Cradle of America: Four centuries of Virginia history.* Lawrence, KS: University of Kansas Press.

Walrath, C. M., Mandell, D. S., & Leaf, P. J. (2001). Responses of children with different intake profiles to mental health treatment. *Psychiatric Services, 52(2),* 196–201.

Walters, J. (2010). *Back on track: Transforming Virginia's child welfare system.* Baltimore, MD: The Annie E. Casey Foundation.

Wraparound Milwaukee. (2013). *Wraparound Milwaukee 2012 year-end report.* Milwaukee, WI: Author.

Wraparound Milwaukee. (2013a). *Report to Milwaukee child welfare partnership council.* Milwaukee, WI: Author.

Wraparound Milwaukee. (2014). *Wraparound Milwaukee 2013 year-end report.* Milwaukee, WI: Author.

Wraparound Milwaukee. (2014a). *Wraparound Milwaukee: One child, one plan.* Retrieved from: http://wraparoundmke.com/.

Youth M.O.V.E. National. (2013). *Annual report: Twenty thirteen.* Hattiesburg, MS: Author. Retrieved from: http://www.youthmovenational.org/images/downloads/YouthMoveNationalannualReportWeb.pdf.

PERSONS INTERVIEWED FOR THIS BOOK

Amy Atkinson
Robert Bloxom
Rebecca China
Betsy Clark
Susan Clare
Walt Credle
Howard Cullum
Michael Farley
Patrick Finnerty
Chuck Hall
Leah Hamaker
Steve Harms
Pat Harris
Shannon Hayworth
William Hazel
Mark Hinson

Lelia Hopper
Edd Houck
John Hughes
Larry Jackson
Cyndi Jones
Bruce Kamradt
Chuck Kehoe
Jane Kusiak
Gail Ledford
Ron Lemley
Rob Lockridge
Kim McGaughey
Charlotte McNulty
William Mims
William Murray
Margaret Nimmo

Greg Peters
Rick Pond
Karen Reilly-Jones
Scott Reiner
Andre Richmond
Wanda Rogers
Alan Saunders
Chuck Savage
Bud Sedwick
Emily Sherwood
Demis Stewart
Eva Teig Hardy
Mike Terkletaub
Dawnel White

Index

About the Authors

Robert Cohen, PhD, is a consultant specializing in children's mental health policy and program development. He currently serves as senior advisor to the Center for Child Well-Being in the School of Social Work at Arizona State University. He previously served as director of the Virginia Treatment Center for Children and professor in the Department of Psychiatry at the Virginia Commonwealth University School of Medicine. Other positions he has held include Associate Commissioner for Policy, Planning and Program Development at the New York State Office of Mental Health and Executive Director of the Society for Community Research and Action. He has been involved in the planning and development of Virginia's Comprehensive Services Act for At-Risk Youth and Families (CSA) since the mid-1980s. He is the author/ co-author of ten books including *Chiseled in Sand: Perspectives on Change in Human Service Organizations* (Wadsworth, 2000), *Beyond Suppression: Global Perspectives on Youth Violence* (Praeger, 2010), and *The Virginia Tech Massacre: Strategies and Challenges for Improving Mental Health Policy on Campus and Beyond* (Oxford, 2015). He has also tried to raise public awareness about critical issues in the child mental health service system in his mystery novel, *Hammond's Choice* (Brandylane, 2008).

Allison B. Ventura, PhD, is a licensed child psychologist specializing in child and adolescent mental health. She is currently an assistant professor in the Department of Psychiatry at the University of Florida, College of Medicine – Jacksonville. She previously served as the clinical assessment specialist at the Children's Mental Health Resource Center at the Virginia Treatment Center for Children at Virginia Commonwealth University.